RIGHT TO ASYLUM: BETWEEN DEMAGOGY AND HYPOCRISY

This book provides insight into the realities of asylum and the right to asylum from the frontiers of refugee law, as observed by a key practitioner, academic and policy-maker in the field.

The book combines expert analysis and first-hand testimony. Written by one of the giants in the field, the first Belgian Commissioner General for Refugees and Stateless Persons, it blends the professional and the personal, to give a candid, compelling account of how asylum law has developed over the last quarter century. It looks back at some of the key cases of asylum, but also forward, suggesting how Europe might address current challenges such as deportation and regularisation.

All lawyers, practitioners and policymakers in the field of refugee law and policy will find this required reading.

Right to Asylum: Between Demagogy and Hypocrisy

Marc Bossuyt

•HART•
OXFORD • LONDON • NEW YORK • NEW DELHI • SYDNEY

HART PUBLISHING

Bloomsbury Publishing Plc

Kemp House, Chawley Park, Cumnor Hill, Oxford, OX2 9PH, UK

1385 Broadway, New York, NY 10018, USA

29 Earlsfort Terrace, Dublin 2, Ireland

HART PUBLISHING, the Hart/Stag logo, BLOOMSBURY and the Diana logo are trademarks of Bloomsbury Publishing Plc

First published in Great Britain 2025

A catalogue record for this book is available from the British Library.

A catalogue record for this book is available from the Library of Congress.

Library of Congress Control Number: 2024946794

ISBN: HB: 978-1-50998-267-7
ePDF: 978-1-50998-269-1
ePub: 978-1-50998-268-4

Typeset by Compuscript Ltd, Shannon

To find out more about our authors and books visit www.hartpublishing.co.uk. Here you will find extracts, author information, details of forthcoming events and the option to sign up for our newsletters.

This book is also available in Dutch
(Tussen demagogie en hypocrisie. Herinneringen van de eerste vluchtelingencommissaris,
Aalter, Ertsberg, 2022, 482 p – ISBN 978-9-46-436924-3)
and in French
(Droit d'asile: louvoyer entre démagogie et hypocrisie. Témoignage du premier Commissaire général belge aux réfugiés,
Paris, L'Harmattan, 2023, 435 p – ISBN 978-2-14-034623-1).

To Kristien, Kristof and Anneleen,
Juliette, Celeste, Felix,
Louie and Viktor

FOREWORD

Marc Bossuyt's passionate and fascinating testimony on his experience as first Belgian Commissioner General for Refugees and Stateless Persons, published 25 years after the end of his mandate, certainly deserves to be translated into English, as his timeliness is striking. It is addressed not only to Dutch-speaking readers and to his French-speaking Belgian compatriots, but to all European readers, even if it means provoking controversy in the current political debates. He is striking above all for his freedom of tone, his firm conviction, and his intellectual honesty.

The work is first a self-portrait, drawn without false modesty, from his beginnings as a student in Ghent and as a doctoral student in Geneva to his consecration as President of the Constitutional Court of the Kingdom of Belgium. Marc Bossuyt has had a triple career. Above all as an academic, committed to his intellectual independence, teaching with great pedagogy, not only in his *Alma Mater* of Antwerp, but also to the most diverse audiences from Butare to Taipei, via Paris and Thessaloniki. I am pleased to note his links with the International Institute of Human Rights in Strasbourg, founded by René Cassin. He was one of the first to receive the diploma of the Institute and to be one of its vice-presidents. His first publications indicate the directions he would follow, with his thesis on *L'interdiction de la discrimination dans le droit international des droits de l'homme* (Bruylant, 1976) and its indispensable *Guide to the 'travaux* préparatoires*' of the International Covenant on Civil and Political Rights* (Martinus Nijhoff, 1987).

His return to Geneva will be done through diplomatic channels, by leading the Belgian delegation to the UN Commission on Human Rights which he will preside over in 1989, a splendid year for human rights, with the adoption of the Second Optional Protocol to the International Covenant on Civil and Political Rights, aiming at the abolition of the death penalty. Marc Bossuyt had prepared this success beforehand as rapporteur of the Sub-Commission on Human Rights, a college of independent experts where he served on several occasions. Having had the privilege of working with him in the final years of the Sub-Commission, I know how much he was appreciated by all his colleagues, including those who were most ideologically distant, at a time when the debates were particularly harsh. He knew how to be the friend to all, expressing himself with great frankness, without hiding his opinions, and accepting criticism equally gracefully. He was particularly attached to the Sub-Commission and did everything to save it, during the 2006 reform, sparing no effort in chairing the last session of the Sub-Commission, when there were only blows to be taken. But that's another story he'll have to tell from the inside on another occasion. According to a subtle balance of posts between Belgium and the Netherlands, Marc Bossuyt alternated with Theo van Boven, within the Sub-Commission, even if it meant ending up intermittently on the Committee on the Elimination of Racial Discrimination where he sat for many years.

Given all these international responsibilities, always fully exercised, one can imagine the work effort and family harmony that it took Marc Bossuyt to assume his important national functions. It is this aspect that the book illustrates in detail, introducing to the subtleties of Belgian political life, with its alliance games – from 'Martens VI' to 'Michel I' – combining linguistic, philosophical and political criteria. As in Switzerland, the high Belgian magistrates thus display a political affiliation, and Marc Bossuyt spent his entire career in the shadow of the VLD, the Flemish Liberal Democratic Party. He was thus appointed Commissioner General for Refugees and Stateless Persons when the UNHCR discharged its operational functions in Belgium to advocate a system influenced by the French model of the 1950s around OFPRA and the Appeals Board. It was a full-time job, both 'administrative, legal and international' for nearly 10 years, between 1987 and 1997, before joining the future Constitutional Court, under the same label.

The heart of the work is this 'return of experience', far from the theoretical constructions, to examine almost day by day, the concrete problems that arise at the head of an embryonic administration, going from four jurists in 1990 to 125 jurists in 1994. This change of scale is still insufficient. To do this, the author uses his annual reports, as well as the press files compiled daily by his services, to revive the climate of the time, with its controversies and polemics. It does not neglect anecdotes that may seem trivial, such as the verses in the Commission General's folkloric 'Revue', alongside analyses of the 'electroshock' of the debates on reception areas and 'special flights' which will later be the prerogative of Frontex. It shows the importance of the press which he carefully distinguishes from public opinion, evokes political manoeuvres and even judicial investigations, such as the criticism of NGOs – in the forefront of which the French-speaking League for Human Rights, saluting the 'warm personality' of Françoise Tulkens who has been judge at the European Court of Human Rights. But he has not spared his criticism of the director of the Centre for Equal Opportunities, thus translating two approaches to the question of asylum, one based on the legal criteria of the 1951 Geneva Convention defining the refugee as such, the other emphasising the social reception of asylum seekers waiting for status and left in an increasingly long grey zone as procedures became congested and guarantees multiply.

Denouncing the 'ostrich policy' of the authorities and the 'cheap demagogy', Marc Bossuyt summed up his position in 1991 in a press article: 'The reduction of the number of illegals is based on three pillars: (a) regular checks on the residence of foreigners; (b) regularisation of integrated illegals; and (c) removal of illegals not integrated' (p 43). In his last interview, at the end of his duties in December 1997, he did not hesitate to denounce a great deal of 'hypocrisy and demagogy' (p 4 and 166), an ambiguous formula found in the title of his work.

Alongside the administrative and political record of his term as Commissioner General, Marc Bossuyt presents a series of emblematic files, presenting in a concrete way the problems of conscience that are at the heart of the individual decision to be taken. The general chapters and case studies alternate in a very lively way for the reader. Marc Bossuyt takes advantage of the retreat of time to measure the legal constraints and diplomatic issues of the time, while providing retrospective insights on sensitive files. This is the case of an Irish priest close to the IRA, Father Ryan, whom the Belgian government refuses to extradite to Britain, to the great displeasure of Margaret Thatcher, but who himself later claimed his role in attacks committed in England. Or even more paradoxically that of the head of the Rwandan Gendarmerie to whom he applied the 'exclusion clause' of refugee status, but who after 11 years of detention in Arusha will eventually be acquitted by the Appeals Chamber of the International Criminal Tribunal for Rwanda. However, the elements on which an administrative decision is based are not the same as those that must constitute criminal evidence, even if this relativity may seem shocking. In this regard, the pages devoted to the Rwandan genocide are particularly dense and sensitive. They alone deserve to be read. He underlines the duplicity of President Juvénal Habyarimana, an 'affable man' whose entourage prepared the genocide with daily propaganda. 'Grand master of the double game', he did not say the same thing to the Ambassador of Belgium as to the Ambassador of France. The President showed himself a devout Catholic, kneeling in the chapel of the Château of Laeken with King Baudouin, then showing himself as a free thinker with President Mitterrand and reciting poems by Prévert. 'In French, he did not say the same thing as in Kinyarwanda' concludes Marc Bossuyt, recalling that 'From the time of their birth, all Rwandans were members by right of the single party' (p 254). All the political crises, from the Former Yugoslavia to the Maghreb, with the rise of the FIS in Algeria, find their echo in the dilemmas of asylum.

Over time, migration crises are multiplying and changing in scale, as demonstrated by the migration crisis of 2015, illustrated by the opening policy of Angela Merkel, closely followed by Brexit. It is here that the book offers a last facet, with its European dimension, involving the policies of the European Union and the jurisprudence of the European Court of Human Rights. Marc Bossuyt revisits the very severe criticisms he had made against the Strasbourg judges, under the title *Strasbourg et les demandeurs d'asile: des juges sur un terrain glissant* (Bruylant, 2010). It is significant that the States themselves, at the high-level conferences in Smyrna and Brighton, denied the European Court the mission of being an 'Asylum Court'. But there are probably procedural and substantive issues. The criticism of the systematic nature of interim measures was itself taken into account by the Court because of abuses which threatened to paralyse the whole system, but this does not detract from the scope of the principle of non-refoulement which has been recalled by international treaties, like the 1984 Convention against torture or the 2006 Convention on enforced disappearance. Reviewing Belgian affairs on all possible grounds, Marc Bossuyt sometimes finds himself on slippery ground, as in the Zairean case of an unaccompanied minor. However, in addition to differences in the interpretation of the concept of 'inhumane treatment', it is the contradiction between the standards of the European Union and the guarantees of the European Convention on Human Rights that is exposed, when Marc Bossuyt deplores the jurisprudence of *MSS v Belgium and Greece*.

These debates are more relevant than ever, like the Belgian government crisis that occurred during the negotiation of the Marrakech Compact of 2018, which with its 360-degree ambition deserved neither this excess of honour nor this excess of indignity, by targeting 'safe, orderly and regular migration', while a second UNHCR Compact deals with refugees, thus avoiding any risk of trivialisation of the 1951 Geneva Convention. The recent Frontex crisis and the negotiations within the European Union to adopt its own 'global pact' refer us to the French debates. The immense merit of Marc Bossuyt in challenging 'postures' like denials, is to pose the problems on the ground of realities, with their ambiguities and contradictions.

Called in turn to chair a commission on removals whose report was presented in 2020, Marc Bossuyt praised one of his predecessors in terms that could apply to himself:

> He was a philosopher who had his feet on the ground, even though he was sometimes on slippery ground. He was not a man to jump to conclusions without considering the needs and realities of the world in which he lived. He believed that the convictions he defended should be the same even if he himself should assume political responsibility for them. He was aware that his positions could have consequences for society, which was a major concern for him. That's what made him so special (p 241).

This is also what makes Marc Bossuyt so original. He did not wish to dissect in the abstract on the opposition between the moral of responsibility and the moral of conviction, but in all transparency and without complacency, to engage in an exercise of 'ego-history' too rare among jurists not to be emphasised. His friends can only wish to see him extend this exercise on the international aspect of his career.

Emmanuel Decaux
Professor Emeritus of the Panthéon-Assas University Paris II
President of the René Cassin Foundation,
International Institute of Human Rights
Former Member of the UN Sub-Commission on Human Rights

TABLE OF CONTENTS

LIST OF ABBREVIATIONS

Newspapers

DM	De Morgen
DNG	De Nieuwe Gazet
DS	De Standaard
FET	Financieel Economische Tijd
GvA	Gazet van Antwerpen
HLN	Het Laatste Nieuws
HN	Het Nieuwsblad
HV	Het Volk
HBvL	Het Belang van Limburg
IHT	International Herald Tribune
LDH	La Dernière Heure
LLB	La Libre Belgique
LM-LL	La Meuse/La Lanterne
LNG	La Nouvelle Gazette
LS	Le Soir
Vl'A	Vers l'Avenir

Political Parties

Agalev	Anders gaan leven (Flemish Ecologists)
cdH	Centre démocrate Humaniste (French-speaking Christian Democrats)
CD&V	Christen-Democratisch & Vlaams (Flemish Christian Democrats)
CVP	Christelijke Volkspartij (Flemish Christian Democrats)

FDF	Front démocratique des francophones (French-speaking Brussels party)
MR	Mouvement réformateur (French-speaking Liberals)
N-VA	Nieuw-Vlaamse Alliantie (Flemish Nationalists)
PRL	Parti réformateur libéral (French-speaking Liberals)
PS	Parti socialiste (French-speaking Socialists)
PSC	Parti social-chrétien (French-speaking Christian Democrats)
PVV	Partij voor Vrijheid en Vooruitgang (Flemish Liberals)
SP	Socialistische Partij (Flemish Socialists)
SP.a	Socialistische Partij Anders (Flemish Socialists)
Vl. Bl.	Vlaams Blok (Flemish extreme right)
VLD	Vlaamse Liberalen en Democraten (Flemish Liberals)
VU	Volksunie (Flemish Nationalists)

Others

ABC	Bureau Conseil (Independent Advisory Board)
AI	Amnesty International
AIG	Inspection générale de la police fédérale et de la police locale (General Inspection of Federal Police and Local Police)
Ann parl	Annales parlementaires
Arr Cass	Judgments of the Cour de cassation
Asadho	Association africaine des droits de l'homme (African Association for Human Rights –Zaire/DRC)
asbl	Association sans but lucratif (non-profit association)
b	born
BBC	British Broadcasting Corporation
BF	Belgian francs
BRTN	Belgische Radio en Televisieomroep (Dutch-speaking Radio and Television)

BSR	Brigade de surveillance et de recherche de la Gendarmerie (Surveillance and Research Brigade, the Judicial Branch of the State Police)
Com	European Commission of Human Rights
CCFIS	Conseil de coordination du FIS à l'étranger (Coordination Council of the FIS abroad – Algeria)
CdE	Conseil d'Etat (Conseil d'Etat)
CERD	Committee on the Elimination of Racial Discrimination
CG	Commissioner General for Refugees and Stateless Persons
CGRA	Commissaire général aux refugiés et aux apatrides
CJRO	Collective Joint Return Operation
CNRO	Collective National Return Operation
Col	Column
CPAS	Centre public d'Assistance sociale (Public Centre for Social assistance)
CRDDR	Comité pour le respect des droits de l'homme et la démocratie au Rwanda (Committee for the Respect of Human Rights and Democracy in Rwanda – Rwanda)
d	deceased
dec	Decision
Doc parl	Parliamentary Documents
DSP	Division spéciale présidentielle (Presidential Special Division – Zaire/DRC)
DST	Direction générale de la surveillance du territoire (General Direction of Surveillance of the Territory – Morocco)
EAW	European Arrest Warrant
EC	European Community
ECHR	European Convention on Human Rights
ENA	Ecole nationale d'administration (National School of Administration – Tunisia)
ETA	Euskadi Ta Askatasuna
EU	European Union

F	Francophone (French-speaking)
FAR	Forces armées rwandaises (Rwandan Army)
FIDH	Fédération Internationale des Ligues des Droits de l'Homme (International Federation of Human Rights Leagues)
FIS	Front islamique du salut (Islamic Front of Salvation – Algeria)
GC	Grand Chamber
GIA	Groupe islamique armée (Armed Islamic Group -Algeria)
GSK	Gents Studentenkorps (Ghent Student Association)
HIV	Human Immunodeficiency Virus
HM	His/Her Majesty
Hon	Honourable
ibid	ibidem (same reference as the one quoted immediately before)
ICTR	International Criminal Tribunal for Rwanda
IHEID	Institut de hautes études internationales et du développement (The Graduate Institute of International and Development Studies – Geneva)
INAD	Person inadmissible to the territory
INSEAD	Institut européen d'administration des affaires (French business school – Fontainebleau)
IOM	International Organization for Migration
IPIS	International Peace Information Service (Antwerp)
IRA	Irish Republican Army
IUHEI	Institut universitaire de hautes études internationales (Graduate Institute of International Studies – Geneva)
JRO	Joint Return Operation
KU Leuven	Katholieke Universiteit Leuven
LiFo	Last in, First out
Lt-Col	Lieutenant-Colonel
LVV	Liberaal Vlaams Verbond (Flemish Liberal Federation)

MB	Marc Bossuyt
M.B.	Moniteur belge (Belgian Official Gazette)
Me	*Maître* (Lawyer at the Bar)
MEP	Member of the European Parliament
MGL	Multiple Grenade Lancer
MINUAR	Mission des Nations Unies pour l'assistance au Rwanda
MP	Member of Parliament
MRAX	Mouvement contre le racisme, l'antisémitisme et la xénophobie (Movement against Racism, Antisemitism and Xenophobia)
MRND	Mouvement national républicain pour la démocratie et le développement (Republican National Movement for Democracy and Development – Rwanda)
N	Dutch-speaking
NATO	North Atlantic Treaty Organization
NGO	Non-Governmental Organisation
NRO	National Return Operation
OE	Office des étrangers (Aliens Office)
OFPRA	Office français pour la protection des réfugiés et apatrides (French Office for the Protection of Refugees and Stateless Persons)
Parl fl	Flemish Parliament
PB	Permanent Refugees Appeals Board
Plen	Plenary
PS	Post-scriptum
Q & Rép	Questions et réponses (Parliamentary Questions and Replies)
RA	Refusal of the status of refugee motivated on the merits
RB	A refusal for not having responded to an information request
RC	A refusal for not having responded to a summons
DRC	Democratic Republic of Congo
RECCE	Escadron de reconnaissance (Reconnaissance squadron)

RER	Réseau express regional (Paris)
RPF	Rwandan Patriotic Front
RTBF	Radio-Télévision belge de la Communauté française
RTL TVI	Radio-Télévision Luxembourg Télévision Indépendante
RTLM	Radiotélévision Libre Mille Collines (Rwanda)
RUCA	State University Centre Antwerp
SARM	Service d'action et de renseignements militaires (Military Action and Intelligence Service – Zaire/DRC)
SO	Ordinary Session
SOS	Save Our Souls
SPF	Service public federal (Federal Public Service, previously Ministry)
SS	Special Session
SRWT	Société régionale wallonne de transport (Walloon Regional Society for Transport)
SVB	Studentenvakbeweging (Student Trade Union Association)
TF1	Télévision française 1 (French television)
TGV	Train de Grande Vitesse (High Speed Train)
UA	University of Antwerp
UCL	Catholic University of Louvain (Louvain-la-Neuve)
UDPS	Union pour la démocratie et le progrès social (Union for Democracy and Social Progress – Zaire/RDC)
UIA	University Institution of Antwerp
UK	United Kingdom
UN	United Nations
UNDP	United Nations Development Programme
UNHCR	United Nations High Commissioner for Refugees
US(A)	United States (of America)
USSR	Union of Socialist Soviet Republics
ULB	Université libre de Bruxelles (Free University of Brussels)

UMA	Union Maghreb arabe (Arab Magreb Union)
UNAMIR	United Nations Assistance Mission for Rwanda
UNIA	Interfederal Centre for Equal Opportunities
UNISOP	Institut universitaire de sondage d'opinion (University Institute of Opinion Polling – Brussels)
Vl.I.R.	Vlaamse Interuniversitaire Raad (Flemish Interuniversity Council)
VTM	Vlaamse Televisiemaatschappij (Flemish Television Society)

Prologue

On 8 August 2021 in Japan, Belgian Bashir Abdi won the Olympic bronze medal in the marathon. On 10 August 2024, he won the Olympic silver medal in Paris. In 1999, Bashir's mother was recognised as a refugee from Somalia in Belgium. Bashir arrived in Ghent in 2002 under a family reunification scheme. Before his mother died of cancer in 2011, he had promised her a medal for his new homeland as a token of his gratitude. In Sapporo and Paris, Bashir kept his promise. A magnificent story. Bashir and the whole of Belgium can be proud of it. Sadly, this kind of success story is rare.

On 23 May 2021, around five hundred foreigners residing illegally in Belgium went on hunger strike. Priest Daniel Alliët once again puts his *Béguinage* church in Brussels at their disposal. The Université Libre de Bruxelles and the Vrije Universiteit Brussel also offer their hospitality. The hunger strikers asked for collective regularisation, without making known the specific characteristics of their personal situation. They want regularisation to be granted by an independent commission based on criteria laid down in a law. Not a word about the pitfalls of this approach.

A hunger strike is the preferred means of testing whether the man or woman newly in charge of asylum in the government can withstand the stress. It lasts as long as its organisers hold out the hope that the politician might give in to blackmail. The strike ended on 21 July 2021. Despite the emotional (and political) pressure, Sammy Mahdi (CD&V), Secretary of State for Asylum and Immigration, proved that he stood firm on principle. Other members of the government had announced that they would resign within the hour if one of the hunger strikers died. Asylum policy is emotionally charged. The media are easily manipulated. Emotional policy is bad policy. It must be based on democratically determined legal rules, in compliance with international obligations. In a State governed by the Rule of Law, these rules cannot be set aside by emotional blackmail.

This is what my book reveals, based on my experience of nine years as Belgium's (first) Commissioner General for Refugees. Several 'asylum mysteries' are revealed.

Introduction

1. A Remarkable Job

This account is based on my experience as Commissioner General for Refugees and Stateless Persons (4 November 1987–5 February 1997), a long time ago. But it seems to me that it was worth writing a book on the subject, so that I could draw lessons that could be used to master problems that persist to this day. It's a remarkable job, and I was the first to do it (for nine years). Previously (until 31 January 1988), the competence to recognise refugees was exercised by the Representative in Belgium of the UN High Commissioner for Refugees (UNHCR). Every three to four years, another UN diplomat (often of foreign nationality) took on this role. Whoever the representative was, he entrusted his closest collaborator, Luc De Smet, with the individual processing of asylum applications. As it happened, Luc De Smet had been my fellow student at Ghent University Law School (1963–68). Since 1973, he had been working at the UNHCR Representation. Gradually, he was assisted by a growing number of collaborators.

In the 1980s, the number of asylum applications in Belgium began to rise. In 1977, there were less than a thousand. From 2,156 in 1984, the figure rose to 7,456 in 1986. It was only several years after the UNHCR had asked to be relieved of the competence to recognise refugees in Belgium, that the Martens VI Government, made up of Christian Democrats and Liberals, resolved to act. Belgian bodies would be set up, inspired by the French model. In the first instance, Belgium would have its own 'Commissioner General for Refugees and Stateless Persons'. Like the UNHCR Representative, he would be independent. His decisions could only be reviewed by a Permanent Refugee Appeals Board (hereafter: Permanent Board). The Commissioner General would have to decide whether foreigners seeking asylum met the legal definition of a refugee as defined by the Geneva Convention of 28 July 1951 on the Status of Refugees: any person with a 'well-founded fear of being persecuted for reasons of race, religion, nationality, membership of a particular social group or political opinion'.

My good friend Luc De Smet asked me if I'd be interested. The position seemed interesting. My academic background seemed relevant to refugee status determination. I had been teaching international law and international organisations at the University of Antwerp (UIA) since 1977. On 1 December 1985, I was promoted to the rank of professor. At the University of Geneva, I had defended my doctoral thesis in international human rights law in 1975. In Geneva, I had gained experience in the workings of UN human rights bodies. For nearly two years (1975–77),

I was a human rights officer at the UN Secretariat. For five years (1981–85), I was one of 26 independent experts on the UN Sub-Commission on the Prevention of Discrimination and Protection of Minorities. From 1986, I represented Belgium at the UN Commission on Human Rights.

The job of Commissioner General had many facets: administrative, legal and international. I had to build up a whole new administration. The most important thing for me was my independence in decision-making. It seemed tailor-made for me. I contacted the Minister of Justice Jean Gol[1] (PRL). The meeting went perfectly. To a PRL parliamentary friend, he announced that he had found 'a rare pearl'. For a long time, I heard nothing more on the subject. The Martens VI Government was in troubled waters, following the Happart affair.[2]

Meanwhile, at the United Nations, Jan Mårtenson, a Swedish diplomat, became Director General (1987–92) of the United Nations Office in Geneva. He combined this function with the leadership of the UN Human Rights Secretariat as Under-Secretary-General. This was the first time that this department was headed by such a high-ranking UN official. He wished to recruit me to function as his 'right-hand man'. At UN headquarters in New York, I had a meeting on this subject with Kofi Annan (Ghana). He was then UN Assistant Secretary-General in charge of personnel (1987–90). Ten years later, he became the first UN official to rise to the top, becoming Secretary-General (1997–2006). Due to budgetary difficulties, there were also delays in recruitment at the United Nations.

On 21 October 1987, the Belgian government crisis came to an end with the advent of the Martens VII Government. This government had the same composition as the previous one (CVP–PSC and PVV–PRL). To my surprise I learned that, at its first Council of Ministers, the new government had on the initiative of Justice Minister Jean Gol proposed my appointment to the King. By royal decree of 26 October 1987, published in the *Moniteur Belge* on 4 November 1987, I was appointed Commissioner General. In fact, I had already taken office the day before. All that remained was for me to inform UN Director-General Jan Mårtenson that I was no longer available. The die was cast. The adventure could begin. Fortunately, I only had to exercise my competences three months later. There was a backlog of 10,000 files. All these files, submitted before 1 February 1988, remained under the jurisdiction of the UNHCR Representative. I could start with a clean slate.

2. How did All this Work Out?

What were the challenges? Who were the allies? What resistance had to be overcome? What successes were achieved? What setbacks had to be overcome? Very

[1] Jean Gol was Minister of Justice from 17 December 1981 to 9 May 1988.

[2] José Happart, mayor of the Fourons, campaigned for the return of his commune to the province of Liège.

quickly, nothing remained of this 'clean slate'. For the first six months, the number of asylum applications did not even exceed 360 per month. Still, this was more than could be processed. Uninterruptedly, for six years, I ended each month with a larger backlog than the previous month! On three occasions, the monthly record for asylum applications was reached: 1,339 in March 1990, 1,736 in September 1991 and 2,960 in June 1993. On 1 October 1993, we reached the sad record of a total backlog (Aliens Office, Commission General and Permanent Board) of 36,164 pending asylum applications.

Right from the start, I was aware of the risk that politicians would one day look for a scapegoat. To be prepared for this eventuality, I always wanted to know the status of the files at the Commission General. How many applications? How many decisions? How many favourable decisions and how many unfavourable? For which nationalities? And within what time frame? Right from the start, everything was accurately recorded at the Commission General. At the University of Antwerp's Faculty of Law, I was the first professor to acquire a computer. At the Commission General too, I wanted to be able to use computers. I was later told that there were more computers at the Commission General than in the entire Ministry of Justice. I had all my opinions and decisions recorded electronically. These computers have been particularly useful in compiling statistics. At the time, the Ministry of Justice, including the Aliens Office, was unfamiliar with computers and statistics. These became an important tool in any discussion of asylum, both externally and internally.

From the outset, I regularly wrote letters and notes warning the Minister of foreseeable developments. As a rule, I didn't publicise them at the time. However, I faithfully mentioned them in my annual reports. This has not been without effect. All too often, early warnings and forecasts became reality in the meantime, with disastrous consequences. The media became important allies. They knew that my door was always open. I always answered their phone calls. Except for the presentation of my annual reports, and sometimes for an interim report, I didn't chase them. Minister of Justice Melchior Wathelet[3] (senior) doubted it: 'I know one thing: before, hardly anyone talked about this issue; since you became Commissioner General, one talks about it all the time'.

Knowing how it all happened is important if we are to learn from it. Better knowledge is needed, as well as a better understanding of asylum issues, which are often mysterious. This story aims to help unravel them. How is it that there are always new asylum crises? How is it that 'civil society' and the relevant authorities are mostly engaged in sterile conversations? Many of today's discussions are, in fact, long-standing. They have lost none of their topicality. Discussions on asylum reveal a lot of demagogy and hypocrisy. I've sometimes said: 'The demagogy comes from the right; the hypocrisy comes from the left'. Navigating between the two was a constant mission. Some discussions now take place at European rather than

[3] Melchior Wathelet (senior) (PSC), Minister of Justice (1988–95), judge (1995–2003) and Advocate General (2012–18) at the Court of Justice of the European Union.

Belgian level. At times, it seems that the European Union (EU) still must travel the same road as Belgium did years ago. It's a difficult process, since not all EU Member States are confronted with asylum issues to the same extent or in the same way.

3. My Story

I tell my story independently, but not uncritically, nor without subjectivity. It's a personal story. Some may not like to remember the positions they took at the time. With actors I've had to fight, antagonism has often long since disappeared. Truth, however, retains its rights: '*amicus Plato sed magis amica veritas*' ('Plato is my friend, but truth is a better friend'). This story can only be useful if it puts its finger squarely on the heart of the matter. Even authorities for whom I have the greatest respect have sometimes, in my eyes, committed missteps. Individual sensitivities must – it seems to me – give way to the general interest to avoid repeating mistakes. Some of the players have left this vale of tears. Almost all of them are retired, emeritus or inactive. This story will therefore hardly do them any harm. That is certainly not my intention.

As is customary, this presentation is divided into chapters. They do not always follow one another in purely chronological order. 'Historical' chapters alternate with the stories of some particularly well-known asylum seekers, before being followed by more 'thematic' chapters. The latter deal in greater detail with problems caused by staff shortages, legislation, deportations, regularisations and Strasbourg case law. Legislative developments concern both the asylum procedure itself and social assistance. The latter is 'the nerve of asylum'. At times, it was as if there was a game of ping-pong between the legislator and the highest courts.

Within each chapter, chronological order is generally followed. However, some events are recounted in certain chapters, while others, taking place at the same time, are recounted in others. There were, in fact, often interactions at different levels with different or the same actors. The main players were: 'the' Minister, sometimes other ministers, the Aliens Office, the Conseil d'Etat, the labour courts, the Public Centres of Social Assistance (CPAS), the Permanent Refugees Appeals Board, Parliament, the UN High Commissioner for Refugees, the Bar, the media, non-governmental organisations (NGOs) and public opinion. All too often, public opinion is confused with the media and NGOs. After I left the Commission General, new players were added, not the least of which were the Aliens Litigation Council, the Strasbourg Court, the Luxembourg Court, and the European Commission. This didn't make things any easier.

Attention to individual cases must always be combined with attention to other issues. It's crisis management all the time. Almost every day, it was necessary to react urgently to one or other acute problem. When I arrived at the Commission General, I could always expect some misfortune or other. It was tiring. It was stressful. It was often frustrating. Above all, it was incredibly fascinating.

After years at the helm, I sometimes wondered how much longer I could go on without exhausting myself, psychologically and perhaps physically. Wouldn't all the effort be wasted? When will one understand that the number of foreigners preferring to stay with us rather than in their own country is inexhaustible? In any case, we're talking about a multitude of people that – even with the most generous policy – far exceeds the possible capacity. Differences of opinion about how many more foreigners Belgium wants to take in are inevitable. But allowing everything to run its course is untenable.

The authority instituted by the new law is not the 'Commission General', but the 'Commissioner General for Refugees and Stateless Persons'. The same applies to 'the Minister' in the Aliens Law. First it was the Minister of Justice, then the Minister of the Interior and then the Minister or Secretary of State for Asylum and Migration. Where the Aliens Law grants decision-making powers to the Minister or Secretary of State, decisions are taken by him or, where the law so authorises, on his behalf by his delegate. From a legal point of view, these are always his decisions, not those of the Ministry or the Secretariat of State.

From a legal point of view, only one person is responsible for making decisions: the Commissioner General. This is the only way to pursue a policy. Particularly in the case of backlogs, it is of the utmost importance to determine priorities in the processing of files. The main factors in determining priorities are the date on which the application was lodged, the nationality (number of applications and recognition rate) of those concerned, and whether they are dependent on public assistance. For a jurisdiction such as the Aliens Litigation Council, pursuing a policy is difficult. Each of the 62 judges on the Aliens Litigation Council is completely independent in his or her decisions. They are independent of the government, as all judges are. Let's hope they are also independent of 'civil society'. They are also independent of each other.

Despite meritorious attempts by the First President and the President of the Aliens Litigation Council, the case law of that Council occasionally takes a different turn depending on the judge, and above all on the linguistic role of the judge concerned. The Commissioner General cannot be divided into linguistic roles. However, this does not prevent him too, whoever he may be, from taking more positive decisions in French than in Dutch. He can ask his French-speaking colleagues to bring their proposals into line with those of their Dutch-speaking colleagues. He cannot force them to do so. Otherwise, his position would quickly become untenable. Anyone who practises law in Belgium knows that these cultural differences exist. Nowhere are they more perceptible than when it comes to foreigners. And this, at whatever level.

4. Some Sensitive Cases

During my nine years in office, 124,136 asylum applications were lodged. Under my personal responsibility, 96,798 individual decisions were taken. Some applications were also processed by the Aliens Office without ever reaching the Commission General. I signed most of the individual decisions and the accompanying letters myself. Almost always, I also signed the long-awaited refugee cards. It was difficult for me to keep up with the preparation of all the decisions and the reasons behind them. In fact, this rarely happened, except for politically or media-sensitive decisions. This was particularly the case when the applicant could be suspected of terrorism. A certain intuition in identifying and handling such cases is welcome. However, these are highly atypical cases.

Among them are the cases of some asylum seekers from the European Union. The first, Patrick Ryan (1988), a Catholic priest suspected of belonging to the Irish Republican Army (IRA), claimed to fear persecution by the United Kingdom. The Basque-Spanish couple Moreno–Garcia (1993–98), followed by another Basque ('Peixotin') and, after the end of my mandate, yet another (Maiztegui), also came from the European Union. Suspected of belonging to the Euskadi Ta Askatasuna (ETA) organisation, these Basques claimed to fear persecution by Spain. In nine years, there has only been one Irish applicant and nine Spanish applicants. I didn't recognise any of them.

Secondly, there are two Islamist asylum seekers. The first, Walid Bennani (1992–97), a leader of the Tunisian Ennahdha movement, was finally recognised by my successor, Commissioner General Luc De Smet (1997–2001). Years later, Walid Bennani became a Member of Parliament for his party in Tunisia. Out of 54 Tunisian asylum seekers, eight were recognised, including one by the Permanent Board. The second Islamist asylum seeker, Ahmed Zaoui (1993–97), a leader of the Algerian Islamic Salvation Front (FIS), was not recognised, in application of the exclusion clause. He was alleged to have committed serious non-political crimes. After many wanderings, he became a New Zealand citizen. Out of 1,395 Algerian asylum seekers, 69 were recognised, including seven by the Permanent Board.

There were also two Rwandans who came to Belgium after the genocide of the Tutsi. Séraphin Rwabukumba (1994–98), a cousin by marriage of President Juvénal Habyarimana, was refused under the exclusion clause. The other, Major General Augustin Ndindiliyimana, chief of staff of the Rwandan Gendarmerie (1995–98), was recognised by the Permanent Board. Before 1994, only 202 Rwandan asylum applications were received in six years. After the genocide, there were 1,389 in three years. By the end of January 1997, I had recognised 897 Rwandan refugees. This put Rwanda in third place after Turkey (1,515) and Zaire (1,211). However, there were far more asylum seekers from Turkey (7,793) and Zaire (16,308) than from Rwanda (1,591).

All the information in this book comes mainly from public sources, such as parliamentary documents and accessible case law. I have never kept a diary. And I haven't even kept track of my agendas. Yet my memory is rarely the only source. More important are my annual reports and the many press clippings. Even in the case of these sensitive dossiers, the press has reported extensively on them. Since 1992, a brochure (*Infojur*) containing relevant press clippings has been distributed daily among my staff. References to sources and additional information are given in footnotes. A major gap in my story is the audio-visual media. Countless times, I have given explanations in both national languages on radio and television. Drawing on these sources, however, was beyond my capabilities.

In some cases, I have supplemented publicly available sources with additional details from my personal documentation, to ensure greater historical and legal accuracy. They help us to better understand the complexity of certain issues and files. These files were closed 20–30 years ago. They may, however, still serve as a 'precedent' for future asylum law. At times, my account goes beyond my term of office. Indeed, insofar as this is deemed relevant, my story continues as far as possible.

5. Other Individual Cases

In nine years, I have confirmed 52,529 negative decisions by the Aliens Office in the admissibility phase. I refused 20,169 asylum applications, 12,147 of which were refused by a decision based on the merits; the remaining 8,022 were refused on technical grounds (such as failure to respond to a summons). In all, I recognised 8,225 refugees of 87 different nationalities. This was only possible by giving my staff three basic rules: (a) follow the practice of the UNHCR Representative; (b) give a wide benefit of the doubt; and (c) opt for a broad interpretation of the Geneva Convention.

In handling individual cases, I saw my responsibility in setting up a system that enabled me to sign decisions in confidence. Decisions were taken on the recommendation of at least one member of staff and checked by a supervisor. I never decided on my own. When a member of staff or a supervisor asked me for an interpretation, I told them what they had to base their decision on. At the end of the day, it was up to them to apply the directives given to them to the best of their knowledge. Right from the start as the Commission General, I entrusted the hearings exclusively to collaborators with a PhD degree or a Master's degree in law. They themselves had to be able to evaluate the files. There was no question of blindly applying directives imposed by the hierarchy.

I rarely deviated from the proposals of my collaborators. They were the ones who interviewed the asylum seekers. They looked them in the eye. They were the ones most familiar with dealing with asylum seekers from particular nationalities. I was not. I didn't feel justified in going against their proposals without having heard the asylum seekers concerned myself. And hearing them myself was simply not feasible. I'm very sceptical about courts that think they can make decisions about asylum seekers without hearing them.

Confidential hearings, held in a special hearing room by experienced staff, give the best chance of revealing the truth. A public hearing is less appropriate.

Asylum proceedings are not criminal proceedings. The authorities do not have to prove the guilt of an asylum seeker. The asylum seeker is not accused of anything. It is an administrative procedure in which the applicant wishes to obtain something from the authority, namely asylum. Consequently, it's up to the applicants to demonstrate – or at least to make credible – that they are eligible. This is not a heavy burden of proof, but their story must be 'plausible'. In criminal proceedings, a rogatory commission would be sent to investigate in the country where the acts were committed. For practical and financial reasons, this is not possible in an asylum procedure. For reasons of principle, an appeal to the authorities in the country of origin is not even permitted. A refugee applicant claims that he or she is being persecuted by this very authority. For this reason, a wide margin is allowed when assessing the credibility of asylum seekers.

Like someone accused of a criminal offence, an asylum seeker is also entitled to the benefit of the doubt. However, they must cooperate fully with the asylum authorities. They must have confidence in the authorities they turn to for asylum. Otherwise, he or she must seek asylum in another country. They may not make fraudulent declarations. They may not use false documents, unless they state that they are false. Any attempt to mislead the asylum authorities may result in the loss of their right to asylum. Being unmasked by lies is the quickest route to refusal. A self-respecting authority cannot allow itself to be mocked. Otherwise, the asylum procedure loses all credibility. If deception were acceptable, it would become a widespread system.

6. Hearing of Asylum Seekers

Is the hearing of asylum seekers difficult? Yes, but not to the extent that some think it becomes a lottery. There are huge differences between the more than one hundred countries of origin. There is great cultural diversity among asylum seekers from all these countries. For this reason, thorough and well-kept documentation by country is very important. To achieve maximum efficiency and high quality, country specialisation is essential. Experience with the specific characteristics of asylum seekers according to their country of origin is even more important. Verbal communication is also important, although it is difficult to reflect this in an audition report. Verbal communication varies greatly depending on the culture of the country of origin. Some speak exuberantly, with a tendency to exaggerate. Others are very reticent and talk only shyly about what they have experienced. Those who have no experience of all this are hopelessly lost.

To take Africa alone: Rwandans and Burundians are not Congolese (at the time, they were still Zairians); nor are they Senegalese, Nigerians, Ghanaians, and so on. All asylum seekers are interviewed at the Commission General only by staff specialised in their country or region. But even within one country, there can be big differences. In Turkey, there are Assyrians, Armenians, Chaldeans, Kurds,

Communists, economic migrants, and now also Gülen supporters. Without experience, it's difficult to discover the truth and make informed decisions. Most jurisdictions do not believe that such specialisation is necessary, with all the unfortunate consequences that entails.

Employees need to be familiar with audition techniques. An audition is very different from a conversation with a friend or acquaintance, or even a casual passer-by. The interviewer dares to ask 'embarrassing' questions. He or she must relate the answers to available documents and previous statements. Every police inspector knows that systematic lying is more difficult than many people think. It's very difficult to stick to a fictitious story consistently. It's not just about the story of persecution. The route of the journey, including means of transport and dates, is also examined in detail. Finally, the person's personality (family, education, profession) is scrutinised. The answer to the following question is of crucial importance: 'What was the decisive factor that prompted you to leave your country?' If you've made up a story, you'll find it difficult to put all three strands together without contradiction. With all these elements, an experienced interviewer will be able to assess the asylum seeker's credibility with full knowledge of the facts. The benefit of the doubt will be given if there is reasonable hesitation. Doubt should not, however, be confused with uncertainty, which is inherent in future developments.

7. The Asylum 'Kitchen'

This story attempts to give a better insight into the asylum 'kitchen'. This has undergone a real transformation. Previously, the image of refugees was that of persons of rare courage who are willing to risk their freedom, physical integrity or even their life to express their convictions. Today, most are 'war refugees', escaping the disruption caused by armed conflict. Subsidiary protection has been introduced for them. This has considerably expanded the number of beneficiaries of international protection. This enlargement of scale has contributed to excesses. Asylum 'cooking' has been transformed into a veritable 'business'. The most extreme form is human trafficking. This is a business organised by criminals who handle millions of euros. It rivals drug trafficking as the world's most lucrative criminal branch. Europol estimates that it generates revenues of €5 billion a year. These unscrupulous human traffickers have no respect for human life. In return for large sums of money, they push their victims into increasingly unsafe boats or into refrigerated trucks. They exploit their victims' despair and rely on the credulity and compassion of many people to keep their clientele.

Although of a completely different order, everything to do with asylum has – in Belgium too – undergone a major expansion. It has become a major source of employment. Just think of the many jobs at Fedasil (over 2,000), the Red Cross, the public assistance centres and the many NGOs. There are also other related organisations, such as UNIA (the Interfederal Centre for Equal Opportunities) and Myria (the Federal Migration Centre). In 2021, it was announced that over 700 additional staff would be recruited. In the legal sector, we must count the State Councillors appointed as reinforcements, the dozens of aliens' judges, and their numerous legal assistants, as well as the several hundred jurists at the Aliens Office and the Commission General. Finally, it's a source of employment for hundreds of lawyers. Many of them must assist asylum seekers *pro Deo* during their internship. Some, quite a few, who call themselves 'specialists', have made this their permanent livelihood, mostly at the State's expense.

The law plays an important role in asylum matters. They involve the application of an international convention, EU directives and laws. These are applied in accordance with legal procedures and under the increasing supervision of courts and tribunals. Many lawyers are highly inventive. To help their clients, they try to find loopholes in the legislation. From time to time, they succeed in convincing courts to follow their theses. When this compromises the smooth running of the asylum procedure, the legislator must intervene quickly to remedy the situation.

Frequently, lawyers conduct asylum proceedings for the sole reason of prolonging their clients' stay in Belgium. The aim is often to obtain residence permits. It is not uncommon for aliens' procedures to be used for purposes other than those for which they were set up. They are sometimes brought solely to obtain or maintain entitlement to social assistance. Lawyers argue that they have the right, even the duty, to defend their clients' interests. They believe that all procedures may be implemented, provided their clients benefit from them. All the legislator must do is ensure that abuses are not possible. This argument would be more convincing if – whenever the legislator tried to combat abuses or simplify a procedure – the Bar Association wasn't turning to the Constitutional Court to have such legislative changes annulled.

According to the rules of professional conduct, the lawyer must act as first judge. To knowingly institute manifestly unfounded proceedings raises questions. Although the right to asylum does not belong to criminal law, but to administrative law, everyone accepts that lawyers may assist asylum seekers. However, legal aid is by no means a prerequisite for recognition by the Commissioner General. When a lawyer sincerely believes that a refusal decision has been taken wrongly, an appeal is justified. This is not the case when a lawyer urges his client to reapply for asylum or other residence permits, even several times. This is even more unjustified when such proceedings are brought solely to block a removal process that has already begun. Admittedly, new facts can arise at any time in the country of origin. Although this is a theoretical rather than a real hypothesis, the lodging of a new application cannot be prohibited for this reason. Without genuinely new and relevant elements, this is an abuse of procedure. How can we justify the fact that some lawyers initiate hundreds of proceedings without ever succeeding? Some only survive thanks to their *pro Deo* actions at the expense of the State. For others, it goes far beyond 'surviving'. Still others, above all, serve political objectives, in line with their ideological fight to destabilise liberal democracy.

Non-jurists generally pay little attention to legal controversies. Yet more attention should be paid. Judges bear a heavy responsibility in society. The consequences of their decisions affect not only jurists. That's why it's not out of place to ask questions about the soundness of the grounds on which far-reaching judicial decisions are based. A societal debate on this subject should not be taboo. Lamentations about the separation of powers are all too often one-sided. Judges must also respect the separation of powers from the executive and legislative branches.

The respect due to the judiciary requires restraint regarding judgments in individual cases. Criticism of general judicial decisions does not, however, jeopardise the rule of law. Uncritical resignation is not required when judges put themselves in the shoes of the competent authority. It is certainly not required when decisions are taken in which judges act as legislators. In asylum matters, this happens from time to time. At the European Court of Human Rights in Strasbourg, it even happens frequently. For this reason, the last two chapters of my book are a little extra, giving an overview of the evolution of that Court's asylum jurisprudence. First, I explain how the Court came to embark on the path of indirect liability for virtual violations. With the help of selected judgments, I then illustrate how this jurisprudence has developed. Not surprisingly, I pay particular attention to judgments against Belgium.

Everyone has the right to lobby for the causes he or she believes in. This also applies to defending the interests of asylum seekers and other foreigners. It's striking that, particularly when asylum applications are under control, the 'foreigners' lobby' is ready for action. They pull out all the stops to undermine the credibility of asylum decisions. The relevant authorities and courts are accused of continually making unjustified decisions. Their incompetence is said to be surpassed only by their inhumanity. Although all this is quite blatant, there are always good souls to believe it. And there is always media ready to turn itself into a megaphone. We can only hope that readers will in future be more reasoned in making up their minds.

1

'*Vox clamantis in deserto*' ('The Voice that Cries in the Desert') (1987–89)

My appointment as Commissioner General by royal decree of 26 October 1987 was published on 4 November. The day before, immediately after the long weekend of All-Saints' Day, I had been invited to the office of the Minister of Justice who wanted to move fast. I met Victor Bricout, his chief of staff (1983–88), Jean Spreutels, his deputy chief of staff (1985–88) and two other members of his staff. At the Ministry of Justice, I met Eugène Frencken, the Secretary General, Stéphane Schewebach, the Refugee Director of the Aliens Office, and Francis Pirard, the Finance Inspector. There were also meetings with officials from the Ministry of Justice to discuss matters concerning the personnel, the buildings and the budget. It was the start of an intense period of preparation for the new refugee bodies: 'We had to get a brand-new public service up and running. A race against time and a battle against an administrative and budgetary imbroglio lie ahead' (*HLN*, 17 November 1987).

1.1. Preparations in a Period of 'Care-taking Business' (November 1987–January 1988)

A multitude of contacts were made with senior civil servants, other important partners and future collaborators. Numerous concerns had to be taken care of, such as renting premises, purchasing furniture, computers, cars, a telephone switchboard, etc. Another complicating factor was the period of 'caretaking business' in which the Martens VII Government found itself since 9 November. Elections were due to be held on 13 December 1987. On several occasions, Justice Minister Jean Gol had to request from the Council of Ministers an exemption from the rules applicable in a period of care-taking business.

I could settle in the vacant office of a director general at the Ministry of Justice, on Place Poelaert in Brussels, opposite the Palais de Justice. From 9 November 1987 on, I shared it with my administrative secretary Rudi Van Hoed. Originally from

Tielt (like my wife), he was to assist me faithfully for nine years. On 19 November, the Minister of Justice surprised me by inviting me into his Cabinet to take the oath, in the presence of Secretary General Eugène Frencken and deputy chief of staff Jean Spreutels. The Minister agreed that I could continue teaching part-time at the University of Antwerp (UIA). I could also continue representing Belgium at the UN Commission on Human Rights. The Secretary General also undertook to examine the social status of the Commissioner General and his deputies.

The position of Commissioner General was at director general level (16), which corresponded to my rank as a professor at the University of Antwerp. My appointment therefore did not imply a promotion. On my request, the Minister of Justice asked Guy Verhofstadt (PVV), Budget Minister (1985–88), whether this new mandate could be fixed at the level of ordinary professor. Economic as he was at the time, he refused. Others, in the new refugee bodies, would jump from levels 10 and 11 to level 15 or even to level 16, as was the case, four years later, at the Permanent Board.

As an independent mandate holder, I was not a state agent. Nothing was settled in this respect, not even my pension rights. Fortunately, my statutory appointment at the university guaranteed me a state pension. Later, under a Flemish decree of 12 June 1991, I would, after six academic years, eventually lose my right to return to a full-time academic post and the corresponding state pension. This decree, which would become applicable to me on 1 October 1997, would incite me to leave the Commission General after nine years in office. Only a few years after my departure, the status of non-permanently appointed mandate holders was settled, along with a considerable salary increase, thanks to the Copernicus reform of Guy Verhofstadt, then Prime Minister (1999–2008).

Even before the new refugee bodies came into operation, I warned in November 1987 in my first contacts with the broadcast media that, without the necessary resources, faster processing of asylum applications would be nothing but an illusion. In *Demain le Monde* (18 January 1988), Michel Moussalli, the UNHCR Representative, agreed with me: 'I fear that the work of the Commissioner General – which some had hoped would be faster – will end up being much slower than ours'. This senior UN official, a Swiss citizen of Lebanese origin, was kind enough to describe my appointment as a 'masterstroke'.

1.2. My First Steps as Commissioner General (February 1988–January 1989)

The solemn handover of responsibilities to the first 'Commissioner General for Refugees and Stateless Persons' took place on 4 February 1988 in the magnificent Egmont Palace. Among those present were Jean-Pierre Hocké (Switzerland), UN High Commissioner for Refugees (1986–89); Jean Gol, Deputy Prime Minister and Minister of Justice; Leo Tindemans (CVP), Minister for External Relations

(1981–89); and Miet Smet (CVP), Secretary of State for Social Emancipation (1985–92).

To the UN High Commissioner, I gave the assurance that the new authorities would apply the Geneva Convention as conscientiously as his delegates had done in Belgium for over 30 years. I also expressed the hope to be able to count on the government to provide me with the necessary resources to carry out the task entrusted to me with the desired speed. The UN High Commissioner then paid a visit to the headquarters of the Commission General, at Rue de la Régence 61, close to the Palais de Justice.

The transfer of powers was widely reported in the press on 5 February 1988:

- Belgium Decides Autonomously on the Recognition of Political Refugees (*DM*).
- Belgium now Decides for itself who is a Political Refugee (*DS*).
- Refugees: Belgium Sets up its own Commission (*LLB*).
- Our Country has 'its' Refugee Commissioner (*LS*).
- Bossuyt Watches over the Borders (*HLN*).

At every opportunity, I insisted in the media on the need to have the necessary means at our disposal:

- I'm already asking myself whether I have enough staff (*GvA*, 8 February 1988).
- Dealing with files quickly is possible if I have enough staff. But now, without a government, I'm probably crying in the desert (*HV*, 12 February).
- A 'Mister Human Rights' for refugees. He's surely lacking in three things: jurists, typists and bailiffs. For the rest, the enthusiasm is there. 'It's up to you to compare what it costs: a procedure for a year and a half or one for six months. If we hire enough jurists, we'll save hundreds of millions of Belgian francs' (*La Cité*, 18–24 February).

In presenting, on 19 July 1988, the Ministry of Justice budgets for 1985, 1986 and 1987, Minister Melchior Wathelet painted a disconcerting picture. He highlighted a series of situations worthy of the nineteenth century:

> The Aliens Office is totally overwhelmed. There used to be an average of 85,000 visa applications, now there are over 200,000. As far as refugees are concerned, there is a crisis. This is leading to acute overcrowding at the Brussels National Airport in Zaventem, where a group of forty asylum seekers is permanently held in appalling conditions.

In June and July 1988, Amnesty International *Belgique francophone* organised a campaign against the new Refugee Law. In a long letter dated 18 August 1988,[1]

[1] *First Annual Report* (1988) 87 (Annex 6).

addressed to Me Eric Gillet, Chairperson of this NGO, I drew his attention to several initiatives I had taken which went beyond what the law required. These included summoning asylum seekers in writing for a hearing, informing their counsel in writing or by telephone, giving reasons for my opinions, communicating my opinions and decisions to asylum seekers' counsel, and giving them access to the files of rejected asylum seekers during the 30-day appeal period. The law provided for such access only during the five days preceding the hearing by the Permanent Board. Contrary to the practice at the Aliens Office, I also allowed asylum seekers' counsel to be present during the hearings. Only later were these practices enshrined in the regulations. However, none of this earned me much recognition.

During an initial contact on 26 November 1987, the Presidents of the Brussels Bar assured me that recourse to the Permanent Board could be avoided if asylum seekers' counsel could have prior access to the files. In practice, this remained wishful thinking. In the above-mentioned letter, I also stated: 'The few months of operation had made me realise more than I could have imagined that many asylum seekers did not have a well-founded fear of persecution within the meaning of the Geneva Convention'. I made mention of fabricated stories, blatantly false declarations, the use of false documents and multiple identities.

On 14 September 1988, I made an initial assessment of my activities. In the first six months of operation, 2,132 asylum applications had been submitted: 25 per cent from Ghana, 14 per cent from India and 11 per cent from Zaire. I said:

> Without more staff, we can expect no acceleration of the procedure. Quite the contrary, as a matter of fact. It is to be feared that the procedure will take even longer than with the Representative of the UN High Commissioner (DS, 15 September 1988).

On 19 January 1989, I reported to the Centre of Consultation for the integration of refugees that 4,476 asylum applications had been submitted since 1 February 1988. The Centre's coordinator, Luk Depelchin, explained that the flow of applications had to be processed more quickly. The headlines on 20 January 1989 were all along the same lines:

- There's Nothing to be Proud of. The situation has certainly improved, but the Commissioner General's departments are sorely lacking in resources (*LLB*).
- Asylum Policy is Flawed because of a Negative Climate and a Lack of Resources (*DM*).
- Fewer Refugees, but their Reception is Going Nowhere (*LS*).
- Refugees Need to be Processed more Quickly (*HN*).
- Asylum Procedures Take too Long (*HBvL*).

1.3. Chairperson of the UN Commission on Human Rights (30 January–10 March 1989)

On 30 January 1989 in Geneva, I was elected Chairperson of the UN Commission on Human Rights.[2] In *La Libre Belgique* the following day, Nicolette Franck wrote of 'the modest, discreet and nonetheless highly competent Professor Marc Bossuyt'. The French newspaper *Le Monde* of 2 February called me 'a competent chairperson, a man of the *seraglio* in the good sense of the word'. On becoming emeritus at the University of Antwerp, I summed up this experience as follows during the ceremony on 28 September 2007:[3]

> It was an unforgettable experience.[4] This session marked the beginning of a growing practice of speeches by high dignitaries [known as 'Distinguished Visitors']. Among others, I received the French Prime Minister Michel Rocard, and the Secretary of State of the Holy See, His Eminence Agostino Cardinal Casaroli. A particularly impressive moment was the speech (27 February 1989) by Hungarian Secretary of State Gyula Horn. In Russian, he denounced human rights violations in Romania. A few months later (on 2 May), by cutting the Iron Curtain between Hungary and Austria, he pointed the way to the West for East-Germans in their small Trabant cars. This caused the Berlin Wall to crumble. At the end of the session, I was asked to appoint a Special Rapporteur for Romania. That this could happen without opposition from the Soviet Union and the German Democratic Republic shows the isolation in which Nicolae Ceaucescu found himself. The session was dominated by a confrontation between the USA and Cuba.[5] We managed to emerge unscathed. At this session, we also succeeded in having two human rights conventions approved without a vote: the Second Optional Protocol to the International Covenant on Civil and Political Rights, aiming at the abolition of the

[2] The Belgian delegation that year was further composed of the Deputy Permanent Representative in Geneva, Dominique Struye de Swielande (later chief of staff, diplomatic adviser, director general and ambassador to Berlin, NATO, Washington DC and Kinshasa); (from New York), Machteld Fostier (currently Secretary to HM Queen Mathilde); and (from Brussels) Paul Rietjens (later director general of the Legal Service of the Ministry of Foreign Affairs). The previous three years, our man from New York was Guy Trouveroy (later ambassador to New Delhi, Cairo, Moscow and London). See M Bossuyt, 'La Belgique et la Commission des Droits de l'Homme de l'ONU (1986–1991)' in *La Belgique et 50 ans de Nations Unies* (Brussels, Ed Vif, 1995) 467.

[3] M Bossuyt, Annex ('At the Crossroads of Law and Politics') in M Bossuyt, *International Human Rights Protection: Balanced, Critical, Realistic* (Cambridge, Intersentia, 2016) 191.

[4] This intense diplomatic experience was only surpassed by my nine days as Chairperson of the Working Group on the Declaration of the 'World Conference Against Racism, Racial Discrimination, Xenophobia and Related Intolerance' in Durban (South Africa) from 31 August to 8 September 2001. Chairing this plenary working group composed of 171 states was the most hectic experience of my professional life. Three days later, during the event known as *9/11*, two aircraft crashed into the World Trade Center towers in New York. See on this conference, ibid, 91–101, and (with S Vandeginste) 'The Issue of Reparation for Slavery and Colonialism and the Durban Conference against Racism' (2001) 22 *Human Rights Law Journal* 341.

[5] R Brody and D Weissbrodt, 'Major Developments at the 1989 Session of the UN Commission on Human Rights' in F Newman and D Weissbrodt, *International Human Rights: Law, Policy and Process* (Cincinnati, Anderson, 1990).

> death penalty,[6] and the International Convention on the Rights of the Child,[7] which was to become the human rights treaty with the largest number of States parties.

On 14 March 1989, a happy Chairperson of the UN Commission on Human Rights reported on the past session at a press conference at the UN Liaison Office in Brussels. With 1,400 people in attendance, the session had been better attended than ever before: 43 Member States, 74 Observer States and 133 NGOs. Two human rights treaties were approved, the first in five years. Negotiations on the Convention on the Rights of the Child had lasted 10 years. I had drafted the Protocol on the abolition of the death penalty when I was Special Rapporteur as a member of the Sub-Commission on Human Rights (1981–85). French Prime Minister (1988–91) Michel Rocard set the tone by referring to 'the unfortunate Romanian people'. Hungarian Secretary of State for Foreign Affairs Gyula Horn's speech on human rights in Romania caused a sensation. He would become Prime Minister of Hungary from 1994 to 1998.

The Commission had been introduced to *glasnost* (transparency). Vladimir Lomeiko, the head of the Soviet delegation (1987–88), had explained to me that *glasnost* was intended to make *perestroika* (reform) irreversible. Belgium, which had become a member of the Commission after an absence of 25 years, was the main sponsor of the resolution on Afghanistan. That's why I was the first head of a Western delegation to be told that the Soviet Union wished to leave Afghanistan. Vladimir Lomeiko warned that, if this happened too quickly, Afghanistan would fall into the hands of Muslim fundamentalists. All this was greeted with a fair amount of incredulity. At the end of the session, Nicolette Franck wrote: 'The Commission has had its merits this year. M. Bossuyt, modestly, attributes them essentially to the change in the international climate, in other words, to the new attitude adopted by the USSR' (*LLB*, 18–19 March 1989).

During my presidency of the UN Commission on Human Rights, two events were to change the face of the world: on 4 June 1989, a student revolt was bloodily put down in Beijing's Heavenly Peace Square; and on 9 November, the fall of the Berlin Wall. It was not usual for the Chairperson of the Commission to undertake action between the annual six-week sessions. It didn't happen this time either. The destructive role played by the Soviet Union for years in human rights matters at the United Nations was soon taken over by the People's Republic of China. Since 15 November 1971, the representation at the United Nations of the Government of the Republic of China (Taiwan)

[6] M Bossuyt, 'The UN Optional Protocol on the Abolition of the Death Penalty' in M deGuzman and DM Amann, *Arc of Global Justice: Essays in Honour of William A Schabas* (Oxford, Oxford University Press, 2018).

[7] M Bossuyt, 'La Convention des Nations Unies sur les droits de l'enfant' (1990) 2 *Revue universelle des droits de l'homme* 141.

had been replaced by that of the People's Republic. It was not until 1982 that China became a member of the UN Commission on Human Rights. At first, the People's Republic of China played a rather discreet role. But this was to change after the events of Tiananmen, with the intellectual technical assistance of excellent Cuban diplomats. These events even had an immediate impact on asylum applications in Belgium.

1.4. A Chinese Misunderstanding (3–5 August 1989)

A few days after the suppression of the student revolt in Beijing, the Minister of Justice announced that residence permits for Chinese nationals legally resident in Belgium would be extended. Suddenly, on 3 August 1989, 300–400 Chinese gathered in front of the gate of the asylum seeker's reception centre Petit-Château. Within three days, 1,800 Chinese came forward (*LS*, 4–6 August 1989). Word had spread that it was easy for Chinese to obtain refugee status in Belgium. Many had naively paid thousands of Belgian francs to travel to Brussels in special buses from the Netherlands, France and Germany. Others had come by cab or in a Porsche, BMW or Mercedes registered in the Netherlands. Bar workers, who had left at 4 am from Maaseik, Bergen-op-Zoom and Sluis, arrived at dawn in their 'work clothes'.

With great difficulty, the gendarmes tried to contain them at the gate of Petit-Château. According to various reports, the operation was organised by the Triads (Chinese mafia-like secret societies). After some confusion, the Aliens Office handed out two sheets of paper: one containing an explanation and the other a summons. Apart from the words 'Wathelet', and 'May present himself or herself on …', these documents were written in Chinese. A stamp with the date of the invitation replaced the ellipsis. There were so many candidates that the convocations ran until January 1990. However, most of these people never showed up. A check of the statistics showed that, over the first nine years of the Commission General, 71 per cent (587/827) of all registered Chinese asylum applications had been lodged in 1989. In nine years, 87 Chinese were granted refugee status, four of them by the Permanent Board. Another group of asylum seekers occupying a very special place were the Ghanaians.

1.5. Ghanaian Asylum-Seeker Networks (April–December 1989)

In April 1989, Willy Kuijpers (VU), Member of the European Parliament, reported that he had brought back some clarifications from his trip to Ghana. He had gone there to find out why 25 per cent of all asylum seekers in Belgium came from this country:

> Ghana is a very poor country. Thousands of Ghanaians leave the country to earn money in Europe. This money is collected by all family members, who sometimes sacrifice their last possessions.[8] Smart guys arrange forged documents and plane tickets. They teach them what stories to tell. A few months ago, Antwerp police discovered 88 Ghanaian prostitutes. They were being put to work in 22 different 'establishments' in the city. I consider this modern slave trade unacceptable (GvA, 27 April 1989).

In an open letter to the Minister of Justice, Willy Kuijpers had complained about the situation at the Zaventem Transit Centre, the huge staff shortage at the Commission General, the fraud by asylum seekers and the existence of organised networks. He concludes: 'No one is served by this way of doing things'.

In *De Standaard* of 3–4 June 1989, I confirmed that the largest group of asylum seekers (1,196 in 1988) came from Ghana. Only two of them had been recognised as refugees:

> The stories they tell are often very stereotyped. The Ghanaian women come and say they used to work in one store or another. One day, crates are delivered. The next day, the police raid the shop, and it turns out that the crates contained weapons for a coup d'état. The ladies were put in a cell. However, they were able to escape to Belgium. They said they had lost their identity papers or that they had been stolen.

I said that Belgium was not the promised land for them. Most of them were unlucky enough to have been intercepted getting off a Sabena plane at the National Airport, en route from Lagos (Nigeria) to Montreal (Canada). I referred to Willy Kuijpers, who said that economic rather than political motives were at play. Recruiters were willing to pay large sums to help Ghanaian asylum seekers realise their dream of making a lot of money in the West.

I returned to it several more times:

- If Ghanaians are to be believed, there must be dozens of coup attempts in Ghana every day (*GvA*, 22 November 1989).
- Among Ghanaians, there are the eternal coup attempts, all of which are said to be committed by hairdressers or seamstresses who have hidden weapons in their beauty huts. Many embroiderers and seamstresses, who were led to believe that they could find work here, end up in prostitution (*Knack*, 13 December 1989).
- If all this were to be believed, Ghana would be a huge ammunition dump. The number of coup attempts would be at least daily. How are we supposed to believe that hairdressers, embroiderers, and seamstresses have all committed coup attempts that have unfortunately failed (*Veto*, 18 November 1991).

[8] These amounts varied between 80,000 and 150,000 BF (€2,000–€3,750).

Earlier, Chris De Stoop[9] had devoted an entire article in the *Knack* on 18 April 1990. It read:

> They are currently the most talked-about group in the red-light districts of Antwerp, Ghent, and Brussels: Ghanaian street and window prostitutes. They apply for political refugee status and 99 per cent of their applications are rejected. There's a huge turnover. They often have good lawyers, and always the same ones. They pay them cash. When they apply for asylum, they serve up their premade stories of persecution for arms trafficking, attempted coup d'état or membership of Jehovah's Witnesses.

On 24 January 1992, *De Morgen* reported that Bob Cools (SP), the mayor of Antwerp (1983–94) had sent the Minister of Justice, on 15 November 1991, a list of three hundred Ghanaian prostitutes who had applied for asylum. The Minister asked for these cases to be given priority. I replied that I would be happy to follow up this suggestion. I pointed out that these files were already being processed speedily.

In the Commission General's first year of operation, more than a quarter of all asylum seekers came from Ghana (1,144/4,476). During the first four years, there was an average of 1,419 Ghanaian asylum seekers per year. From 1992 to 1993, this number dropped to an average of 986 per year. In the last three years, they averaged just 159. In my last year (1996), their percentage of the total number of asylum applications fell to just 0.5 per cent (67/12,395). Out of a total of 8,129 Ghanaian asylum applications, there have been – in nine years – 64 recognitions, to which the Permanent Board added 10. The overall recognition rate for Ghanaians was therefore 0.78 per cent.

By prioritising the processing of Ghanaian asylum applications, their share of the total could be reduced from 25 per cent in 1988 to 0.5 per cent in 1996. For years, however, I had to watch hundreds of young Ghanaian women abusing the asylum procedure to engage in prostitution. Tolerating this was considered humane. It's incomprehensible how this situation has proliferated for so long. Ghanaian asylum seekers arrived in Belgium at Brussels National Airport, where – even before the new Refugee Law came into force – the reception conditions were a source of great concern.

1.6. The Reception Conditions 'Crying Vengeance to Heaven' at the National Airport

Under the new Refugee Law, the Minister, or his delegate (the Aliens Office), could refuse entry to asylum seekers who did not have the documents required to

[9] On 23 October 1993, we were together at the British Embassy in Brussels to greet Diana, Princess of Wales. She left a big impression.

enter the Kingdom. Against such a refusal, an 'urgent request for reconsideration' could be submitted to the Minister or his delegate. In such cases, an opinion was sought from the Commissioner General. A favourable opinion was binding on the delegate if he had taken the decision, but not when the Minister had taken it himself.

Practical experience showed that in Belgium there was only one border where asylum seekers could not enter without being checked, and that was at the National Airport. The law imposed very short deadlines (24 hours), both for asylum seekers to submit their urgent request for reconsideration, and for the Commissioner General to give his opinion. This did not prevent a considerable amount of time elapsing between the submission of an asylum application and the issuing of a binding decision, especially in the case of an urgent request for reconsideration. This time could be even longer if, in the event of a negative decision, the foreigner concerned had to be deported. In the meantime, these foreign nationals had to remain at the National Airport without any decent reception facilities.

1.6.1. 'Caretaking Business' under Martens VII (November 1987–March 1988)

On 10 November 1987, a week after my appointment, I had written to Justice Minister Jean Gol about the need for better reception conditions at the National Airport:

> It is essential that the necessary measures to guarantee the reception of refugee candidates in conditions compatible with human dignity be taken in good time, in order to avoid situations that could damage the reputation of our country and compromise the functioning of the new law.

I went to the National Airport on 15 December 1987, accompanied by my two Deputy Commissioners, Christian Bayi and Marc Bonte, appointed that same day. The following day, I sent letters to Herman De Croo (PVV), Minister of Communications (1981–88), to the Minister of Justice and to the Secretary of State for Social Emancipation. I reported that the reception conditions did not even meet a minimum standard.

On 5 March 1988, I drew the attention of Wivina Demeester (CVP), Secretary of State for Public Health (1985–88), to the very worrying situation in the 'SOS' premises in Zaventem: 'From both a moral and a public health point of view, this situation is totally unjustifiable, and the combination of the two factors is frankly worrying'. The premises were previously used to receive travellers stranded at Zaventem. There were still two small Saniport premises, which carried out the functions entrusted to it under the International Health Regulations. With a maximum capacity of eight people, these premises were in no way suited to receiving dozens of asylum seekers. On 18 March 1988, the Secretary of State for Public Health expressed the wish to make the building previously used for quarantine purposes (building 127) available for asylum seekers as soon as possible.

In the media of 19–20 March 1988, the UNHCR Representative denounced the situation at the National Airport. He said that the Belgian authorities could have foreseen the reception problems at Zaventem a long time ago. Interviewed on RTBF radio's *La Une* on 19 March, I explained that at least one temporary reception centre should have been available by 1 February. We couldn't wait any longer. On 25 March, the Interministerial Committee decided that three days later the necessary work would begin, which would last around 45 days.

That same evening, I was a guest on a Humanist Federation programme broadcast live on BRTN TV. The host, Johan Anthierens, tried to blame me for the reception conditions that were 'crying to heaven'. He asked me if I was going to resign if the centre wasn't ready within 45 days. Not without irritation, I replied that it wasn't me, but the government that had to take responsibility. Immediately after my appointment, I had drawn attention to this indecent situation.

1.6.2. Repelling Responsibility under Martens VIII (May 1988–December 1989)

The 28-place Transit Centre 127, decided on 25 March 1988, was not finally inaugurated until 1 December 1988. The expansion to 80 places, decided on 22 December 1989, would become operational in March 1990. It was a long ordeal.

The Martens VIII Government took office on 9 May 1988. On 31 May, in a letter to the new Minister of Justice, Melchior Wathelet, I expressed the hope that the reception centre would open quickly. From 1 June to 1 November inclusive, the opening of the new reception centre was postponed from month to month. On 21 October, a reader of *Het Laatste Nieuws* described the situation at Saniport as follows:

> Great was my astonishment when I opened the door and found nothing but coloured people with few clothes (men and women). A horribly unpleasant smell seized me. The place was a sight to behold. Dirt was piling up. Unworthy of an international airport!

In the media on 2 December, I learned that the Minister of Justice and the Secretary of State for Social Emancipation had finally, the previous day, inaugurated an airport transit centre for asylum seekers in Melsbroek. It could accommodate 28 people.

In the case of an urgent request for reconsideration of a decision to refuse entry, I always delivered my opinion within the legally prescribed 24-hour time limit. The Minister generally took these decisions himself. An initial negative ministerial decision was often followed by a second, following an urgent request for reconsideration. This meant that a refusal decision would take dozens of days to become enforceable. The Aliens Office assumed responsibility for the 28 places at the transit centre. For the remainder, it tried to shift responsibility to other ministerial departments.

This again led to unacceptable situations. On 19 October 1989, the Minister of Justice described the humanitarian and health situation in the transit zone as 'intolerable'. The simultaneous arrival of some 40 Angolan and Ghanaian asylum seekers had caused panic:

> Asylum seekers live in their own filth. It's an old and monotonous story. Next to Saniport's small premises, Belgium boasts fine chocolates, and we sell special beers. Here, we're seized by smells of human sweat, leftover food, and toilet odours. In one corner, there's half a meter of stinking garbage. One toilet looks like it hasn't been cleaned in ages. Perhaps these people had valid passports to begin with. However, they had lost them on arrival (*HN*, 21 October 1989).

In consultation with Jean-Luc Dehaene, Minister of Communications (1988–91), the Minister of Justice called in the Belgian Red Cross. Some 50 beds were set up at the airport. On 15 and 29 November 1989, the Brussels Chamber of Indictment visited the airport to rule on the 'deprivation of liberty' of 37 rejected asylum seekers. In the meantime, nine of them had been put back on a plane, eight had managed to escape and five others had their applications declared admissible. There were now around 70 asylum seekers in the transit zone. On 30 November, the Chamber of Indictment ruled that the rejected asylum seekers were not in a state of deprivation of liberty since they could board any plane.

On 31 October 1989, I wrote to the Minister of Justice to point out the need for a clear allocation of responsibilities within the government. Only the Minister of Justice had the means to influence the length and number of people held at the border. He could do so by refusing or not access to the territory, by following or not my favourable opinion, by allocating enough staff and by taking the initiative to amend the law. On 24 November, the Minister of Justice replied that he was not responsible for the infrastructure at Zaventem, nor for the actual reception of asylum seekers. The Minister felt he could no longer tolerate being systematically made the scapegoat for certain situations over which he had no control, either budgetary or legal.

Also on 24 November, the Council of Ministers mandated the Minister of Justice, in collaboration with his colleagues in Communications and Social Emancipation, to set up a working group tasked with proposing an extension of accommodation capacity for asylum seekers. On 22 December 1989, the Council of Ministers approved an 80-bed extension to the transit centre for asylum seekers. This extension, which became operational in March 1990, was sufficient to temporarily accommodate the number of asylum seekers retained that year.

1.7. 'Refugee Policy Collapses' (May–December 1989)

On 11 May and 8 June 1989, I presented my *First Annual Report* (1988) to the House of Representatives and the Senate respectively. Compared with 1987, the number of asylum applications had fallen slightly (-9 per cent). At the National Airport, there were far fewer asylum applications (-86 per cent). I complained that the procedure was too slow: 'Right from the start, Mr Bossuyt ("not easy to discourage") shouted "daredevil": "We should be handling 230 cases a month, but we can only take 120, due to lack of staff"' (*La Cité*, 1 June 1989).

On 24 May 1989, the Minister of Justice answered questions in the House during the exchange of views on this report. He was particularly opposed to any interference with his powers. He felt that the procedure was no longer credible since asylum seekers were rarely expelled from the country. He agreed that the procedure took too long. He also said that he was up against the Finance Inspector. The latter felt that the backlog was not serious enough to justify temporary recruitment.

In *De Standaard* of 3–4 June 1989, Pol Van Mossevelde wrote that the new Refugee Law was working differently from what had been envisaged at the Palais d'Egmont. Staff shortages remained a serious obstacle to handling the ever-increasing mountain of backlogs. On 7 June, Piet Van Brabant wrote in *Het Laatste Nieuws*: 'Wathelet sounds the alarm. The overloaded Aliens Office has absolutely no control over the situation. The Minister considers the situation to be dramatic'.

In the same newspaper, on 27 June 1989, I questioned the feasibility of a proposal by Guy Verhofstadt, Chairperson of the PVV (Flemish Liberals) (1989–92), who wanted to distinguish between migrants according to their degree of integration. I preferred to distinguish between foreigners who were in the country legally and those who were in it illegally. This distinction is based on a legal criterion that can be objectively verified. I thought it was worrying that, as the Minister of Justice had pointed out, the Aliens Office had collapsed. In an editorial on the same day, Piet Van Brabant wrote: 'It is a highly unhealthy and dangerous state of affairs that thousands of illegal immigrants are roaming our country, for want of a well-equipped administration, on the fringes of society, bordering on criminality'.

In *Le Vif/L'Express* of 8 December 1989, I acknowledged that 'the situation was catastrophic'. In the same article, under the headline 'The Alert Rating. An Explosive Situation', Bernard Detry, who oversaw asylum issues in the Justice Minister's office, told Carine Vassart: 'In 1988, out of more than 2,500 decisions concerning all foreigners, only 400 were repatriated. Only firmness can discourage mass arrivals, but this is difficult to reconcile with humanitarian principles … Reception facilities are rapidly saturated'. That same day, Secretary of State for Social Emancipation, Miet Smet, told *Le Soir*: 'In fact, we only react when there are difficulties'.

The eyes of Bernard Detry, magistrate at the Mons Public Prosecutor's office, were opened when he took part in international consultations on asylum. He discovered that not only Belgium, but other European countries, were facing a sharp rise in asylum applications. These other countries, however, were more aware of the urgent need for drastic measures. He gradually tried to convince the Minister – not without difficulty – that my warning signals were not intended to undermine his position. The only objective was to try to save the Minister and the country from further misfortune.

In the *Knack* of 13 December 1989, Chris De Stoop wrote, under the headline 'There was no more Room in the Inn': 'As expected and predicted, Belgian refugee policy has collapsed. From the very first days of his appointment, Mr Bossuyt, crying out in the desert, had foretold the present catastrophe'. And he quoted me:

> They only discover the problem when the newspapers mention it. During the first two months of the new Refugee Law, an asylum seeker could enter in the morning and already receive an order to leave the country the same day. Now, the Aliens Office gives them a small piece of paper which they must return within six months. In Switzerland and the Netherlands, the number of staff is automatically increased as the number of asylum seekers rises. Here, we're always five years late. We're always one war behind. The Swiss receive 175 extra members of staff. This would cost half a billion BF [€12.5 million] but would save one billion [€25 million] for reception. Belgium is not yet the most disastrous country. Switzerland is running at 25,000 asylum seekers, France at 60,000 and Germany at 100,000.

1.8. The Asylum Crisis in Switzerland

It is striking that for the first two years of the Commission General's activity (1988–89), there are more newspaper clippings available concerning the asylum situation in Switzerland than in Belgium. Asylum in Switzerland was in a state of permanent crisis. The media were paying close attention. A subscription to the *Journal de Genève* proved to be a good investment. Peter Arbenz, Director of the Swiss Federal Office for Refugees (1985–93), fulfilled an unenviable role as the country's first 'Mister Refugees'.

I was very familiar with Switzerland. I had lived in Geneva for six years. I had been a doctoral student (1969–73) at the Graduate Institute of International Studies (IUHEI). I worked as a human rights officer for almost two years (1975–77) in the Human Rights Division of the United Nations Office in Geneva. There I met my wife Kristien, a midwife at the Cantonal Hospital. Our son Kristof was born there on 12 February 1976. From 1981 onwards, I spent at least four to six weeks a year taking part in UN human rights sessions. I knew what fate awaited Belgium if the necessary measures were not taken in good time. Meanwhile, the processing of asylum applications continued. A particular one was that of Patrick Ryan.

2

Patrick Ryan, an Irish Asylum Seeker[1] (7 September–25 November 1988)

In my first year as Commissioner General, I was confronted with a very special asylum application. On 7 September 1988, an Irish citizen, Patrick Ryan (b 1930), applied for asylum in Belgium. He had been a Catholic priest in the Republic of Ireland and later in Great Britain. Back in Ireland, he collected money for African countries. He also did this in support of Irish activists opposing the British presence in Ulster. In 1977, he was arrested in Geneva and deported to Madrid.

On 28 June 1988, in Benidorm, he took a bus bound for Brussels. Two days later, the local police in Uccle (in the Brussels region) arrested him. The police found in his possession, among other things, manuals on explosives, 52 watches and five 'Memoparks'. On 1 July 1988, an arrest warrant was issued for falsifying documents and breaching the Law of 28 May 1956 on explosive substances and mixtures. On 6 September 1988, the examining magistrate issued an arrest warrant based on the announcement of a British extradition request.[2] The following day, Ryan applied for asylum.

2.1. The Asylum Application Intersects with the Extradition Request

On 15 September 1988, a new warrant was issued for his arrest on charges of conspiracy and criminal association. On 20 October, the British Embassy notified him of an extradition request. He was suspected of conspiracy to murder and

[1] M Bossuyt, 'Father Ryan, an Irish Asylum Seeker in Belgium (1988)' in K Lemmens, S Parmentier and L Reyntjens (eds), *Human Rights with a Human Touch: Liber Amicorum Paul Lemmens* (Antwerp, Intersentia, 2019) 223.

[2] The extradition request referred to the following offences: 'On various days between 21 May 1975 and 1 July 1988 conspired with other persons unknown to murder other persons and between 1 February 1986 and 1 July 1988 to cause by explosive substances explosions of a nature likely to endanger life or cause serious injury to property in the United Kingdom; on 30 June 1988 had in his possession or under his control certain explosive substances namely 52 switches containing integrated circuits, 5 "Memopark" timing devices, 14 dowels and a "ROBBE" receiver'.

possession of explosive substances with intent to endanger life or property in the United Kingdom.

On 20 October 1988, the Aliens Office refused him residency on the grounds that he could endanger public order or national security. He was suspected of being an active member of the Irish Republican Army (IRA) and was carrying a false passport. Other grounds for refusal included: having applied for asylum even though he did not meet the criteria for it; having stayed in several countries, namely Italy, France and Spain, and having left the latter country in the absence of fear within the meaning of the Geneva Convention; having submitted his application after the expiry of the eight working days following his entry into the Kingdom; having deliberately attempted to mislead the Belgian authorities by confusing and incomplete declarations concerning his multiple activities and travels.

Imprisoned in Saint-Gilles prison, Ryan appeared before the Chamber of Indictment of the Brussels Court of Appeal. He referred to Article 6 of the Extradition Law of 1 October 1833, which stipulates that 'the foreigner may not be prosecuted or punished for any political offence prior to extradition'. Belgium had adhered to this principle in Article 7 of the Extradition Treaty it had concluded with the United Kingdom on 29 October 1901, and in its reservation to the European Convention on Terrorism of 27 January 1977. Ryan stated that the United Kingdom was requesting his extradition to prosecute and punish him because of his political, ideological, national, or religious conviction. He referred to publications in the British press which described him as a dangerous terrorist. This would prevent a 'fair trial', as required by Article 6 of the European Convention on Human Rights (ECHR).

2.2. My Recommendation: Send Ryan to Ireland (14 November 1988)

On 28 October 1988, Ryan submitted an urgent request to the Minister of Justice, Melchior Wathelet, for reconsideration of the decision to refuse him residency in Belgium. In my (non-binding) opinion of 14 November,[3] I examined the reasons given by the Aliens Office for refusing Ryan's residence in the country. As his application had not been lodged more than three months after the event that had led him to declare himself a refugee (the extradition request), the fact that he had spent more than three months in one or more other countries could not validly be invoked. Nor was his application late, having been submitted the day after he became aware of the extradition request. He could not have been expected to apply

[3] My opinion was published in the *First Annual Report* (1988) (*Doc parl*, *Chambre*, 1988/89, N° 871/1, Appendix 1, 98), and in the (1991) 1 *Revue belge de droit international* 200.

for asylum before the events had occurred that had prompted him to lodge his application. As the person concerned was the subject of an extradition request and did not know whether he would have access to the asylum procedure, his confused and incomplete statements concerning his numerous activities and travels could not necessarily be considered as the result of a deliberate intention to deceive the Belgian authorities. Since he invoked grounds such as his religion, nationality, membership of a certain social group or political opinions, it was not possible, at this stage of the proceedings, to conclude that his application was manifestly unrelated to asylum criteria.

The fact that he was in possession of a forged (British) passport could hardly lead to the conclusion that he might compromise public order or national security. Since he was suspected of being an active member of the IRA, I felt that the Minister had not exceeded his discretionary powers in this matter. Responsibility for public order or national security rests with the Minister of Justice. However, Ryan had not applied for asylum because of a well-founded fear of persecution by his State of nationality (the Republic of Ireland). There was nothing to suggest a priori that the Irish authorities would refuse him protection. I referred to the UNHCR Guide to Procedures and Criteria for Determining Refugee Status (1979), which states that:

> [A]n applicant's well-founded fear of persecution must be in relation to the country of his nationality. As long as he has no fear in relation to the country of his nationality, he can be expected to avail himself of that country's protection. He is not in need of international protection and is therefore not a refugee.

For all these reasons, I have given the Minister of Justice an unfavourable opinion of Ryan's stay in Belgium as an asylum seeker. As for his removal, I added the following to my unfavourable opinion:

> However, in view of the fact that he claims to fear persecution on the grounds of his religion, nationality, membership of a particular social group or political opinions in the United Kingdom because of his activities against that country's policy in Northern Ireland, it would seem appropriate, in the event of removal, that the person concerned be directed to the country of which he is a national, namely the Republic of Ireland, whose authorities are in a better position to assess the validity of this fear than the Belgian authorities.

The Minister of Justice learned of this opinion via the media on 16 November. As was clear from his press release, he was indisposed. Yet the notice had been sent to him, as usual by fax, on Monday 14 November at 4.45 pm, the day before King's Day. Although this was not customary, it had also been communicated to him barely 15 minutes later by courier to his Cabinet. I drew his attention to the fact that I did not consider my opinions to be confidential. At the express request of one his lawyers, Me Georges-Henri Beauthier, the notice was faxed to Ryan's Belgian counsel on 16 November at 11.54 am. His counsel immediately sent it to the media. On 17 November 1988, the Minister of Justice rejected the urgent request for reconsideration.

2.3. Favourable Opinion of the Court on Extradition to the United Kingdom (17 November 1988)

The pleadings on the British extradition request took place on 3 November 1988 before the Chamber of Indictment. Submissions were made by three lawyers[4] from the Brussels Bar, two from the London Bar, one from the Paris Bar and one from the Dublin Bar. On 17 November, the Chamber of Indictment gave a favourable opinion[5] to the British request for extradition of Patrick Ryan. The Chamber considered that the facts referred to by the British government could constitute the offence of criminal association, punishable under Articles 323 and 324 of the Belgian Penal Code. Such an offence is also referred to in Article 1, 1°, of the Extradition Treaty of 29 October 1901. The activity had taken place outside the territory of the United Kingdom but had materialised on UK territory. As one of the constituent elements of the offence had been committed on that territory, the offence was presumed to have been committed there in its entirety.

Regarding Article 6 of the Extradition Law of 1 October 1833,[6] the Chamber considered that the facts were neither a political offence 'by its nature', nor an offence 'connected' to a political offence, nor an offence qualified as a 'mixed' political offence, since they had not directly undermined the country's political institutions or the political order of the requesting State. The Chamber also referred to Article 13 of the European Convention on the Suppression of Terrorism, which stipulates that any State may reserve

> the right to refuse extradition in respect of any offence mentioned in Article 1 which it considers to be a political offence, an offence connected with a political offence, or an offence inspired by political motives, provided that it undertakes to take into due consideration, when evaluating the character of the offence, any particularly serious aspects of the offence.

The Chamber believed that the possession of electronic equipment with the aim of causing injury to persons and damage to property was an element which made it possible to establish the 'particularly serious aspect' of his behaviour. Finally, it did not appear that his situation would be aggravated by his surrender to the requesting State on grounds of race, religion, nationality, or political opinion. Considering that the conditions laid down in the Law of 15 March 1874 and in the Extradition Treaty between Belgium and the United Kingdom had been met, the Chamber issued a favourable opinion on the extradition of Patrick Ryan.

[4] The other Belgian lawyers were Me Jacques Hamaide and Me Luc Walleyn of the Brussels Bar.

[5] The 'secret' opinion of the Chamber of Indictment [Bruxelles (ch mises acc – avis), 17 novembre 1988 (Ryan P)], was published in the *Journal des Tribunaux* (1989) 125.

[6] Supplemented by the Laws of 15 March 1874 and 3 July 1985.

2.4. Ryan not Extradited: Thatcher is Furious with Martens

Despite the favourable opinion of the Chamber of Indictment, the Minister of Justice Melchior Wathelet decided, on Friday 25 November 1988, not to extradite Ryan to the United Kingdom.

2.4.1. The Transfer to Ireland (25 November 1988)

That evening, Ryan, who was in the third week of his hunger strike,[7] was transferred to his country of nationality (Republic of Ireland), arriving at around 10.50 pm. Ryan (58 years old) had been refusing to eat since 3 November and drink since 24 November. He had lost 12 kg. At the military airport in Melsbroek, he was put on a military plane with, in the words of former Minister Jean Gol, 'the honours due to his rank'.[8] On the night of Monday to Tuesday, 29 November 1988, he left the clinic where he had been resting, to go to a religious institution.

Although this was formally a decision taken by the Minister of Justice, it was in fact taken the same day by the Council of Ministers. According to the press release from the office of Prime Minister Wilfried Martens, which referred to 'the decisions and opinions of the Belgian courts and the opinion of the Commissioner General', the facts were very imprecisely circumscribed, and the arrest warrants did not contain the constituent elements of the punishable offence of criminal association. In fact, this was the only charge which, based on the exequatur, could have allowed extradition to the United Kingdom.

In his *De Memoires*,[9] Prime Minister Wilfried Martens wrote that this was done 'after a brief but intense deliberation'. According to External Relations Minister Leo Tindemans,[10] Deputy Prime Ministers Philippe Moureaux (PS) and Hugo Schiltz (VU) were the most opposed to extradition. He himself was in favour of extradition but was unable to inform the British before the military aircraft landed in Ireland. When the British Foreign Secretary, Sir Geoffrey Howe, heard of the decision, he suddenly hung up with a '"Thank you" – end of story'.[11]

At 3 am on Saturday 26 November 1988, the Commissioner of Dublin City Police received four extradition requests concerning Ryan. The reasons given were

[7] According to *Le Monde* (26 November), he had said: 'If I am extradited, it will be in a coffin'; *Tipperary Sun* quoted in the *Knack* (7 December).

[8] *Doc parl, Chambre*, SS 1988, 21 (29 November 1988).

[9] W Martens, *De Memoires: Luctor et emergo* (Tielt, Lannoo, 2006) 793.

[10] L Tindemans, *Een Politiek Testament: Mijn plaats in de tijd. Dagboek van een minister* (Tielt, Lannoo, 2009) 546.

[11] ibid 547.

the same as those in the requests to Belgium. Before Irish Attorney General John Murray had a chance to examine the case,[12] the media predicted that he would reject the requests on the grounds of insufficient evidence. The *Sunday Tribune*[13] and the *Sunday Independent* of 27 November referred to a government source. The *Sunday Press* of the same day wrote: 'Attorney General to block British bid on Father Ryan. The indications in Dublin last night were that the Irish Attorney General will refuse the request'.

2.4.2. Margaret Thatcher Furious and Jean Gol Unleashed

The Belgian decision was strongly criticised in the United Kingdom.[14] Prime Minister Margaret Thatcher (1979–90) was furious. On 29 November 1988, an 'outraged' Jean Gol[15] in the Foreign Affairs Committee of the Belgian House of Representatives criticised the decision not to extradite a person accused of terrorism in the United Kingdom to that country. In his view, this ran counter to the policy pursued to date of European cooperation to combat terrorism within the framework of the European Legal Area.

Justice Minister Melchior Wathelet stated that the decision was taken on legal grounds. On 22 and 26 September 1988, the Chambre du conseil of the Brussels Tribunal of first instance had granted exequatur to the extradition requests. This was confirmed by the Chamber of Indictment on 12 October. However, the exequatur was limited to the charge of criminal association. This charge is vague and could even be considered *obscuri libelli* (unclear wording) under Belgian law. Moreover, the British notion of 'conspiracy' did not entirely correspond to that of criminal association, which requires organisation. Other charges were less vague but had not been granted exequatur.

A mission to London on 29 and 30 November 1988 by eight Belgian senators to study methods of combating terrorism received a particularly cold reception. On meeting the delegation, British Home Secretary Douglas Hurd expressed his 'disappointment' at the decision and his 'bitterness' at not having been informed until Ryan was already on his way to Ireland (*DS*, 1 December 1988).

[12] John Murray, Attorney-General (1987–91), Judge at the EU Court of Justice (1992–99), Judge at the Supreme Court (1999–2015), Chief Justice (2004–11). In 1995, Melchior Wathelet joined him in Luxembourg.

[13] 'Irish Government sources are sceptical of the chances that the extradition will be granted, in view of the vague charges of conspiracy which the British applied to Belgium'.

[14] 'Belgium Angers Thatcher with Ryan Decision' *The Times* (28 November 1988); 'Why the decisions have to go to the Belgian cabinet; when decisions are reached in the political forms, the reasoning is likely to be political' (29 November 1988). 'COWARDS' *The Sun*, quoted in *DM* (1 December 1988). Ivan Lawrence MP said in the British Parliament on 6 December: 'We are all shocked and hurt by the cowardly behaviour of our friends, the Belgians. The Belgian Government just did what was necessary to get the problem off their plate, which is as near an act of cowardice as I have ever seen any government perform' (vol 143, col 232).

[15] *LLB* (30 November 1988): 'Déchainé, Jean Gol a parlé d'Eurotrouille, d'Europanique, d'Eurodérobade, d'Euroblabla'; *Le Monde* (1 December). *Doc parl, Chambre*, SS 1988, 18.

During the weekend of 2–3 December 1988, the European Council was held on the island of Rhodes (Greece). In the run-up to this meeting, Manu Ruys published an opinion in *De Standaard* on 1 December under the title 'Misplaced pride'. In his opinion, there was no reason for Prime Minister Wilfried Martens 'to back down or apologise'. Among other things, he pointed out that it had not been forgotten that

> Mrs Thatcher, in her hatred of Irish separatism, made the cold-blooded decision to let IRA fighters – imprisoned on hunger strike – die in their cells … and how unarmed Irish nationalists – who it was not proven were going to commit an attack – were murdered in the street in Gibraltar by British secret agents.

Manu Ruys was referring to the death on 5 May 1981 of Bobby Sands (and later of nine other Irish nationalists) after a 66-day hunger strike in the Maze prison in Northern Ireland, and to the murder of three IRA members in Gibraltar by the British Special Air Service on 7 March 1988.[16]

At the Rhodes European Council, British Prime Minister Margaret Thatcher had harsh words for the Belgian and Irish governments, accusing them of cowardice. She was dismayed: 'our confidence is shaken'. After the meeting, Prime Minister Wilfried Martens said: 'The meeting was lively and warm, at least for me'. He was 'happy' to have had the opportunity to provide her with all the information she needed to understand the Belgian legal system. The Irish Taoiseach, Charles Haughey,[17] had not at all appreciated Thatcher's aggressive remarks in the House of Commons: 'This will reduce the chances of Ryan being extradited to Britain'.

2.5. Virulent Reactions in the Irish and British Parliaments (December 1988)

During a debate in the Irish Parliament on 6 December 1988, Irish MPs wondered whether in such a climate Ryan could expect a fair trial in the United Kingdom: 'The British Prime Minister was unable to mention his name without using the word "terrorist" in the same sentence'. Irish MP Peter Barry declared:

> In prevailing circumstances, it is very difficult to allow people to be extradited to Britain since they still occupy part of our national territory. In those circumstances, I have a difficulty, in that, to my mind, extraditing people to the North or Britain recognises the right of the British to be in Ireland and to impose their will and laws on our country, flouting our aspirations and the constitutional position of this State.

[16] In its judgment *McCann et al v the United Kingdom* of 27 September 1995, the Grand Chamber of the European Court of Human Rights in Strasbourg would condemn (by 10 votes to 9) the United Kingdom in this case on the grounds of a violation of Art 2 ECHR (the right to life).

[17] Charles Haughey, Prime Minister (Taoiseach) (1979–82; 1987–92) for Fianna Fáil.

By 28 November, there had already been criticism in the British Parliament of Prime Minister Margaret Thatcher's statements on Ryan. It was feared that they would make a fair trial impossible. Tony Benn[18] referred to what his fellow MP Michael Mates had said the previous day: 'one of the most wanted terrorists has been let free, and many still believe that the Irish Republic is a safe haven for some terrorists'. Referring to Thatcher's reaction ('I entirely agree with my Hon Friend'), he concluded:

> When a senior member of the House says, and it is confirmed by the Prime Minister, that that person is a terrorist, it is impossible from that moment for that man to have a fair trial. The BBC broadcast these comments and all the newspapers picked them up.[19]

After Rhodes, there was also much criticism in the British Parliament. On 5 December 1988, Liberal Democrat leader Paddy Ashdown declared:[20]

> What the Prime Minister did was cheered to the echo by the extremists in the North who would wish to see undermined our capacity to review the Anglo-Irish Agreement and the relations between the Irish Government and the British Government at their worst possible level because they know that would damage the fight against terrorism (column 70).

On 6 December, Tony Benn declared: 'the confusion, which began with the political evasion by the Belgian Cabinet, was turned into chaos last week by the prejudicial tantrums of the British Prime Minister' (column 174). Thatcher replied that it was clear that the present arrangements for extradition between the United Kingdom and Ireland were not working well. She felt that attention ought to be given to that (column 177).

2.6. British Rage Prevents a Fair Trial: No Extradition by Ireland

In the Irish Parliament, the Attorney General[21] declared on 13 December 1988, that he believed there was sufficient evidence on two of the charges to

[18] Tony Benn, Labour politician, member of the House of Lords (as Viscount Stansgate) (1960–63); MP (1963–2001); Minister (1961–66 and 1974–79).

[19] Michael Mates reacted: 'Strictly, I should have said, "Ryan is the man the security forces most want in connection with serious terrorist offences"' (vol 143, col 722). John Fraser MP (vol 143, col 910) and Eric Heffer MP (vol 143, cols 913–14) also referred to these statements on 14 December 1988.

[20] Paddy Ashdown MP (1983–2001), Leader of the Liberal Democrats (1988–99), High Representative in Bosnia and Herzegovina (2002–06).

[21] The Irish extradition Law of 1987 requires the Attorney General 'to direct that a warrant for the extradition of a person from the State shall not be endorsed unless, having considered such information as he deems appropriate, he is of the opinion that there is a clear intention to prosecute that person, founded on the existence of sufficient evidence (*Dáil Eireann*, vol 385, 13 December 1988, 1201).

prosecute Ryan.[22] This could be done in Ireland, without a jury.[23] He also pointed to references to Ryan in the British media 'often expressed in intemperate language and frequently in the form of extravagantly worded headlines'.[24] Nor could he ignore the statements made in the British Parliament. They were widely and fully reported in the media and carried weight with potential jurors. He felt they had the effect of creating prejudice and hostility manifestly and inescapably, to the point where it would not be possible for a jury to approach the issue of Ryan's guilt or innocence free from bias. He felt that the resulting prejudice was 'irredeemable': 'The right to a fair trial includes a right to protection against the creation of prejudice or animosity in the minds of potential jurors'.[25]

On 14 December 1988, Labour leader Neil Kinnock[26] told the British Parliament concerning Margaret Thatcher: 'It is clear that, by her manner in Parliament and at Rhodes, the Hon Lady had squandered the opportunity to secure Patrick Ryan's extradition' (column 764).

In her memoirs,[27] Thatcher wrote that the case of Patrick Ryan demonstrated 'how little we could seriously hope from the Irish'. She could not understand why the Belgian government had not followed the advice of the Brussels Court of Appeal and had flown Patrick Ryan back to Ireland on a military plane:

> Ryan, a non-practising Catholic priest, was well known in security service circles as a terrorist; for some time, he had played a significant role in the Provisional IRA's links with Libya. The charges against Ryan were of utmost seriousness, including conspiracy to murder and explosive offences. In June 1988 we had asked the Belgians to place him under surveillance. They, in turn, pressed us strongly to apply for extradition. So, the application was made in close collaboration with the Belgian authorities. The Belgian court which considered the extradition request gave an advisory opinion, which we knew to have been favourable – something which the Belgian Government never denied – to the Minister of Justice. The latter then took the decision to the Belgian Cabinet. The Cabinet decided to ignore the court's opinion and to fly Ryan to Ireland, only telling us afterwards. Presumably, this political decision was prompted by fear of terrorist retaliation if the Belgians co-operated with us.
>
> We now sought the extradition of Ryan from the Republic; but this was refused, initially on what seemed a technicality, though the Irish Attorney General later suggested that Ryan would not receive a fair trial before a British jury. I wrote a vigorous protest to Mr Haughey. I had already taken up the matter personally with him and with the Belgian Prime Minister, M Martens, at the European Council in Rhodes on Friday 2 and Saturday 3 December 1988. I told both how appalled I was. I was particularly angry with M Martens of how his government's attitude contrasted with all the

[22] ibid 1202.
[23] ibid 1206.
[24] ibid 1204.
[25] ibid 1205.
[26] Neil Kinnock MP (1970–95), Leader of the Labour Party (1985–92), EU Commissioner (1995–2004), Member of the House of Lords (since 2005).
[27] M Thatcher, *My Downing Street Years* (London, Harper Press, 1993) 413.

co-operation we had given Belgium over those British people charged in relation to the Heysel Football Stadium riot affair. I was unconvinced and unmoved by M Martens' explanations. His government had clearly taken its decision in contradiction to and in defiance of legal advice. As I warned him I would, I then told the press of my views in very similar terms. But as a Belgian Government under the same M Martens later showed at the time of the Gulf War, it would take more than this to provide them with spine. And Patrick Ryan is still at large.

2.7. PS: No Cowardice, but Fair Sharing of Responsibility

In October 1989, the Director of Public Prosecutions in Ireland announced that he had decided not to take legal action against Ryan. In 1989, Ryan stood as a candidate for the European Parliament in the Munster constituency with the support of Sinn Fein (a left-wing party working for Irish reunification). Despite obtaining over 30,000 votes, he was not elected. Accused of receiving stolen goods, he was tried in 1993 by a special criminal court in Ireland but acquitted.

On 24 September 2019, more than 30 years after his removal to Ireland, Ryan (then 89) made his voice heard. And how?! In an interview with the BBC,[28] he admitted to having been linked to most of the bombings of which he had been accused by Margaret Thatcher, such as those in Hyde Park and Brighton. The Hyde Park bombing, on 20 July 1982, claimed the lives of four members of the Household Cavalry. An attack 2.15 hours later the same day in Regent's Park killed seven members of a military music chapel. The attack on the Grand Hotel in Brighton on 12 October 1984 claimed the lives of five participants in the Conservative Party conference held there.

In his BBC interview, Ryan said his only regret was that he had not been more effective:

> *To go back to what Thatcher accused you of being involved in any of the incidents that she …*
>
> I would say most of them. One way or another, yes, I had a hand in most of them. Yes, she was right.
>
> *So, when she linked you to Hyde Park, to Brighton, she was right?*
>
> Absolutely, 100 per cent, Oh, yes.
>
> *And now, when you look back, do you have any regrets?*
>
> Oh, I have, yes, big regrets. Of what nature? I regret that I wasn't even more effective. Oh yes, absolutely. I would have liked to have been much more effective than I actually was. But we didn't do too badly, no.

[28] BBC, *Spotlight on the Troubles. A Secret History.*

For years, Ryan travelled all over Europe before being arrested in Belgium at the request of the British authorities.[29] As an Irish citizen, not persecuted by the Irish government, he had no need of international protection. Had the British authorities succeeded in providing solid evidence of his responsibility for terrorist activities, one might have expected that Ireland could have done nothing but extradite him to the United Kingdom. His lawyers had pleaded with me against his eventual return to Ireland.[30]

Despite the vagueness of the charge,[31] the competent Belgian authority gave a favourable opinion on the British extradition request. Personally, I couldn't admit Ryan to the asylum procedure in the absence of persecution by his national authorities. However, I didn't want my unfavourable opinion to be used to support his extradition to the United Kingdom. For this reason, my advice was to return him to Ireland rather than to the United Kingdom. After a lively discussion by the Council of Ministers,[32] this advice was followed. By arresting him,[33] Belgium was cooperating with the British authorities to combat terrorism. The Irish authorities were undoubtedly better placed than Belgium's to assess his fear. Rather, it was up to them to decide whether to extradite him to the United Kingdom.

The Belgian decision was not guided by a fear of reprisals. It was based on an equitable division between its own responsibilities and those of Ryan's country of nationality. In this way, Belgium fully discharged its international obligations towards both the United Kingdom and Ryan's individual rights. British reactions, both in the press and in Parliament, and not least from the Prime Minister, were particularly virulent. This prevented the Irish government from granting the British extradition request. In Belgium, the case had raised awareness of the existence of a Commissioner General for Refugees and Stateless Persons, who exercised his mandate independently, as provided for by law.

[29] Wathelet: 'although he was previously arrested, neither France, the Netherlands nor Switzerland had extradited Patrick Ryan' *Le Monde* (1 December 1988).

[30] In a note of 9 November 1988, Ryan's Irish lawyer wrote: 'I have no doubt that Fr Patrick Ryan, if deported from Belgium to Ireland, would eventually be extradited to England if the Authorities in England so requested'.

[31] Wathelet: 'the qualifications as worded by the British authorities were very vague' (*LLB*, 30 November 1988). 'However, the British demands only speak of various days and of having conspired with unknown persons to commit murder on others. These accusations are therefore too vague, according to the Belgian Government' (*LS*, 30 November 1988). Wathelet: 'No one can dispute that the charges were extremely vague' (*LS*, 1 December).

[32] According to *De Morgen*, the Ryan decision was 'very sensitive' (26–27 November 1988). It was 'a difficult delivery' (28 November 1988).

[33] Jean-Claude Matgen: 'And to say that this whole affair could not have happened if the Belgian police had not arrested Ryan but had content itself, as the English had asked them, to monitor his retirement in Uccle pending a possible meeting of IRA activists' (*LLB*, 1 December 1988).

3

'Nerves are Getting Tighter and Tenser' (1991–92)

A cumbersome asylum procedure and a painful shortage of staff led to ever-increasing backlogs. This was exacerbated when, at the end of 1991, asylum seekers from Eastern Europe arrived in increasing numbers. Increasing pressure on reception facilities led to the repartition of asylum seekers throughout the country. This policy provoked growing public resistance. Nerves became increasingly tense. A small glimmer of hope, however, was offered by the introduction of simplified procedures and staff reinforcements, which became operational on 1 October 1991, making a fresh start possible.

3.1. 'The Commissioner General has Ideas but no Staff' (1990)

In the *Knack* of 10 January 1990, I declared that the problem of asylum had a European dimension, and that it was at this level that the solution had to be found. That same day, Vic Anciaux (VU), Brussels Secretary of State (1989–95), visited the Petit-Château accompanied by Miet Smet, Secretary of State for Social Emancipation, and me. The Brussels Secretary of State explained that asylum seekers who were not recognised as refugees had to be expelled from the country without delay. In an op-ed piece on 28 January in *Le Soir*, entitled 'Political refugees, a real problem', he insisted that the Minister of Justice and the Commissioner General should be provided with sufficient staff.

3.1.1. 'Time for Action' (March–July 1990)

A growing concern:

> Miet Smet, Secretary of State for Social Emancipation:
>
> Continually extending the reception of asylum seekers is not a solution. The only helpful measure is a rapid legal procedure that separates genuine refugees from the rest. And let's just send the others back (*Knack*, 28 March 1990).

Dirk Achten ('Time for action'):

> The gracious Minister of Justice Melchior Wathelet is nowadays the most beleaguered member of the government. The influx of would-be political refugees is soaring. The situation is fast becoming untenable. The procedure for recognising political refugees must be drastically shortened. 'It's time to deliver'. The situation is deteriorating too fast (Editorial, *DS*, 2 April 1990).

In *Le Soir* of 11 May 1990, Martine Vandemeulebroucke referred to my *Second Annual Report* (1989). This report spoke of a year and a half's backlog at the Aliens Office and four years at the Commission General. In *Le Vif/L'Express* of the same day, under the headline 'Asylum in Chaos', I declared:

> In April 1989, the Aliens Office was relieved of the militiamen[1] at its disposal. The result: new arrivals are offered an appointment nine months later. To reduce the number of applications, we need to increase the number of staff at the Aliens Office and the Commission General. The government is now aware of this. This was not the case six months ago. Finally, we need to effectively remove people whose applications have been rejected. There's no point in setting up procedures if nobody then has the courage to apply them.

Based on a report published by the Secretary of State for Social Emancipation, *La Dernière Heure* of 25 May 1990 referred to the 8,112 asylum applications in 1989 as 'the record of the decade'. On 1 June, the Council of Ministers approved a draft bill from the Minister of Justice concerning asylum. In future, urgent requests for reconsideration would be submitted directly to the Commissioner General. In the July 1990 issue of *Amnesty Nieuws*, I pointed out, under the heading 'The Lack of Staff at the Commission General Costs the State a Lot of Money', that 1989 had been 'catastrophic'. I also pointed out that Belgium was the only European country that did not take a fixed quota of recognised refugees under the UNHCR mandate.

3.1.2. 'The Commissioner General at the Wailing Wall' (2 October 1990)

The newspapers of 3 October 1990 echoed the interim report I had presented the day before. The main headlines were:

- Commissioner General at the Wailing Wall. Bossuyt: 'Wathelet Holds the Strings too Tightly in his Hands'. Procedure too Cumbersome, not Enough Staff (*DM*).
- Fortune Hunters are very Expensive. The Administration is too Weak to Cope with the Flow of Fake Political Refugees (*HLN*).

[1] The term used in Belgium for conscripts doing military service.

- SOS from the Commission General, which is Bursting at the Seams (*LM-LL*).
- There's Improvement, but it's not Byzantium (*LLB*).
- Asylum seekers are causing a record year (*DS*).

The message of 2 October 1990 may be summarised as follows:

- Right from the start, I issued warnings. There was a risk of things getting out of hand because of a painful lack of personnel. I wasn't listened to. Things got out of hand.
- Since Easter 1990, the procedure has gone more smoothly, but not enough to clear the backlog. In the first eight months of 1988, 707 decisions were taken; in the first eight months of 1990, 2,751. The Civil Service audit estimates that 46 statutory civil servants are needed, whereas there are barely 16. Of the 39 temporary civil servants required, 10 are missing. Of the 40 jurists required, there are only 4 jurists civil servants and 20 jurists militiamen.
- The procedure is too cumbersome. The Minister is too concerned about his own competence. This slows down the procedure. Simplifications will come, but not enough. Many asylum applications must be examined twice by the Aliens Office, twice by my services and once more by the Permanent Board. Very complicated and time-consuming.
- The Commission General costs (the equivalent of) €1.25 million and the reception of asylum seekers (the equivalent of) €50 million. Every franc invested in the Commission General brings a saving of 10 BF to Social Emancipation. In France, the budget was tripled to the equivalent of €37.5 million. The number of files processed rose from 3,000 to 9,000. The number of asylum seekers dropped from 7,000 to 4,000.

A clear-sighted comment came from journalist Gabrielle Lefèvre ('Refugees: A Puzzle'):

> At the Aliens Office, there are a few more staff, not enough computers and not many ideas. At the Commission General, there are ideas and computers, but no staff … (*La Cité*, 11 October 1990).

3.2. 'Great Hordes of East Europeans' (November–December 1990)

To make matters worse, many asylum seekers came from Eastern Europe, especially Poland and Romania. On 21 November 1990, I gave an interview to Reuters. Referring to it, *Het Belang van Limburg* of 22 November asked: 'Is a New "Curtain" Needed to Prevent the Mass Exodus of East Europeans?' Warning about migration from Eastern Europe, I replied: 'I have a feeling that this will happen, and we are not prepared for it. It could become a major crisis'. In the *Gazet van Antwerpen* of the same day, I pointed out that most of them came to Belgium for economic reasons. The following day, the Secretary of State for Social Emancipation added that most Eastern Europeans needed help in their own countries. The same newspaper wrote: 'Ever since he took up this post, the Commissioner General has been shouting in vain that our country is heading straight for catastrophe'.

In 1989, there were 253 Polish asylum seekers. An annual record was reached in 1990 with 1,089 Polish asylum applications. In nine years, out of 2,678 Polish asylum applications, there were 25 recognitions (0.9 per cent). Of these, 20 concerned applications submitted before 31 December 1989.

In 1989, there were 234 Romanian asylum seekers. This number grew each year (1,755 in 1990; 2,384 in 1991; and 3,338 in 1992) to reach an annual record in 1993 with 5,071. In nine years, out of 15,831 Romanian asylum applications, there were 427 recognitions, of which 51 were by the Permanent Board. The recognition rate for Romanians, which was 14 per cent (286/2,055) for applications submitted before 31 December 1990, was only 1 per cent (141/13,752) for subsequent applications.

In response to *Humo*'s question of 5 December 1990, who asked me if there were 'great hordes of Eastern Europeans' in the queue and if they could not be treated quickly, I replied:

> It is especially the Polish and Romanian applications that have experienced a strong increase. We must interview them all. You can't just say, 'Oh, Sir, you're Polish. I don't bother to interview you'. In addition, many Romanians mention political persecution. When I took office, I said we can't process 5,000 asylum applications. It's going to triple. It's going to take two, three years before we're able to say to newcomers, 'Well, you're not a refugee'. But in the meantime, they're here. It's strange that the authorities still don't understand that this is an area where you can't afford a backlog'.

On 13 December 1990, Prince Philippe held a working meeting on aliens' policy at the Royal Palace in Brussels. Stéphane Schewebach, Director of Refugees at the Aliens Office and I participated. Ascending to the throne on 21 July 2013, King Philippe received me on 17 January 2014 at the same royal palace in a farewell audience. A week earlier, I had been admitted to emeritus status as President of the Constitutional Court.

On 14 December 1990, HM Baudouin, the King of the Belgians (1951–93), received me in audience at the Château of Laeken. That was the second audience he gave me. The first time was on 20 September 1985 at the royal palace in Brussels, following my appointment as Belgian Representative to the UN Commission on Human Rights, on the proposal of Leo Tindemans, Minister for External Relations. The audience took place less than a month after the signing of the royal decree (27 August 1985) appointing me and more than one month before its publication (22 October).

My first conversation with King Baudouin was on 9 October 1967. It was during a reception on the 150th anniversary of the founding of the University of Ghent by HM William I, the King of the United Netherlands (1815–30). As Secretary General of the Ghent General Students' Association (Gents Studentenkorps), I was – and still after protest – the only student to be invited. It was before May 1968. King Baudouin had noticed that there was among the guests someone, without a robe, at least 20 years younger than all the others. As with any encounter with King Baudouin, I was very impressed.

At the end of December 1990, I said:

> Belgium is Overwhelmed: Since Easter, the situation has improved. The Aliens Office has received from the authorities the means to operate. Since July 1990, things have become complicated, mainly because of the influx of East Europeans, especially Romanians. It should not be forgotten that, if a thousand Romanians have arrived here, 10,000 have settled in Austria and more than 30,000 in Germany (*LLB*, 19 December 1990).
>
> I Warned in Time: The lack of a backlog of new refugee cases was a unique opportunity to address the refugee problem. This opportunity was missed by the shortsightedness of the Budget and Civil Service administrations and the inability of the Belgian system to react quickly to urgent problems. I recognize the problems of Secretary of State Miet Smet. For me, having a backlog means 'files piling up'; for Ms Smet, it means 'people wandering the streets'. I have a problem with lack of cupboards to put files in. Ms Smet has a problem with lack of beds to put people in (Ann Ghijs, *HV*, 29–30 December 1990).

Finally, in 1990 there were 12,915 asylum applications (a growth of 58 per cent). The Ghanaians (1,541) had retreated and were overtaken by the Turks (1,674) and the Romanians (1,755). Half of the asylum seekers came from Eastern Europe. This weighed heavily on the reception facilities. The Secretary of State for Social Emancipation called for a more flexible procedure for asylum seekers from countries that are 'not dangerous'. This will be done with the 'double 5 per cent rule' introduced by the Law of 18 July 1991 (see below p 46–47 and p 203–207).

3.3. Third Annual Report (9 April 1991): 'Extreme Generosity does not Solve Anything'

On 10 April 1991, newspapers echoed the presentation on the eve of my *Third Annual Report* (1990). Some headlines:

> Five Years of Waiting (*DS*; *HBvL*); Growing Influx …' (*LLB*); The Long Wait Continues (*LS*); Growing Mountain of Cases (*HLN*); Asylum Cases Piling up (*HV*); Worrisome Influx (*LDH*); Backlog rises to 15,000 (*GvA*).

According to *Le Soir*, 'the Commission General's backlog chart looked like a Himalayan whose downward slope would never be seen'.

I considered the situation to be politically and budgetary unacceptable. Four areas needed intensive work:

a. An extension of the staff cadre to 60 statutory members.
b. An amendment to the law to simplify the recognition procedure.
c. A rapid ratification of the Dublin and Schengen Conventions.
d. An effective removal of rejected asylum seekers.

I described the latter area as 'the most delicate but nonetheless unavoidable'. I added:

> The problem of refugees is too dangerous a subject for demagogy. I don't want the extremism of a Vlaams Blok [extreme right], for example. But extreme generosity doesn't solve anything either. The Secretary of State Miet Smet receives for the reception of asylum seekers the equivalent of €100 million, while she is faced only with the consequences of a biased situation. Almost nothing is done about the real causes of this situation (*DM*).
>
> Human tragedies in refusals become more acute when asylum seekers have had to wait so long, and their children are fully integrated (*HV*).
>
> If everyone who received my reports, had read them, the situation would be totally different (*GvA*).

3.4. Removing Illegal Aliens and Repartition of Asylum Seekers (1991–92)

As a university professor, I published in *De Standaard* of 21 April 1991 an Opinion entitled 'Reducing the Number of Illegal Foreigners by an Active Policy':

> It is time to abandon the policy of resignation. So far, we have adopted the policy of the ostrich: not to carry out checks on the stay of foreigners, nor to regularise illegal aliens, nor to remove them from the territory. The reduction of the number of illegals is based on three pillars: a) regular checks on the residence of foreigners; b) regularisation of integrated illegals; and c) removal of illegals not integrated. Conclusion: the longer the wait for implementation, the higher the number of illegal immigrants increases and the greater the chance of seeing the problem addressed in an emotional rather than rational way. The risk thus becomes all the greater as the path will be open for cheap demagogy that underestimates the complexity of the phenomenon of immigration and proposes solutions that are neither humanly nor socially founded.

More specifically on removals:

> Individual removals are very expensive (in most cases one must provide additional plane tickets for two accompanying policemen, and it is enough for the person concerned to resist for the captain to refuse transport). There is a fear that collective removals will generate a lot of opposition. When it concerns the execution of individual decisions, such opposition is unfounded.

3.4.1. The Charters of Edith Cresson (8 July 1991)

On 8 July 1991, Edith Cresson (PS), Prime Minister of France (1991–92), spoke on French television TF1 about the deportation of illegal migrants:

> I understand very well that a pilot does not accept that an extremely agitated person enters his plane. We should not use regular lines. You call them charters. With charters people go on vacation at lower prices. There, it will be totally free, but it will not be for holidays. It will be to take people back to their country once justice has established that they are not entitled to be in our country.

Her words provoked an outcry. Three days later she stated that the word 'charter' had not been her choice but that of a journalist.

When asked about this, I replied:

> My position is that the two taboos (removal and regularisation) must be broken simultaneously. Removal is a matter of being consistent. Illegal is illegal; to act otherwise is to ignore its own legislation. Moreover, illegal residence is also a criminogenic factor. It automatically leads to evasion of tax and social legislation. Unfortunately, the way in which illegal foreigners must be deported is very inflated in the media. In essence, Ms Cresson is on the right track with her ideas. Provided that any decision to deport is taken individually, the system of joint removal is useful and probably necessary. A pilot who expects difficulties, can always refuse to transport the person concerned. With special charter planes, we don't have these problems (*DM*, 13 July 1991).

Me André De Becker, Chairperson of the Dutch-speaking League for Human Rights, was outraged: 'A strong sample of cynicism' (*Panorama/De Post*, 19 July 1991).

3.4.2. The Lint Reception Centre Hype (5 September 1991)

On 5 September 1991, a programme *Panorama* was broadcast on BRTN TV from Lint (see below p 194). The atmosphere was overheated. The Red Cross's plan to turn the former cloister of Bethany into a reception centre for 150 asylum seekers was met with strong protests. In accordance with the repartition plan for asylum seekers in the various municipalities, the municipality of Lint wanted to accept only seven asylum seekers. Two editors commented on the programme:

> Paul Goossens: The scum led by Filip Dewinter [Vl.Bl.] made it a foul scene. Anger and shame are here. But above all there is a need to think lucidly. After the sad event in Lint, there is no doubt that the problem of migrants is easily flammable (*DM*, 7 September 1991).
>
> Marc Platel: Panorama colleagues proved conclusively with their daring report that television is a social lever. It was good adult television. Excellencies now know that there is a social conflict. The atmosphere in the tiny town of Lint is overheated, even sickly. Hospitality is a human virtue, but the host must have sufficient means

> to receive the guests. He should not send too many of his guests to his friends and acquaintances who may already have their own guests or do not want his own (*HBvL*, 9 September 1991).

On Sunday 8 September 1991 (during a study day in Mol on radical democracy), Louis Tobback (SP), Minister of the Interior (1988–94), made some strong criticisms of the reception policy pursued. The next day, SP Chairperson (1989–94) Frank Vandenbroucke continued:

> What Louis [Tobback] said on Sunday is the well-thought-out view of both himself and the Socialist Party. All illegals must be deported. Only genuine political refugees can still be accepted. The SP fully supports Commissioner General Marc Bossuyt. The government also needs to support him better. If Prime Minister [Wilfried] Martens had given the money for his new newsroom to Bossuyt, he could have recruited enough jurists.

On the same day, Johan Leman, chief of staff of the Royal Commissioner for Immigration Policy, Paula D'Hondt (CVP), said that she was keeping away from the whole affair: '"Too bad", but she had no jurisdiction over refugees'. On 28 December 1991, however, the Royal Commissioner stated that she was concerned about the problem of refugees, although they were not migrants. She did not want these people to be considered migrants: 'Their presence can only be temporary. I believe that those who are not recognised as refugees should be sent back, but in humane conditions'.

La Libre Belgique of 10 September 1991 dedicated, under the title 'Asylum Seekers: A Wave that Shakes Belgium', a whole page to the controversy triggered by Minister Louis Tobback. He proposed a list of countries whose nationals could no longer be considered refugees. Secretary of State Miet Smet explained that she had introduced into the new law – which would come into force on 1 October – a procedure to identify those who are 'economic refugees'. In his commentary, Jean-Claude Matgen observed:

> It is surprising, however, that Mr Tobback's sudden interest in a problem that the government of which he is a member seems to have long cared about. As far as we know, the boisterous MP of Leuven rarely (more rarely anyway than Ms Smet) denounced the cruel lack of means attributed to the Commissioner General. It would be a mistake to respond with an excess of tolerant naivety to the challenge of the massive influx of foreigners (especially from Eastern Europe), pushed out of their country not by fear but by hunger or the hope of a better future. But a withdrawal in us would not make any more sense.

Patrick Martens wrote:

> Under the dance of numbers behind which hides a lot of human misery among the guests and as much official agitation among the host, and apparently also because of the upcoming elections, the nerves in several places are increasingly tense (*HBvL*, 10 September 1991).

Referring to the upcoming elections, Minister Louis Tobback said in the same newspaper:

> Why should I keep my mouth shut? Because there will soon be elections? This would imply that I should from now on, and until then, go on vacation? In June 1989, I agreed with the proposed policy of 1 per 1,000 ie 10,000 per 10 million population. There are now 1,700 a month. That's 20,400 on an annual basis.

In the *Knack* of 24 September 1991, I complained that the media was always talking about 'political refugees'. Yet, most often they were 'asylum seekers'. Experience had also shown that most of these asylum seekers were not 'refugees'.

3.5. The Law of 18 July 1991 Comes into Force (1 October 1991)

Finally, there was a glimmer of hope. The procedural simplifications introduced by the Law of 18 July 1991 came into force on 1 October. The reinforcements of personnel decided on 26 April becoming operational, it was a new start. During the months of July and October, 28 new jurist civil servants and eight new jurist militiamen took office. The UNHCR Representation in Brussels organised a training week on three occasions.

On the entry into force of the new law, *La Libre Belgique* once again devoted a whole page to this problem, under the title 'Refugees: Means Certainly but for what Policy?' In my opinion, the repartition of asylum seekers presented a threefold disadvantage: (a) those that organise the reception of asylum seekers are discouraged in the face of the opposition from the local authorities; (b) xenophobia arises in the four corners of the country; and (c) it makes repatriation, if not impossible, very difficult and painful. I asked if it was normal for us to spend the equivalent of €62.5 million for the 15,000 asylum seekers who arrive with us, and only the equivalent of €625,000 for the 15 million refugees who haunt the world. For a thousand times more refugees, the contribution is a hundred times less than for asylum seekers: ie, for each asylum seeker Belgium spent more than €4,000, while for each refugee in the world, it contributed €0.04 (100,000 times less per person).

In terms of the resources available, there was progress. However, there was a need to further streamline the process. I felt that the 'double 5 per cent rule' was better than the Swiss system. Switzerland had drawn up a list of safe countries whose nationals were considered a priori profiteers. Me Vincent Lurquin, Chairperson of the Movement Against Racism, Anti-Semitism, and Xenophobia (MRAX), said the Geneva Convention was 'scorned'. Overturning the burden of proof by the 5 per cent rule was 'a real blunder, it was purely illegal'. With an 'illegal law', this lawyer created a new legal category. His view was also in opposition to the opinion of the UNHCR Representative of 3 July 1991 that the double 5 per cent rule was not contrary to the Geneva Convention (see below p 203–207).

The *Gazet van Antwerpen* of 1 October 1991 also devoted an entire page to the entry into force of the new law. That newspaper spoke about the European problem, probably the most acute in the 1990s. I was not in favour of adapting the Geneva Convention: 'Belgium recognises about 500 refugees a year. That's not the problem. The problem is the 13,000 applications and the complicated law and procedures to achieve that result'.

Two days earlier, on 29 September 1991, the Volksunie members of the Martens VIII Government had resigned. There was a strong fight between the Communities over arms exports to the Middle East. The remaining government, Martens IX, would be the last of this name. Elections took place on 24 November 1991. It was a 'Black Sunday'. Vlaams Blok won at the expense of the government parties. This far-right party rose from two to 12 seats in the House of Representatives. Nationally, it won 6.6 per cent of the vote (+4.7 per cent). In the electoral district of Antwerp, it became the largest party with 20.68 per cent. There was discussion about the causes of this result. Dissatisfaction with immigration was generally perceived as an important factor. The fact that the government had allowed the asylum procedure to go awry will not have helped.

Two months later, on 22 January 1992, my remarks on 'charters' caused quite a stir (see chapter five). Two weeks later, on 7 February 1992, Walid Bennani, an Islamist leader in Tunisia, filed an asylum application (see chapter four). It became a legal duel with the Minister of Justice. Supported by the Conseil d'Etat, I managed to prevent Bennani from being expelled from the country. Because of the slowness of the Conseil d'Etat, he had to wait a long time for his recognition.

4

Walid Bennani, an Islamist Refugee from Tunisia (1992–97)

Walid Bennani (b 1956) applied for asylum in Belgium on 7 February 1992. He graduated in 1976 from the National School of Administration (ENA) in Tunis. He worked at the Ministry of Transport and Telecommunications. He was dismissed in 1981.

4.1. Ennahdha: A Democratic Fundamentalism?

Since the early 1980s, Bennani has been an active member of the Ennahdha Movement. It is a radical Islamic religious movement that wants to make Tunisia an Islamic State. Two currents existed within the Movement: some wanted a purely religious movement; others retreated into hiding and formed militias for weapons and guerrilla warfare in military camps abroad (mainly in Sudan).

The Ennahdha Movement had been based in Belgium since at least 1986. The Belgian section was headed by Mohamed Merghini, a professor of Islamic religion in Charleroi. In Belgium, the Movement was not a problem. A State Security report of 24 March 1992 described the Movement as follows:

> According to Ennahdha, the law should be made by oulémas (judges of Islam), tourism gradually suppressed, banks should lend without interest and women should be veiled/enclosed. In economic terms, it advocated 'democratic socialism' that would guarantee private property and participation in the means of production. It says to be committed to democracy but places Islam 'above all else'. It openly aims for the seizure of power but is divided as to the method to be used: either to educate the population, through gentleness, to adopt the values of Islam; or to change the regime through the 'Islamic Revolution' to establish Sharia law'.[1]

The Tunisian Constitution prohibited any movement or grouping based on religion, race, language, or region. Successive requests from Ennahdha to grant the Movement legal status were denied. When the leaders first asked for the legalisation of the Movement, they were sentenced to five years in prison. Bennani

[1] State Security Report of 24 March 1992.

was also arrested as a member of Ennahdha. He was pardoned after three years in prison. Between 1984 and 1988, the Movement was tolerated under the strict supervision of the Tunisian authorities.

The Tunisian State Security Court sentenced several members of Ennahdha in 1987. Bennani was sentenced to 20 years in prison. But the general Amnesty Law of 27 June 1989 also benefited Bennani, although he was still prohibited from participating in a religious organisation. When, in December 1989, members of Ennahdha asked again for the legalisation of the Movement, several of its leaders were arrested. Bennani then hid for several months before leaving his country for Algeria. On 27 May 1991, while he was hiding there, his photo was published in the *La Presse* newspaper with those of other people wanted by the Tunisian authorities. When he learned at the beginning of January 1992, after a brief illegal stay, that members of the Tunisian police had infiltrated Algeria in search of members of Ennahdha, he left that country.

4.2. False Passport: Refusal of Access to the Territory (14 February 1992)

On 7 February 1992, Bennani flew from Algiers to Belgium with an impressive record. When his passport turned out to be false, he disclosed his identity and declared himself a refugee. On 12 February, Amnesty International sent a letter to Justice Minister Melchior Wathelet in which they confirmed Bennani's statements. On 14 February, the Aliens Office refused him access to the territory. That same day,[2] Bennani introduced an urgent request for reconsideration.[3] The next day, 15 February 1992, a telex from Interpol Tunisia requested his extradition and the investigating judge of the Tribunal of first instance of Ben Arous issued an international arrest warrant. Bennani was suspected of complicity in an attack on the Ben Arous Transmission Centre and Tunisian telecommunications facilities.

4.2.1. My Favourable Opinion (19 February 1992)

On 19 February 1992, I gave an opinion in favour of his access to the territory. As to the use of a false passport, I considered that Bennani's application and his counsel's letter sufficiently demonstrated that the intention to deceive the Belgian authorities was not established. Bennani had produced documents showing that

[2] His lawyers were Me Georges-Henri Beauthier and Me Mustapha El Karouni of the Brussels Bar.

[3] Since the legislative amendment of 18 July 1991 (which entered into force on 1 October), the urgent request for reconsideration was, in accordance with Art 63/2, §2, of the Aliens Law, no longer addressed to the Minister of Justice but directly to the Commissioner General (*Fourth Annual Report*, 1991, §55).

his safety was in danger if he returned to Tunisia or Algeria. The examination of the possible applicability of the exclusion clause[4] had to go hand in hand with the examination of the substance of his application. I stated that 'he was clearly someone who had to flee his country for political reasons. The opening of an admissibility procedure has nothing to do with possible sympathy for his political ideas'.[5]

4.2.2. The Minister Disregards My Favourable Opinion (25 February 1992)

There was close consultation within the government, with the Tunisian Embassy in Brussels and the Belgian Embassy in Tunis. The Minister was really besieged by the Tunisian Ambassador. The question arose whether this would weigh more heavily than the warnings of humanitarian organisations. On 25 February 1992, the Minister of Justice overruled my favourable opinion by dismissing the urgent request for reconsideration. According to the Minister, his application was fraudulent and did not meet the criteria set out in the Geneva Convention. He deduced from the Gendarmerie's report of 7 February 1992 that Bennani had only disclosed his identity after the officials responsible for border control had ascertained that his passport had been falsified. It was only at that time that he applied for asylum. In addition, the Minister felt that the exclusion clause should be invoked. Suspected of committing an explosive attack, Bennani was the subject of an international warrant.[6]

The next day, the instruments of an extradition treaty between Belgium and Tunisia were exchanged. A French language newspaper came out firmly against Bennani's asylum application. The government's decision was described as 'responsible' and my favourable opinion as 'inexplicable'.[7] The Royal Commissioner for Immigration Policy, Paula D'Hondt, also joined the Minister: 'The competent Minister must look after the interests of the State. And Commissioner General Bossuyt for the sake of refugees. I'm not a jurist. I take a pragmatic position'.[8]

[4] Art 1, para F: 'The provisions of this Convention shall not apply to any person with respect to whom there are serious reasons for considering that: a) He has committed a crime against peace, a war crime, or a crime against humanity, as defined in the international instruments drawn up to make provisions in respect of such crimes; b) He has committed a serious non-political crime outside the country of refuge prior to his admission to that country as a refugee; c) He has been guilty of acts contrary to the purposes and principles of the United Nations'.

[5] *GvA* (24 February 1992).

[6] By the Law of 18 July 1991, the Minister of Justice retained the possibility of overriding the Commissioner General's opinion by a reasoned decision but only within a strict period of five working days (*Fourth Annual Report*, 1991, §24). Since the Law came into force (1 October 1991), this has been done in less than 1% of cases (previously less than 10% of cases) (ibid §57). When, from 15 July 1992, the Minister of the Interior (instead of the Minister of Justice) became responsible for aliens' policy, he did not disregard any favourable opinion of the Commissioner General (*Fifth Annual Report*, 1992, §44).

[7] Gilbert Dupont, *LDH* (26 February 1992): 'Fake Refugee, Real Terrorist'.

[8] *DM* (27 February 1992).

It seemed pragmatic to sacrifice an individual for the sake of the State. According to Bennani's lawyer, the Royal Commissioner was contaminated by the fantasy that every Islamic was a fundamentalist.[9] She lost sight of the fact that her competence was in immigration policy. Judging individual asylum applications did not belong there.

Between 20 and 28 February 1992, humanitarian organisations wrote several letters in support of Bennani's access to Belgian territory. The Minister was asked not to extradite him to the Tunisian authorities as this would put his safety and even his life in danger. On 23 March 1992, I sent these letters to the Minister of Justice stressing the importance of 'urgent action' by Amnesty International on 20 February, which reported recent allegations of torture of members of the Al-Nahdha Movement in Tunisia: 'At least 8,000 *Al-Nahdha's* supporters were arrested this past year. Most of them had been kept in a prolonged incommunicado. Hundreds were wronged and at least nine political prisoners died, probably under torture'.[10]

4.2.3. The President of the Tribunal Assists: Deportation Ban (9 March 1992)

On 26 February 1992, the UNHCR Representative in Belgium, Ruprecht von Arnim, sent a letter to the President of the Tribunal of first instance in Brussels:[11]

> I had Mr Bennani interviewed by one of my colleagues, and we have concluded that the evidence put forward by the person concerned about his political commitment is true and certainly capable of bringing him under the benefit of Article 1 of the Geneva Convention on the Status of Refugees. The Tunisian authorities have indeed requested the extradition of Mr Bennani based on so-called criminal acts, but none of this could be verified. In this situation, we will apply the 'in dubio pro refugio' rule.[12]

On 27 February, Bennani asked the President of the Tribunal of first instance in Brussels, in the form of an interlocutory order, to suspend the execution of the

[9] ibid.

[10] Amnesty International, 'Urgent Action' (20 February 1992). In its March 1992 report 'Tunisia: Prolonged Incommunicado Detention and Torture', Amnesty International added: 'Hundreds of prisoners have claimed to have been tortured, their complaints have rarely been investigated by the Tunisian authorities and have not resulted in sanctions'.

[11] If the Minister decides to return the refugee applicant to the country from which he has fled and where he claims that his life or liberty is threatened, the person concerned has the possibility of bringing an appeal to the President of the Tribunal of first instance within two working days. The latter will then have to give a decision, in the form of an interlocutory order, within 15 days. If the request is rejected, the President of the Tribunal may still grant a maximum of one month for foreign nationals to be admitted to another country (*Third Annual Report*, 1990, §33). After the legislative amendment of 18 July 1991, this procedure was maintained only when the Minister disregarded a favourable opinion of the Commissioner General (*Fourth Annual Report*, 1991, §55).

[12] *DM* (28 February 1992).

Minister's refusal. He says his life and safety would be in danger as soon as he was returned to Tunisia or Algeria. Pending the decision of the Conseil d'Etat, he asked for permission to leave the transit centre and be given a temporary residence permit. On 28 February, Bennani was sentenced by the Tribunal of first instance of Ben Arous Court to a maximum of five years for 'passive complicity'. This sentence is for 'a person who has knowledge of a plan allowing to fear the commission of [certain offences] has not notified the public authorities'. Such an offence is unknown in Belgian law.

In his order of 9 March, the President of the Tribunal of first instance of Brussels noted that the applicant had been an Ennahdha activist in Tunisia for many years. This was evidenced by the written testimony of several persons with responsibilities at the level of the international sections of Amnesty International, 'whose good faith and intellectual integrity cannot be questioned'. Extracts from the international press suggested that the rights of political prisoners in Tunisia would not always be guaranteed:

> Whereas a body of consistent evidence indicates that the applicant was engaged in political activities in Tunisia, which led to his being sought by the Tunisian authorities; that these elements make plausible the elements put forward by him concerning his political commitment and his right to fall under Article 1 of the Geneva Convention on the Status of Refugees.

The President of the Tribunal of first instance of Brussels prohibited in an interlocutory order the enforcement of the decision of refusal:

> We state that there are serious indications that the applicant's statement that his life or liberty would be threatened if he were returned to Algeria or Tunisia, the country he fled, is accurate; consequently, we prohibit the execution of the decision of 25 February 1992 against the applicant or the deprivation of his freedom on this count.

4.2.4. The Conseil d'Etat also Helps: Suspension of the Order (17 March 1992)

On 6 March 1992, Bennani filed a request with the Conseil d'Etat for annulment of the implementation of the ministerial decision of 25 February, rejecting his urgent request for reconsideration. In its judgment of 17 March,[13] the Conseil d'Etat considered that the applicant had given a plausible explanation of the use of a false passport which the Commissioner General had accepted. The application for recognition of refugee status seemed to coincide with the presentation of the passport. At that time, the applicant had provided the reasons for his application. He was in possession of documents establishing his identity and intent to apply for

[13] CdE, No 39.015 (17 March 1992) *Jurisprudence de Liège, Mons et Bruxelles* (1992) 834, note of E Gillet, 'Les candidats réfugiés dans le maquis du référé'.

refugee protection. In addition, the Minister did not consider the reasons why the Commissioner General did not consider the applicant to be a terrorist.

On the auditor's assent,[14] the Conseil d'Etat concluded that the plea appeared serious, and that the decision was not sufficiently reasoned. The Conseil d'Etat considered that the danger to the applicant, if he was sent back to his country, was not contested, nor contestable and justified the serious damage which was difficult to repair. In accordance with Article 17, §2, of the coordinated Laws on the Conseil d'Etat, the latter ordered the suspension of the execution of the ministerial decision rejecting the urgent request for reconsideration.

In accordance with Article 18 of the Laws on the Conseil d'Etat,[15] on 21 March 1992 Bennani asked the Conseil d'Etat to take provisional measures, namely: 'on a provisional basis, to say that the applicant may leave the Transit Centre 127 freely and thus enter Belgian territory and that the Belgian State will be ordered to give the applicant a provisional residence permit'. This request was rejected on 27 March,[16] on the assent of the auditor, by the Conseil d'Etat since it had already, in its judgment of 17 March, suspended the implementation of the decision of removal.

4.3. Access to Territory, to Leave within Five Days (7 May 1992)

After three months at the Transit Centre in Melsbroek, Bennani was allowed to enter the Kingdom on 7 May 1992. The Aliens Law, as amended on 18 July 1991, provided in Article 74/5, §5, that the duration of detention in a specified place at the border could not exceed two months. However, there was an agreement to go beyond that, to allow the UN Representative to find another country that could grant him political asylum. However, these efforts proved unsuccessful.

On the same day (7 May 1992), Bennani received a decision refusing him stay in the territory. This refusal was based essentially on the same grounds for refusing him access to the Kingdom:

> The personal declaration of the person concerned, recorded in the Gendarmerie report of 7 February 1992, according to which 'he wanted to seek political asylum in France', confirms that he did not declare himself a political refugee until after the Gendarmerie discovered the falsification of his passport. Thus, not spontaneously applying for asylum at the passport control post, the person concerned tried to enter the Kingdom by trying to deceive the Belgian authorities.

[14] Martine Vandemeulebroucke (*LS*, 12 March 1992): 'The Minister is not the Refugee Commissioner'.

[15] This Article allowed the Conseil d'Etat to take all necessary measures to safeguard the interests of the parties or persons who have an interest in the solution of the case, except for civil rights measures. It was repealed by the Law of 20 January 2014.

[16] CdE, No 39.091 (27 March 1992).

According to the Minister's delegate, the presence in Belgium of one of the main representatives of the Ennahdha Movement, a radical Islamist movement known for its violent actions in Tunisia, constituted, by virtue of his very role as leader within this Movement, a definite risk to public order or national security for Belgium.

4.3.1. I Invoke All Possible Arguments (21 May 1992)

On 11 May 1992, Bennani filed an urgent request for reconsideration. That same day, Bennani's lawyer sent me a letter about the situation in Tunisia and Algeria. The letter referred more specifically to the case of Raouf Labiri. As a supporter of Ennahdha, this man had fled to Belgium after being arrested several times. His asylum application had been denied. In 1991, he returned to Tunisia, believing in the legalisation measures that were periodically announced. After being tortured for three weeks, he died in prison of a heart attack. These facts have been confirmed by reports from Amnesty International.

Bennani had learned from friends that members of the Tunisian police, infiltrated in Algeria, were on his trail. Eight members of Ennahdha were arrested on 6 and 7 May in Algeria for expulsion. These facts were confirmed by Amnesty International, which noted other similar situations. Bennani had in his luggage files prepared before his arrival in Belgium. They justified the functions he exercised, and the discrimination he had been subjected to. He could not apply for asylum in Algeria since that country does not grant asylum to nationals of the Arab Maghreb Union. In addition, he was wanted by Tunisian police officers who would obtain his extradition immediately. He could not leave Algeria without carrying false documents. In Belgium, he never hid his identity. The fact that he first wanted to apply for refugee status in France does not mean that his application was fraudulent. This intention shows that his sole purpose was to flee his country and Algeria to seek refugee status in a State of law, in this case Belgium. Nothing, neither in his conduct nor in the reports of international organisations, has come to invalidate Bennani's assertions, quite the contrary.

At his hearing by my collaborators on 15 May 1992, Bennani stated that the Movement was moderate, Islamic leaning but not fundamentalist, and that he and his members had never refused to engage in dialogue. He added that Islamic culture was the basis, but freedom of opinion and expression was essential: 'The party leadership has always imposed a peaceful and democratic course of action. A seizure of power will be done by legal and democratic means and certainly not by armed struggle'. At the same hearing, Bennani stated that he had not participated in any way in the attack on the Djebel Transmission Centre. This would have been completely inconsistent with his membership of the League for Human Rights in Kasserine, of which he had been treasurer since 1986, and with his contacts with embassies and Amnesty International.

On 21 May 1992, I delivered an ample reasoned opinion to the Minister of Justice on Bennani's stay in Belgium. In considering his application fraudulent with reference to Bennani's false passport, the Minister's delegate persisted in presenting the facts in a manner that was formally contradicted by the various judicial or quasi-judicial bodies. For the first time in this case, the danger to public order and national security was invoked. These reasons were not cited by the Minister's delegate in his decision on12 February, nor by the Minister of Justice in his decision on 25 February. They were only invoked after the Commissioner General, the Representative of the UN High Commissioner for Refugees, the President of the Tribunal of first instance and the Conseil d'Etat had refuted all other grounds. For this reason, I considered that the credibility of this ground was seriously undermined by the delay with which it was invoked.

Moreover, those grounds could only be validly invoked in cases where there was a risk that the person concerned could take actions capable of compromising public order or national security in Belgium. By claiming that Bennani, by his very office as leader of Ennahdha, constituted a danger to public order or national security, the Minister's delegate gave a scope that amounted to voiding the concept of refugee within the meaning of the Geneva Convention. Moreover, the State Security report of 24 March 1992, which was communicated to me on 12 May, did not mention any personal participation of Bennani in violent actions. For this reason, I found that the Aliens Office had exceeded the discretion of the executive in this matter. My opinions should not be influenced by the sympathy or antipathy of the Belgian government or public opinion regarding the views expressed by the refugee applicants who apply for asylum in Belgium.

4.3.2. The Minister Persists (27 May 1992)

Overruling my opinion once more, the Minister of Justice rejected, on 27 May 1992, the urgent request for reconsideration of the decision to refuse residence and establishment in the territory. The Minister was still of the view that the application was fraudulent. Although the falsification of the Tunisian passport and the obtaining of a Belgian visa under a false name could be justified, the intention to deceive the Belgian authorities was, according to the Minister, established. It appeared from the Gendarmerie report that he first wanted to seek asylum in France, which was confirmed by the fact that he had 13,200 French francs (€2,012). He declared himself a refugee only after the discovery of falsification of the passport.

The grounds relating to public order or national security were not previously invoked, since the Minister had considered that the provisions of the Geneva Convention were not applicable. He felt that there were serious reasons to believe that he had committed 'a serious non-political crime outside the country of refuge prior to his admission to that country as a refugee'.[17] In so far as the Conseil d'Etat had held that such an argument was a matter for consideration of the merits, the Minister was entitled to invoke it for the first time in order to rely on the applicability of Article 33, §2, of the Geneva Convention.[18]

The Minister relied on the following motivation:

> Because of his leadership of the Ennahdha Movement, he supports its ideology and action and consequently the use of violent acts. To this extent, by his presence in Belgium, Mr Walid Bennani is likely to compromise public order or national security by risking being at the origin of violent acts as perpetrated by this Movement.

This decision was not notified to Bennani until 29 June 1992. He was ordered to leave the territory within five days with a ban on travelling to Luxembourg and the Netherlands. According to the UNHCR Representative, sending him back to his country of origin was excluded. On 28 May, he gave an overview of the reactions of different countries to his request to take over Bennani's case if he was refused asylum by Belgium. In addition to a few countries that were still waiting but were not encouraging, a dozen countries had refused.[19] The headquarters of the UN High Commissioner for Refugees in Geneva even believed that there was no reason to transfer the problem to another country. On 4 June, the UNHCR Representative sent a letter 'to whom by right' confirming that 'Walid Bennani is a prima facie refugee under the Geneva Convention, subject to final procedure. In this situation, any Belgian national authority is requested to provide him protection and assistance'.[20]

On 26 June 1992, the press office of the Tunisian Embassy in Brussels sent a letter to the editor-in-chief of the *Le Soir* newspaper following an article published the same day. This article referred to the Ennahdha Islamist Movement, whose members were heavily repressed in Tunisia. According to this article, several active members of Ennahdha had been easily welcomed by Germany, France, Sweden and Switzerland long after Bennani's arrival in Belgium. The article ended with a quote from Bennani: 'I am not here to harm Belgian interests, but to work clearly to make possible the return to Tunisia of opponents like me'.

According to the Embassy of the Tunisian Republic, the Ennahdha Movement had been

> the object of much leniency and many gestures to lead it to abandon its violent and totalitarian character. Notwithstanding the criminal acts committed and its notorious

[17] Art 1, para F, al b, of the Geneva Convention.

[18] Art 33, para 2: 'The benefit of the present provision may not, however, be claimed by a refugee whom there are reasonable grounds for regarding as a danger to the security of the country in which he is, or who, having been convicted by a final judgment of particularly serious crime, constitutes a danger to the community of that country'.

[19] *LDH* (16 July 1992): 'The UNHCR has contacted some 20 countries. The only country that responded positively was Luxembourg, but the Belgians did not want to because it was too close'.

[20] Martine Vandemeulebroucke (*LS*, 26 June 1992): 'Refugee Undesirable in Belgium because too Political'.

> collusion with a violent international fundamentalist chain, the prosecution of this Movement in Tunisia remains respectful of the law.

The Embassy observed that Bennani was the subject of an official request for extradition: 'Walid Bennani is not a mere political leader of this Movement. He was charged with involvement in the organisation of serious acts of sabotage of public property'.

4.3.3. Waiting for Suspension (25 June 1993) and Annulment (23 September 1997)

A year later, on 25 June 1993, the Conseil d'Etat ruled on the suspension of the ministerial order of 27 May 1992 to leave the territory within five days, notified to Bennani on 29 June 1992:

> Considering that the applicant produces a file of documents which show, in his opinion, that if he was forced, in one way or another, to return to his country, he could be subjected to inhuman or degrading treatment within the meaning of Article 3 of the European Convention on Human Rights; that he adds that extradition between the countries of the Arab Maghreb Union, of which Algeria and Tunisia are members, is not subject to any restrictions; that, at the state of the case, these assertions were not contradicted.[21]

The Conseil d'Etat ordered the suspension of the execution of the order to leave the territory, since the execution of the contested decision caused damage which was difficult to repair.

On 21 November 1994, I granted refugee status to his wife and two children: 'His own wife, who had been tortured in Tunisia, arrived in Belgium with their two children in 1994, after fleeing clandestinely, and she was immediately granted refugee status'.[22]

Le Soir of 5–6 October 1996 announced that the Tunisian newspaper *La Presse* connected Bennani to the assassination of Minister of State André Cools (PS) on 18 July 1991. Two Tunisians were charged with this crime. Bennani denied having been associated with it: 'Because Tunisia does not succeed in getting me extradited, it tries at least to bring me before the Belgian justice system in a case with which I have nothing to do'. He refused to be heard on 24 October 1996 by Véronique Ancia, the investigating judge of Liège, since he was informed that she would be accompanied by a Tunisian judge.

On 23 September 1997, more than five years after the Minister of Justice had, on 27 May 1992, rejected Bennani's urgent request for reconsideration and refused

[21] CdE, No 43.475 (25 June 1993).
[22] *LS* (5–6 October 1996).

him residence and establishment in the territory,[23] the Conseil d'Etat annulled this ministerial decision. As regards the fraudulent nature of its application, the Conseil d'Etat considered that, what authorised the Minister to refuse access to the territory was not so much that he attempted to access it fraudulently but that his refugee application was fraudulent:

> In other words, what makes the application manifestly based on reasons other than asylum is an attempt to deceive the authorities 'at the time of the refugee declaration', that's to say, on the circumstances likely to support their decision: evidence of alleged persecution, political, philosophical, ethnic, or religious affiliation, etc.[24]

The Conseil d'Etat considered that it did not appear that the applicant had used the false passport to deceive the Belgian authorities on the refugee status he applied for. Referring to the State Security report of 24 March 1992, the Conseil d'Etat considered that the plea against the invocation of danger to public order or national security was serious:

> Considering that this information does not necessarily allow to infer that the applicant has opted within the Ennahdha Movement in favour of violence whose ideology he would endorse, and that his mere presence in Belgium constitutes a threat to public order or national security.

This decision was notified to Bennani on 29 September 1997.

4.4. Finally Recognised, but Tunisia Insists (19 November 1997)

On 19 November 1997, Commissioner General Luc De Smet recognised Bennani as a refugee. On 6 December Bennani received his refugee card. On 19 January 1998, the Minister of the Interior filed (belatedly) an appeal to the Conseil d'Etat for the annulment of the Commissioner General's decision of 19 November 1997 recognising Bennani as a refugee. Immediately before the opening of the proceedings, by letter of 10 February 1998, the Minister withdrew his appeal. In its judgment of 30 September, the Conseil d'Etat declared the appeal abandoned.[25]

In the context of new requests for extradition by the Tunisian authorities, several Belgian authorities were asked to arrest Bennani. On 5 October 1998, the National Magistrate asked the Commissioner General for more information on the specific reasons that had found recognition of Bennani as a refugee. On 9 October, the Commissioner General replied: 'The file has been subjected to an

[23] The Conseil d'Etat decided in its judgment No 58.979 of 3 April 1996 to reopen the debates and set a hearing on 15 May.

[24] CdE, No 68.259 (23 September 1997).

[25] CdE, No 76.011 (30 September 1998).

extremely thorough examination, *taking into account* all the elements in these *comprehending* elements advanced to argue the extradition request'. He did not find grounds for withdrawing his recognition decision.

On 16 March 2000, the Commissioner General again confirmed to the Ministry of Justice that the extradition to Tunisia would clearly be contrary to Belgium's international obligations under Article 33 of the Geneva Convention. On 27 March, the Minister of Justice rejected the Tunisian request for extradition. With Tunisia once again requesting his extradition, on 3 August 2001 the Ministry of Justice asked the Commissioner General whether the person concerned still had refugee status.

4.5. PS: People's Representative in Tunisia (2011–19)

After Ben Ali, who had been President of Tunisia since 7 November 1987, was ousted from power on 14 January 2011, Bennani returned to Tunisia. He was elected People's Representative for the Ennahdha Party in the electoral district of his birthplace Kasserine from 22 November 2011 to 2 December 2014 and again for a second term from that date until 13 November 2019. In the 2011 elections, Ennahdha became the largest party with 37 per cent of the vote. In 2014, the party obtained 27.73 per cent and in 2019 19.63 per cent.

5

From the 'Charters' Incident to a 'Revue' (January 1992 to May 1993)

At the end of January 1992, some of my comments raised a lot of emotion. I said that we should not exclude the use of charters to repatriate rejected asylum seekers and other illegal residents. Because, among other things, of an influx of asylum seekers from the Former Yugoslavia, the progress made since 1 October 1991 could not be maintained. On 15 July 1992, responsibility for aliens' policy was transferred from the Minister of Justice to the Minister of the Interior. In June 1992, however, the snowball effect began again. Gigantic efforts would be needed to stop it. Many young jurists at the Commission General, including some 40 militiamen, did not care. As there is sometimes need for relaxation, they organised a '*Revue* of the Commission General'.

5.1. 'My Charters' (22 January 1992)

On the evening of Wednesday 22 January 1992, in a meeting room of the *Het Laatste Nieuws* newspaper in Brussels, I gave a presentation on the problem of foreigners staying irregularly in Belgium to a meeting of the Board of Directors of the Flemish Liberal Federation (LVV).[1] I was a member of that board myself. After explaining how the asylum procedure works, I got on one of my favourite hobby horses: 'It doesn't make sense to have a procedure to determine who can stay and who can't stay, when those who can't stay can stay anyway'. This was greeted with murmurings of approval.

Then I explained the difficulties in implementing an effective policy of removal. One of them is transportation. Aircraft are the most appropriate means of transportation, but regular airliners are not always appropriate:

> For some countries, there are no direct line flights from Brussels. Take, for example, Ghana. In the first four years of operation of the Commission General, there were more than 5,500 Ghanaian asylum applications. This is more than 13 per cent of all asylum

[1] The Liberaal Vlaams Verbond (LVV) founded in 1913, was chaired (1982–93) by Camille Paulus. He was vice-president (1971–93) of the University of Antwerp (UIA) and then Governor (1993–2008) of the province of Antwerp.

> applications. Their recognition rate was less than 1 per cent. Consequently, 99 per cent of these 5,500 asylum seekers should have been repatriated to Ghana. There are no direct flights between Brussels and Accra.
>
> In addition, it sometimes turns out that when a failed refugee applicant is brought on board, he is recalcitrant and even starts singing. The commander of the flight will say quite easily: 'Excuse me, I can't take him. The safety (and comfort) of my passengers come first'. For these reasons, it is not justified to exclude special flights, regardless of whether you call them 'charters' or not.

No one seemed offended by these explanations. A meeting of the LVV-board is obviously held *in camera*. Only members of the Board of Directors participate. It was a meeting between about 30 'companions' (Liberals are not 'comrades'). I spoke in confidence.

Friday morning 24 January 1992, 6.34 am, my bedroom in Edegem (near Antwerp):

> Ring, Ring. A sleepy voice picks up the phone and says: 'Hello?'
>
> *Mr Bossuyt?*
>
> Yes …
>
> *Mr Bossuyt, Radio BRTN. Is it correct that you said illegal aliens should be deported by charter?*
>
> Me? What? Where did you get that?
>
> *It's in the newspaper, Mr Bossuyt.*
>
> How? What newspaper?
>
> *On the front page of this morning's* Het Laatste Nieuws.
>
> Oh yes! Oh my God! Sorry. I was still asleep Maybe you can call me back in five minutes.
>
> *Sure, Mr Bossuyt, but it's for the news of 7.00 am.*

I brush my teeth. I'm thinking for a while. In essence, my answer will be: 'Yes, I said it. What's wrong with it?' The phone rings again. This will be one of the most chaotic days of my term as Commissioner General. After the telephone conversation, I hurried to the Commission General: 'There, all the Belgian media fall on me'.[2] I could address all the print media and radio stations. The four TV stations (BRTN, VTM, RTBF and RTL) also lined up On the news, they broadcast the images of the interviews I had granted.

The stumbling block was Laurent Panneels. In the *Het Laatste Nieuws* newspaper of 24 January 1992, he wrote an article entitled 'Expulsion by Charter. For Refugee Commissioner Bossuyt: "The Only Way to Reduce the Number of Illegal Immigrants"'. The article was illustrated by my photo taken in my office next to my computer, under the portrait of Queen Fabiola. The subtitle stated: 'Commissioner

[2] *DS* (25–26 January 1992).

General for Refugees Marc Bossuyt in the Footsteps of the Socialist Prime Minister of France Edith Cresson'. In the same newspaper's editorial, René Adams wrote under the title 'A Commissioner in Distress': 'It is striking that a man who is deeply serious and involved and who pursues a difficult balance between legislation and humanitarian principles is now appealing for help'.

5.1.1. Reactions to an 'Electroshock' (25–26 January 1992)

Under the title 'Justice Angry with Bossuyt', Laurent Panneels wrote that the Cabinet of Justice Minister Wathelet had reacted in a 'very angry' way to my remarks. The Cabinet had set the upper speed: 'This is very serious. We can only react decisively. It is very difficult for us. Bossuyt had better deal with the backlog of 9,000 cases attributable to him' (*HLN*). I replied:

> What I said is not so new. I'm not denying what I said. I have always addressed the issue of the expulsion of illegals in my annual reports. That may sound very loud now that we are starting to do several things, but we must be prepared to accept the consequences of what we decide and do. I have consistently raised the issue of my backlog in my annual reports. It is the consequence of the lack of means to fulfil my mandate (*HLN*).

Royal Commissioner Paula D'Hondt said she did not want to comment on my proposal. However, she felt that I had committed 'a serious ethical error':

> The deportation policy is entirely within the jurisdiction of Justice Minister Melchior Wathelet. The latter cannot react since the government has resigned and the Minister must act with restraint since he is called upon to form a new government [since 19 December 1991] (*DS*).

The Minister's office did not show much restraint. The Royal Commissioner also said: 'It is necessary to be able to discuss what Bossuyt said, but in an appropriate and discreet forum [such as at a closed meeting perhaps (MB)]' (*HV*).

The Royal Commissioner went so far as to claim that I had interchanged the notions of 'refugees' and 'illegals'. Fortunately, she was aware (at least on 9 September and 28 December 1991) (see above p 45) that there was a distinction between 'refugees' and 'migrants'. Her chief of staff, Johan Leman, found it 'Too bad'. On 27 February 1992, however, she pronounced herself on a decision concerning a particular refugee (Walid Bennani) (see above p 50–51).

In his first interim report (1 July 1994), Johan Leman, who would succeed her as Director of the Centre for Equal Opportunities, had already counted asylum seekers among migrants (*cf* below p 139–141). As chief of staff, he put another layer in the same newspaper:

> I am shocked that a colleague can express himself in such a way. Marc Bossuyt has fallen in my esteem. He, an academic, should know that one cannot express oneself on such a complex subject with only slogans. He must stick to the separation of powers.

> The function of Bossuyt [an administrative authority! (MB)] belongs to the judiciary [sic]. His remarks touch on areas of jurisdiction that belong to the executive and legislative branches. Where does our democratic system go if some people think they can do anything and say anything? Have our academics fallen so low that they lack respect when speaking of human beings? (*HV*).

To Laurent Panneels, he declared that he had 'studied a little too long and that he felt too good an intellectual to lend himself to certain remarks and reactions' (*HLN*).

Under the heading 'I Stand by what I Said', I said:

> It is my legal competence to say what I consider necessary for a good refugee policy. I talk about it at least twice a week, in front of any audience. This time, there was a journalist in the room. I did not know that. I am not responsible for the sensational way in which my remarks were presented. It is up to the media to know how to do it (*HV*).

Martine Vandemeulebroucke wrote under the title 'Charter Expulsions for Illegal Immigrants?':

> Marc Bossuyt's statements were like an electroshock. Don't we create a risk of drift? Response from Marc Bossuyt: 'Is it a taboo to talk about return by charter? It is hypocritical to say that one can expel the illegals only one by one; how many is inadmissible? Four? Seven? Twenty? There is no point in having a deportation procedure if 90 per cent of the illegals stay here' (*LS*).

Michel Marteau wrote under the title 'The Charter of Discord':

> Not everyone likes the way Mr Bossuyt sees things. In Melchior Wathelet's office, there was talk of serious statements that in no way bind the Minister. Mr Bossuyt spoke for himself and was certainly not mandated to do so [I was an independent agent (MB)].

I replied:

> I don't see why, for fear of being accused of this or that, I would refrain from using realistic language about the problem of illegals. And I have no sympathy for the extreme right, I beg you to believe (*LDH*).

Jean-Claude Matgen wrote under the title 'Charters for Illegal Aliens?':

> Me Jean-Yves Carlier refers to Article 4 of Protocol No 4 to the ECHR which is clear and short: 'Collective expulsions of foreigners are prohibited'. Mr Bossuyt talks about individual decisions, but I don't think we can separate decisions and enforcement (*LLB*).

Under the heading 'Deportation of Failed Asylum Seekers: Dirty?', in an opinion published in *De Morgen* on 28 February 1992, I examined the context of the charter incident. Regarding the ECHR, I referred to a decision of the European Commission of Human Rights of 3 October 1975. This decision (*Becker v Denmark*) concerned Denmark's grouped removal of 199 Vietnamese children to Vietnam. In that decision, the European Commission defined the concept of 'collective expulsion' as

> any measure of the competent authority compelling aliens as a group to leave the country, except where such a measure is taken after and on the basis of a reasonable and objective examination of the particular cases of each individual alien of the group.[3]

In an interview with RTBF Radio, my opponent, Me Georges-Henri Beauthier,[4] claimed that my proposal was contrary to the prohibition of 'collective expulsion'. He apparently had never heard of *Becker v Denmark*. He originally believed that I was referring to *De Becker v Belgium*.[5]

On 5 February 2002, the European Court of Human Rights concluded (by four votes to three) that Belgium had violated this ban in the *Čonka* case. On 5 October 1999, Prime Minister Guy Verhofstadt ordered the departure of the plane which would repatriate a Slovak couple with dozens of others. The Court considered it problematic that in the orders to leave the country 'the only reference to the personal circumstances of the applicants was to the fact that their stay in Belgium had exceeded three months' (§61). In this case, the Prime Minister had shown great determination. The government took note that day at 4.30 pm of an interim measure by Strasbourg against their expulsion. This was confirmed by fax at 6.10 pm. By 5.45 pm the plane had left.

5.1.2. Firmness Appreciated (Editorials of 27 January 1992)

Raymond De Craecker wrote under the title 'Expulsion and Esteem':

> Our country is experiencing a fight between commissioners: Royal Commissioner Paula D'Hondt considers that Commissioner General Marc Bossuyt has committed a serious ethical error by declaring his point of view on the defaulting policy of expulsion in a period during which the competent Minister of Justice cannot react. Her chief of staff says he is shocked and adds: 'Bossuyt is down in my esteem'.
>
> In my esteem, however, Bossuyt went up. He maintains his point of view. He does not follow the lead of many politicians, cabinet members, officials, etc who unscrupulously follow the air of time. This nation clearly lacks figures of rectilinear authority, who are not only concerned with paperwork but also subsequently with the effect of their interventions. The Refugee Commissioner seems to be one of them (*DNG*).

Michel Marteau wrote under the title 'Common Sense is Dangerous':

> A well-known moderate man, who claims to have no sympathy for the far right, says out loud what most people think. But Mr Bossuyt was wrong to use the word 'charter'.

[3] M Bossuyt, *Strasbourg et les demandeurs d'asile: des juges sur un terrain glissant* (Brussels, Bruylant, 2010) 97.

[4] See J-C M, *LLB* (28 January 1992): 'M Bossuyt: la suite dans les idées'.

[5] This was the first Belgian case (concerning a French-speaking journalist who collaborated during the war) and the second case ever before the Strasbourg Court. That case was dropped on 27 March 1962.

> Would he have said 'by air' or 'by special plane' his message would have been better passed among the professional indignants (*LDH*).

Jean-Claude Matgen wrote under the title 'Clumsy, Mr Bossuyt':

> If he took the risk of such strong words, it is perhaps to open the eyes of the political class on the seriousness of an increasingly acute problem. We are surprised, and we regret that he chose this path and defended a point of view that all those for whom Human Rights still have a meaning cannot share (*LLB*).

5.1.3. The Dust is Settling

The satirical weekly *Pan* wrote, under the title 'Charters: The False Scandal':

> The brave Bossuyt has only repeated what he has been saying for years and which he notes every year in his annual report. His proposals seem realistic. Probably too much for the demagogic-angelic couple [Mel]Chior-D'Hondt (29 January 1992).

Gabrielle Lefèvre brought real relief under the title 'Fake Scoop, Real Problem':

> Marc Bossuyt has been defending and teaching human rights for twenty years. He was Chairperson of the UN Commission on Human Rights. He is Vice-President of the International Institute for Human Rights in Strasbourg. He continues to teach this subject while undertaking effectively and under very difficult conditions the hard work of defending the rights of asylum seekers. The trial he was given in some newspapers was therefore quite surprising. A journalist from *Het Laatste Nieuws* assisted, without having informed Mr Bossuyt, at a closed meeting at the *Liberaal Vlaams Verbond*. He thought he was holding a scoop when Mr Bossuyt spoke about the 'charter solution' for repatriating failed asylum seekers. He had already analysed his arguments in *De Standaard* of 21 April 1991, the *Gazet van Antwerpen* of 7 June, De Morgen of 14 July and in a tribune of *La Libre Belgique* of 16 December. Consequently, no scoop! (*La Cité*, 30 January 1992).

Edith Cresson spoke on 8 July 1991, so I could not walk in her footsteps on 21 April (*DS*) and 7 June 1991 (*GvA*). Presented in a less sensational way, my remarks had escaped the attention of some at the time.

Letters from readers of *Het Laatste Nieuws* of 5 and 6 February 1992 were encouraging:

> Bravo for Marc Bossuyt, who at least dares to draw logical and realistic conclusions. The indignation of the Minister of Justice and Paula D'Hondt is perceived by people as ridiculous. Her right-hand man, J Leman, considered himself too intelligent to react to the proposal of Marc Bossuyt (from Tielt-Wingene).
>
> I can only commend Mr Bossuyt for his courage in making this issue a topic for discussion (from Furnes).
>
> With Marc Bossuyt, we finally have someone who dares to echo the opinion of most of the Belgian population and who says what Belgians think about the problem of migrants. I wish Mr Bossuyt much courage and perseverance in his difficult task. He deserves congratulations (from St Nicolas).

> He reminds me of Diogenes.[6] He was walking around in broad daylight with a lamp and said he was looking for a man. If Diogenes met Marc Bossuyt, he would certainly say: 'Finally, a Man, and even someone with common sense' (from Deurne).

5.1.4. The House Justice Committee (28 January 1992)

On Tuesday morning 28 January 1992, a dozen members of the House Justice Committee visited Transit Centre 127 in Melsbroek and the Petit-Château in Brussels. The Commission was chaired by Laurette Onkelinx (PS),[7] a young and promising politician. The press of 29 January gave a broad account of this visit:

> Patrick Martens ('Asylum Seekers Welcome Parliamentarians for a Day', *HBvL*): The direct confrontation with applicants from Africa, Asia and Eastern Europe – and for once not a distant conversation in the Parliamentary House – impressed parliamentarians.
>
> Alain Vanbuyten ('Near the Promised Land', *HV*): Although the two centres were deeply cleansed, it remained an image of desolation. We have noted a great history of human misery, scattered families, and long days of waiting for a frequently negative response.
>
> Alain Heyrendt ('Marc Bossuyt Assumes', *LLB*): The morning was foggy and cold. It smelled of bad cooking, soapy water, and resignation. The women's shower was not lit or heated. Through a window, one sees drying clothes and punctured football balls dotted a rare grass enclosure. At the Petit-Château, the scenery was hardly less hopeless.

In the afternoon, I presented to the Commission my *Third Annual Report* (1990). This would be my last annual report presented in the House and published as a parliamentary document. It was supplemented orally by data concerning the fourth year of activity (1991):

> The parliamentarians were waiting for Marc Bossuyt at the corner of the gallery: he did not escape. In his conclusion, he did not forget 'the most delicate but nonetheless unavoidable removal from the territory of rejected asylum seekers', and so much for the emotional reactions. 'We can no longer be too watchful about the practical modalities of implementation', he said.[8]

I did not go back on what I said a few days ago about charters. I stated that there was no solution if failed asylum seekers were not forced to leave the territory. I conceded that the way in which my remarks were presented was not conducive to a serene debate on the issue of refugees: 'This subject is too sensitive to make sensationalism'.

[6] Diogenes, Greek philosopher (404–323 BC).

[7] From 1992 to 2014, Laurette Onkelinx did hold uninterrupted ministerial positions, including Minister President of the French Community (1993–99)' Deputy Prime Minister (1999–2014)' Minister of Health (1992–93, 2007–14), Employment (1999–2003), and Justice (2003–07) in the Federal Government.

[8] Alain Heyrendt, *LLB* (29 February 1992).

5.1.5. PS: Frontex's' 'Special Flights'

Who would have thought that there would now be monthly 'special flights' taking off from several EU countries to different countries of origin of illegal foreigners? This is now the official policy of the European Union executed by Frontex (the European Border and Coast Guard Agency). These flights are mainly used for (a) foreigners who cannot, or can hardly, be removed due to strong resistance; (b) large groups for the same destination; (c) large families who, because of limitations imposed by airlines, are not permitted to board a commercial flight; and (d) a Member State participating with a limited number of persons, when another country organises a return operation. Frontex finances the costs of such operations up to 80 per cent.

It is to be regretted that special flights became possible only after the death of a young Nigerian woman, Semira Adamu (b 15 April 1978; d 22 September 1998), during the sixth aborted attempt to bring her back to Togo on an airliner. If there had not been a taboo on 'charter' removals, she would not have paid with her life. This price was paid because emotional arguments took over rational arguments. It also led to the resignation (on 26 September 1998) of a particularly competent minister, Louis Tobback, who was the architect of a responsible immigration policy. Then it became clear that an airliner was not always the most appropriate means of removing recalcitrant illegal aliens from the territory (*cf* below p 68 and 91 and chapter eighteen, p 234–241).

5.2. Progress could not be Maintained (June 1992–April 1993)

In June 1992, I noted progress. However, an influx of asylum applications from a dislocated Yugoslavia contributed to reverse this trend. In the rare cases of an unfavourable opinion concerning applicants from the Former Yugoslavia, I had them accompanied by a recommendation of non-expulsion. From the beginning of 1992, I gave priority to the processing of other asylum applications. I proposed establishing a 'displaced person' status for persons of the Former Yugoslavia. On 23 November 1992, the Minister of the Interior followed up.

5.2.1. An Influx of Ex-Yugoslavs

On 18 June 1992, I presented my *Fourth Annual Report* (1991). Thanks to better awareness of the political world and public opinion, there was progress. A positive point was the reinforcement of staff, but only 10 per cent of my collaborators were statutory. The procedure was speeded up because, since 1 October 1991, for many decisions, the Minister's personal intervention was no longer required. The number of asylum applications fell from an all-time high of 1,756 in September 1991 to an average of about 1,200 per month. The backlog was still large: there were

20,000 asylum applications pending, including 12,000 at the Commission General. I insisted on a greater acceleration of the procedure. I dealt with the most recent entries (LiFo: Last in, First out). The Aliens Office did not follow this procedure. I was suggesting that a temporary residence permit be granted to ex-Yugoslavs. In the meantime, the best I could do was not to prioritise their urgent requests.

On 10 November 1992, I received a threatening letter in the mailbox of my private home. According to the *Gazet van Antwerpen* of 12 November, I took my place 'in a line of high-ranking people who were dedicated to the integration of foreigners'. Paula D'Hondt and parliamentarians Luc Dhoore (CVP) and Jef Sleeckx (SP) also received one.

On 30 December 1992, the *Gazet van Antwerpen* related that in 1992 I expected to cross the threshold of 17,000 asylum seekers. In the same newspaper, Boudewijn De Muynck relativised this record number:

> If the Commissioner General had not picked it up again, probably few people would have noticed. An exorbitant excitement would have been inappropriate. It would have been shameful to lament as if a generally prosperous society were not able to treat these men, women, and children humanely. The response to refugee flows is to ensure that they no longer must flee.

On 8 February 1993, I wrote to the Minister of the Interior about the policy of deportation:

> If effective deportation to the country of origin were to take place, it would appear that, in a considerable number of cases, the duration of the 'legal' stay in Belgium has resulted in integration making any removal measure irresponsible, socially, humanitarian, and (presumably) also political. The media attention given to orders to leave the territory not really justified – even more so to effectively implemented forced removals to the country of origin – can discredit aliens' policies. Consequently, the policy of deportation must be applied as a matter of priority against illegal immigrants and rejected asylum seekers who have not been in Belgium for a very long time and who can be returned to countries where the political and economic situation is not abnormally bad.[9]

5.2.2. Status of Displaced Persons from the Former Yugoslavia

In *De Morgen* of 18 February 1993, I explained the status of displaced persons from the Former Yugoslavia established at the end of 1992:

> Since the beginning of the conflict (spring 1991), I have been giving favourable opinions for most urgent requests for reconsideration. Since 1 October 1991, I have added the following clause in the rare cases of an unfavourable opinion:
>
> *'In view of the current events in Yugoslavia, however, the Commissioner General recommends that any removal from the territory be suspended'.*

[9] *Sixth Annual Report* (1993) 43.

> Since the Aliens Office continued, despite the deterioration of the situation, to issue orders to leave the territory, I decided at the beginning of 1992 to give priority to applications submitted by the many other nationalities. After the Dehaene Government took office on 7 March 1992, I proposed granting asylum seekers from the Former Yugoslavia a provisional residence permit. In August 1992, the Minister of the Interior (responsible since 15 July 1992) decided to establish a simplified procedure for granting temporary residence rights to displaced persons from the Former Yugoslavia. On 3 September 1992, I asked to clarify the status of those whose urgent request for reconsideration was pending. On 23 November 1992, the Minister decided to grant them 'displaced person status'.[10]

From November to December 1992, I had provided the Aliens Office with lists of applications by asylum seekers from Croatia (131), Kosovo (229), Bosnia and Herzegovina (270) and [Northern] Macedonia (379). On 13 July 1993, I asked the Aliens Office to obtain lists of persons who had been granted the status of displaced persons. On 6 August 1993, I was told that it was not possible to follow up on my request 'in view of the confidentiality of the files'. The Office did not keep statistics on this. At the end of 1993, the Aliens Office had issued 3,880 declarations of arrival of displaced persons.[11] With the introduction of displaced person status, their situation during the conflict was resolved. They could stay in Belgium without having to follow the asylum procedure. There was still much to read in the media about the Former Yugoslavia. However, this is a monotonous story that I will not repeat here.[12]

In a debate in Leuven on 2 April 1993, I stated that the backlog in the processing of files was 'phenomenal'. About 30,000 files were 'somewhere' in processing.[13] At the beginning of May 1993, the *Burgerkrant*, the monthly magazine of the VLD (Flemish Liberals), published under the title 'The Snowball of Asylum Seekers Must Stop' an interview by Bart Somers in which I stated:

> We don't have a refugee problem but a refugee applicants' problem. The absence of effective deportations works like a magnet on potential asylum seekers. We have a procedure to determine who can and cannot stay in the country. What is the point of such a procedure if rejected asylum seekers can still stay? Stop all this and open the borders for all.

[10] Such a status was established by Council Directive 2001/55/EC of 20 July 2001 on minimum standards for giving temporary protection in the event of a mass influx of displaced persons. On this subject, a UNHCR official, Periclis Kortsaris, defended his doctoral thesis under my supervision at the University of Antwerp in 2003. Following the Russian invasion of Ukraine on 24 February 2022, the EU Council decided on 4 March 2022 to make this directive operational.

[11] *Sixth Annual Report* (1993), 14.

[12] See *Fifth Annual Report* (1992) §§46–74; *Sixth Annual Report* (1993) §§36–54; *Seventh Annual Report* (1994) §§34–63; *Eighth Annual Report* (1995) §§40–64; *Ninth Annual Report* (1996) §§55–73. M Bossuyt, 'Le CGRA et les personnes déplacées de l'ex-Yougoslavie' [1995] *Revue du droit des étrangers* 467.

[13] *GvA* (3 April 1993).

5.3. The 'Revue' of the Commission General (8 May 1993)

In Belgium, humorous 'revues' consisting of several sketches is a tradition at universities. In the administration, it's rare. The (bilingual) 'Revue'[14] of the Commission General of 8 May 1993 at the parish centre of Kraainem (near Brussels) was a real event. No wonder with a staff composed largely of 40 militiamen, most of whom were jurists. Some excerpts from that Revue give an impression of the young, student and humorous atmosphere that reigned there.

5.3.1. The Fictional Press Conference

The Revue began with a (fictional) press conference attributed to me on the opening of a new reception centre for asylum seekers at the national airport:

- *Introduction: The Bossuyt Centre, named after its founder Refugee Commissioner General Bossuyt, was opened today in Zaventem. At his request, we transmit in full his inaugural speech.*
- Bossuyt: Ladies and gentlemen, I am honoured to be able to open the Bossuyt Centre today. I sincerely thank my friends in the press for their support in choosing the name of the Centre. With this new initiative, the star of the Commission General will sparkle even more. The Bossuyt Centre is indeed an innovative project in the field of asylum in Belgium and Europe. It meets all the needs and necessities of the modern refugee. The days of castles and containers are over: 'The new refugee has arrived'. The Centre is divided into three classes. The wealthiest asylum seekers will now be able to enter the first class, the VLD-lounge, where openness is one of the essential points. In the middle class, the Paula D'Hondt lounge, there will be pantagruelist meals for the guests. The man or woman who wants a little adventure can enter our third class, the Louis Tobback lounge. Each lounge will be led by its own hostess. If Belgium wants to maintain its status as an attractive asylum country, the culinary aspects cannot be neglected.
- *Journalist: Is repatriation of asylum seekers to certain countries reasonable?*
- Bossuyt: Naturally, naturally. I'll use Africa as an example. Some time ago, I was on mission in an African country. I took the opportunity to investigate alleged human rights violations in that country. Well, during a cocktail party on the terrace of my host, the Minister of Interior and Security of the country concerned, in the shade of palm trees and with the sweet murmur of the

[14] Theatre, composed of different elements of a different nature, such as singing, dancing and sketches, usually comic or satirical.

Indian Ocean in the background, I asked for clarification on the veracity of these international complaints of torture. He formally assured me that there were no violations of fundamental rights. Consequently, no objection.

- *Journalist: Could you say something about the interview rooms in the new centre?*
- Bossuyt: Interview rooms? What do you mean? Why interviews? Who is interviewing? I am the only one who gives interviews on behalf of the Commission General. I will make available to you the compilation of my television interviews, entitled '*The Best of the Boss*'.
- *Journalist: Can you lift a corner of the veil already with regard to your Centre's future plans?*
- Bossuyt: If in the next legislature I can count on sufficient support from Parliament, I think that a cooperation agreement with Sabena and Air France is not excluded. After a period of minority participation, the Bossuyt Centre will take over this privatised airline. This will lead to the creation of *Bossuyt Airlines*'.

Then two collaborators sang to the tune of '*M'n Airhostess*' ('My Airhostess') by Will Tura:

When I was a little boy,
At the babysitting school,
I dreamed of a plane
With a lot of people in it.
I was naturally the pilot.
I was the chief on board.
And now that I'm grown up,
My dream comes true:
These are Bossuyt Airlines.
Monday, we fly to Accra.
Tuesday night, we land in Kinshasa.
Wednesday, I'm already in Bombay.
And Thursday, back
Empty at home.
How do you become a passenger?
It starts with a grey file.
You're telling an hour-long story.
It's submitted to Infojur.
Then you wait another year or two
And you get my stamp
With a letter from Tobback in hand.
Then you get to Bossuyt Airlines.
On Friday, we fly to Warsaw.
Saturday, I land in Islamabad.
Sunday, in Ankara.
And in the evening, back to Melsbroek.
My flights are very successful.
There are six a day.
I've also organised charters.

With support of the Minister.
Every flight is full.
Lode[15] makes it work.
Engines at full power, all wings out.
These are the Bossuyt Airlines.

5.3.2. A Monologue on Statistics

A monologue was attributed to me concerning my statistics:

> Oh yes, my statistics. I think one can do anything with statistics. I must confess I haven't convinced Louis Tobback yet. Last week, I was at his office, when he said to me: 'Marc, my boy, your statistics are like a bikini: it shows a lot, but it hides the essential'. Anyway, I'm happy with my statistics. Let's take this example: the highest line shows the number of minutes I appeared on the VTM news for the period 1989–1990: 19.5 minutes; the lowest line shows for the same period my appearances at the RTBF: no less than 14 minutes. At the end of 1990, I bought a new suit … And here, on the following diagram, we directly see a spectacular rise in my television performances. What is surprising is that this increase is much greater on francophone television. This is why I conclude that my Walloon friends of the RTBF are more fashion conscious than those of VTM: from 14 minutes to 27.5 minutes. In 1991, I appeared 13.5 minutes more on TV. Per minute of film, I denounce twice the lack of staff. In 1992, Wallonia learned 27 times more than in 1990 that the Commission General was recruiting staff.

This monologue was illustrated by a 'Song of Statistics' to the tune of '*Ze is mijn lief*' ('She is my lover') by Helmut Lotti:

In the evening, when I'm still here,
At night, when everything is quiet,
I take my calculating machine
And I count my RAs.[16]
Because at night, I'm always concerned.
So, at night, I check everything.
I count all my decisions
And pray to God with all my heart to be with me.
If my stats are good,
Otherwise, I'm completely blocked,
Because I'm Commissioner General,
Thanks to the language of statistics.
At night, after pressing a button,
At night, I see where the problem lies. […].
No peaks too high

[15] The first name of an employee who processed applications from countries with a very low recognition rate.

[16] RA refers to a reasoned decision on refugee status refused on the merits of the case.

In my statistics,
Because I'm Commissioner General,
Thanks to the language of statistics.
They are unique
My two-colour stats,
Exceptionally attractive.
Even at university,
They are exclusively mine,
My productivity statistics,
My stats.
I thank the Lord for my statistics.

5.3.3. The Ghanaians at Petit-Château

The Revue ended with a song about Ghanaian asylum seekers[17] in Petit-Château to the tune of Leonard Bernstein's 'I want to be in America':

Accra-City, Ashanti land,[18] my
Country with tropical fruits,
With a lot of coconut
And the sounds of the tam-tam.
Accra City, city of hunger, my country
Of tropical diseases,
With all your gossip,
And your green army uniforms.
Where bullets kill and soldiers
Murder. Give me, in the heart of Brussels,
Home of Entertainment and Pleysier.[19]
I'm so good at the Petit-Château.
For a Ghanaian it's a real gift
To be able to live in the Petit-Château.
I'll never leave the Little Castle.
I also love Kumasi.[20]
Your flight's at 2.30.
Hundreds of girls still pure.
Hundreds of people in the house.
As an aperitif at the Petit-Château,

[17] In the first year of operation (1988) of the Commission General, Ghanaians accounted for more than 25% of total asylum applications. They were the most important nationality from 1988 to 1989, the third in 1990 (after Romania and Turkey) and 1991 (after Romania and Zaire) and the fifth in 1992 (after Zaire, Romania, the Former Yugoslavia, and India). Their recognition rate was less than 1%. While in principle the staff at the Commission General were specialised by country or geographical region, in the early years many of them also had to process Ghanaian asylum applications.
[18] A Kingdom in Ghana.
[19] Bob Pleysier was the director of the Petit-Château.
[20] Second town of Ghana, capital of the Ashanti.

No sour rum but a sweet pinot.
More manioc at the Petit-Château,
Everything at the Petit-Château.

The staff members who had organised this Revue had – for three months now – been answerable to a memo of 26 January 1993 (see chapter nine). This memo introduced an evaluation system to measure their productivity. Participation in the Revue did not provide them with additional points. Yet no discomfort was noticeable. To say it with a famous expression: 'The atmosphere was good'. I would say even more: 'The atmosphere was excellent'. Three months after this Revue, in July 1993, the Basque-Spanish couple Moreno–Garcia applied for asylum in Belgium. Suspecting that they had assisted ETA, Spain had requested their extradition. This affair created much excitement and dragged on for several years.

6

The Basque-Spanish Couple Moreno–Garcia (1993–98)

The Basque-Spanish couple Moreno–Garcia applied for asylum in Belgium in July 1993. Luis Moreno Ramajo (b 1961) and Raquel Garcia Arranz (b 1962) had been staying in Vilvorde (near Brussels) with Basque friends since March 1992. They led a 'peaceful life'.[1] At the informal request of the Guardia civil of 17 July 1992, a static observation measure was undertaken in respect of them. The observation was stopped for lack of a Spanish international mandate.[2] It was not until 20 May 1993 that such a warrant was issued by an investigating judge in Madrid. The couple was accused of 'being members of an ETA terrorist association which, by seeking to separate the Basque provinces of Spain, was committing attacks on persons and property in which there were 800 deaths'. They would have taken care of the infrastructure for three members of the '*Viczaya* commando' belonging to this organisation. They would have housed them and carried weapons for them.

6.1. Unfavourable Opinion of the Court on the Extradition Requests (23 July 1993)

On 28 May 1993, the Spanish authorities requested their provisional arrest. They were arrested on 15 June. On 2 July, the Chambre du conseil of the Tribunal of first instance of Brussels granted the exequatur in respect of 'criminal association for the purpose of committing crimes'. On 16 July, the Chamber of Indictment of the Brussels Court of Appeal declared the arrest warrants enforceable.[3] On 23 July, the same Chamber gave opinions on the extradition requests.[4] Referring to the

[1] See the order of 8 December 1993 of Godelieve Halsberghe, President of the Tribunal of first instance, for interim measures.

[2] [1994] *Tijdschrift voor Vreemdelingenrecht* 27.

[3] Because the Chambre du conseil had been presided over by Judge Bruno Bulthé, who in his capacity as investigating judge had issued the arrest warrant, the Chamber of Indictment declared the order null and void, but – after evocation – still enforceable (*DS*; *LS*, 22 July 1993).

[4] Their lawyers were Me André De Becker and Me Marleen Vanlouwe of the Brussels Bar and Me Paul Bekaert of the Bruges Bar. The reader of this chapter will understand why on Monday afternoon 30 October 2017, Charles Puigdemont, President of the Government of Catalonia, was at the door of Me Paul Bekaert in Tielt.

undoubtedly political character of the crimes charged and the absence of features which would give the facts a particular gravity, the Chamber issued an opinion unfavourable to the requests for extradition. The Chamber held that the Belgian reservation concerning politically motivated facts, as mentioned in Article 13 of the European Convention on Terrorism of 27 January 1977, was applicable.[5] Referring to a consistent practice,[6] Minister of Justice Melchior Wathelet could have immediately refused the extradition requests. Spain 'would not have been happy but all the subsequent difficulties could have been avoided'.[7] To tell the rest of the story now will take several more pages.

6.2. 'A Slap in the Face':[8] Further Examination of their Asylum Application (29 October 1993)

Raquel Garcia and Luis Moreno each applied for asylum on 5 and 13 July 1993 respectively. On 23 September, the Aliens Office declared them inadmissible because they had filed their application more than eight days after their entry into the Kingdom. Their stay was considered illegal because they did not report to the commune for registration. On 24 September, they filed urgent appeals against these refusals to stay.[9] On 18 October they were heard by my collaborators, respectively in the prisons of Saint-Gilles and Forest. They denied having housed members of

[5] According to G Vermeulen and T Vander Beken, 'The Extradition of Basques to Spain: Legal Reflections on a Political Affair' (1995–96) *Recente Arresten van de Raad van State* 211, this Convention has only been in force since 26 March 1995 between Belgium and Spain, as has the Schengen Implementation Agreement of 19 June 1990. They consider that the advice previously given by the Chamber should have been given based on the bilateral extradition treaty of 17 June 1870. In this case, the extradition request would not have been admissible, because the facts (accommodation and transport) do not fall under Art 2 of that bilateral treaty. The facts would have been punishable only under Art 339 of the Penal Code (concealment) for which this treaty does not provide for extradition. They also dispute that these facts fell under Art 1 of the European Convention on Terrorism. If they fell under that Article, they could not be considered a political offence. According to Belgian law, the facts cannot be considered as 'attempt' or 'participation'. Art 339 of the Penal Code does not even cover participation. See *DM* (16 March 1996) and the interview of Frank De Moor, with these two authors in *Knack* of 13 March 1996: 'Everyone was wrong'.

[6] See C Van Den Wijngaert, 'La Belgique et l'exception pour infractions politiques en matière d'extradition: analyse critique de la pratique judiciaire et administrative' [1979] *Revue du Droit Public* 858: 'extradition was never granted after a negative opinion, and extradition was often refused despite the favourable opinion of the Court of Appeal' (cited in my decisions of 16 February 1994 denying refugee status to Moreno and Garcia).

[7] In my conversation with Misjoe Verleyen (*Knack*, 16 March 1994).

[8] The erroneous headlines in the newspapers of 4 November 1993 (*DS*: 'Supporters of ETA Recognised as Candidate-Refugees. Bossuyt's Decision Implies that Spain is Violating Human Rights'; and *HN*: 'Asylum for two Basques. The Decision around ETA Suspects is a Slap in the Face for Spain') contributed to the violence of the Spanish reactions.

[9] As of 1 June 1993, my (non-binding) opinions on 'urgent requests for reconsideration' were replaced by (binding) further examination decisions (admissible application) or confirmatory refusal of access or residence (inadmissible application) on 'urgent appeals'.

the commando. It was in January 1992, following a raid on their home during their absence, that they decided to leave Spain.

Since, as nationals of a Member State of the European Union, they did not need permission to stay in Belgium and in view of the political nature of the charges, I considered, in my further examination decisions of 29 October 1993, that the alleged delay in their refugee application was not a sufficient ground for refusing their stay. Their fear of persecution appeared only on 2 July 1993, when they were notified of the extradition requests.[10]

In addition, the extradition requests were based on a statement by Juan Ramón Rojo, who had been mistreated after his arrest, as was reported by a Spanish medical examiner.[11] I also referred to the report[12] by Professor Pieter Kooijmans,[13] Special Rapporteur of the UN Commission on Human Rights, and to Article 3 ECHR and Article 15 of the UN Convention against Torture and Other Cruel Treatment or Punishment of 10 December 1984.[14] In view of 'the seriousness of the charges and the unquestionably political nature of the reasons for the facts relied upon', I felt that further consideration of their applications was necessary.[15] The Minister of the Interior, Louis Tobback,[16] was sympathetic to my decisions: 'In his place, I would have done the same'. He conceded, however, that it was politically embarrassing for our relations with Spain.[17]

Having noted in a press release of 12 November 1993 that there were several hundred asylum applications in Belgium every month from persons who clearly had no political motive, I was saying that refusing applications with obvious political grounds for a purely formal reason (such as the late date of the application) without substantive examination (with the guarantees prescribed by the

[10] The reasons for this further examination decision were published in [1994] *Tijdschrift voor Vreemdelingenrecht* 30.

[11] The report of 29 January 1992, referred to 'mistreatment': 'there are recent abrasions and bruises on the face, arms, forearm, hand, trunk and lower extremities'. The official medical examiner at the Audiencia Nacional had found 'bruises, hematomas, abrasions'. The Audiencia Nacional, a special court in Madrid with jurisdiction over the entire Spanish territory is, inter alia, competent for acts of terrorism.

[12] This report (E/CN.4/1993/26, § 401, e) of 15 December 1992 stated in respect of Juan Ramón Rojo: 'arrested at his home in Basauri by civil guards on 29 January 1992. He was insulted, threatened with a firearm, pulled about by the hair, and hit on sensitive parts of the body'.

[13] Professor Pieter Kooijmans had meanwhile become Minister of Foreign Affairs of the Netherlands (1993–94). He later became a judge (1997–2006) at the International Court of Justice.

[14] Art 15 of the Torture Convention: 'Each State Party shall ensure that any statement which is established to have been made as a result of torture shall not be invoked as evidence in any proceedings, except against a person accused of torture as evidence that the statement was made'.

[15] I found it excessive to consider my decision a slap in the face for Spain. Referring to the admissibility decisions taken by the Aliens Office and myself since 1 February 1988, I said: 'I would have already given 21,000 slaps to 108 countries (*DM*, 5 November). Referring to these remarks, on 16 November 1993 the Spanish Ministry of Foreign Affairs informed the Belgian Ambassador in Madrid, Thierry Muûls, that it was unacceptable for a Member State of the European Union to be put on an equal footing with all the states on the planet.

[16] Louis Tobback, Minister of the Interior since 1988, had been responsible for aliens' policy since 15 July 1992 (by the transfer of aliens' policy from Justice to the Interior).

[17] *DM* (5 November 1993).

accompanying law) would not increase the credibility of the asylum procedure.[18] I pointed out that I had not claimed that Spain was requesting these extraditions for political reasons. However, the facts of which the parties concerned were accused were undoubtedly of a political character, as the Appeal Court had already ruled.

In protest at my decision, on 29 November 1993, Spain blocked all initiatives on the right to asylum at the Council of Ministers for Justice and the Interior of the European Union in Brussels. That same evening in Madrid, Prime Minister Jean-Luc Dehaene (1992–99) promised his Spanish counterpart Felipe González (1982–96) that the government would appeal if I recognised as refugees the two imprisoned Basques. Interior Minister Louis Tobback declared his full agreement with the Prime Minister. He nevertheless felt that as Commissioner General, in whom he had full confidence, I should be able to work freely.[19] Magda Aelvoet in the House and Frans Lozie in the Senate (both Agalev) orally asked the question: 'How could he still conduct an asylum procedure objectively, after the Prime Minister's remarks?' On 2 December 1993, Minister Louis Tobback replied: 'I know him well enough to know that he will not be so influenced'.

In *Het Volk*[20] of 2 December 1993, I stated that the Prime Minister's remarks were not likely to guarantee serenity. They showed, however, that I acted independently. In a point of view, *De Morgen* on the same day regretted the serious disruption of the political debate and the rapidity with which Belgium, President of the European Union, had yielded to Spanish pressure: 'Poor, poor European Union, if it can only take a structural form on corpses'. Two parliamentarians from the Basque nationalist party Herri Batasuna referred to political blackmail never seen from Madrid.[21]

6.3. A Thunderbolt: The President of the Tribunal Releases them (8 December 1993)

In her order of 8 December 1993, the President of the Tribunal of first instance of Brussels, sitting in interim proceedings, referred first to the unfavourable opinions of the Chamber of Indictment and to my further examination decisions. She noted that the government had not yet taken a decision on the extradition requests and that my decision, which she described as the overriding interest, could take several more months. She ordered the immediate release of the two applicants[22]

[18] *Knack* (24 November 1993).
[19] *Ann parl, Chambre*, 1993–94, 3 December 1993.
[20] 'A State appeal against a refugee determination is highly unusual'.
[21] *DM*; *LS* (3 December 1993).
[22] [1994] *Tijdschrift voor Vreemdelingenrecht* 27, with note from L Denys, 'Extradition to the Country of Origin of a Refugee Applicant, a National of a Member State of the EC' 39. According to *Vers l'Avenir* of 10 December 1993, the Minister of Justice appealed against this order. On 7 December 1994, the Brussels Court of Appeal upheld the order of the President of the Tribunal.

and imposed a penalty payment equivalent to €1,250 to be paid to each of the applicant parties per day of delay. The applicants had to settle in and register in the province of Brabant. They were released the same evening.[23]

This made the news of the day in the Belgian media of 9 December 1993:

> The Judge Orders the Release of the Basques, The Judge Releases the Basques, The Basques have Difficulty in Actually Finding Freedom (*DM*); ETA Suspects are still Free (*HN*); Belgium Releases two ETA Suspects (*DS*); Justice Releases the Basques after a Lot of Hesitation, After Recognition, Extradition Becomes Impossible (*GvA*); A Tug of War over the Release of the Basques, The Basques still Released (*HLN*); and The Judge for Interim Measures Orders the Release of the two Basques (*LLB*).

Het Nieuwsblad of 2 December had published for the first-time photos of the young Basque couple (both 31 years old). From 9 December, these photos appeared in several newspapers, including *El País*.[24] From now on, Basque asylum seekers had a face.

In Spain, the indignation was great. According to the Spanish government, the whole affair was unacceptable, both politically and legally. It was an interference of Belgian justice in Spanish justice.[25] On Saturday 11 December 1993, *El País* published a long interview with me, including a photo. I emphasised that I had not spoken at all about persecution in Spain. All of this was to be part of the examination of the merits on which I could not provide any information. I expressed the hope that Spain did not doubt that Belgium was a State of law. According to the same newspaper, the Professional Association of the Spanish Judiciary expressed its indignation at the decision of a Belgian judge, which was based on an unacceptable questioning of the safety of the Spanish judicial system.[26] Also in the same newspaper, there was an article according to which the Spanish government had hidden from Professor Pieter Kooijmans the medical reports concerning Juan Ramón Rojo, the couple being accused on the basis of the latter's statements.[27]

Since the statements of the Belgian Prime Minister on 29 November 1993 in Madrid could give the impression that the decisions I had to take would be influenced by considerations of political expediency, on 6 December I asked the Representative of the UN High Commissioner for Refugees three

[23] *Ann parl, Chambre*, SO 1993–94, 9 December 1993.

[24] On 11 December 1993, a photo of the couple in freedom holding the *El País* newspaper of 9 December 1993 appeared in *El País* and in several Belgian newspapers.

[25] *El País* (9 December 1993). According to *El País* of 10 December 1993 (with the photo of Jean-Luc Dehaene), '*La actitud belga, calificada de "disparatada", "insolita" y "rechazable"*' (crazy, unusual, and regrettable). According to *Knack* (15 December 1993), the Spanish Minister of Justice spoke of 'a dismal and incoherent decision which can only be described as a sequence of absurdities. We have not seen such a glaring error anywhere else'.

[26] '[L]a indignación que produce la decisión de una juez de Belgica, por cuanto se funda en el inadmisible cuestionamiento de la seguridad del sistema judicial de Espana'.

[27] On 2 November 1992, the Spanish government informed Professor Pieter Kooijmans that no injuries had been observed in any of the 28 prisoners (including Juan Ramón Rojo) about whom he had requested information.

questions pursuant to Article 57/23*bis*, §2, of the Aliens Law. On 13 December, this Representative, José Maria Mendiluce (by coincidence, himself a Spanish Basque), answered these questions as follows:

a. The Geneva Convention does not allow an asylum application to be rejected on the sole basis of the nationality of an applicant without examining the data specific to his asylum application.
b. The granting of asylum cannot be regarded as unfriendly towards another State and should not involve any political qualification of the nature of the applicant's country of origin.
c. Spain is a democratic country that protects human rights and is a party to all legal instruments for the protection of human rights. Some abuses of rights in the context of the repression of terrorism denounced by non-governmental organisations are isolated cases condemned by the Spanish authorities.

Those answers strengthened my position in the decisions I had made and that I was going to make next.

On the initiative of five political groups, the European Parliament adopted, on 16 December, by 69 votes to 13, with 4 abstentions (and in the absence of 449 MEPs!), a resolution on my declaration of admissibility for asylum applications by two alleged members of the terrorist organisation ETA. According to this resolution, a Member State of the Union could in no case envisage granting political refugee status to a national of another Member State.[28]

In a press release of 17 December, I noted that no Belgian authority had taken a decision in this case which indicated a lack of confidence in Spanish justice. I noted that the reactions to these decisions resulted from a lack of understanding caused by a lack of familiarity with the specific characteristics of both the extradition procedure and the Belgian asylum procedure, and in particular concerning access to the latter procedure. According to Martin Gerritsen of Amnesty International, 'the weight on Marc Bossuyt's shoulders was heavy'.[29]

6.4. Spanish Relief: Moreno–Garcia not Recognised (16 February 1994)

In 'a very remarkable decision' of 16 February 1994,[30] I denied Moreno and Garcia refugee status. Referring to experts in this field, the *Knack*[31] made mention of a

[28] In *De Morgen* on the same day, Willy Laes, former chairperson of AI Belgium, published an open forum entitled 'A State of Law can also Violate Human Rights'. According to MEP Lode Van Outrive (SP), the European resolution was contrary to the Geneva Convention (*DM*, 18 December 1993: 'Concern for Human Rights is not Interference').

[29] *Wordt Vervolgd* (Amnesty International – Nederland) (July–August 1994).

[30] [1994] *Tijdschrift voor Vreemdelingenrecht* 31.

[31] 16 March 1994.

decision formulated in an extremely precise manner which could be found as it is in the manuals. The decision referred to the above-mentioned doctrine, case law and practice, as well as to the background as regards both extradition and asylum procedures. I noted that there are many known cases in which extradition was not granted despite a favourable opinion from a Chamber of Indictment, but not the reverse. I felt, however, that it was not for me to proceed with the recognition of refugee status solely to prevent a deviation from this constant practice. I also noted that an application by a citizen of the European Union, who in principle can stay legally in any Member State of the Union, was not applicable if there was no request for extradition. Finally, I stressed that, in the present case, it was for me decisive that in my opinion it had not been convincingly demonstrated that in Spain, a Member State of the European Union, ETA sympathisers are persecuted based on their ethnic origin or political conviction and not based on the charges against them.[32]

Recognising that in the light of recent information,[33] the existence of a fear of ill-treatment on the part of the persons concerned could not be excluded, I considered that the exceptional public attention given to this case both in the context of bilateral relations between Belgium and Spain and in that of the European Parliament, it was possible to assume that the fear expressed in the present case by the persons concerned was not justified in the present circumstances.

Except for the reports – as always correct – in *El País* (18 and 19 February 1994), these refusal decisions did not give rise to much controversy in the Belgian media. In the *Knack* of 6 March, Misjoe Verleyen devoted a long article to this case with subtitles: 'The Case of Two Suspects Lingers. All jurisdictions are Passing the Buck'.[34] The Permanent Board would wait almost two years.

6.5. Permanent Board Takes its Time (Until 12 January 1996)

On 18 February 1994, Moreno and Garcia appealed to the Permanent Board against my refusal of 16 February 1994. At its hearing on 17 May, the Permanent

[32] In a letter dated 13 December 1993 to Foreign Minister (1992–94) Willy Claes (SP), with a copy to the Prime Minister (in view of the EU summit in Brussels the following weekend), I had warned him that a possible extradition decision – by the Minister of Justice in defiance of the opinion of the Chamber of Indictment – might be annulled or at least suspended by the Conseil d'Etat. I complained that the Belgian government gave the impression of having more confidence in the Spanish authorities than in the Belgian authorities. In the same letter, I asked about Juan Ramón Rojo. According to Misjoe Verleyen (*Knack*, 24January 1996), this request was forwarded to Spain on 3 February 1996. My decision and that of the Permanent Board were taken without a reply from the Spanish authorities.

[33] Referring to the Amnesty International *Annual Report 1993* (384) and the report (E/CN.4/1994/31, §§482–99 and, esp §§485–87) of (since 1998 Sir) Nigel Rodley, UN Special Rapporteur on Torture. He later became a member (2001–16) of the UN Human Rights Committee.

[34] See also *HN* (25 March 1994): 'The Basques Wander: At Easter, the Young Son Comes to Visit'.

Board heard the applicants and their counsel. The debates were reopened on 12 September. However, it was not until 12 January 1996 that the Permanent Board declared the appeals unfounded.

In its refusal decision, the Permanent Board referred to the answer given by the UNHCR Representative on 13 December 1993 to my questions. After referring again, inter alia, to the *US Country Reports on Human Rights Practices for 1994*,[35] the Permanent Board concludes that,

> the prosecution of the appellants was criminal in nature; extradition is sought for acts of common law, namely being part of an armed band, and for the offence of unlawful association;
>
> it may be accepted that the facts of common law in question, if they could be proved in respect of the appellants by the competent Spanish authority, are politically motivated but, having regard to information provided, the normal course of judicial proceedings will not be obstructed by reason of a ground of the Geneva Convention of 28 July 1951, nor will the possible execution of the sentence be influenced for the same reason.[36]

The same day, immediately after the decision of the Permanent Board, Justice Minister Stefaan De Clerck[37] (CVP) ordered the arrest of Luis Moreno (on 12 January 1996). On 23 June 1995, he had succeeded Melchior Wathelet in this position.[38] Raquel Garcia, who had managed to go underground, was arrested on 22 January 1996 at the headquarters of Herri Batasuna in Auderghem (Brussels). A glass door was broken, and their eight-year-old son was held for six hours by members of the Gendarmerie Surveillance and Research Brigade (BSR). Minister Stefaan De Clerck later described this as 'unfortunate'. According to Bert Cornelis, the way in which the Basque couple was deprived of their freedom did not correspond to the usual gentleness of our customs (*HLN*, 26 January 1996).

Questioned in the House of Representatives by Geert Bourgeois (VU) on 18 January 1996, the Minister of Justice conceded that this was not an easy case.[39] On 27 July 1993, at the request of the couple's lawyer, Stefaan De Clerck had intervened as a member of the House of Representatives with Minister Melchior Wathelet to prevent them from being extradited.[40] On 19 January 1996, it became public knowledge that two Basque parliamentarians had informed the office of the Minister of Justice that the Audiencia Nacional had ruled on 29 December 1995

[35] US State Department, Washington DC (1995) 969.

[36] Quoted literally in the House of Representatives (*Ann parl*, SO 1995–96, 1073) (25 January 1996), by the Minister of Justice. On 18 January 1996, the Minister described these decisions as 'particularly well-reasoned' (ibid 1018).

[37] Stefaan De Clerck, Minister of Justice (1995–98 and 2008–11).

[38] On 23 June 1995, Melchior Wathelet became Minister of Defence until 3 September 1995. On 18 September 1995, he became a judge at the Court of Justice of the European Union in Luxembourg. Stefaan De Clerck was strongly criticised for this appointment.

[39] *Ann parl, Chambre*, SO 1995–96, 1018 (18 January 1996). On 17 January 1996, 21 Flemish MPs (belonging to CVP, SP, VLD, Agalev and Volksunie) insisted on non-extradition (*DS*; *GvA*, 18 January).

[40] *Ann parl, Chambre*, SO 1995–96, 1017. P Deltour, *DM* (13 January 1996) with a picture of this letter in *DM* from 16 January; *DS* (17 January); *HN* (23 January).

that Juan Ramón Rojo had been ill-treated on 29 January 1992. It was under physical pressure that he had made the statements incriminating Moreno and Garcia. On 10 January 1996, the investigating judge in Bilbao had ordered the arrest of eight members of the Guardia Civil.[41]

6.6. The Turning Point of Stefaan De Clerck: Extradition Granted (22 January 1996)

On 22 January 1996, the Minister of Justice nevertheless decided to extradite the two Basques to Spain.[42] He said he wanted to wait five days before proceeding with the extradition to give them the chance to challenge his decisions at the Conseil d'Etat. On 23 January, their lawyers requested the suspension and annulment of these decisions and their immediate release. That same day in the Senate, Bert Anciaux (VU) called the Minister of Justice's decision 'scandalous'.[43]

On 25 January, MPs Geert Bourgeois (VU), Patrick Dewael (VLD), Frans Lozie (Agalev), Serge Moureaux (PS)[44] and Francis Van den Eynde (Vl Bl) questioned the Minister of Justice in the House.[45] They all criticised the extradition decision. Geert Bourgeois began his enquiry with these words: 'So, you did it anyway'. According to him, the decision was made by the Minister of Justice (and not by the government), because the Prime Minister had been severely burned in this matter at the time in Spain by his counterpart Felipe González.[46] Again, the Minister of Justice admitted that he was experiencing emotional difficulties with this file. Finally, he had to assume his political responsibility based on the dossier:[47]

> Although I know very well that many deeply human aspects must be taken into account and that these people do not pose any danger to the community here, I have nonetheless cited our international obligations and our commitment to our European partners.[48]

[41] See the Opinion of Didier Rouget (Paris V): 'Rule of Law and State Reasons' (*LLB*, 6 February 1996) and *Le Monde* (16 February): 'Franco is not quite Dead'.

[42] All the Belgian newspapers of 23 and 24 January 1996 spoke about it, with headlines such as: 'Angry Reactions everywhere' (*DM*); 'A Highly Discussed Extradition' and 'More than three Years of Anxious Waiting' and 'It's the Suspense' *(LLB)*; 'De Clerck Decides ... almost. But not Really ... and not Immediately' (*LS*).

[43] *Ann parl*, Senate, SO 1995–96 (23 January 1996).

[44] It was mainly the criticism of a member of the majority calling for the Minister's resignation that weighed 'De Clerck in Tight Locks' *DS*; *HV*; *HLN*; *GvA* (26 January 1996).

[45] *Ann parl*, *Chambre*, 1066–78 (25 January 1996).

[46] ibid 1067. Patrick Dewael said: 'The Moreno-Garcia case is politically charged to the point that the government and more particularly the Prime Minister [Jean-Luc] Dehaene prefers not to be confronted with it' (ibid 1068).

[47] ibid 1072. *DS*; *HN* (19 January 1996); *DM*; *LS* (20 January 1996).

[48] *Ann parl*, *Chambre* (n 45) 1075.

On 25 January, Yves Desmet wrote in a point of view in *De Morgen*, under the title 'Masterly', that Stefaan De Clerck would receive a place of honour in the political history of this small country. He launched a political sophistry with a logic that ends with a blood-chilling beauty. In the same newspaper, under the title 'Coward', Geert Van Istendael wrote that he had seen on television a man who knew he was doing something he should be ashamed of but could not say. According to him, Stefaan De Clerck was acting under the pressure of Jean-Luc Dehaene, who could not help but bend the rules of law: 'For him, it is a nervous tic'.

On 26 January, 5,000 Basques marched through the streets of Bilbao protesting against the possible extradition of the Moreno–Garcia couple. In *Het Nieuwsblad* on 27 January, Pol Van Den Driessche wrote that the reversal of Minister Stefaan De Clerck, who at the same time betrayed something schizophrenic, took place on the instruction of Jean-Luc Dehaene not to spoil – by upsetting the Spanish authorities – his still underlying European ambitions. Under the title 'Remembering the Duke of Alba', he continued:

> The danger is relatively small that the King of Spain, Juan Carlos, will send a descendant of Duke Fernando Alvarez of Toledo – known as the terrible Duke of Alba – to lead troops to the Southern Netherlands to come and take Moreno and Garcia with the halberd stock's strike force.

After the Council of Ministers on 26 January, Prime Minister Jean-Luc Dehaene declared: 'De Clerck has assumed his responsibilities. I'm used to covering people who take responsibility'. He says he was outraged by the Opposition's comments as if the decision to extradite had anything to do with his European ambitions, 'if ever he had such ambitions'.[49]

6.7. 'The Conseil d'Etat Disavows the Minister' (1 and 5 February 1996)

On 29 January 1996, at a hearing after which Luis Moreno could briefly hug his mother, who had come from Spain, the first auditor of the Conseil d'Etat recommended that the extradition order be suspended.[50] He considered that the facts charged did not fall under the European Convention on Terrorism. On 1 February, with extreme urgency, the President of the Conseil d'Etat, Gustaaf Baeteman, ordered the suspension of the extradition decision. He considered that

[49] *DM*; *HLN*; *LLB* (27 January 1996). The newspapers of that day wrote that the Spanish Minister of Justice would have given guarantees for a new procedure and that the couple's lawyers had filed a petition with the European Court of Human Rights.

[50] *HN*: 'We have New Hope'; *El País* (30 January 1996). According to Yves Desmet in a point of view in *De Morgen*: 'Stefaan De Clerck had demonstrated a mental flexibility that even a simple weathervane could not imitate'.

'the immediate implementation of the contested decision would have irreversible consequences and would deprive of any effect a judgment of the Conseil d'Etat which would annul the contested decision'.[51]

'It was expected, but it is nonetheless worth mentioning':[52] four days later (5 February), the Conseil d'Etat confirmed the ordered suspensions.[53] The Conseil considered that no data had been put forward which would lead to another judgment with regard to the considerations[54] of the suspension judgments taken with extreme urgency.[55] The Conseil stressed that the serious and hardly repairable damage which was taken into account in the suspension judgment did not imply any word of criticism towards Spanish justice.[56] The Minister of Justice immediately released the Basque couple.

In a comment under the title 'A Blamed Minister', Luc Neuckermans wrote that the public humiliation of the young minister (aged 45) by the Conseil d'Etat had created a big weakness in his authority. Even after a few centuries, Flanders had not forgotten history. The couple enjoyed the sympathy of certain sections of the population as fighters for an ideal in which the Flemish also recognised themselves: 'The brutality of the Spanish occupiers and oppressors was instilled in us from an early age by the history books and comics'. Under the title 'The Spanish Fury', Yves Desmet[57] wrote that the evidence with which Spain supposes that its logic must be followed, suggests that in Madrid it is still considered that this small country is only a distant Spanish province. In *De Morgen* also, Edi Clijsters[58]

[51] CdE, Nos 57.973 and 57.974 (1 February 1996).

[52] Dirk Achten, *DS* (6 February 1996): 'This proves that there is still room for independent and respectable jurisprudence'.

[53] *LS* (6 February 1996).

[54] These were the following considerations: (a) the definition of the facts listed in the international arrest warrant and those on which the extradition order is based – the facts of Art 1, (e) and (f), of the Convention on Terrorism – did not correspond; and (b) the attacked order did not set out the reasons why the facts should not be qualified as a political offence. According to Vermeulen and Vander Beken (n 4) 225 and F Verbruggen, 'Ook zonder Madrid en Dublin blijft de uitlevering van Moreno en Garcia mogelijk, als Spanje een degelijk dossier heft' [1997] *Panopticon* 165, there was confusion between the facts and the qualification given therein. See also H Das and M Pertegás Sender, 'Moreno and Garcia: Law and Diplomacy' (May 1996) *Vlaams Jurist Vandaag* 4.

[55] CdE, Nos 58.012 and 58.013 (5 February 1996).

[56] In a comment, Verbruggen (n 54) 168 later wrote that, since the Conseil d'Etat had only noted that the Minister had not sufficiently explained why it was not a political offence, the extradition of Moreno and Garcia remained possible, 'if Spain has a good dossier'. He felt that, if Spain had only an inadmissible witness statement, it had no support to stand by and that, with its request for extradition, it had made a serious political mistake.

[57] *HN* (6 February 1996).

[58] Edi Clijsters (ibid) wrote that, according to the newspaper *El Mundo*, sympathy in Flanders for Basque nationalism also led to considerable duplicity towards ETA. In short: 'We are *all* terrorists. If it does not bring about a new 80-year war'. In *Le Soir* (12 February 1996), Leo Marynissen, editor-in-chief of *Het Volk* wrote: 'From the not-so-distant past, we know what it means to be considered second-class citizens in one's own country. Flanders fought peacefully for its autonomy, without using the weapon of attacks and murders. Unlike ETA, Flanders hardly uses barbaric methods to achieve these ends. Over the years, she has learned that tenacity and patience enable great things'.

asked himself the question: 'Will a New Spanish Armada soon Appear in Front of our Shores?'[59]

Spain was shocked by these historical references to Spanish rule in the sixteenth century: 'What does the Duke of Alba have to do with all this?'[60] According to *El País* of 9 February 1996,[61] the conflict with Spain recalled the old days of the '*Tercios de Flandes*'[62] in a country where children who do not want to sleep are still told that the Duke of Alba will come and pick them up. The Spanish government reacted with unusual anger:[63] the Spanish Ambassador was recalled to Madrid and the Belgian Ambassador was summoned to the Ministry in Madrid.[64] He was told that judicial cooperation between the two countries was suspended.[65]

In the Belgian Parliament, Prime Minister Jean-Luc Dehaene was questioned, on 8 February 1996, by the same deputies as on 25 January, with Didier Reynders (PRL-FDF) in addition, but excluding Serge Moureaux (PS). The Prime Minister fired a gun through the arc of the Spanish Armada:

> In no case will the Belgian Government admit that the functioning of the Belgian Justice is contested by Spain. If, because of a decision of the Conseil d'Etat, the application of judicial cooperation is denounced and endangered, we will react immediately and let it be known that this is unacceptable to us.

On 24 May 1996, the Minister of Justice promised the Spanish Secretary of State for Security that the freedom of movement of the Moreno–Garcia couple would be restricted so that they could not flee Belgium.[66]

6.8. Minister Backs Down: Extradition Withdrawn (2 October 1996)

On 27 September 1996 in Dublin, the Ministers of Justice of the European Union signed the Convention on Extradition between Member States of the European Union. This Convention allows extradition for any offence that provides for a

[59] *DM* (7 February 1996).

[60] *LLB* (15 February 1996).

[61] Under the title 'Con los vascos y contra Castilla', W Oppenheimer referred to the 'fantasma del Duque de Alba'.

[62] The army in Flanders of King Philip II of Spain.

[63] *El País* (6 February 1996) referred to '*El error belga*': 'For the highest Administrative Tribunal, cooperating with ETA and providing cover and transport to one of its murderous commandos are not offences provided for in the European Convention on Terrorism' (*DS*, 7 February). *HN*: 'Spain Reacts Furiously'; *LS*: 'Spain very Critical' and 'Madrid between Anger and Misunderstanding'; *GvA*: 'Angry Madrid' and 'Tense Relationship with Spain'.

[64] *IHT* (7 February 1996): 'Spain Recalls Belgian Envoy After Basque Extradition Move'.

[65] *El País* (6 February): '*Espana suspende la cooperación judicial con Bélgica*'. Reaction of *HLN*: 'Our Bandits are Safe in Spain'; *LLB*, 'It's an Escalation', 'Spain is Raising its Voice'; *DM* (10 February) 'Spain Suspends the Schengen Agreement with Belgium'; see *El País* (10, 13, 17 and 18 February).

[66] *Ann parl, Chambre*, SO 1995–96, 1177.

sentence of at least one year without requiring double criminality, without exception for political offences and applicable to its own nationals.[67] Minister of Justice Stefaan De Clerck had previously travelled to Madrid to meet his Spanish colleague Margarita Mariscal de Gante. They had agreed to bring this Convention into force between themselves on an expedited basis. In Dublin, the Spanish Minister of Justice declared her willingness to submit a new application for Moreno and Garcia. She said, however, that she would await the decision of the Belgian Conseil d'Etat. Paul Bekaert did not worry about the fate of his clients:

> The procedure before the Conseil d'Etat can only consider the previous legal situation. With a new extradition procedure, we can expect a new judicial carousel. Belgium and Spain especially want to avoid repetitions of the *Moreno–Garcia* affair in the future.[68]

On 2 October 1996, Minister of Justice Stefaan De Clerck decided to withdraw the ministerial decree of 22 January 1996 granting the extradition of the applicants to Spain: 'Having regard to the signing of the Convention on Extradition between Member States of the European Union, done at Dublin on 27 September 1996; Having regard to all the modified circumstances'.

In an oral question from Senator Bert Anciaux, the Minister of Justice replied on 24 October 1996, that the Extradition Convention of 27 September 1996 would be applicable only after ratification and only on subsequent applications.[69] As regards the *Moreno–Garcia* case, according to the Minister, there were no commitments made to Spain. On 22 May 1997, the Conseil d'Etat[70] rejected the requests of Moreno and Garcia, considering that by this ministerial withdrawal the action for annulment was moot. It would still take more than six years before Moreno and Garcia attracted attention again. Before that, there will still be two Basque exiles, one in Venezuela and the other in Mexico, who will come to seek asylum in Belgium.

[67] *LS* (28 September 1996): 'Europe is Less and Less a Land of Asylum'. Verbruggen (n 54) 163 was particularly critical of this Convention: 'a blind trust in foreign institutions testifies to a reckless naivety'.

[68] *DM* (27 September 1996): 'The Fate of the Basques is not in Danger by the Agreement'.

[69] *Ann parl*, Senate (24 October 1996).

[70] CdE, Nos 66.363 and 66.364 (22 May 1997).

7

No Longer 'Mop under an Open Tap' (1993–94)

Five days after the 'Revue' of 8 May 1993, I sounded the alarm loudly. The asylum procedure was overwhelmed. Twenty days later, on 28 May 1993, the Dehaene I Government (CVP/PSC; SP/PS) decided, under the leadership of Minister Louis Tobback, to take strong measures. From October 1993 there were signs of progress. In Limburg, the Sikh Indians who came to pick fruit there, posed a particular problem. From January 1994, the number of asylum applications decreased considerably. I was a candidate in the European elections of 12 June 1994. On 10 October 1994, Johan Vande Lanotte (SP) succeeded Louis Tobback (until 23 April 1998) as Minister of the Interior.

7.1. A Break in the Dyke and Quicksand (13 May 1993)

At the press conference on 13 May 1993, the atmosphere was not as good as it had been at the Revue five days earlier. In presenting my *Fifth Annual Report* (1992), I was not avoiding big words. According to *De Morgen* of 14 May, I did not miss superlatives and I was not afraid of pictorial language. I was talking about a breaking of dykes, quicksand, skidding, snowballs, alarm bells and the biggest asylum crisis.[1] I had 120 staff members, including 40 militiamen and barely 12 statutory civil servants. I stated that the number of staff had to be tripled (*GvA*, *LDH*).

I was aware that there was criticism: 'Why is this Bossuyt getting nervous?' Reference was made to the number of asylum applications in Germany: they had grown from 57,400 in 1987 to 443,000 in 1992. I took as a reference the number of asylum applications in France: from 60,000 in 1989, it had fallen by half

[1] The headlines in the newspapers were eloquent: 'Bossuyt Warns against a Breakup of a Dyke', 'Largest Asylum Crisis in Belgian History', 'Bossuyt: "Concerned but not Desperate"' (*DM*); 'The Stack of Asylum Applications is Huge. A Pessimistic Commissioner General' (*DS*);' Alert Call for more Resources and Staff: Snowball of Asylum Seekers' (*HLN*); 'Warning Cry: This is the Biggest Asylum Crisis Belgium has ever Known' (*GvA*); 'The Snowball Effect must be Removed from the Asylum Procedure' (*HBvL*);' We are Sinking Deeper into the Quicksand' (*HV*); 'Asylum Procedure "Slipping". Refugees: 30.000 Late Files' (*LS*); 'Alarm Signal Fired' (*Vl'A*).

(27,486 in 1992).[2] Belgium was about to receive more asylum applications than France, which has a surface area 20 times larger (*DM*, *GvA*). I complained that the measures taken were always too late and never sufficient (*Vl'A*). The under-resourcing of my services was 'an ancient evil that prevented me from sleeping already five years earlier, when I presented my *First Annual Report*' (*DS*):

> All the warning cries expressed earlier are nothing compared to the present. We are desperately sucked into the quicksand. It is not the rise in asylum applications that is causing them to slip. It's the other way around. It is because the processing of cases fails, that the number of applications increases. This snowball effect must be stopped (DM, DS, LDH). The competent Minister, Louis Tobback, is aware of the problems. I have an excellent cooperation with him (*DM*, *HV*, *HLN*).

On 19 May 1993, the Minister informed me that I would receive enough staff to handle a normal flow of refugees and to absorb the backlog accumulated with contractors:

> I also want a firm commitment from Bossuyt on the work that will be done. If he is talking about four cases per day per jurist, I demand that this be done. He must not come and complain that there will only be two (*HLN*, 19 May 1993).

On 27 May 1993, *Humo* published a long interview with Jaak Smeets in which I explained the reasons why Belgium had started to lose control of the asylum procedure since April 1992:

> Thanks to the new procedure which entered into force on 1 October 1991, the number of asylum applications fell by 25 per cent in the week and by 45 per cent in the three months. The refugee applicants understood this: 'It's no longer like before here'.
>
> From April to May 1992, two new phenomena emerged: the situation deteriorated in Zaire and the Former Yugoslavia; the number of appeals against the decisions of the Aliens Office increased from 29 per cent to 71 per cent. The number of urgent appeals filed with me rose from 200 to 1,200 per month. I was able to get 750 reviews a month. The Aliens Office failed to keep up with this pace in its notifications of decisions based on these opinions.
>
> The number of asylum applications rose from 1,125 per month to 2,400. The snowball effect was triggered. It was like mopping under a tap that was left open. The great tragedy was that Minister Louis Tobback did not become competent until 15 July 1992, thus after the procedure began to slip. The famous breakage of the dyke had begun.

I observed that 'refugee flows' were not a natural phenomenon. The differences between the Netherlands and Belgium demonstrated this. It is as if these two countries were separated from each other by an ocean:

> Two years ago, there were 1,821 Sri Lankans in the Netherlands and 91 in our country. The Netherlands had 1,710 Somalis, we had 80. The Netherlands had 816 Ethiopians,

[2] In 1993, the number of asylum applications in France dropped by 3.6% to 26.507 (*Le Monde*, 26 January 1994).

> we had 70. While we had the world record of Ghanaians, and we received proportionally many more Indians, Pakistanis and Nigerians. This shows that the Netherlands has some channels that we don't have and vice versa.

I also pointed out the 'absurd situation' offering foreigners two ways to come to Belgium:

> The legal way: you ask for a visa; you will wait several months; you will not have the assistance of a lawyer; you will not be able to appeal; you will not have a reasoned decision and you will not be assisted in the meantime by a CPAS.
>
> And there is the illegal way: you go to Belgium; you go to the Petit-Château, and you declare yourself a refugee. You will be confronted with someone who will say: 'I'm giving you a piece of paper. Please come back in a few months because now I don't have time to interview you'. In the meantime, you will be supported by a CPAS, you will receive the assistance of a lawyer, you will receive a reasoned decision, and, if you do not like it, you can appeal once or twice.

7.2. My Alarm is Heard (28 May 1993)

This time my alarm was heard. On 28 May 1993, the Council of Ministers granted recruitment authorisation to the Aliens Office for 100 contractual civil servants, of which 23 were university trained.[3] For the Commission General, there were 186 contractual civil servants, of which 138 were university trained. To ensure the training of all these new employees, I insisted that recruitment be spread over three streams. A royal decree of 25 June 1993 provided for recruitment on 1 July 1993, 1 October 1993 and 1 January 1994. On 2 July 1993, the training of the first group of newly recruited jurists began. Recruitment results for the first two streams were particularly successful. The success was such that, at my request, the third-tier staff were not recruited. I had predicted that this would not be necessary, but the Minister did not dare believe me.

On 2 July 1993 at the Château of Laeken, King Baudouin received in audience Stéphane Schewebach, the Administrator General of Public Security,[4] preceded immediately by me. This was the third time that King Baudouin had received me in audience (*cf* above p 41). During his visit to the Payoke organisation in Antwerp on 28 October 1992, the King made a commitment to the victims of trafficking in women. This time he made it clear that he wanted to influence asylum policy. With his death in Motril (Spain), less than a month later, on 31 July 1993, this initiative also died.

[3] 'Tobback Requests 200 Additional Officials for Asylum Policy' (*HBvL*, 27 May 1993); 'New Measures' (*Vl'A*); 'More Staff' (*HLN*); 'Additional Money and Civil Servants' (*GvA*); 'Three Hundred more Civil Servants' (*DS*); 'Bossuyt Receives Additional Staff' (*DM*, 29 May 1993).

[4] The Administrator General of Public Security was responsible for both the Aliens Office and State Security.

In a letter to the Minister of the Interior, on 23 July 1993 I returned to the policy of removals (*cf* below chapter eighteen, p 234–241):

> Any improvisation must be avoided in terms of policy of removal. The actual removal of one applicant rather than another may not depend on incidental factors. A carefully considered policy of removals may not, once defined, be challenged by any media interest. It must be accompanied by a policy of regularisation. Here too, it is appropriate to stick to the principles defined in advance in an objective manner; without this, these principles will be disaggregated in the very near future. As soon as it becomes known that politics give way to media interest, petitions or hunger strikes, this type of action is encouraged to such an extent that their multiplication makes all politics impossible. To maintain the required flexibility and avoid new legal procedures, a regularisation policy must be developed in the form of an administrative practice or prescriptions rather than in the legislative form.[5]

On 30 September 1993, the Minister of the Interior explained several measures already taken while also announcing additional measures. The amendment of the Aliens Law by the Law of 6 May 1993 and the strengthening of staff were of great importance. He also announced the creation of a waiting list in which all asylum seekers would be registered. On 5 October, an additional closed centre with a capacity of 120 people was opened in Walem. Jean-Claude Matgen (*LLB*, 1 October 1993) made a distinction between 'useful and dangerous measures'. He counted Walem among the dangerous measures. The Printrak facility to discover double or multiple applications had an immediate result: in the first six days, out of 427 asylum seekers, it had uncovered 54 (11 per cent).[6]

On 14 October 1993, I stated that the measures taken were 'neither superfluous nor excessive but necessary'.[7] I also drew attention to a 'cascading effect' that caused backlogs to move from one authority to another. For the first time in a long time, I had hope. There were 'signs of progress': the number of asylum applications had dropped from 3,076 in August to 2,507 in September. However, I was not completely satisfied: I regretted that there was a delay in some recruitments since I could not expand my premises in the Shell building at rue Ravenstein 60. I had to move to the North Gate on 1 January 1994. I was very critical of the CPAS. I found it

> very disturbing that mayors and deputy-mayors openly decided not to respect the law. They continued to assist people who had been refused asylum and who were therefore illegally in the territory. They refused to assist new asylum seekers who were still in the process and were legally staying in the country.

[5] *Sixth Annual Report* (1993) §138.

[6] 'Printrak Fights Fraud: A Fingerprint Comparison Must Uncover Asylum Fraud' (*HLN*, 1 October 1993). On a written question from MP Claude Eerdekens (PS) of 27 October 1993, the Minister of the Interior reported that identity fraud was found mainly among Indians (23.5%), Romanians (18%), Zairians (14%), Ghanaians (14%) and Nigerians (11%).

[7] *LLB* (15 October 1993): 'We have lost control of asylum applications. Yet the Commissioner General had predicted it'.

7.3. Sikhs: Fruit Pickers in South Limburg (1993–94)

In July 1992, the Minister of Employment and Labour (1992–99), Miet Smet, had, at the insistence of the city of Saint-Trond, facilitated the employment of asylum seekers in the collection of fruit. I cautioned the Minister that this could be a magnet for asylum seekers with no fear of persecution. The Minister refuted this in a letter dated 9 September 1992. On 14 April 1993, the Minister of the Interior informed his colleague that he had noted with regret that her denial was contradicted by the facts. Meanwhile, the number of Sikh asylum applicants had risen from an average of 73 per month in 1991/1992 to an average of 400 per month from March to August 1993. The observation made on 23 June 1993 by the Belgian Ambassador in New Delhi, Cristina Funes-Noppen,[8] was particularly relevant: 'There are 900 million inhabitants in India!'

I stated that 'there was an indisputable link between employment opportunities for fruit pickers from India and the rise of asylum seekers from India' (*DM*, 15 October 1993). Yet only 6 per cent were declared admissible and less than 0.5 per cent accepted as refugees. Now the city of Saint-Trond felt that there were too many Sikh asylum seekers in its territory. According to *Het Belang van Limburg* of 15 October 1993, there were 1,700 refugee applicants in South Limburg, including 1,400 in Saint-Trond. At the Halmaal Red Cross, a hundred mattresses had disappeared; they were for sale at 3,000 BF (€75) per piece. Out of 20 homes inspected by the fire department, only five were in good condition. The mayor (1977–94) of Saint-Trond, Jef Cleeren (CVP), no longer registered foreigners, unlike seven other municipalities in South Limburg. It was a complete about-face: in March 1992, he had demonstrated against raids on foreign workers.

On 10 November 1993, MP Jan Peeters (SP) asked an oral question on the massive violation by employers of the agreed protocol for the fruit-picking sector. The Minister of Employment and Labour was also outraged by these abuses. As of 1 October, refugee applicants could only obtain a work permit when their application was declared admissible.[9] When asked why there was a concentration of Sikhs in the Saint-Trond area, I replied on 4 March 1994:

> Sikhs are excellent at picking fruit, it seems. They are satisfied with a miserable salary, poor housing conditions, etc. It is by declaring themselves refugees that they come to do this work. The asylum procedure is not designed to organise the labour market in general, nor the fruit-picking market in Limburg in particular.

[8] In 1984, she had successfully lobbied in Geneva for my re-election to the UN Sub-Commission on the Prevention of Discrimination and the Protection of Minorities (C Funes-Noppen, *Chroniques impertinentes* (Brussels, 180 editions, 2021) 18.

[9] *Ann parl, Chambre*, SO 1993–94 (10 November 1993); ibid Senate (2 December 1993). See also the circular of 26 April 1994 concerning provisional employment permits for refugee applicants (asylum seekers) (*MB*, 30 April 1994).

According to the Secretary of the Belgian Fruit Growers' Organization: 'Sikhs could be given a place to sleep over a fridge. With Spaniards, it would not work' (*DM*, 10 August 1994).

In *De Standaard* of 2 April 1994, Jeroen Wils mentioned a consultation with the Indian community which had taken place in Antwerp between the governor of the province of Antwerp and Dirk De Winter, the excellent Ambassador for immigration policy. There was also a meeting in Brussels between the Minister of the Interior and the Indian Ambassador. I felt that the fruit growers were sending the wrong signal by repeating that they wanted to put asylum seekers to work. I pointed out that in 1993 there were 3,111 Indian asylum applications in Belgium and 78 in the Netherlands. As if there were a Berlin Wall between the Netherlands and Belgium.

On 1 June 1994, the Minister of the Interior made a rather cynical statement:

> Sikhs are no longer coming. There is no more persecution or torture. There is no more poverty. Meanwhile, we went to India to explain that there is no longer work in Belgium for asylum seekers and that their applications are currently processed in half a year (*DM*, 2 June 1994).

On Sikhs in Saint-Trond, I stated in *Dag Allemaal* of 14 June 1994:

> The Mayor of Saint-Trond came to protest a few years ago with the fruit growers to welcome more Indians. At one point, there were more Indians than inhabitants in Saint-Trond. These are human beings, not discards. We can't use them, squeeze them a little and then throw them in the trash! I cannot continue to recruit jurists to listen to the fake stories of people who are not even persecuted, but who come to pick fruit to help farmers in distress. I'm not prepared to pay for it. It's not my job to offer cheap workers. The Indians coming here have nothing to do with the situation in India. This is the consequence of the situation in Limburg where they can earn a little money and the lax way in which we send back illegals. Or more correctly, 'don't send them back'.

The number of Indian asylum seekers collapsed completely (from 400 per month in 1993 to 7 in July 1994). I said: 'It seems they understood' (*GvA*, 6 September 1994). In nine years of activity, I counted 8,460 Indian asylum seekers. Thirty-seven Indians were recognised as refugees (0.43 per cent), five of them by the Permanent Board. Think of the number of jurists we had to hire to process all these Indian applications, assisted by lawyers and interpreters ….

7.4. Candidate in the European Elections (of 12 June 1994)

On 28 December 1993, Senator Herman Suykerbuyk (CVP) published an open letter in which he accused me of an 'intellectual conflict of interest' (*DS*, 11 January 1994). For him, it was unacceptable for me to take fourth place on the VLD-list in the European elections of 12 June 1994. On 12 January 1994, *De Standaard* wrote: 'Bossuyt has an ethical problem'. Interior Minister Louis Tobback, however, reacted with a smile:

> I always have difficulties when someone is on another list. The Commissioner General has the right to stand for election. His job is temporary. No one can blame him if he explores the possibilities of another job. He will take steps to ensure that there is no ethical problem.

Questioned in the House of Representatives on the same day by MP John Taylor (CVP), the Minister replied:

> I am particularly satisfied with the way the Commissioner General works and the work of the Commission General. He is a loyal partner. In case of a new law, I will organise the function of Commissioner General differently. Now even his status and pension are not settled. At the head of such an institution, there would then be a Commissioner General appointed for life. I personally think he picked the wrong party, but he has the right to do that anyway.[10]

In a letter to Senator Herman Suykerbuyk on the same day, VLD-Chairperson (1992–95) Guy Verhofstadt wrote:

> We cannot at the same time impose the ethics of independent judges on someone and deny them the corresponding status. I have the utmost confidence in Marc Bossuyt's sense of responsibility. I have no doubt that the management, or the operation and decisions of the Commission General will not be influenced by partisan political considerations (*DS*, 29 January 1994).

On 14 March 1994, the Minister of the Interior sent me a kind note with the following words: 'As I have already told you: "You would waste your time in Europe". But I will do what is necessary to prevent this misfortune'. He kept his word. He was himself elected, even from last place on the SP-list.

On 31 March 1994, in response to a question from Senator Paul Pataer (PS), Minister Louis Tobback replied:

> The law does not impose restrictions on the political commitment of the Commissioner General. He has an independent status, and he receives no orders from the government. As a public servant, he has the right to speak, and he has no duty of silence. I am not shocked by the fact that he is going to proclaim his opinions somewhere. I have the impression that Mr Pataer would react differently if the Commissioner General had expressed views that he liked. The Commissioner General made a fundamental mistake by joining the party of Mr Herman De Croo,[11] but everyone has his weaknesses.

[10] *Ann parl, Chambre*, SO 1993–94 (12 January 1994).

[11] Reaction of the satirical weekly *Père Ubu* of 28 April 1994: 'The VLD, the party of Mr De Croo. This will improve relations between Herman [De Croo] and Guy [Verhofstadt]'.

The *Pan* of 30 March 1994 dedicated, under the title 'The Cynicism of Marc Bossuyt', a long article to my candidacy:

> This ambitious professor from the University of Antwerp owes his fame to the fact that after having been entrusted with several missions in the defence of human rights, the government then suddenly bombarded him Commissioner General.

This appointment was compared to that of Fons Verplaetse as Governor (1989–99) of the National Bank.

On 20 April 1994, the satirical newspaper published my reaction:

> In my capacity as Professor of International Law at the University of Antwerp and Belgian Representative to the UN Commission on Human Rights, I did not feel my appointment as Commissioner General as a 'bombardment' but rather as an opportunity to render a perilous service to my country in circumstances that were likely to prove difficult. I do not think I was wrong, either about the perilous nature of this mission or about the difficulty of the circumstances. And by the way, the position of Commissioner General has very little in common with that of Governor of the National Bank.
>
> I am still not a 'former expert on human rights', but in 1992, I found my seat back, for a four-year term, as a member of the UN Sub-Commission on the Prevention of Discrimination and the Protection of Minorities.[12]
>
> The Commissioner General can only reform the negative decisions of the Aliens Office in a way favourable to asylum seekers. Even if he wanted to, he could not therefore 'take advantage of this precedence over the Aliens Office to conduct a very harsh policy towards refugee applicants'. Those who are refused on the merits, may always lodge an appeal with the Permanent Board.
>
> [Referring to my previous publications] I said that there was no 'mental reconversion' or 'new discourse'. The discourse does not and will not vary. However, I'm aware that, having agreed to run for office, some people will have different perceptions of my speech. It is not to be confused.

In response to this right of reply, *Pan* wrote that it was unhealthy for a senior state official to appear on an electoral list. It was undemocratic for me to abuse my official duties for propaganda purposes. *Pan* seemed unaware that, like the Deputy Commissioners, I was not an 'agent of the State'. Our status wasn't even settled. There was incompatibility with a political mandate but running for office – a fundamental political right – was not.

[12] After six years (1986–91) on the Commission on Human Rights as head of the Belgian delegation. The eight years (1992–99) at the Sub-Commission would be followed by four years (2000–03) as a member of the UN Committee on the Elimination of Racial Discrimination (CERD). Then again three years (2004–06) as a member of the Sub-Commission, finishing there as Chairperson of its last session (2006). The Sub-Commission was replaced in 2008 by an Advisory Committee of the Human Rights Council. This Council replaced the Commission in 2006. After my presidency of the Constitutional Court (2007–14), I became a member (2014–19) and then Vice-Chairperson (2020–21) of CERD.

At the beginning of June 1994, *Fuga*, a bimonthly published by the Centre of Concertation for the integration of refugees, published an interview with five candidates in the European elections,[13] including myself:

> When the fight against illegal immigrants is successful, we will see that certain immigration needs must be met. Keeping illegals as such is forbidden. No grey area, but it's black or white. Any illegal person arrested must be regularised or repatriated.
>
> It is difficult to compare the figures for recognition rates between different countries. Just because there are applications from the same nations does not mean they are from the same population groups. Among the Turks, we must deal with a wide variety of origins: Armenian, Christian, communist, economic. Each country does not receive the same categories in the same proportion.
>
> If the Afghans who are now welcomed in Pakistan arrived at a Red Cross centre in Belgium, it would cost 120 billion BF (€3 billion) per month. It doesn't cost as much in Pakistan.
>
> If the process to determine which country will have to process an application takes longer than the process to determine whether the person concerned is a refugee, it would be better to choose the last alternative. I would very much like Dublin and Schengen to come into force, so that I can demonstrate how these conventions do not work.
>
> The authorities are not doing enough to educate the population, explaining the reality as it is on the ground. We are afraid of a whole series of organisations and lobby groups monopolising information intended for the public. It is desirable to have a greater input from organisations in the definition of policy and a greater participation of the authorities in the debate. A dialogue is necessary.

In the weeks leading up to the European elections, the opinion polls gave a perspective of a fourth and even a fifth seat for the VLD. On election day, 12 June 1994, the VLD obtained only 18.4 per cent or 10 per cent less than expected by the polls. The VLD won only three seats: Annemie Neyts, Willy De Clercq and Mimi Kestelijn-Sierens. The latter had the advantage of being a CVP defector. Some thought the pollsters were wrong. Others believed that the way in which the VLD campaigned had cost it a lot of credibility in a few weeks. The VLD campaign, entrusted to Wim Schamp, would remain in history as that of the '13 degrees' (the difference between the left eye and the right eye): the faces of all candidates had to be presented at 13 per cent oblique. According to Wim Schamp, Guy Verhofstadt received nothing but praise for this at the presentation of the campaign from both the board members and the candidates: 'Only Marc Bossuyt, who figured on the list in a place that would be a battleground, felt that we were not doing justice to his face by putting it oblique'.[14] In *Het Laatste Nieuws* of 2 June 1995, political editor Luc Van der Kelen wrote that all those who followed Guy Verhofstadt blindly were doubly guilty.

The whole campaign was characterised by an excess of appearances, rhetoric and lightness and a lack of content, seriousness and solidity. For example, it was

[13] The other candidates were Anne Van Lancker (SP), Jan Van Erps (CVP), Magda Aelvoet (Agalev) and Willy Kuijpers (VU).

[14] W Schamp, *10 jaar Politieke Campagnes: een huurling vertelt* (Antwerp, Hadewijch, 1996) 254.

claimed that the number of asylum seekers continued to rise. In fact, this number fell from 3,058 in June 1993 to 1,010 in May 1994. It was therefore not surprising that the fruits of this decline benefited Minister Louis Tobback. As I said after the municipal elections of 9 October 1994: 'It didn't hurt him' (*DM*, 11 October 1994).

7.5. 'A Small Fracture in the Tourmalet' (3 February 1994)

On 11 January 1994, the Minister of the Interior was able to announce a considerable drop in the number of asylum applications. This number had fallen from 3,058 in June 1993 to about 1,400 in November and December 1993. The Minister found this number still too high. The number of applications under another identity dropped from 13.6 per cent in the third week of September, when Printrak started, to 3.9 per cent in the last week of December 1993.

Not without pride, the Minister of the Interior said in the Senate on 3 February 1994: 'For the first time, there is a small fracture in Mr Bossuyt's Tourmalet'.[15] With that plastic expression, he indicated that I was winning my fight against the backlog of asylum applications. For the first time since I took office as Commissioner General, there were more decisions than I had received in appeal. The overall backlog of 36,000 asylum applications pending on 1 September 1993 had fallen on 1 February 1994 to 33,000.

The Law of 6 May 1993 entered into force on 1 June 1993. From that date on, the Aliens Office was no longer obliged to take new decisions after my opinions on urgent appeals. The introduction of such a remedy automatically suspended the enforceability of the order to leave the territory. When the decision of inadmissibility was confirmed, the order to leave the territory became enforceable again once I had notified my confirmatory decision. This led to a considerable acceleration in the procedure. The new law also provided that, once I had declared my decision 'enforceable notwithstanding any remedy', suspension by the Conseil d'Etat was no longer possible.

On 3 March 1994, King Albert II received me in audience at the royal palace in Brussels. Almost 20 years later, on 21 July 2013, I co-signed, as President of the Constitutional Court, his act of abdication.

In *De Standaard* magazine of 4 March 1994, Gilbert Roox described the road to be taken to an interview with me as follows:

> It is not easy to find the Commission General in the middle of the scaffolding behind the Brussels North Station. There's a line outside the Commissioner General's office. He works in a glass aquarium without curtains. He is proud that, despite the move, his department has continued to operate without interruption.

[15] On questioning by Maurice Didden (CVP), with interventions by Nelly Maes (VU), Paul Pataer (SP), Germain Dufour (Ecolo), Jef Ulburghs (Agalev) and Ludo Dierickx (Agalev), *Ann parl*, Senate (3 February 1994) 1070.

In this interview, I said:

> In the next two years, we will refuse more asylum seekers than in the past six years. With all the consequences it will bring. What we do not need is a proliferation of action committees and civil society initiatives such as those we have seen emerge recently. This could eventually make any policy of removal impossible. If a consistent policy of removal is not pursued, 'we mop under an open tap'. The illegals will continue to flow in and our whole system will be on a downward slope. A policy of removal can only be implemented if at the same time many rejected asylum seekers are regularised. But first, the pressure must be released into the pressure cooker. And unfortunately, we're not there yet.

After referring to my letters of 8 February and 23 July 1993 to the Minister of the Interior on the policy of expulsion and regularisation, I added:

> What is a reasonable time? Does it include recourse to the Conseil d'Etat? I don't think so. An applicant of a nationality with a success rate of 0.1 per cent who brings an appeal to the Conseil d'Etat, this is no longer reasonable. I do not think it is possible to invoke a long stay, after being rejected for years. An important question is whether the applicant is dependent on the CPAS or not.
>
> *All these criteria, will you put them in a legislative text?* In no case. This should remain a discretionary competence of the Minister of the Interior. If we introduce a new procedure for this, there will once again be a hassle and an endless waste of administrative time. I dare not think about it: first, five years of recognition procedure, then five years of deliberation on regularisations. For us, that would be the end. No, the decision must remain with the Minister. It is not a right, as is the case with the refugee status. Regularisation is a favour.

In a contribution to *De Standaard* of 9 April 1994, under the title 'Economic "refugees" are migrants'. I considered that it was not justified that Belgium had to spend the equivalent of €125 million on the reception of asylum seekers, 90 per cent of whom were not refugees. This contrasted sharply with the equivalent of €625,000 in our contribution to the UN High Commissioner for Refugees to help welcome 17 million refugees worldwide.

On 1 June 1994, a few days before the European elections, an optimistic Minister of the Interior announced that with less than 1,000 asylum applications a month the flow of asylum sekers was slowly coming under control. On 14 June 1994, two days after the European elections, *Dag Allemaal* published, under the title 'At the Commission General, Marc Bossuyt was mopping under an open tap', a long interview with me:

> For years I cried in the desert. For the first two years, we had to work with four jurists. Now there are 150. But it is not enough to refuse asylum. We also must remove rejected applicants.
>
> There are probably 5 billion people in the world who have less income than we do. We cannot afford to attract all these people. There are also those who take advantage of these illegal workers. It undermines our social system. No one pays social contributions for these people. No one pays tax contributions for them.

> At the golden age of Ghanaian applications, it was always about coups d'état or attempted coups d'état. The applicants were not directly associated with it, but their partner was. Those were made up stories. There must be a plausible minimum.
>
> Some asylum seekers receive more per month than the unemployed. It's looking for trouble. The problem of asylum seekers is not inevitable: we do not have to suffer this. Are we building a European Fortress? Strange fortress in which 600,000 illegals enter every year (laughs). It is a very porous fortress.

On 14 July 1994, the Court of Arbitration[16] annulled the legislative provision excluding the possibility of requesting a suspension from the Conseil d'Etat, when the Commissioner General had declared enforceable 'notwithstanding any remedy' its decision confirming the inadmissibility decision of the Aliens Office. Subsequently, it would appear that this judgment was an important step towards further slippage in the asylum procedure. On 15 July 1994, the Minister for the Interior announced to the Council of Ministers that the number of asylum seekers had fallen. The number of repatriations and voluntary returns had increased. In *Humo*[17] of 21 July 1994, Jan Hertoghs gave the floor to lawyers on the issue of asylum seekers. In a reaction published two weeks later, I remarked that this article was characterised by 'an uncritical reflection of a unilateral and biased presentation of things. It was full of outrages'.

On 10 October 1994, Johan Vande Lanotte became Minister of the Interior. In a letter dated 25 October 1994, his predecessor, Louis Tobback, who had become Chairperson of the SP, expressed to me 'his appreciation for the mutual cooperation that had made it possible to force a major breakthrough in the asylum policy'. This appreciation was reciprocal. In retrospect, it was this cooperation that made it the most exciting time of my professional career. A year earlier, on 4 November 1993, Ahmed Zaoui, a leader of the Islamic Salvation Front (FIS) in Algeria, had applied for asylum.

[16] In its judgment No 61/94, the Court of Arbitration annulled Arts 32 and 33 of the Law of 6 May 1993, having inserted in the Aliens Law a second paragraph of Art 69*bis* and the second paragraph of the newly inserted Art 70. In a legal commentary, I gave a harsh criticism of this judgment: see M Bossuyt, 'La Cour d'arbitrage: Contrôle d'égalité ou contrôle d'opportunité? A propos de la faculté de suspension par le Conseil d'Etat des décisions confirmatives du Commissaire général aux réfugiés et aux apatrides' [1996] *Revue trimestrielle des droits de l'homme* 467.

[17] Under the title: 'If Mobutu flees to Belgium, He Immediately Receives Political Asylum. His Victims Almost Never'.

8

Ahmed Zaoui, an Islamist Asylum Seeker from Algeria (1993–97)

On 4 November 1993, Ahmed Zaoui (b 1960), a professor of Islamic science at the University of Algiers, applied for asylum in Belgium. Since 1991 he had been a member of the Islamic Salvation Front (FIS).

8.1. Zaoui and the FIS in Algeria

The FIS is an Orthodox Islamic movement founded in 1989 in Algeria. In June 1990, the first free elections were held in Algeria for provincial and municipal bodies. The FIS won 54.2 per cent of the vote and a majority in more than half of the municipalities and two-thirds of the *wilayas* (departments).[1] Since June 1991, Zaoui had been a member of the FIS National Council and Vice-President of the Council's Information and Propaganda Bureau.

In the first round of general elections on 26 December 1991, the FIS recorded very good results. Zaoui won 42.45 per cent of the vote in his constituency of Cheraga. The FIS was expected to win an overwhelming majority in the second round. For fear of an Islamic dictatorship, the elections were cancelled, and the second round abolished. On 11 January 1992, President Chadli Bendjedid (1979–92) was forced to resign. The military set up a Supreme Council of the State to govern the country for two years. After President Mohammed Boudiaf came to power (16 January–29 June 1992), Zaoui pleaded, at a public meeting on 17 January 1992, for the continuation of the second round of parliamentary elections. Arrested that evening, he was released 48 hours later. Shortly after, he fled to Morocco for the first time. He remained hidden there for fear of being condemned in Algeria to complete isolation in the Sahara, as had happened to his father. Imam and president of the *wilaya* of Medea, his father had been imprisoned from 18 January 1991 for five months in a camp in Reggan.

On 9 February 1992, the Supreme Council of the State declared a state of emergency. A year later, it was extended indefinitely. On 4 March, the FIS was banned

[1] Amnesty International (March 1993), 'Algeria, Degradation of Human Rights in a State of Emergency'.

and dissolved by the courts. Several leaders of the movement were imprisoned; others were forced into exile. On 2 April, the Tribunal of Chera sentenced Zaoui by default to three months in prison. On 14 July he appealed to the Court of Appeal of the same city.

On 1 March 1993, after a year in hiding in Algeria, Zaoui left on foot, and without any identity document, again to Morocco. On 24 April, the Moroccan Territory Security Division (DST) arrested him in a hotel in Oujda. He was released after three days. On 14 July 1993, the judgment of the Chera Tribunal was overturned by the Court of Appeal, and he returned clandestinely from Morocco to Algeria. During this period, he lived with various friends. He remained in Algeria because he had no means of transportation to seek asylum in Europe.

On 27 July, the Special Court of Algiers sentenced Zaoui to capital punishment. According to the Algerian newspaper *El Moudjahid* of 28 July 1993, he was one of four operatives from a terrorist group of six on the run.[2] At the beginning of August 1993, Zaoui left again for Morocco. On 28 October, he left Morocco because he was wanted by the DST based on an Algerian extradition request. A day later he sailed for France. On 2 November, he went by car to Belgium, where he arrived in the evening. He did not apply for asylum in France 'because there were many Algerians in that country'.

8.2. First Asylum Application: Exclusion Clause Applied (10 August 1994)

On 4 November 1993, on the day of his application for asylum, the Aliens Office refused him residence in Belgium. He had been in France since March 1993 and had left that country without fear within the meaning of Article 1, paragraph A, al 2, of the Geneva Convention. The next day Zaoui filed an urgent appeal against this decision.[3] On 16 November, he was heard at the Commission General.[4] On 6 May 1994, Deputy Commissioner Xavier De Beys decided that a further examination of his application was necessary:

> In view of the evidence in support of his conviction by the Special Court, it is necessary at this stage of the proceedings to declare the person's fears credible. Only a further examination of his application will raise the question of the applicability of the exclusion clause[5] provided for in Article 1, para A, al 2, of the Geneva Convention of 28 July 1951.

[2] 'Seven Individuals Involved in Terrorist Acts Appeared Yesterday before the Special Court of Algiers' (*El Moudjahid*, 28 July 1993).

[3] Since 31 May 1993, the 'urgent requests for reconsideration' that resulted in an opinion of the Commissioner General were replaced by 'urgent appeals' that resulted in a decision by the Commissioner General.

[4] His lawyer was Me Georges-Henri Beauthier.

[5] See above p 56 (n 18).

On 10 August 1994, the same Deputy Commissioner excluded him from refugee status.[6] He referred to information that he had since May 1994 joined the Islamic Armed Group (GIA). It was an organisation that sought to take power through intimidation and terror. The political nature of the motivation of the GIA's acts of terrorism did not prevent the application of the exclusion clause of the Geneva Convention. An indirect participation in the decision, preparation or execution of actions which could be classified as serious crimes of common law was established on his part. He could not benefit from the provisions of the Geneva Convention.

8.3. The Permanent Board Confirms the Exclusion Clause (18 May 1995)

On 24 August 1994, Zaoui filed an appeal against this refusal decision before the Permanent Board. The appeal noted that the decision had not challenged the persecution fears he had raised. If he were to return to Algeria, he would be immediately imprisoned, most likely tortured, taken to a 'death row' as described in the European Court of Human Rights' judgment *Soering* (see below p 264–265), and executed. He wanted to say that he had not rallied the GIA cause. Since he had never been invited to respond to rumours about such a serious charge, he had not been able to exercise his right of defence on the matter.

At the beginning of 1995, Mrs Zaoui and their three sons also arrived in Belgium. They had fled from Algeria via Syria. From 17 January to 28 February 1995, the household lived in Liège. They applied for asylum on 1 March after Zaoui was arrested by the Belgian authorities.[7] They did not know that their application was late. Mrs Zaoui referred to her mental situation, her fatigue and the illness of her children.

Zaoui was suspected of conspiracy, complicity in the production of false documents and receiving such documents in connection with a terrorist organisation. The press described him as an important leader of the GIA in Europe. Mention was made of rivalry between the FIS and the GIA.[8] Zaoui would have moved during the summer of 1994 from the FIS to the GIA. He would have been part of the caliphate, the (shadow) government of the GIA. The GIA professed threats against Belgium. Four days later, on 8 March 1995, it was announced that the FIS also demanded his release. The head of the FIS in Belgium, however, condemned

[6] I was prevented, given my participation in Geneva at the session of the UN Sub-Commission on the Prevention of Discrimination and the Protection of Minorities.

[7] 'Ahmed Zaoui, Leader of the GIA, was in Belgium Unhindered for a Year and a Half' (*DM*; *LLB*, 7 March 1995). 'It was at the Head of the GIA that the Belgian Police Struck' (*LLB*; *DS*; *GvA*, 8 March 1995).

[8] *Le Monde* (15 September 1995): 'The Islamic Salvation Front Condemns the Attacks in France'.

these threats. Foreign Affairs Minister Frank Vandenbroucke[9] warned travellers to North Africa and the Middle East, which caused a great deal of discontent in Tunisia, Morocco and Israel.

On 18 May 1995, the Permanent Board upheld the refugee exclusion decision.[10] The Permanent Board referred to the exclusion clause of the Geneva Convention and to Article 14 of the Universal Declaration of Human Rights.[11] These two provisions guarantee the right of States to refuse the reception of individuals who threaten the security of their population.

From an attestation by Rabah Kebir, the FIS's representative in Europe and the United States, it appeared that Zaoui was presented as one of the FIS's 'most important personalities'. The Permanent Board held him responsible for the actions perpetrated on behalf of that organisation. The file did not contain any evidence of a public position taken by the applicant by which he dissociated himself from the acts referred to above. The line between the GIA and the FIS was often blurred:

> [T]he two movements resorted to violence and covered several nebulous groups with varying allegiances; an indication of this ambiguity can be seen in the fact that the applicant and other FIS leaders were taken among the ministers of the caliphate government that the GIA was planning to institute.

The targets and processes of members and supporters of the FIS military wing were not significantly different from those of the GIA. They organised, perpetrated and claimed attacks, murders and other crimes of common law. Such acts and actions are unquestionably covered by Article 1, paragraph F, of the Geneva Convention. The Permanent Board considered that there were indications that Zaoui, notwithstanding his denials, was directly involved in such acts:

> In this regard, in addition to the aforementioned condemnation by the Special Court of Algiers, journalistic sources present the applicant as the organiser of a maquis in the region of Medea and the author of a sermon during which he promised death and imprisonment to all Algerian communists and democrats in case of victory of the FIS in the second round of the legislative elections.

The Permanent Board was aware that serious human rights violations were being blamed on the Algerian authorities. This did not exonerate the liability of opponents who committed or were complicit in acts referred to in Article 1, paragraph F, of the Geneva Convention.

[9] Frank Vandenbroucke was Minister of Foreign Affairs from 10 October 1994 to 22 March 1995.

[10] His lawyer was Me Xavier Magnée of the Brussels Bar, who considered him 'a philosopher, a kind man' (*GvA*, 10 March 1995).

[11] Art 14, §2: 'This right [to seek asylum and to enjoy in other countries asylum] may not be invoked in the case of prosecutions genuinely arising from non-political crimes or from acts contrary to the purposes and principles of the United Nations'.

8.4. Brussels Court of Appeal: Four-Year Conditional Sentence (26 November 1995)

As part of a large-scale raid carried out by State Security and the Gendarmerie, which took place on 1 March 1995, 15 searches took place at the homes of Algerians suspected of being fundamentalists. Weapons of war, grenades, ammunition and logistical material were found and confiscated. Thirteen alleged Algerian fundamentalists – including Zaoui – were arrested. On 14 June, they were referred to the Brussels Correctional Tribunal by the Chambre du conseil.[12] The charge against Zaoui mentioned 'criminal association (as a leader), concealment and incitement to crime'. The Public Prosecutor, represented by Michèle Coninx, described him as 'the undisputed intellectual and moral leader of the GIA' and demanded the maximum penalty of five years for criminal association.

Before the start of the trial on 5 September 1995, there was a kind of 'psychosis' in Belgium following four incidents[13] and in France in the previous two months.[14] Zaoui had admitted to being a member of the FIS[15] but had no connection with the GIA, an armed fundamentalist Muslim movement that was fighting the Algerian government with arms in hand. He was defended by three Brussels lawyers[16] and by Parisian lawyer Me Jacques Vergès.[17] On 3 October, the Correctional Tribunal, chaired by Claire De Gryse, sentenced the five defendants to sentences ranging from a year and a half to five years. Two defendants received only light sentences and five, including the main accused Zaoui, were acquitted for lack of evidence. As regards the fact that he was in possession of falsified residence documents, the Correctional Tribunal admitted the state of necessity, given his precarious residence situation.

Observers welcomed this judgment as 'courageous, nuanced, well-motivated, exemplary, solid, and impartial' (*LS*; *LLB*, 4 October 1995). In a comment to the

[12] According to the *Journal de Genève* (6 March 1995), it was 'an arsenal of war': 'grenades, cartridges of various calibres, chargers and silencers, binoculars equipped for night vision, camouflage gear, handcuffs, phones, cell phones and transceivers'.

[13] On 25 July 1995 in the metro (RER Saint-Michel) in Paris (8 dead and 117 wounded), on 17 August in Place Charles de Gaulle (Etoile) (16 wounded) and failed attempts on 26 August near Lyon on the track of the TGV Paris–Lyon, and on 3 September in a market in Paris.

[14] 'The Tension is Mounting around the GIA. But Ahmed Zaoui Assures us that Belgium has nothing to Fear' (*LLB*, 1 September 1995); 'GIA: a Tense Climate for a Delicate Trial' (*LLB*, 2 September); 'Psychosis and Politics Mark the Trial of the GIA' (5 September); 'The Maghreb Community Warns against Hysteria because of the GIA Trial' (*DM*, 13 September).

[15] On the eve of the speech, Alain Heyrendt wrote a comment under the title 'Justice and Islamism': 'The men arrested in March dream for the Muslim world of a fundamentalist theocracy without any connection with our conceptions of life in society. We may fear that the replacement of a corrupt secular power by the authority of fanatical devotees does not bode well for the future' (*LLB*, 3 September 1995).

[16] Me Xavier Magnée, Me Fernande Motte de Raedt and Me Gilles Vanderbeck.

[17] 'The Gia trial Attracts the Best Lawyers' (*DS*, 4 September 1995); 'According to Me Vergès, Zaoui is like an Opponent of Pinochet', 'Me Vergès Accuses Algiers of the Attacks in Paris' (*LS*, 8 September), and the reaction: 'The Algerian Embassy Indignant' (*LS*, 11 September).

newspaper *De Morgen* of 4 October 1995, under the title 'The Rule of Law Works', Pol Deltour spoke of 'a well-reasoned judgment and of great serenity, characteristics that differ acutely from the sometimes-simplistic amalgam that others – although armed with public authority – have thought it necessary to make around this GIA affair'.[18] The prosecution appealed against the five acquittals.

On 6 November 1995, the Palais de Justice in Brussels was once again transformed into a fortress for the appeal trial of Zaoui and seven others.[19] In its judgment of 20 November 1995, the Court of Appeal sentenced Zaoui to four years of suspended imprisonment. The Court found that the criminal association was established because the accused

> had rented apartments under false names and had subscribed to telephone lines. In addition, they had registered a car on behalf of a banned member, while others used it. At several of the defendants premises, investigators found pamphlets that referred to the GIA. Weapons caches, foreign currencies and maps could hardly justify legitimate purposes.

According to section 322 of the Criminal Code, 'Any association formed for the purpose of harming persons or property is a crime or an offence that exists by the sole fact of the banned organization'. The Court ruled that Zaoui was the mastermind behind this dangerous organisation that was ready to attack people and property. This was evident from his contacts with wanted terrorists, as well as from his personality, culture, degree and activities that gave him some authority. With his suspended imprisonment sentence, there was no longer a basis for his judicial detention. He was transferred to the Aliens Office, which locked him in the Saint-Gilles prison because of his illegal stay in Belgium.[20]

8.5. Second Asylum Application: No New Elements (7 June 1996)

On 18 April 1996, Zaoui filed a second asylum application. He referred to an article in the *El Ansar* newspaper published by the GIA on 5 January in London. In this article, he was accused of having denounced Abdel Haq Layada, the emir of the GIA, to the Moroccan DST. This emir was one of the leaders of the GIA that Zaoui met during his stay in Oujda in March 1993. Later, the emir was arrested by the Moroccan authorities.

[18] He referred to the Minister of the Interior, Johan Vande Lanotte, who had lost his way by speaking before the trial of 'GIA terrorists' (see also *DS*; *HLN*, 9 September). He felt that it was urgent to clarify 'the role of the Belgian State Security in judicial cases such as that of the GIA' (*DM*, 4 October 1995).

[19] The Court was presided over by Francine De Ceuleneer, the Public Prosecutor was represented by Advocate General René Marchal and the defence was held by the same three Brussels lawyers; Me Jacques Vergès was announced but did not come.

[20] In search of a third country, attempts were made to send him to Sudan but without success (*DS*, 21 February 1996; *LLB*, 8 March 1996).

On 26 April 1996, the Advisory Commission for Foreigners issued an opinion against his expulsion. On 23 May, the Aliens Office again refused Zaoui's stay and establishment in the territory. The newspaper article did not sentence him to death. Therefore, there were no serious indications of a well-founded fear of persecution. He claimed to have been informed of the threats made against him by compatriots. According to the Aliens Office, such a rumour could not be verified.

On 30 May 1996, Zaoui filed an urgent appeal. During his hearing by my collaborators at the Saint-Gilles prison on 6 June, he denied that the GIA had condemned him at his request to prove his innocence. He explained that between his arrest in March 1993, when he allegedly denounced Abdel-Haq Layada to the Moroccan authorities, and his death sentence, three years had passed. According to him, the GIA had in the meantime been very close to the FIS for tactical reasons. However, a rupture occurred between the two organisations shortly before the date of the GIA's communiqué. As a result, the GIA would have sought to eliminate members of the FIS influential in political dialogues.

On 7 June 1996, I confirmed the decision of the Aliens Office of 23 May concerning the refusal of residence and establishment in the territory. I believed that his request did not bring anything to reconsider his exclusion from the benefit of the Geneva Convention. However, I considered that, given the situation in his country of origin, it was not appropriate, under the present circumstances, to return him to Algeria.

On 13 July 1996, mention was made of Zaoui's lawyers' complaint that he had already spent 216 days in pre-trial detention and 312 days in administrative retention. On 31 October, the Cour de cassation overturned the judgment of the Chamber of Indictment which had confirmed his retention. Zaoui had to be released. Because this did not happen immediately, he began a hunger strike on 4 November. After being deprived of liberty for more than a year in the Saint-Gilles prison, Zaoui was released on 20 November. He was placed under house arrest. By 11 December, he was still looking for a country of asylum.

8.6. Benothmane's 'Suicide' (29 November 1996)

Meanwhile, on 26 July 1996, the FIS in Washington and Paris announced the death under torture of Benothmane Bouasria. It was widely reported in the media of 27 and 29 July. On his way to Canada, he had been arrested in Zaventem nine months earlier (5 October 1995). He had applied for asylum five days later. He declared that he did not belong to the FIS. The FIS representative in Belgium even refused to issue a certificate supporting his application. On 13 October, the Aliens Office refused him access to the territory. I confirmed this on 28 December. He did not address himself to the Conseil d'Etat. On 15 July 1996, he was escorted to Barcelona, where he was brought back to Algiers.

Interior Minister Johan Vande Lanotte asked the Algerian government for explanations through diplomatic channels. On 17 August 1996, *Le Soir* asked the question: 'Why does Algiers not Answer Brussels?' Two months later, on 23 November, Benothmane, supposedly dead, appeared on Algerian television in an interview. He said he was arrested at the Algerian–Libyan border with a fake Danish passport. On 24 November, the Belgian Ambassador met him in Algiers. On 26 November, I learned from official Belgian sources that Benothmane had been found alive. The story of his death under torture turned out to be a manipulation of the FIS. I recommended that such information be treated with greater caution in the future.

A few days later, it was announced that Benothmane had jumped out of a window on 29 November 1996 after being questioned by the investigating judge at the Mostaganem Tribunal. He died two days later. According to an Algerian source, he committed suicide. His admission on television that the announcement of his death was a FIS scheme, would have led him to commit suicide. The FIS would have wanted to scare European governments to better protect their asylum seekers. His brother, who was staying in Belgium and who was a collaborator of Zaoui, would have been associated with it. It was probably the publicity given to this story that ultimately cost him his life.

8.7. Hot Potato Sent to Switzerland (1997–98)

In November 1997, Zaoui left Belgium with his wife and children to travel via Germany to Switzerland. Immediately after his arrival he applied for asylum in Switzerland. The media wondered if Zaoui had left under an agreement between Brussels, Algiers and Bern. Yet, there were no pointers in this direction:

> On the other hand, a less flamboyant and less glorious thesis for the Belgian authorities, Zaoui has left Belgian territory in recent weeks to reach Cologne and meet clandestinely Rabah Kébir, Chairperson of the FIS executive body abroad. Whatever the subject of this meeting, Zaoui then demonstrated that he could leave Belgium and travel without hindrance in Europe despite his house arrest.

From December 1997, he lived under police surveillance in Saint-Gingolph in the Swiss canton of Valais, near the French border.

The Swiss authorities were reluctant to welcome Zaoui. Belgium was not prepared to take him back and bring him into the 'Schengen area'. This led to a dead end. Since there was no takeover agreement between Belgium and Switzerland, the latter country could not force Belgium to take over Zaoui:

> In fact, for Zaoui, two scenarios are possible: Switzerland refuses him political asylum, which seems to be a given and tries to send him back to Belgium. This solution no longer seems to embody Switzerland's preferred path. Another solution: they let him marinate in the Valais until the arrival of a new letter of request from Judge Le Loire, this time addressed to Switzerland. Zaoui is imprisoned, charged, and possibly extradited. This is the most plausible scenario.

French judge Roger Le Loire was investigating him for conspiracy. In this context, a request for a hearing had been made to the Belgian authorities on 1 October 1997. In May 1998, the French judge charged Zaoui with terrorist activities against France. Among other things, he was suspected of having been associated with the attacks in the Paris metro on 25 July 1995. The French judge accused him of 'criminal association, complicity in the production of falsified documents, receiving falsified administrative documents in relation to a company having the objective of disturbing public order'.

On 30 March 1998, Zaoui had reported that he was chairing the provisional bureau of the FIS Coordinating Council abroad (CCFIS). On 8 October 1997, he had stated that he no longer recognised the authority of the FIS's executive body abroad. In Saint-Gingolph (Switzerland), Zaoui received many visitors from the Islamic fundamentalist milieu. The Swiss authorities noted this with suspicion. The Swiss federal police investigated the extent to which Zaoui's activities could endanger the security of the Swiss State: 'It is thus clear that the situation of "Brother Zaoui" does not in any way prevent him from carrying out intense political activity, which is certainly not illegal, but worries the Swiss Valais authorities' (*LLB*, 23 April 1998).

On 29 October 1998, he was arrested in Switzerland. On the same day he was put on a plane with his sick wife and four children to Burkina Faso. It was the only country willing to accept him. Switzerland would have granted him a monthly allowance of 1,500 Swiss francs.

8.8. Burkina Faso (1998–2000), Malaysia and New Zealand (2002–14)

After Zaoui left for Burkina Faso, the Belgian media lost interest in him. *Wikipedia* tells us what happened to him later.[21] I think it is worth briefly telling the rest of his story.

In 2000, he left Burkina Faso with his family for Malaysia. On 13 November 2001, he was sentenced in Paris by default to three years of a conditional sentence for participation in a criminal group in preparation for terrorist acts. When the Algerian police chief visited Malaysia to study police methods, Zaoui decided to leave the country. On 4 December 2002, he arrived in New Zealand via Vietnam with a false South African passport. Upon his arrival in New Zealand he applied for asylum there.

When his name appeared in the media, he became the subject of media attention and debate. Initially, he was denied refugee status under the exclusion clause. In March 2003, he received a security risk certificate from the New Zealand

[21] En.wikipedia.org/wiki/Ahmed_Zaoui.

Intelligence Service. After his arrest, he was held for 10 months in a maximum security prison. In August 2003, the New Zealand refugee appeal body declared the French and Belgian trials 'unsafe'. That body considered that these trials had not provided evidence that he had committed, conducted, or participated in any act of violence or terrorism. He was granted refugee status. In October 2003, he was transferred to a minimum security prison. When the Supreme Court ordered, in February 2004, that his lawyers should receive a summary of his case, they responded to it point by point.

The government of New Zealand maintained that it had information that showed that he was a 'credible risk'. In September 2004, Prime Minister Helen Clark connected his name with Al Qaeda. Later she acknowledged that she was probably going too far. On 20 October, a biographical book about him was presented. On 9 December 2004, the Supreme Court of New Zealand authorised him to provide bail. This Court allowed him to stay in a Dominican convent.[22]

In October 2005, he published a book (*Migrant Birds*) with 24 poems in Arabic and English. The twenty-fifth poem ('He will come back, the one I'm waiting for') was described by Emma Neale, editor of *The Best New Zealand Poems 2004*, as the most important of the year in New Zealand. He became a celebrity. On 13 September 2007, his security risk certificate was withdrawn. His wife and four children, who had been illegally staying in Kuala Lumpur (Malaysia) since 2000, joined him in New Zealand on 26 October 2007. In 2009 he went to Massey University to study. He worked for a Muslim association and opened a kebab stand. In 2012 he moved to Auckland. He was granted New Zealand citizenship in May 2014.

[22] Helen Clark, Prime Minister of New Zealand (1999–2007); Administrator of the United Nations Development Programme (UNDP) (2009–17).

9

'Malaise at the CG' and 'Asylum Seeker "Deceased"' (1994–95)

On 16 November 1994, *La Libre Belgique* and *Le Soir* reported a great scandal. I would have encouraged my staff to make refusal decisions. They could have obtained 'points' through negative rather than positive proposals. This was the cause (for almost two years) of great unease at the Commission General. On 1 February 1995, I could finally announce some good news: the number of asylum applications had dropped, as well as – for the first time in seven years – the backlog. On the other hand, ecologist senators had, on 5 May 1995, some frightening news: an asylum seeker, to whom I had refused asylum, had perished in the prisons of N'Djili (Zaire).

9.1. 'Malaise at the Commission General' (16 November 1994)

The (French-speaking) League for Human Rights had thus discovered a great scandal. It concerned a memo which was almost two years old (dated 26 January 1993) to assess the productivity of jurists at the Commission General:

> Marc Bossuyt Challenged (*LLB*). Unease among the Jurists of the Commission General: the Rule Must be Refusal. The Asylum Application, a Game of Fools for All? (*LS*).

According *to La Libre Belgique* and *Le Soir* of 16 November 1994, I reacted as follows:

> Refugee Commissioner Denies Encouraging the 'Tough' in his Department (*LLB*). Marc Bossuyt is Hardly Moved (*LS*).

The next day, the Dutch-speaking newspapers hastened to repeat this information:

> Jurists Gain Points by Denying Asylum Seekers (*DM*); The Point Allocation System Upsets the League (*HLN*); A Refugee Points System (*DS*); A Bonus for Jurists who Keep Refugees out (*HN*).

9.1.1. The System of Awarding Points

In *La Libre Belgique*, I explained to Jean-Claude Matgen that the chosen weighting tried to consider the difficulty of the proposed draft decisions. It was only an indicator that should not be overemphasised. For the sake of good administration, efforts had been made to improve efficiency. Critics with political motives contributed to undermining this. Facing Martine Vandemeulebroucke in *Le Soir*, I noted that in my administration there were only four jurists in January 1990, in June 1993, 50 and today (in November 1994), there were 125. I make efforts to put more structure in the house. I tried to imbue my will with guidelines without interfering directly in the files. My Deputy and I rarely stopped a file.

According to the League, this was a 'blatant violation of the fundamental principle of the right to access to fair justice'. In a letter dated 17 November 1994 addressed to the Chairperson of the francophone League for Human Rights, André-Marie Servais, I declared myself 'dismayed that an organisation that is supposed to embody and defend human rights is aiding and abetting a sneaky scheme to release an internal memo without even notifying its author'.

I felt that in this way the frustrations of three anonymous collaborators (militiamen or contractual civil servants) were exploited without regard for the respect of the principle of adversarial debate. If I really wanted to encourage my employees with a 'bonus' to make negative decisions, I would have done so at the phase of admissibility. At this level, 80 per cent of decisions were taken and there was no longer any suspensive appeal. Only 20 per cent of the decisions were taken on the merits and an appeal to the Permanent Board was possible.

As an appeal body in respect of admissibility, I gave reasons for both my positive and negative decisions. For this reason, the same weight was given to both types of decision. At first instance on the merits, I gave reasons only for my negative decisions. The Aliens Office, which acted as first instance on admissibility, also gave reasons only for its negative decisions. Since only my negative decisions taken at first instance on the merits were reasoned, generally quite extensively, they were given more weight than positive decisions. Moreover, an erroneous estimate in the negative direction may have more serious consequences than in the positive direction. The reasons for a negative decision must be convincing to hold before the Permanent Board from a legal viewpoint. There is almost never an appeal against a positive decision. Article 57/6 of the Aliens Law provided that 'Decisions refusing to recognise or confirm refugee status, as well as those withdrawing refugee status, shall be *reasoned*'. Reasons were not prescribed for recognition decisions. A refugee has never asked for his recognition to be annulled because it was not motivated.

9.1.2. My Impeachment Requested

The francophone League, as well as Ecolo and Agalev, asked for my dismissal. On 23 November 1994, the Minister of the Interior, Johan Vande Lanotte, responded to the interpellations of MPs Denis Grimberghs (PSC) and Henri Simons (Ecolo):

> The impression cannot be created that employees are evaluated on the result of their work rather than on its quality. The conversation with Mr Bossuyt reassured me. He has done a tremendous job. I maintain my trust in him. I'm sceptical of people who have left a service and then they're unloading their bile.

In the *Knack* of 23 November 1994, I explained that experience tells us that when we measure who does much and who does little, more work is done. I found it insulting to my staff to suggest that they were refusing refugees for half a point more. I was not surprised that the attack came from the francophone side: 'Bad faith was obvious'. The francophone League was in favour of a much laxer refugee policy than that provided for in the Geneva Convention. In the weekly *Panorama* of 24 November 1994, I stated that 'the idea of measuring productivity objectively deserves to be followed in other jurisdictions. This could only be beneficial to their functioning'.

In an article in *La Cité* of 1 December 1994, Anne-Françoise Moyson quoted the 'overzealous' Marc Bossuyt as saying:

> I'm sending a message to my staff that they're here to address the backlog, not to sit back and relax. [And, referring to my curriculum vitae], I am insensitive to all pressures, no matter where they come from, even if they are international.

On the enquiry of Senator Frans Lozie and at the request of Senator Paul Pataer, Interior Minister Johan Vande Lanotte replied:

> The note was read very selectively. Evaluations are needed. That's one of the things we must consider. Negative decisions must be better motivated. The evaluation system was not well explained. Various elements have not been sufficiently emphasised (7 December 1994).

This could have been useful for critical parliamentarians and other outsiders, but it was an internal memo. It was only intended for employees of the Commission General. They were familiar with the comings and goings of the Commission General. Senator Lozie nevertheless felt that I should be relieved of my duties. Senator Pataer felt that to strengthen my independence I had to be appointed for life.

In a letter of 9 December 1994 addressed to the Chairperson of the francophone League for Human Rights, Minister Johan Vande Lanotte wrote:

> I see no reason to doubt the impartiality of the Commissioner General. Your very detailed conclusions are based on a too unilateral and too quick reading of an internal note. A better analysis of the note itself and its application could have already led you to other conclusions. There is no objective evidence that the Commissioner General acts in a biased manner or decides on asylum applications without first being concerned about the application of the Geneva Convention. I hope that in the future you will examine matters more thoroughly before making serious charges.

In *Le Vif/L'Express* on the same day Valérie Colin painted my portrait under the title 'The Man that Loved Figures':

> He walks around like a caged lion in his vast North Gate headquarters in Brussels. When he was appointed Commissioner General in November 1987, the instrument of his policy, the Commission General, simply did not exist. 'Seven years ago, we had no premises, no Bic, no phone. And lots of people piling up, for whom reasoned opinions had to be delivered within 24 hours ...'
>
> Without question, he is the man of the situation. Even his critics – who criticise its lack of flexibility, its lack of sense of compromise – agree that he has succeeded, in record time, in making the Commission General operational, and then transforming this 'craft' structure into a large company. If the Commission General now has high-performance computer scientists, interpreters capable of translating the languages of 125 nationalities, libraries that provide documentation on so many countries, a reception service that provides, all day long, more than 200 visitors, it's thanks to Bossuyt ...
>
> 'In the midst of the economic crisis, he went out of his way to obtain budget and reinforcements of staff' says an elder from the house. How? The man is a skilled negotiator. He's brilliant, convincing, charming. King Baudouin offered him three audiences; King Albert II did it once. But the Commissioner General proudly attributes his success to his perfect knowledge of the figures ...
>
> As for the League's critics, he simply shrugs his shoulders. He taxes his accusers of 'obvious bad faith' and 'disconcerting lightness'. To criticisms of the severity of his administration, he replies: 'Either the Commission General is filled with incompetent staff members incapable of saving thousands of lives in danger, or it must be admitted that asylum seekers are attracted to Belgium for reasons unrelated to the Geneva Convention'.
>
> For those close to him, he is a skilful man with the temperament of a leader who generally avoids open conflicts. The man sins a little by excess of confidence. Bossuyt admits that his young administration is still lacking in consistency: 'But it functions ... This year we have mastered the flows ... But who knows what the future holds for us?' Clairvoyant, Bossuyt has also learned to moderate (publicly) his enthusiasm.

9.1.3. 'Accusations Out of Ignorance, if not Bad Faith'

On 12 December 1994, I gave a press conference on the criticisms addressed to me.[1] I charged the League with 'allegations out of ignorance, if not bad faith'. I explained at length the evaluation system, which had been presented in a bad light. Gross counting of decisions of a different nature would lead to meaningless results. It is also important to know that, in the proceedings on the merits, there

[1] 'Marc Bossuyt's Response to Criticism' (*LDH*); 'Marc Bossuyt Happy and Worried' (*LLB*); 'Bossuyt: "Criticism on the Points System is not Justified"' (*DM*); 'Bossuyt Denies Bias' (*HV*); 'My Note is Interpreted Maliciously' (*Vl'A*); 'Refusal of a Refugee Application Requires more Work' (*FET*); 'Bossuyt Defends the Points System' (*GvA*, 13 December 1994). See also the *Fifth Annual Report* (1994) Annex II, 127.

was one summons per day, whereas there were three in the admissibility proceedings. Reasoned refusals on the merits (RA) were given a weighting of 1.2. The weighting given to refusals based on not responding to an information request (RB) or a summons (RC) was lower (0.2 and 0.1, respectively). For decisions in admissibility, all of which (positive or negative) were reasoned, a coefficient of 0.4 was granted. And a coefficient of 0.6 to recognitions, because a brief motivation was sufficient. This purely internal motivation was not publicly available. Since there was no appeal against recognitions, there was no need for reasons that might be submitted to the Permanent Board for critical examination.

These criticisms came from supporters of a procedure in which the Commissioner General would only take a first decision which could be appealed before a jurisdiction. I feared that excessive 'jurisdictionalisation' would lead to a situation like that in the Netherlands.[2] Our northern neighbour in 1994 expected 52,500 asylum applications compared with 14,500 expected in Belgium! I acknowledged that there was a malaise at the Commission General. The collaborators were disillusioned by the actions of some of their former colleagues. There was also unease because, as of 12 December 1994, the contractual civil servants still did not know whether their contract would be extended on 1 January 1995.

The bad faith of the francophone League was clearly manifested in the *Knack* of 23 November 1994. One of its spokesmen said: 'Bossuyt does not want to exceed a monthly quota of 5 per cent recognitions'. In the *Knack* of 14 December 1994, I replied with precise figures:

> The percentage of favourable opinions or further examination decisions in the admissibility phase was 24% in 1991, 18% in 1992, 16% in 1993 and 20% in the first ten months of 1994. The percentage of recognition decisions on the merits was 24% in 1991, 25% in 1992, 27% in 1993 and 27% in the first ten months of 1994. This sufficiently shows that the French-speaking League does not hesitate to spread misinformation in this area.

This incident helps to understand how – after more than 20 years of attempts – it had not been possible in Belgium to properly measure the workload of courts and tribunals.

In an opinion in *Het Laatste Nieuws* on 24 December 1994, Laurent Panneels wrote under the title 'Efficient':

> The positive shift in an efficient and rapid approach to the processing of applications in the fight against the influx of asylum seekers must be attributed above all to the work of Commissioner General for Refugees Marc Bossuyt, who in a relatively short period of time made the Commission General an administration working effectively with modern means and especially with sufficiently motivated men. Bossuyt has demonstrated in our own country that governments can do solid work when excessive red tape is avoided and a transparent public service with motivated staff is given a chance.

Such appreciation allowed a merry Christmas, which, with what was about to happen (chapter eleven), was welcome.

[2] In *Panorama* on 15 December 1994, Minister Johan Vande Lanotte declared: 'The Dutch did not move, while we have accelerated the procedures'.

9.2. Finally, Some Good News (1 February 1995)

In a note dated 9 January 1995 addressed to the Chairperson of the francophone League for Human Rights, I stressed that a faster procedure was not a more restrictive procedure. The percentage of applications declared admissible by the Aliens Office had dropped from 38.1 per cent to 6.7 per cent. At the Commission General, however, the percentage had doubled from 7.1 per cent to 14 per cent. The number of recognised refugees increased every year from 311 in 1988 to 1,507 in 1994. Asylum applications from those who were not refugees under the Geneva Convention were more frequently refused in the admissibility phase. So, the refusal was faster. Previously, refusals were usually decided in the merits phase. The criteria and guidelines for the application of the Geneva Convention were unchanged. Even after the last legislative changes, the asylum procedure had far more guarantees than before I took office. Previously, decisions were not reasoned, there was no appeal procedure, neither in admissibility nor on the merits, and the Conseil d'Etat was not competent, not even in annulment.[3]

On 1 February 1995, I was finally able to announce some good news: for the first time in seven years, the number of asylum applications was down[4] and the absorption of the backlog[5] was successful.[6] I pointed out that 'the asylum procedure was proceeding more quickly but was not more severe'.[7] A multitude of figures demonstrated this:

- The recognition rate as well in absolute[8] as in relative[9] figures increased.
- The rate of admissibility at the Aliens Office had decreased but at the Commission General it was increasing.[10]
- More than 93.1 per cent of the recognitions were decided by the Commissioner General and 6.9 per cent by the Permanent Board.
- In 92.5 per cent of cases, the Permanent Board upheld the decisions of the Commissioner General.

[3] *Seventh Annual Report* (1994) Annex I, 118.

[4] From 14,340 in 1994 to 26,883 in 1993. Already on 10 January 1995, this had been reported in *La Libre Belgique* ('Asylum: it is in Free Fall') and on 28 January in *De Morgen* ('The Number of Asylum Applications Reduced by Half').

[5] From 35,475 on 1 October 1993 to 25,750 on 31 December 1994.

[6] 'Drastic Drop in Asylum Applications' (*HV*); 'Significant Drop in Arrivals' (*LS*); 'Fewer in 1994' (*LDH*); 'Half as many' (*LNG*, 2 February 1995).

[7] 'The Asylum Procedure is Faster, but Certainly not Tougher' (*GvA*); 'Fewer Refugee Applications, More Recognitions' (*HN*; *DS*); 'Not More Severe, but Much Faster' (*HBvL*; *DM*); 'Not More Severe' (*FET*); 'The Examination of Refugee Applications has not Become More Stringent, Procedures have been Expedited' (*LLB*); 'A Faster Procedure is not More Restrictive' (*Vl'A*, 2 February 1995).

[8] 1,507 in 1994 compared with 1,610 in 1989, 1990 and 1991 taken together.

[9] From 24% in 1991 over 25% and 27% up to 30% in 1994.

[10] 21% in 1994 compared with 16% in 1993 and 18% in 1992.

Some of my sentences received special attention:

- I am Commissioner General for Refugees, not for illegal aliens or clandestine migrants.
- As long as I am Commissioner General, any refugee within the meaning of the Geneva Convention will be recognised, regardless of whether they are numerous or not.
- Neither the Geneva Convention nor the human rights treaties require slow procedures. Neither the government, nor Parliament, nor public opinion want it.
- I have the impression that there are some who are unhappy that the number of asylum applications has dropped. From the lawyers who have made it their livelihood, I can understand that. From others, I find it less intelligent.
- Why were there 52,500 asylum seekers in the Netherlands last year and 14,500 in Belgium?[11] Because in the Netherlands they have no Commissioner General.
- It now costs six billion Belgian francs (€150 million) to welcome asylum seekers. I guess that's enough, right?

Apparently, not everyone was happy with this positive news, and some felt it was time to put some roadblocks in the way. Within a week, a first salvo was launched.

9.3. 'Failed Asylum Seekers Ill-Treated' (1995)

On 7 February 1995, the media reported accusations made by Senator Germain Dufour (Ecolo).[12] He claimed that failed asylum seekers had been mistreated on their return to Zaire. These charges were based on the statements of an asylum seeker in the Netherlands. He presented himself as a former officer of the 'Garde civile' of Zaire. The honourable senator was criticising the frivolity with which these files were dealt with when human lives were at stake.[13] This information gave rise to a series of reactions.

9.3.1. Reactions to Senator Germain Dufour's Accusations (February 1995)

The Ambassador of Zaire in Brussels, Jean-Pierre Kimbulu,[14] asked Senator Germain Dufour to give him a list of the persons who were eliminated or tortured when they returned. He said that if the Senator could find one, he would resign as Ambassador. He also said that one could buy in Matonge (Ixelles) the plans of the

[11] The foreign countries seen from the Netherlands do not really differ from those seen from Belgium.

[12] In an open letter to Frank Vandenbroucke, Minister of Foreign Affairs, MEP Claude Desama (PS) expressed his support for Senator Germain Dufour (*Vl'A*, 16 February 1995).

[13] Martine Vandemeulebroucke, *LS* (7 February 1995).

[14] Marie-France Cros, *LLB* (8 February 1995).

prison of Makala, the detention centre of the Garde civile and the military camp Tshatshi. These plans could help Zairean asylum seekers to answer questions about their alleged imprisonment. For its part, Sabena indicated that for those who were removed, it used the code INAD ('inadmissible') on the passenger lists. These lists were only forwarded to the captain, the in-charge flight attendant and the station manager. The names of Zairean citizens who were staying illegally in Belgium, were never communicated to the Zairean authorities.

In a press release of 7 February 1995, I stated that the accusations emanated from a person who did not inspire much trust. As an asylum seeker in the Netherlands, he had an interest in making such allegations to increase his chances of recognition. On 2 February 1994, the Ministry of Foreign Affairs informed me that the Zairean security services did not harass returned asylum seekers.[15] A confidential report of 13 September 1993 from the European Community embassies in Kinshasa went in the same direction. The Ministry gave assurance that the Belgian Embassy in Kinshasa was appropriately monitoring the situation of asylum seekers who had been returned. Statements such as those made by Senator Germain Dufour appeared unfounded after verification by the Embassy. I also pointed out that the admissibility rate in Belgium for Zairean asylum seekers was higher than for other nationalities and that the recognition rate was higher than in other countries.

In *Le Soir Illustré* of 15 February 1995 ('Curious Practices at Sabena'), Philippe Brewaeys continued to accuse Sabena. After the return to Kinshasa of 43 Zairians from France, the Netherlands, Germany and Belgium, on 19 July 1995, Floribert Chebeya, founder and Chairperson of La Voix des Sans Voix, confirmed that Sabena had never communicated to the Zairean security services the lists of returned asylum seekers. He was very critical about the behaviour of the French police.

9.3.2. 'Marie-Louise Dead in N'djili Jails' (April 1995)

On 5 May 1995, Senator Germain Dufour and Senator Frans Lozie gave a press conference in which they announced that an asylum seeker refused in Belgium (Marie-Louise T) had died in Zaire on 1 April. She was allegedly sent back on 29 September 1994 from Zaventem to Kinshasa. She had not benefited from the guarantees of an asylum procedure. The press of 6 May 1995 reported this extensively under the following headings:

- Marie-Louise's Fatal Return to Zaire. Rejected Refugee Candidate in Zaventem, Ms T Died in N'Djili Jails (*LLB*).

[15] I also referred to the letters I had written on this subject to the Minister of Justice on 10 December 1991, and to the Minister of the Interior on 30 March 1993. After a meeting in the office of the Minister of the Interior on 19 April 1993, I insisted on 7 and 29 July 1993 on receiving more information from the Minister of Foreign Affairs.

- A Zairean Woman Died in Prison in Kinshasa. Brussels–Kinshasa: Deadly Return for a Repressed. A Smudge Follows a rather Strange Refoulement Procedure (*LS*).
- Zairean Refugee Applicant Returned Died in Suspicious Circumstances (*DM*).
- Zairean Woman Died after Expulsion. Belgian Asylum Policy Berated (*GvA*).
- Rejected Refugee Applicant Killed in Zaire (*HLN*).

The two senators, 'shocked by this tragic adventure', claimed to have 'tried for a month to reconstruct the plot of the tragedy'. They claimed that this asylum seeker had not stayed at the Transit Centre in Melsbroek, but in the INAD area in Zaventem. According to them, no trace of her asylum application could be found. They didn't bother to contact me. Yet, as the *Gazet van Antwerpen* wrote: 'A simple phone call to the Refugee Commissioner Professor Marc Bossuyt was enough to reconstruct what had happened'. *Het Laatste Nieuws* had also contacted me.

Immediately it appeared that at least their claims about her asylum application and the Transit Centre were false. She had applied for asylum on 28 August 1994, the day after her arrival in Zaventem. She had been refused entry by the Aliens Office on 1 September 1994. Assisted by an interpreter and a lawyer, she was heard by one of my staff on 8 September at Transit Centre 127 in Melsbroek. On 16 September, I made a confirmatory refusal decision. On 19 September, she refused to sign the decision notified to her. She did not appeal to the Conseil d'Etat, either for suspension or annulment. The hearing revealed several contradictions and implausibility in her account. Thus, she claimed at the Commission General that her husband was a law student, while at the Aliens Office he was a student in agronomy. At the Commission General, she claimed to be a member of the UDPS,[16] although she had not previously mentioned it.

Moreover, she had already come to Belgium in 1991 and returned to Zaire without fear. She had French travel documents under a different identity. These frauds went hand in hand with the falsification of Belgian, French and Swiss stamps. The experience of the Commission General shows that documents produced by Zairean asylum seekers were very rarely authentic. In the present case, it was obvious that the young sister of the person concerned, who had produced the document attesting to her death had, in her capacity as an asylum seeker in the Netherlands, every interest in making believe that this alleged fact was true. The letter accompanying this document read as follows:

> My dear cousin Cocotte,
>
> It is with great regret that I draw your attention to the death of your older sister Marie-Louise T, caused by the repatriation of Zairians to Kinshasa, that is to say … because of the non-acceptance of her political asylum at the border in Zaventem … Arriving in Kinshasa, after a few hours, she disappeared for months … On 1 April 1995, while a

[16] Union for Democracy and Social Progress, founded on 15 February 1982 by Frédéric Kibassa Maliba, Etienne Tshisekedi, Vincent Mbwakiem and Marcel Lihau.

> morgue worker was checking the bodies, he suddenly recognised your older sister by the name of the T family that was on the white button … around her neck. As he knew one of our family members … he came to warn us … She was later found to have died because of injuries, rape, and the way she stayed in the prison with the torture of military personnel … My condolences and courage, courage, courage, courage.
>
> Your cousin, Denis.

9.3.3. 'I Read too Many Detective Novels' (May 1995)

In a press release of 10 May 1995, I first observed that there was no evidence of a causal link between the alleged fact and its repatriation six months earlier. In the light of all the fraudulent elements found in the context of her asylum application, I considered that the alleged fact would prove more than likely fanciful. This had already been demonstrated with other allegations made at this press conference. I had asked the Ministry of Foreign Affairs to verify this information. In any case, I felt that spreading these kinds of statements, without making the slightest effort to verify them beforehand, was being light-handed. If such statements had come from me, 'the frivolity with which these files were dealt with, when human lives are at stake' would no doubt have been strongly denounced. On 11 May 1995, Martine Vandemeulebroucke of the *Le Soir* newspaper reported on this press release by noting that I was perhaps reading too many detective novels. *La Libre Belgique* of 12 May and *De Morgen* of 17 May also reported my press release.

9.3.4. 'Marie-Louise Risen' (June 1995)

On 8 June 1995, *La Libre Belgique* brought news about the Zairean asylum seeker claimed to be dead. In the Kinshasa newspaper *Le Soft* of 29 May, she explained that she had indeed declared herself a refugee in Belgium. She and her children were housed in the transit centre where they were fed 'like little princes'. According to three senators from Agalev and Ecolo, on the contrary, 'the situation there was worse than in a concentration camp'. When she arrived at N'djili airport, there had been some complications with soldiers and security agents. Five hours later, she and her children were released without having been beaten or molested. *Le Soft* concluded that the death of this failed asylum seeker was 'a made-up story'. Ambassador Jean-Pierre Kimbulu said that the allegations made by the two Belgian parliamentarians were 'as fanciful as they were light'. In a press release of 9 June, I stated that I was 'dismayed by the cavalier and light-hearted manner in which some public officials and media outlets had been able to lay their accusations concerning this incident'.

On 10 June, the *Gazet van Antwerpen* ('The Zairean Dead is Alive and Well'), *Het Laatste Nieuws* ('The Dead Zairian is Alive') and *De Morgen* ('The Zairean

Dead Gives an Interview') mentioned this press release. *Le Soir* was waiting until I had received a letter from the Ministry of Foreign Affairs. In a letter of 11 July 1995 two Zairean human rights organisations (La Voix des Sans Voix and Asadho) confirmed that Marie-Louise T was still alive. They also checked that there was no mention of her death in the morgue registers in Kinshasa.

9.3.5. The Seventh Annual Report (1994): (27 July 1995)

Le Soir mentioned the resurrection of Marie-Louise only in addition to its report of the presentation, on 27 July 1995, of my *Seventh Annual Report* (1994). The report, 'full of statistics and pie charts', highlighted the decline in asylum applications. *Vers l'Avenir* was not reassured by my obsession to divide my statistics by nationality. However, the determination of refugee status is based on the fear of persecution by the country of nationality. *La Dernière Heure* mentioned the large number of languages for which interpreters had to be found. Some of these languages are little known, such as Bissan, Ibo, Ga, Fulah, Farsi, Kibunda, Lobi, Peul, Punjabi (needed in 3,745 cases), Twi, Wala, Wolof, Zarma and Zacaca. This cost more than the equivalent of €300,000, three times as much as in 1992. *De Morgen* wrote: 'The Field of Asylum Seekers can Present Tangible Results'. I complained about the growing differences between my decisions in admissibility and those of the Aliens Office. I also complained about my status, that 90 per cent of my civil servants were on contract, and the many prejudices I felt towards my services.

At that time, there was also the application of a Rwandan VIP, following the genocide of the Tutsi in Rwanda. On 6 April 1994, the Rwandan presidential plane was shot down in Kigali. It carried Juvénal Habyarimana, President of Rwanda (1973–94), and Cyprien Ntaryamira, President of Burundi (1994). They returned together from Dar-es-Salaam (Tanzania). It was this shooting that triggered the genocide. On 22 November 1994, Séraphin Rwabukumba, a cousin of the wife of the late President of Rwanda, applied for asylum in Belgium.

10

Séraphin Rwabukumba, Cousin of the Rwandan President (1994–98)

On 22 November 1994, Séraphin Rwabukumba (b 1949) applied for asylum in Belgium. He is a cousin of Agathe Kanziga, the widow of Major General Juvénal Habyarimana. He was President of Rwanda from 5 July 1973 until his death on 6 April 1994. In the elections he achieved ever better results: 98.99 per cent on 24 December 1978, 99.97 per cent on 19 December 1983 and 99.98 per cent on 19 December 1988. In Belgium, this raised no questions. It was admitted that he enjoyed great popularity.

10.1. A Cousin of President Juvénal Habyarimana's Widow

Rwabukumba's father was the brother of Agathe Kanziga's father. He is therefore her (first) cousin. In Africa, and in Rwanda in particular, cousins are often referred to as brothers and sisters. He was often referred to as the President's brother-in-law. His brother, Elie Sagatwa, who was the President's private secretary, died with him on the presidential plane. Rwabukumba studied humanities followed by a year of economics at the National University of Rwanda in Butare. At the age of 20, he started working at the National Bank, where he finished in management positions. In Kigali he became an important businessman. He ran a company called La Centrale, which mainly exported tea, milk and coffee.

According to a note from the Belgian State Security, the brothers-in-law of President Juvénal Habyarimana were also the leading figures in the famous Zero network:

> The Zero Network was a systematic destabilisation undertaking with the objective of sabotaging peace negotiations. It was the work of a group of people who included those closest to the President, including the three brothers-in-law of the Head of State who, according to our sources, were the heads of this 'network'.[1]

[1] State Security Report of 9 January 1995 concerning Séraphin Rwabukumba. On 11 April 1995, State Security authorised me to refer to its notes in this case.

The report of the Commission of Inquiry of the Belgian Senate[2] referred to the '*Clan de Madame*', called '*akazu*' (literally the 'little house'): 'The most important members of this group were her brothers, Colonel Pierre-Célestin Rwagafilita, Protais Zigiranyirazo and Séraphin Rwabukumba, her cousin Elie Sagatwa, and her best friends Colonel Laurent Serubuga and Noël Mbonabaryi'.[3]

President Juvénal Habyarimana's in-laws were a clan with significant political influence in Rwanda:

> It is generally accepted that the real power during the last years of the Habyarimana regime belonged to his in-laws and no longer to President Habyarimana himself. One of the theories explaining the attack on the President's plane is that the in-laws felt that Habyarimana wanted to make too many concessions to the opposition and the Tutsi rebels. The sharing of power would have resulted in his in-laws losing their privileges.

10.2. Departure from Rwanda in a French Military Plane (9 April 1994)

Rwabukumba left Rwanda on 9 April 1994 in a French military aircraft. Then he crossed several countries. From Rwanda, he travelled to the Central African Republic, then to France and Belgium, then again to France, the Central African Republic, Cameroon and Kenya. He finally returned to Belgium on 4 November 1994, via France. He was not accompanied by his wife, nor by his six children. He was also responsible for the three children of his brother Elie Sagatwa. Five of his nine children were in Madagascar at the time of his asylum application; the four youngest children were with his wife in Nairobi.

When Rwabukumba arrived in Belgium, he carried a Rwandan passport, issued in Kigali in 1992, and valid until 1997. He also had a second passport, issued by the Rwandan Embassy in Paris on 19 July 1994 and valid until 1999. In addition, he had a Belgian visa, valid for 90 days and issued by the Belgian Embassy in Bangui (Central African Republic) on 4 November 1994. This raised questions from the Belgian media.[4]

[2] Report made on behalf of the Parliamentary Commission of Inquiry into the events in Rwanda, by Mr Mahoux and Mr Verhofstadt on 6 December 1997, *Doc parl*, Senate, 1997–98, 1–611/7, Appendix 2, C, 13 (Extracts from G Prunier, *The Rwanda Crisis. History of a Genocide* (London, Hurst & Co, 1995).

[3] ibid 141.

[4] *FET* (20 August 1997): 'The Belgian honorary consul in the Central African Republic, Etienne Lamarche, issued a Belgian visa to Séraphin Rwabukumba after the Rwandan genocide in 1994 without having followed the prescribed procedures. Rwabukumba is considered one of the brains of the genocide. Lamarche, honorary consul in Bangui since mid-May 1994, issued visas to some Rwandans suspected of having played a role in the genocide. In a telephone reaction, Lamarche says he remembers nothing. He can no longer consult the files because, during the unrest in the Central African Republic, the honorary consulate was looted'.

10.3. Further Examination of His Asylum Application (28 February 1996)

Rwabukumba's asylum application, lodged on 22 November 1994, was declared inadmissible on 1 December by the Aliens Office *without* order to leave the territory. According to that Office, his application was clearly based on grounds unrelated to asylum, because it was fraudulent. Moreover, after leaving his country he had resided for more than three months in another country. He had left the last of these countries without fear within the meaning of Article 1, paragraph 2, of the Geneva Convention. He also failed to apply for asylum when he was in Belgium on 19 May 1994.

On 5 December 1994, Rwabukumba filed an urgent appeal against the refusal decision by the Aliens Office. Accused of being part of the 'death squads', he feared being executed immediately on his return to Rwanda. This would have been the case for several members of his family. He denied having committed or participated in any crime, either in his country or abroad. He also contested being a sponsor of the Radiotélévision Libre Mille Collines (RTLM)[5] or a probable actor in a resumption of hostilities.

Before coming to Belgium, he spent a few months in several African countries trying to reunite his family. At the beginning of May 1994, he went to France for urgent surgery. Immediately after his discharge from hospital, he came to Belgium for physiotherapy. Finding it impossible to return to his country, he applied for a Belgian visa. According to him, Tutsi threatened him all over the world because he was part of the Habyarimana family. All his assets in Rwanda were allegedly intentionally destroyed after the Rwandan Patriotic Front (RPF) took power. Belgium was the first country in which he stayed at a fixed address after fleeing Rwanda. In addition, he owned a property in Belgium.

He was heard at the Commission General on 15 May 1995. On 28 February 1996, I decided that further examination was necessary. A possible application of the exclusion clause in Article 1, paragraph F, of the Geneva Convention requires an examination of merits.[6]

10.4. 'Not a Land of Asylum': Application of the Exclusion Clause (29 March 1996)

Between December 1994 and the further examination decision of 28 February 1996, I received dozens of letters from Rwabukumba and his counsel.[7] These

[5] On RTLM, see A Thompson (ed), *The Media and the Rwanda Genocide* (London, Pluto Press, 2007).

[6] See above p 50 (n 4).

[7] Me Luc De Temmerman of the Brussels Bar.

letters emphasised his innocence and the fact that he was in no way associated with the genocide. They also denounced the false statements published about him and the situation in Rwanda. He hoped that I would ignore these claims, which he said emanated from the current regime and were strongly anti-Hutu inspired. In his letters and during his hearing at the Commission General, he contradicted the accusations made against him. That he belonged to the *Akazu*, the Zero Network or the death squads were, according to him, only myths and an unwarranted accusation on the part of the new regime and journalists who did not know what they were talking about. His counsel strongly attacked international sources, the press and institutions that continually spoke of genocide against the Tutsi minority and the moderate Hutu, programmed and planned by previous authorities. No one had shown any plan or document that could have demonstrated that.

Generally, Rwabukumba was considered the financier and banker of the '*Interahamwe*'. He would have bought weapons for them. Yet, he claimed to have no connection with them and certainly not in the purchase or distribution of weapons or rearmament of the ex-FAR (Rwandan Armed Forces). To prove this, he authorised the investigating judge to check his bank accounts. He said that he had occasionally paid money to the National Republican Movement for Democracy and Development (MRND) out of sympathy, without ever having been a member. Although it was generally accepted that he was one of the leading figures in the death squads, he claimed to be unaware of their existence.

On 29 March 1996, I denied him refugee status. In my decision, I noted that multiple sources, although of very diverse origin, were consistent in the attribution to Rwabukumba of 'a discreet but extremely influential role at the very heart of the Rwandan regime, which committed a premeditated and systematic genocide'.[8] Among these sources, I quoted Colette Braeckman,[9] Jean-Pierre Chrétien,[10] Filip Reyntjens,[11] André Guichaoua,[12] African Rights,[13] Els De Temmerman,[14] François Misser[15] and Mark Heirman.[16] These writings all mentioned Rwabukumba explicitly by name concerning his membership of the *Akazu*, the Zero Network, the *Interahamwe* or the RTLM.

[8] According to the Preliminary Report (annexed to document S/1994/1125 of 4 October 1994) of three independent experts (from Mali, Guinea and Togo), appointed pursuant to UN Security Council Resolution 935 (1994), 'there exists overwhelming evidence to prove that acts of genocide against Tutsi group were perpetrated by Hutu elements in a *concerted, planned, systematic and methodical* way' (§44).

[9] C Braeckman, *Rwanda: histoire d'un génocide* (Paris, Fayard, 1994) 104.

[10] J-P Chrétien, *Rwanda: les médias du génocide* (Paris, Karthala, 1995) 23 and 47.

[11] F Reyntjens, *L'Afrique des Grands Lacs en crise* (Paris, Karthala, 1994) 190.

[12] A Guichaoua, *Les crises politiques au Burundi et au Rwanda (1993–1994)* (University of Lille, Karthala, 1995) 268 and 765.

[13] African Rights, *Rwanda: Death, Despair and Defiance* (London, African Rights, 1995) 64, 66 and 102.

[14] E De Temmerman, *De doden zijn niet dood – Rwanda, een ooggetuigenverslag* (Grand-Bigard, Globe, 1995) 88.

[15] F Misser, *Vers un nouveau Rwanda?* (Brussels, Luc Pire and Karthala, 1995) 23; and F Misser, 'Radio la mort' *Témoignage chrétien* (3 June 1994).

[16] M Heirman, 'Ruanda: Het land van duizend leugens' *IPIS-brochure* No 79 (Antwerp, 1995) 32 and 51.

In that decision, I noted that the massacres committed in Rwanda in 1994 had been described as genocide and crimes against humanity. The exclusion clause is applicable if there are 'serious reasons' for considering that the person committed one of these crimes. The asylum procedure does not require the establishment of formal evidence as required by a criminal procedure. The exclusion clause may also apply to accomplices or members of criminal organisations found collectively responsible for such acts, provided they have acted with knowledge of the criminal objectives pursued.[17]

I considered that, even if the person concerned had not been directly involved in serious crimes against humanity, that circumstance would be irrelevant, since he knowingly encouraged and facilitated them by his material assistance. I considered that

> for such a person Belgium could not be a land of asylum where the person concerned could in peace reap the fruits that his family had accumulated in the exercise of a power that was guilty of the worst violations of human rights, including genocide and mass killings.

Under the exclusion clause, I denied him the benefit of the Geneva Convention.

10.5. 'Negationist': The Permanent Board Confirms Exclusion Clause (4 March 1998)

On 11 April 1996, Rwabukumba appealed to the Permanent Board against my refusal. According to him, my decision was based on unconvincing documents. Those articles, books and reports were part of sources identified as pro-RPF or were in any case without any basis.

According to Rwabukumba, he should have been arrested, charged, or at least placed at the disposal of the Belgian or international authorities if he had been guilty of the acts that were alleged against him. All his bank accounts had been scrutinised by the Belgian authorities, who had been unable to identify any movement that would support the theory that he was the 'big financier'[18] of the former Rwandan regime. There was no 'serious reason to consider' that he had participated in any way in genocide or crimes against humanity. I had committed an obvious abuse of the law in that I had used legal provisions for a politically position.

[17] F Schnyder, *The Status of Refugee in International Law* (Leyde, Sijthoff, 1966) 277.

[18] K Vidal, *DM* (17 July 1998): 'Séraphin Rwabukumba is considered to be the banker of the genocidal regime. He was head of the currency department of the Central Bank of Rwanda. He systematically extorted businessmen. According to the Governor of the National Bank, he was the pivotal figure in the arms and drug trade. He was also one of the most important shareholders of the "broadcast of hatred", *Radiotélévision des Mille Collines* (RTLM). He maintains his innocence: "On those days, I had a fever of 40° and I was in bed". During his hearing by the Permanent Board, he shot himself in the foot by questioning the genocide'.

According to the Permanent Board, which confirmed my refusal on 4 March 1998, there was no reason to doubt the reality of the genocide.[19] There were numerous reports of genocide against the Tutsi population. The Permanent Board did not give any credence to the negationist argument put forward by the appellant. The report of the Parliamentary Commission of Inquiry into the events in Rwanda confirmed the pre-eminent role played by the applicant at the highest spheres of power in Rwanda prior to 1994. A State Security note of 9 January 1995 unambiguously concluded that Rwabukumba played a predominant role in the faction that organised and funded the *interahamwe* militias and other death squads.

The Permanent Board recognised, however, that there was a risk that 'commentators could mix, make hasty or biased judgments, or even engage in disinformation campaigns'. In this case, however, all the authors agree; for the most part they are personalities whose scientific qualities are unanimously recognised. The only condition for the application of the exclusion clause is the existence of 'serious reasons'. Although not criminal evidence, 'there is a body of evidence upon which the Commissioner General could validly base his decision in the absence of any serious evidence to the contrary'.

The Permanent Board found that the applicant had not contributed in good faith to the establishment of the facts of which he wished to contest the relevance:

> The applicant endeavours to veil the exact nature of his activities between 1990 and 1994, as well as during the period immediately following his flight in April 1994; this attitude leads him to deny the evidence, from the very reality of the genocide to ancillary points such as the advantages he derived from his relationship with the President in the management of his affairs or even the importance of these, which he seeks to minimise; the credit that can be given to its denials is reduced to nothing.

The Permanent Board concluded that he could not benefit from international protection under the Geneva Convention. It did not recognise the applicant as a refugee.

10.6. A Web of Asylum Applications

The following can only be understood by learning about the interference with the asylum applications of Rwabukumba's close family members. Before the decision of the Permanent Board, several members of his family had arrived in Belgium. After leaving Kigali in June 1994, his wife with three of their children (born 1982, 1983 and 1990 respectively) and two children (born 1985 and 1987) of his brother-in-law Elie Sagatwa arrived in Belgium on 8 December 1994 with a valid visa.

[19] Referring to the State Security report (n 1) 141.

On 29 December 1994, she filed an asylum application. On 13 January 1995, the Aliens Office refused her the stay but *without* order to leave the territory:

> Her application had to be rejected on the grounds that she was in solidarity with her husband and that the applicant arrived in Belgium from Kenya, the last country where she stayed and left without fear.

On 12 March 1996, I decided that further examination was necessary. Two weeks later, I refused her refugee status on 29 March 1996, the day I made the same decision about her spouse:

> The fears of persecution she claims to have in her country of origin are 'the consequence of the serious human rights violations committed in Rwanda' by her husband's membership in the Zero Network of which she was aware and which she admitted and approved.[20]

Three of her children's asylum applications were refused three days later on 1 April 1996.

My refusal decision, against which she filed an appeal on 11 April 1996, was confirmed on 4 March 1998 by the Permanent Board, on the same day as the refusal decision concerning her husband. By her failure to cooperate, she herself had become unable to establish that she had reasonable grounds to fear persecution on one of the grounds set out in the Geneva Convention:

> That, in fact, the only certain element available to the Permanent Board is the existence of a conjugal relationship between the applicant and a person suspected of participating in crimes against humanity and the preparation of genocide, which does not, as such, correspond to any of the criteria justifying the granting of international protection under the Geneva Convention;
>
> That for the remainder, it cannot be inferred from the applicant's remarks that she would be at risk of persecution because of her political convictions, since they are non-existent in her view; that she acknowledges that her sisters have returned to the country and are not worried.

At the time Rwabukumba's asylum application was pending before the Permanent Board, two of his children and a dependent daughter of Elie Sagatwa were in Germany. Another daughter of Rwabukumba was in France. For these children, Rwabukumba had asked the Aliens Office, on 3 July 1997, to have them come and have their files examined together. For another daughter, born in 1980, who was in Germany and had applied for asylum, he had already applied for family reunification on 23 December 1996. Based on Article 36 of the Convention implementing the Schengen Agreement, this request was welcomed on 25 June 1997. She arrived in Belgium on 30 July 1997. She applied for asylum on 19 August.[21]

[20] I was referring to decision (No 50266) of the French Appeals Commission concerning Madame Jean-Claude Duvalier, the wife of the former President of Haiti (CdE, France, 3 July 1992, reg 81962).

[21] Art 36 of the Convention of 19 June 1990 implementing the Schengen Agreement of 14 June 1985 on the gradual abolition of checks at their common borders (*M.B.*, 15 October 1993): 'Any Contracting

10.7. Order to Leave the Territory: The Conseil d'Etat Blows Hot and Cold (13 May 1998)

The order to leave the territory was notified to Rwabukumba and his wife on 13 May 1998. The removal order involved both parents and their children. On 14 May, the parents brought an appeal to the Conseil d'Etat against this order. According to them, it constituted an interference in their right to respect for private and family life (Article 8 ECHR). They noted that both their daughter's application for asylum on 19 August 1997 and that of Rwabukumba's mother were still pending.

The Conseil d'Etat noted that at no time in the proceedings had the presence in Belgium of the appellant's mother (then 82 years old) been invoked. The Belgian authorities could therefore not be accused of not having taken this element into account. His minor daughter, for whom an application for family reunification had been made on 23 December 1996, had been in Belgium since 30 July 1997. For a little less than a year, she lived under the same roof and was indeed part of family life in Belgium.

The Conseil d'Etat considered that the order to leave the territory, taken on 13 May 1998, was clearly an interference in the right to respect for family life enshrined in Article 8 ECHR, their daughter's asylum application still pending. Removal of the applicants from the territory would constitute a serious and hardly repairable prejudice. The applicants argued that 'the removal of their minor child would break up this family that was already wounded by the war and deprive them of any contact with their daughter'.[22] In its judgment of 29 May 1998, the Conseil d'Etat decided to suspend the execution of the order to leave the territory, notified to the applicants and valid for three of their children. This suspension was lifted on 4 December 1998.[23]

The three children whom I had refused on 2 April 1996, reintroduced asylum applications on 23 July 1998 on their own behalf. These were also rejected by the Aliens Office on 24 August. In an urgent appeal filed on 26 August, Commissioner General Luc De Smet confirmed the refusal decision in all three cases on 13 January 1999. They had not put forward any new evidence to establish a personal fear of persecution within the meaning of Article 1 of the Geneva Convention. According to the Commissioner General, they could be removed to Rwanda. However, he drew the Minister's attention to the fact that they were minors under their national law.

Party responsible for processing an application for asylum may, for humanitarian reasons, based in particular on family or cultural grounds, ask another Contracting Party to assume that responsibility provided that the asylum seeker so desires. The Contracting Party to which such a request is made shall consider whether it can be granted'.

[22] CdE, No 73.957 (29 May 1998).

[23] CdE, No 77.386 (4 December 1998).

On 21 January 1999, the three children, represented by their mother, filed a request for a suspension with extreme urgency before the Conseil d'Etat concerning the confirmatory decision of the Commissioner General. They claimed that the refusal of their first refugee application, as well as that of their father, was based on the exclusion clause. According to them, this clause could in no case be extended to the family members of the persons concerned. The disputed decision could not refer to a decision based on an exclusion clause.

However, the mother had expressly indicated that, if granted refugee status, she wanted it to be extended to her children. When, on 4 March 1998, the Permanent Board refused to recognise her as a refugee, this decision was ipso facto extended to her minor children. Consequently, according to the decision of the Conseil d'Etat of 28 January 1999, there was no lack of reasons in the decision of the Commissioner General of 13 January 1999 concerning the second asylum application:

> Contrary to the applicants' contention, the mother's application for asylum was not rejected based on Article 1, para F, of the Geneva Convention, but because she had not established that she remained away from her country for fear within the meaning of Article 1, para A, al 2, of the aforementioned Geneva Convention; that her arguments were contradicted by the facts and therefore not serious.[24]

10.8. PS: Regularised, and Almost a Belgian Citizen

Despite the refusal decisions concerning Rwabukumba as well as his wife and children, the Rwabukumba family could reside in Belgium undisturbed, much to the displeasure of the victims of the genocide.[25] In Kigali too it was misunderstood:

> Rwandan President [since 2000] Paul Kagame[26] this week called for more support from the international community, especially from European countries, in arresting those responsible for the genocide: 'There is still much to do'. Kagame accused some countries of tolerating suspects. He mentioned among others Séraphin Rwabukumba, who resided in Belgium. Complaints were filed against him by the Rwandan Government, non-governmental organisations, and citizens.[27]

It seems that Rwabukumba's stay was regularised in 2001,[28] but he did not become Belgian.

[24] CdE, No 78.447 (28 January 1999).

[25] Yves Bastin quoted Gasana Ndoba: 'Today, it is the victims who raze the walls, not the suspects. Every day, victims meet alleged executioners in the subway, at the CPAS, at the Commission General' (*LNG*, 25 July 1997).

[26] Previously (since 1994) Vice-President of Rwanda. About Kagame, see S Kinzer, *A Thousand Hills: Rwanda's Rebirth and The Man Who Dreamed It* (Hoboken, NJ, Wiley, 2008).

[27] 'Regio kort. Rwanda' (*DM*, 18 April 2002).

[28] *HLN* (27 October 2009). In 2009, he claimed to have an indefinite residence permit (Colette Braeckman's diary, *LS*, 20 August 2009).

On 27 October 2009, referring to *Le Soir*, *Het Laatste Nieuws* reported:

> Séraphin Rwabukumba, the brother-in-law of the assassinated Rwandan President Habyarimana, and a relative of the executioners of the genocide in that African country, asked for his Belgian naturalisation. His wife and children have already obtained Belgian nationality.

On 24 January 2011, *Het Laatste Nieuws* continued:

> Séraphin Rwabukumba, a brother-in-law of the assassinated Rwandan President, Juvénal Habyarimana, does not provisionally receive Belgian nationality. This was decided by the Brussels Court of Appeal. The man had made an application in 2006, but after the negative opinion of the Public Prosecutor's Office, first the Tribunal of first instance in Brussels and now the Court of Appeal decided that more clarity was needed first.

11

I Recognise Both Too Many and not Enough Refugees (1995)

A judicial inquiry was opened concerning recognitions that would be unjustified, especially for Lebanese and Zairians. Searches took place on 21 March 1995 throughout the country. The search at the Commission General was under the watchful eye of the media. Later, all this turned out to be 'much ado about nothing'. At the same time, criticism was levelled at me for not recognising enough refugees. I responded to all these criticisms.

11.1. 'Schemes at the Commission General'

On 21 March 1995, searches were carried out in several places, including the Commission General, which was then located in the North Gate building (150 Boulevard E Jacqmain since mid-December 1999: 6 Boulevard Albert II).

11.1.1. Search at the Commission General (21 March 1995)

On 2 February 1995, at the insistence of Jean-François Pirot, who – as Adviser – was the most senior French-speaking official at the Commission General, I disclosed certain documents to the BSR. Referring to Article 29 of the Code of Criminal Procedure,[1] he told me that the BSR was investigating Zairean asylum seekers' channels. I asked to be able to explain the context of this communication.

In fact, the context consisted of a rather strong personal antagonism between the Adviser and the French-speaking Deputy Commissioner Xavier De Beys. The Adviser, who was very familiar with asylum issues, belonged to the conservative wing of the Christian Democrats (PSC). He was in favour of a strict asylum policy. The Deputy Commissioner, who did not excel in his knowledge of asylum

[1] Art 29, §1: 'Every constituted authority, every official or public officer … who, in the performance of his duties, shall acquire knowledge of a crime or offence, shall be required to give immediate notice to the Prosecutor'.

issues, belonged to the progressive wing of the same party. He was in favour of a broader recognition policy. This context also included relations of good neighbourliness between Jean-François Pirot and 'first marshal' Aimé Bille[2] of the BSR, to whom he had complained. That first marshal wanted to investigate all this. Jean-François Pirot provided him with information. In the two months preceding the searches, he had no less than 40 telephone contacts with the first marshal. He then forwarded a file to the investigating judge Jacques Pignolet. In his own words, the first marshal had been working for a long time with the investigating judge.

On the morning of 21 March 1995, I was invited to go to the headquarters of the BSR. According to *De Standaard*, I had been 'intercepted' a few hours before the searches. A major operation was under way. I was questioned at length about the functioning of my services. It emerged that many of the suspicions were based solely on peccadillos. The attention to issues of little importance was striking. I was asked if it was 'normal' for the Deputy Commissioner to take home at night the *Le Soir* and *La Libre Belgique* newspapers. The first marshal had to buy his newspaper himself. I was asked if I had received any gifts. I replied that once I had received a small frame: it was a gift of good relationship, from the Gendarmerie.

In the early afternoon, I was able to accompany the investigating judge and about 20 investigators in a raid on the Commission General. A press photographer was waiting for us there.[3] A team from the Flemish commercial TV station VTM made a filmed report of this sensational operation. Investigators confiscated 130 files relating to asylum seekers. The headlines in the press said it all:

> Scheming around Asylum Cases (*DS*); The Brussels Public Prosecutor's Office on the Trail of Human Trafficking in Zaire, Trafficking in Human Beings Leading to the Commission General (*DM*); Search at the Commission General for Refugees (*LS*).

It was first reported that 'The Deputy Commissioner General [*sic*] was arrested'.[4] Later it appeared that this was incorrect.

On 23 March 1995, two Zairians were arrested. One, who presented himself as a lawyer, allegedly helped Zairean asylum seekers who had escaped from the transit zone. The other, Joseph Sita Nsoni Zeno, allegedly provided imaginary stories to Zairean asylum seekers. On 15 April 1995, in the context of these searches, mention was made of the arrest on 11 April of a Lebanese man named Camille Harb. Six days later he was released by the Brussels Chamber of Indictment of the Court of Appeal of Brussels.

[2] He was '*premier maréchal des logis*', a non-commissioned officer of the BSR, the Judicial Branch of the Gendarmerie, with the rank of first sergeant.

[3] See the photo of Paul Bolsius subtitled: 'Marc Bossuyt, Commissioner General for Refugees, leads the BSR to his Service for Search' (*DS*, 22 February 1995).

[4] Jeroen Wils, *DS* (22 February 1995).

11.1.2. Fraud in the Asylum Procedure (April 1995)

On 5 April 1995, during the visit to the Commission General of Johan Vande Lanotte, Minister of the Interior (since 10 October 1994), I addressed him in the following terms:

> Everyone at the Commission General knows that we are constantly confronted with fraud. It is not surprising to us that people outside the Commission General should be paid for their interventions at the Commission General. There is, on the other hand, no evidence that anyone at the Commission General was paid to assist in the examination of refugee applications. I remain firmly convinced that no one at the Commission General has ever committed an act of corruption.
>
> Some investigative acts were clearly based on mere gossip, mostly by former employees of the Commission General. If we consider the means used to verify the validity of this gossip, we do not understand how important crimes have still not been solved in Belgium.[5] Especially in the context of a judicial inquiry, it is necessary to know how to balance things and to avoid confusion between, on the one hand, indications – as weak as they are – of criminal wrongdoing and, on the other hand, regrettable gossip, inspired by frustration, personal pettiness, or antagonism.

In view of the great interest in fraud in the context of the asylum procedure, I forwarded, on 6 April 1995, to Prosecutor Benoit Dejemeppe a list of 6,616 asylum applications. This concerned applications in which I had taken confirmatory decisions in connection with urgent appeals lodged in 1993 and 1994 based on the fraudulent nature of those applications. This concerned 44 per cent of the 14,777 confirmatory decisions. I had also learned that the Aliens Office had informed the Office of the Prosecutor that the fingerprint check had revealed that undeniable fraud had been found in a few hundred cases.[6] I had no idea what that Office had done with these cases of fraud in the asylum procedure.

The charges of fraud led to numerous insinuations about the operation of the Commission General. In addition, Jean-François Pirot complained to *La Libre Belgique* on 5 May 1995 of his transfer from the Commission General to the General Police of the Kingdom.[7] He considered this transfer as a sanction and said that it had affected his honour. He said he was outraged by the laxity of the Commission General. The next day[8] I reacted by saying that Jean-François Pirot felt uncomfortable since his opinions were rarely shared by the sections called upon to examine asylum applications. The Adviser had conceived a certain bitterness in the fact that neither the Minister of the Interior nor I had seen fit to

[5] According to Jean-Claude Matgen (*LLB*, 21 April 1995): 'A sentence that shocked the investigators'.

[6] *LNG* (13 April 1995) 'Printrak Stalks Cheaters': 'Printrak has Uncovered 560 Frauds on 21,015 Fingerprints'. Printrak was the computer system that had been identifying fingerprints for a year and a half.

[7] Jean-Claude Matgen: 'A Former Advisor of Bossuyt Accuses'.

[8] Jean-Claude Matgen, 6 May 1995: 'Bossuyt Defends his Office. The Evils of which he is Accused come from a Suspicious and Petty Relentlessness'.

warmly defend his note on the admissibility rate considered too high for Zairean refugee candidates.

The (francophone) League for Human Rights organised the leak of this note of 9 September 1993 in *Le Soir* of 6 November 1994, together with the memo of 26 January 1993 on the evaluation system. The 'Pirot Note' reported an 'unsustainable admissibility percentage' of 42 per cent for Zairians compared with 27 per cent for other nationalities. The note also drew attention to the much higher percentage of admissibility of the French-speaking section of Africa compared with that of the Dutch-speaking section.[9] It stressed that 'Refusal is the rule; further examination must be the exception'. This was the subject of much criticism. Curiously, there was more criticism of the Commission General where 53 per cent of the decisions taken concerning Zairean asylum seekers were negative, than of the Aliens Office where 89 per cent of the decisions taken at first instance concerning Zairean asylum seekers were negative. The note was signed by Jean-François Pirot. I allowed it to be released because I felt that my staff should know his viewpoint.[10]

On 23 November 1994, the Minister of the Interior, Johan Vande Lanotte, replied to the interpellations of MPs Denis Grimberghs (PSC) and Henri Simons (Ecolo) that he considered the note 'slightly unnuanced'. On 7 December 1994, he replied to an enquiry by Senator Frans Lozie and a question by Senator Paul Pataer that he did not agree with the contents of the note. Ecolo and Agalev asked for my resignation. That the Aliens Office, which reports directly to the Minister of the Interior, had declared only 11 per cent of these Zairean applications admissible, did not cause any problems for anyone. Nor for the Minister. Not even for the League. I had initially refused Jean-François Pirot's transfer application dated 23 February 1995, knowing that a judicial inquiry was under way at his instigation. After the searches, his position at the Commission General had become untenable.

On 31 May 1995, I informed the investigating judge that I had completed the administrative investigation initiated by the searches he had ordered. I gave him 14 notes concerning that investigation. When Aimé Bille, the first marshal, asked for additional notes, I sent them to the investigating judge on 15 June 1995. In my covering letter, I pointed out that in an administrative asylum procedure, the hearing of the applicants is done at the Commission General exclusively by university trained civil servants, almost all jurists. I was struck by the fact that during a judicial proceeding the hearing of my collaborators, my deputies and me was entrusted to first marshals of the Gendarmerie. If he had approached me beforehand, it would have been possible to avoid serious disruption in the operation of the Commission General which had caused it significant harm and prejudice to the public interest.

[9] *LDH* (13 December 1994).
[10] Anne-Françoise Moyson, *La Cité* (1 December 1994).

11.1.3. Sita and the 'Zairean Network'

As regards Sita's action in Zaire, it should be noted that he was known as an opponent of President Joseph-Désiré Mobutu (1965–97). Between 1986 and 1989, he had been detained a few times and even for an entire year at the premises of the Military Action and Intelligence Service (SARM) in Kinshasa.[11] On 1 August 1990, I recognised him as a refugee.

In a letter dated 4 October 1993 addressed to the President of the Permanent Board and to me, the Chairperson of the UDPS in Kinshasa, Frédéric Kibassa Maliba, had designated him as 'his personal and direct representative for all testimony, intelligence and information concerning the members working in the clandestine structures of the UDPS, placed under the direct responsibility of the National Presidency of the UDPS in Zaire'. On 24 November 1994, the National Secretary of the UDPS confirmed to me once again that the '*clandestins*'[12] were under the jurisdiction of Sita.

An internal note of 18 May 1995 concerning the 54 Zairean files seized showed that the applications were declared admissible in 16 cases by the Aliens Office and in 35 cases by my intervention. These 35 cases consisted of 16 favourable opinions and 19 confirmatory decisions taken on proposals from 15 different protection officers. In 24 cases, recognition was given on the proposal of 10 different protection officers. In five cases there were substantiated refusals; 24 applications were still being processed. There was no indication that officials at the Commission General were involved in fraudulent practices.

Out of a total of 149 Zairean refugee recognitions between 1991 and 1994, there were in 44 files 70 certificates issued by 24 persons who had intervened on behalf of the UDPS. With nine certificates, it was Sita who intervened most frequently. During these four years, nearly 12,000 Zairean asylum applications were submitted. Sita was the only one with a document designating him as the UDPS representative. He himself had acknowledged that it was difficult for him to refuse such certificates to his compatriots.

The note stated that such a certificate was only one element in determining whether an asylum applicant was a refugee. It could not turn an inconsistent file into a positive decision. If it was not ruled out that Sita sometimes issued non-credible certificates, this did not prevent others from having value. It would be a mistake to believe that a case in which Sita intervened would ipso facto be fraudulent. In no case was it found that any member of the Commission General acted unlawfully.

[11] *La Meuse* (23 and 29 March 1995). Sita was presented as 'close to [Etienne] Tshisekedi' (*LDH*, 29 March 1995).

[12] 'Some people working in the arcana of power are secretly operating on behalf of the UDPS by providing them with information'.

11.1.4. Harb and the 'Lebanese Network'

Regarding Camille Harb's interventions in certain Lebanese cases, an internal note dated 15 May 1995 stated that he presented himself as a lawyer, without specifying the Bar to which he belonged, and as vice-chairperson of the Lebanese League for Human Rights. For a time, he often accompanied a lawyer who intervened on behalf of Lebanese asylum seekers. He was present at meetings at the Commission General with Amnesty International's delegate in Lebanon and with the (francophone) League for Human Rights in Brussels. Gradually, he lost the confidence of my collaborators by his untimely visits, by his multiple requests on the evolution of the processing of files of Lebanese asylum seekers, and by his presentation of documents of which he was mostly the sole author. At the beginning of 1993, it was recommended that employees adopt a reserved attitude towards him.

Based on internal notes from several collaborators, on 31 May 1995 I drafted a very elaborate note on the 25 asylum applications in which Harb and/or befriended lawyers intervened. At the outset, it was noted that the Lebanese applications did not excel by their number (930 or 0.9 per cent of the total number of applications) or by their abusive character (a recognition rate of 18 per cent compared with an average of 7.5 per cent). Over a period of two and a half years, it concerned 16 families. Only two of these families filed applications after Deputy Commissioner Xavier De Beys took office on 1 August 1992.[13] It was therefore completely unfounded to claim that he was involved in a Lebanese network.[14] Of these 25 asylum applications, 11 were declared admissible by the Aliens Office and 12 on the proposal of eight different protection officers of the Commission General. For two asylum applications, I made a confirmatory decision of inadmissibility.

As for the processing on the merits, only one file concerning a couple was awaiting a decision at the Commission General. It was a complex case of a surgeon in a Brussels hospital. For this asylum applicant, I had made five requests for information to the Ministry of Foreign Affairs to determine whether the exclusion clause should be applied. Except for six asylum applications involving two families, all other asylum applications had led to a refusal decision. One of these other decisions was revised by the Permanent Board. After examination, it turned out that for one family greater caution would probably have been welcome. The decision was taken by the French-speaking Deputy Commissioner. At that time, for six weeks, he exercised the full powers of the Commissioner General. At that time I was prevented because of my participation in the European elections. The Deputy

[13] The French-speaking Deputy Commissioner admitted having gone to a restaurant with Harb on three occasions for a modest meal: one evening, in the company of his wife, where the refugee issue was not discussed; a second time, before a conference of Harb's brother, a priest in Lebanon, at the Commission General; and a third time, in the company of a befriended lawyer, without addressing the general situation in Lebanon. This is what Anne De Graaf called in her bold title in *Het Laatste Nieuws* of 24 March 1995: 'Asylum Lawyers very Generous for Civil Servants'.

[14] J-C M, *LLB* (23 March 1995): 'File Traffic: Personnel Involved?'.

Commissioner was therefore responsible for assessing the various elements of the case. He could also assess to what extent humanitarian and compassionate considerations could influence the decision and/or to what extent the benefit of the doubt could be granted.

The note stressed that my mission as Commissioner General was to protect refugees. It could not be confused with that of a police service. I had neither the means nor the vocation for it. A margin of error benefiting the applicant was allowed. Appeals to the Permanent Board and/or the Conseil d'Etat are provided for. Even though I had taken more than 20,000 decisions in 1994, the rate of difference in assessment by the appeal bodies was much lower than that between the various bodies in the judiciary.

11.1.5. In the End, it was 'Much Ado about Nothing' (2000–01)

More than five years after the beginning of the investigation, the Brussels Correctional Tribunal, at its hearing on 23 May 2000, dealt with the charges against Harb. The latter was prosecuted for attempted corruption of a civil servant by having offered three meals and a small painting. He was also being sued for claiming the title of lawyer without being registered with the Bar Association. His counsel filed a new exhibit, revealing his status as a lawyer at the Beirut Bar. The substitute prosecutor acknowledged that the BSR had exceeded its role in the investigation. He reduced Harb's interventions to those of a lobbyist. The lunches and the gift were to be placed in a social context related to this role. The corruption attempt was not established. Harb complained bitterly of the harassment of the investigators. They had tried to make him confess that he had paid civil servants at the Commission General. Which he always denied. After deliberation, Harb was acquitted.

Another year later, on 27 June 2001, the Sita case was dealt with by the Brussels Correctional Tribunal. The prevention of forgery in writing in respect of some certificates from 1992 and 1993 was considered established. Their purpose was to obtain refugee status for different persons. Considering the possibility of amendment of the accused and the concern not to hinder his professional future, the Tribunal of first instance ordered the simple suspension of the sentence for five years. This doesn't even figure on his criminal record.

11.1.6. The First Marshal and the X Witnesses (1996–2001)

Meanwhile, the first marshal Aimé Bille had taken care of something else. In 1996, in the aftermath of the *Dutroux* case,[15] he and warrant officer Patrick De

[15] Marc Dutroux was arrested on 13 August 1996 and sentenced to life imprisonment on 22 June 2004.

Baets began hearing the so-called 'X witnesses'. This was the result of the green telephone line opened by Neufchâteau investigating judge Jean-Marc Connerotte. On this line, citizens could communicate information about paedophilia. One of these witnesses gained a great reputation in the media: Regina Louf, alias 'X1'. In 1997, tensions rose between the investigators and their chiefs. Colleagues of theirs were responsible for a 'rereading' of witness X's statements. Subsequently, in July 1997, the De Baets–Bille team was removed from the investigation. They were not allowed to continue to investigate criminal records. On 26 August 1997, a judicial charge against them for forgery in writing was entrusted to investigating judge Jacques Pignolet. For a long time, the first marshal had worked closely with him. On 17 February 1998, the last 'rereading' was sent to the investigating judge.

When Commissioner General Luc De Smet became aware of the ongoing investigation concerning first marshal Aimé Bille, he referred, on 6 July 1998 in letters addressed to the Prosecutor General of the Brussels Court of Appeal and to the Commander of the Gendarmerie, to the searches on 21 March 1995. In particular, he referred to the letters I had addressed to investigating judge Jacques Pignolet. In these letters I contested that the investigation concerning the Commission General could be conducted in an objective, impartial manner and without prejudice by the said first marshal.

On 20 May 1999, I was heard by investigators from the Control Committee of the Police. I admitted that first marshal Aimé Bille had not committed unlawful acts. His behaviour towards me had been correct. I complained about the media leaks and the scale of the action that I considered out of proportion. I was wondering about the appropriateness of the numerous searches and surveillance missions. I was referring to the obstinacy, the frustrations and the mean-spiritedness of the first marshal. He seemed especially motivated by the idea of attacking at all costs personalities he thought important. I was under the impression that the non-commissioned officers of the Gendarmerie were conducting investigations without much control from their hierarchical authorities. It was at the request of these non-commissioned officers that the magistrates ordered the missions entrusted to them.

In response to an oral question from Senator Frans Lozie, Minister of Justice Marc Verwilghen replied on 23 December 1999 that the first marshal could receive new judicial missions, but only outside the district of Brussels.[16] The Prosecutor General of the Brussels Court of Appeal continued to oppose the assignment of such tasks to warrant officer Patrick De Baets. According to an internal Gendarmerie investigation, completed in 2000, the two gendarmes had not committed any mistakes. On 30 March 2000, however, the Prosecutor General considered that there was a breach of trust between the judiciary and them. They had to stay away from criminal investigations. The investigating judge Jacques Pignolet concluded, on 21 January 2001, that nothing could be put in their charge.

[16] *Ann parl*, Senate (23 December 1999).

11.2. Criticism from All Sides (1994–95)

Johan Leman, the Director of the Centre for Equal Opportunities, criticised me continuously about whatever. Lawyers even formed a non-profit association (asbl) to file a criminal complaint against me. Another critic accused me of carrying out expeditious recognitions – before the end of 1995 – to 'embellish' my statistics. A platform was also offered to a former employee who had been dismissed, to blacken his former employer.

11.2.1. The Leman Centre (1994)

From time to time, Johan Leman felt an urge to criticise me. By the time of the incident concerning the charters, when he was chief of staff of the Royal Commissioner for Immigration Policy (1989–93), he had already expressed himself (on 25 January 1992) in a very pretentious way in my regard (see above p 62–63). Once director of the Centre for Equal Opportunities and the Fight Against Racism (1993–2004) there was already (according to *De Standaard*) in his interim report of 1 July 1994, 'a notable shift from the traditional problem of migrants to that of asylum seekers'. He himself said: 'As long as I'm allowed, I'll deal with asylum seekers'.[17]

He was particularly shocked by the refusal of visas to Rwandans and their lack of reception. In a correction dated 15 July, he specified that he pointed 'at the work of the Commissioner General, therefore of Marc Bossuyt'. In a reaction published on 26 July 1994, I wrote that it should be known that I had no jurisdiction in issuing visas to foreigners, any more than the Centre. The same was true for the reception of asylum seekers. In addition, since my arrival, I had given only seven unfavourable opinions after refusals to stay or enter of Rwandans and 96 favourable. As to the merits, I had refused only three Rwandans with a reasoned decision and recognised 125 Rwandan refugees.[18] Further, at a written question of Senator Germain Dufour dated 20 July 1994, the Minister of Foreign Affairs replied that his colleague from the Interior had developed a special procedure for the flexible and rapid processing of visa applications submitted by Rwandan nationals.

In his *First Annual Report*, presented on 16 December 1994, Director Johan Leman spoke of my rather particular way of applying the law on the publicity of administrative acts. According to him, an asylum seeker should receive a copy of the hearing report. In a note dated 9 January 1995, I reminded him that the Aliens Law only prescribed access to the file during the appeals phase (*cf* above p 16 and p 141–143). From the outset, however, I granted this access, within the time

[17] *DS*; *LLB* (1 July 1994).
[18] *DS* (1 and 15 July 1994).

necessary to bring an action before the Permanent Board or, once the suspension procedure was initiated, before the Conseil d'Etat.

In this report, Director Johan Leman considered it necessary to join the criticism of the 'points system' at the Commission General:

> We note the same concern for profitability as at the Aliens Office. Civil servants could get 'good points' which would lead to a kind of 'negative decision bonus'. This is unheard of in a constitutional State.[19]

There's no need to come back on this.

According to the Leman Centre, there was at the Commission General 'a relative deterioration in the quality of interviews on admissibility'.[20] In a press release dated 19 December 1994, I replied that there was no basis for this claim. On the contrary, many efforts had been made to further improve this quality. The Centre complained that it was not consulted by the government in connection with the asylum problem. The same Centre, however, did not even include me in its working group on aliens' law, including the asylum procedure. It was therefore not surprising that the Centre's reports clearly lacked objectivity and expertise. Rather than meddling in a negative way with the problems of a few thousand asylum seekers, I felt that the Centre would do much better to give priority to the concrete problems posed by tens of thousands of illegal aliens and hundreds of thousands of immigrants. In the absence of any constructive proposal to reduce the number of illegal aliens, I pointed to a bias that hindered a balanced approach to the problem of foreigners.

In an initial reaction to the *First Annual Report* of the Centre, I said on 16 December 1994 that it should focus on the problems of migrants and illegal aliens. And that Johan Leman had better leave the asylum seekers to me.[21] For illegal aliens and migrants, there was no other independent body. For refugees and candidate refugees, the legally competent independent body was the Commissioner General. In addition, according to Article 57/28 of the Aliens Law, I had to report on my mission every year. Among other things, this report was to enable me 'to give a general assessment of the situation of refugees in Belgium and to make any suggestions [that I thought] appropriate in this area'.[22]

In a press release of 21 December 1994, Director Johan Leman stated that he did not wish to debate any issues. In my reply, I wrote that I found his repeated criticism irritating. It was obviously more comfortable to criticise if the other person did not react. The former student of the Jesuits of the Saint-Barbara College in Ghent (Rhetoric B 1963) did not appreciate the action of the Dominican father.

[19] The not-so-subtle title of his press release ('Asylum Seekers: Refusing the Policy of Good and Bad Points') sounded controversial. See above p 110–114.

[20] *LS* (17 December 1994).

[21] *HLN* (17 December 1994): 'Leman, Stay with your Migrants'.

[22] Explanatory statement of the Law of 14 July 1987 amending the Aliens Law (*Doc parl*, *Chambre*, 1986/87, No 689/1, 15).

I asked whether it was in the interests of the fight against racism to make public criticisms of me based on unilateral information. A bidding war between the Centre and the Commissioner General to see who could give the most virulent criticism of government policy would not necessarily be appreciated. I exercised my own responsibilities, true to my principles, independently, but with restraint, rather than acting as a non-governmental lobby group.

11.2.2. The asbl 'Aid to Political Refugees' (29 June 1995)

On 29 June 1995, Me Frédéric Clément de Cléty told a press conference that he and three other lawyers[23] were going to establish an asbl 'Aid to political refugees'. This non-profit association aimed to file a criminal complaint for 'coalition of civil servants'[24] against Xavier De Beys, the French-speaking Deputy Commissioner, Jean-François Pirot, former Adviser at the Commission General, and me. We were accused of violating the Geneva Convention, the ECHR, the Constitution, the Law on access to the territory and the Law on publicity of the administration.[25]

In a response to *La Libre Belgique* of 1 July 1995, I informed them that I had written to the President of the Brussels Bar on 2 February 1995 to complain about the behaviour of Me Frédéric Clément de Cléty. He was guilty of actively soliciting customers. He asked my staff to pass on his business card to asylum seekers. I didn't know how the President of the Bar responded to that complaint. I found the charges against my services to be contradictory. After Jean-François Pirot had left the Commission General, he accused it of laxity. Now, I was criticised for being overly harsh. I could have added that, as the context of the 21 March 1995 searches indicated, I could hardly imagine collusion between Xavier De Beys and Jean-François Pirot over anything.[26]

Apparently, the lawyers of the new association were very unhappy with the way in which I was applying the Law of 11 April 1994 on the publicity of the administration.[27] For the Commission General, the search for truth is a primary objective. That is why, until I had taken a decision, access to the file was not granted before the hearing had taken place. It is, in fact, essential to be able to

[23] Me José Saels, Me Michel Graindorge and Me Suzanne Hage of the Brussels Bar.

[24] Art 233 Penal Code: 'When measures contrary to laws or royal decrees have been agreed, either in a meeting of individuals or bodies depository of any part of the public authority, or by deputation or correspondence between them, the guilty parties will be sentenced to imprisonment of one month to six months'.

[25] *Vl'A* (1 July 1995).

[26] He became well known in August 1996 as the lawyer of Michel Nihoul, who was prosecuted as a sidekick of Marc Dutroux.

[27] On this Law, which came into force on 1 July 1994, see the *Eighth Annual Report* (1995) 64. Regarding the indication of the name, quality, address and telephone number of the treating official (Art 2, 3°, of that Law), I considered that my collaborators, while having no power of decision, should be protected against possible external pressures. For a long time already, the decisions mentioned the possibilities of appeal (Art 2, 4°).

verify the concordance between the account of the facts given during the interview with the Aliens Office and that produced at the Commission General.

A few weeks after the opening of the closed centre in Walem, the Bar Association had initiated an interim procedure before the President of the Tribunal of first instance in Mechelen. On 6 January 1994, the President ruled that lawyers should be informed by fax 48 hours before the hearing and that the file, together with an independent interpreter, should be made available to them no later than one working day before the hearing. The Minister of the Interior was dismayed by this judgment: 'Judges Make Asylum Policy Impossible'. It seemed impractical to find sworn interpreters for every possible language on the globe, whenever the lawyer wished to speak with his client:

> If that is the meaning of the Rule of Law, I will go to another country. This would cost no less than 1 billion BF (€25 million), but in this way the authorities are condemned to impotence.[28] The implementation of the government's asylum policy is continually thwarted. It is obstruction, through ignorance or bad faith. If this absurd decision is upheld, I will have to amend the Law (*DS*, 12 January 1994).

A decision to the contrary was taken on 18 January 1994 by the President of the Tribunal of first instance in Turnhout. He observed that these were not defence rights such as in criminal matters. This was an administrative procedure in which the refugee applicant is 'assisted' by a lawyer. It is not possible to grant access to the file to lawyers without jeopardising the discovery of the truth. A sworn interpreter was not always possible either.

On 21 January 1994, the National Judicial Commission expressed its 'great irritation'. The Interior Minister's criticism of the judge in Mechelen was considered an attack on the Belgian judiciary: 'Any comment constitutes inappropriate pressure on the independence of the judge. The citizen's trust in justice is undermined. All the Minister must do is appeal'.[29]

On 3 February 1994, the Minister of the Interior asked the Senate: 'Who is under attack here? This is an absurd judgment. If I found that judgment correct, I would not have appealed'. In its judgment of 29 November 1994, the Court of Appeal of Antwerp, following a joint appeal by the Minister of the Interior and the Minister of Justice, amended the interim decision of the President of the Tribunal of Mechelen. According to *Gazet van Antwerpen* of 22 December 1994, the Minister of the Interior was 'particularly happy' with this decision.

For its part, the Conseil d'Etat had already ruled in its judgment of 23 February 1994 that 'no violation of its rights of defence can be inferred from the circumstance [that the asylum seeker] did not have access to the file to prepare his hearing at the Commission General'.[30] Later, with specific reference to the Law

[28] 'Minister Tobback: "The Decisions of the Malinois Judge are Absurd"' (*HLN*, 12 January 1994).
[29] 'Tobback under the Fire of Magistrates' (*GvA*, 22 January 1994).
[30] CdE, No 46.256 (23 February 1994).

of 11 April 1994 on the publicity of administrative acts, the Conseil d'Etat also stated in its judgment of 13 November 1995:

> That a possible violation of this Law does not ipso facto render illegal a decision taken by the administrative authority based on these documents; that this Law does not require that this right be exercised by the services of the Commission General or by the decision-making of the Commissioner General or one of his Deputies before the hearing of the refugee applicant.[31]

Thus, my interpretation was supported by both the judiciary and the highest administrative court.

11.2.3. Pieter De Gryse: 'Embellish' (November 1995) and 'Blacken' (April 1996)

In *De Morgen* of 27 November 1995, Pieter De Gryse knew that I had taken the personal initiative to suddenly recognise Bosnians, en masse, to 'embellish' my asylum statistics. In a reaction from the same newspaper of 30 November, I pointed out that the percentage of recognition for 1995 at the Commission General was, with 30.09 per cent (1,116/3,709), already higher than ever. I also stated that, even if the 49 admissible Bosnian asylum applications, introduced between 1991 and 1993, all led to recognition before the end of 1995, the recognition percentage would only increase by less than 1 per cent. 'What is called "embellish *en masse*"'. I also stated that the backlog of files was not only for 'this year', but for seven years 'one of my major concerns'. I felt that, although 'peace is in sight', the Bosnians who had found refuge in Belgium for three or four years should not be sent back against their will. In my view, this criticism showed that some people were more concerned about taking the opportunity to constantly discredit the asylum procedure than about the fate of these war refugees.[32]

In a parliamentary question of 8 December 1995, Senator Bert Anciaux (VU) held that this was 'a genuine denial of the seriousness and professionalism that the Commissioner General was claiming'. In his reply, published on 8 April 1997, the Minister of the Interior, Johan Vande Lanotte, declared that the questionable practices invoked of embellishing the asylum statistics were non-existent. He expected the honourable Member, like himself, to respect the legal independence guaranteed to the Commissioner General.[33]

[31] CdE, No 56.225 (13 November 1995); *Journal des Tribunaux* (28 September 1996): the Conseil d'Etat added that 'the contested decision does not rule on the merits of a criminal charge or on the applicant's civil rights; that Article 6 of the Convention for the Protection of Human Rights and Fundamental Freedoms is not applicable in this matter'.

[32] He would become director (2002–10) of 'Vluchtelingenwerk Vlaanderen' (a Flemish NGO defending the interests of asylum seekers) and political director (2010–18) of Groen (the Flemish ecologists).

[33] *Q and Rep*, Senate (8 April 1997) Application No 62. The recognition rate during the first 10 months of 1995 was 29.9% (up from 30% in 1994). Decisions taken in November and December 1995 raised this percentage to 30.8% (+0.9%).

In *Humo* of 30 April 1996, Pieter De Gryse offered, under the title 'Fleeing is no Longer Possible', a platform to a former employee of the Commission General to allow him to criticise his former employer. His contract had not been extended because his productivity was too low. No attempt had been made to verify with me the veracity of his statements. The man claimed to handle 16 cases a month, when in fact he only handled six.[34] By stating that 'Asia was not in the Commission General's area of focus', he lost sight of the fact that among the top 15 countries for recognition, there were seven Asian countries: Turkey (1st), Vietnam (4th), Iran (5th), Lebanon (11th), Iraq (12th), Syria (13th) and Afghanistan (15th).

This former employee of the Commission General felt that employees should have a good legal training. Eighty employees, including the 14 statutory staff, had received legal training; 36 contract workers had another university training. The Independent Advisory Board (ABC) had recommended not only recruiting lawyers to avoid excessive 'legalism'. He also claimed that the jurisprudence of the Commission General was not systematically available. However, all the reasoned decisions taken since 1988 could be consulted on screen and in the internal library of the Commission General. They were listed in chronological order by country.[35]

In July 1995, a second Rwandan VIP applied for asylum in Belgium. It was Major General Augustin Ndindiliyimana (b 1943), the former Chief of Staff of the Rwandan Gendarmerie (1992–94). I refused his refugee application. However, the Permanent Board recognised him. He was subsequently extradited to the International Criminal Tribunal for Rwanda in Arusha (Tanzania). He was sentenced at first instance to 11 years, 3 months and 19 days in prison (the length of his pre-trial detention). On 11 February 2014, he was acquitted on appeal.

[34] He rightly said that I carefully hold a record of the 'productivity' of my collaborators and that by pressing a button I could see this on my screen.

[35] '"Flight is no Longer Possible?" Commissioner General's Right of Reply' *Humo* (14 May 1996).

12

Augustin Ndindiliyimana, Head of the Rwandan Gendarmerie (1995–98)

In January 1995, the former Chief of Staff of the Rwandan Gendarmerie, Major General Augustin Ndindiliyimana, applied for asylum in Belgium. He had received military training at the Infantry School in Arlon (1968) and at the Brussels War School (1972–74). He had been Minister for Youth and Sports (1982–89), Minister for Transport (1990), Minister for the Presidency (1991) and Minister for Defence (January–April 1992). In July 1992, on the proposal of the opposition, he was appointed Chief of Staff of the Rwandan Gendarmerie. He was promoted to Major General on 1 January 1994 under the Arusha Accords. During the genocide, which began after the attack on President Juvénal Habyarimana's plane on 6 April 1994, he continued to serve as Chief of Staff of the Gendarmerie. He was relieved of this post on 5 June, being appointed ambassador in Bonn (Federal Republic of Germany). He left Rwanda on 17 June. After a transit to Kinshasa, he arrived in Brussels on 2 July 1994.

12.1. My Refusal for Omission (9 May 1996)

Introduced in January 1995 (six months after his arrival in Belgium), his asylum application was nevertheless declared admissible by the Aliens Office in March 1995. However, on 9 May 1996 I refused his application on the merits, because he had seriously failed in his duty by committing, 'at least by omission', the worst violations of human rights and that he had 'knowingly condoned' serious crimes against humanity.[1] After references to the writings of Alain Destexhe,[2] François-Xavier Verschaeve,[3] the CRDDR,[4] Filip Reyntjens,[5] Alexandre Goffin[6] and

[1] Marie-France Cros (*LLB*, 24 May 1996): 'Bossuyt Throws a Stone in the Pond'.
[2] A Destexhe, *Qui a tué nos Paras* (Brussels, Ed Luc Pire, 1995) 182.
[3] F-X Verschaeve, *Complicité de génocide* (Paris, Ed La Découverte, 1994) 104.
[4] The Committee for the Respect of Human Rights and Democracy in Rwanda, Brussels, note of 9 May 1995.
[5] F Reyntjens, *Rwanda: Trois jours qui ont fait basculer l'histoire* (Paris, L'Harmattan, 1995) 55 and 76.
[6] A Goffin, *Rwanda, le 7 avril 1994: Dix commandos vont mourir* (Brussels, Ed Luc Pire, 1995) 100.

African Rights,[7] I first repeated seven paragraphs similar to those contained in my decision of 29 March 1996 concerning Séraphin Rwabukumba.

As regards Ndindiliyimana specifically, the reasons continued as follows:

> That, as the highest ranking military officer in Rwanda (the only surviving Major General),[8] and in addition the Chief of Staff of the Gendarmerie in charge of the protection of civilians in particular, he seriously failed in the duties of his office and was thus guilty, at least by omission, of the worst violations of human rights that took the scale and forms of a true genocide, resulting in the death of hundreds of thousands of innocent civilians.
>
> That his responsibility is all the greater since the Rwandans in general, and the Rwandan military in particular, are particularly respectful of the hierarchy and that a firm attitude of the person concerned could have changed the course of history at these crucial moments.
>
> That, in view of the important functions occupied by the person concerned, his liability was incurred, whatever his direct involvement in certain specific events, especially since it is not possible to identify any indication of the applicant's public position by which he has dissociated himself from the acts referred to above.

I also referred to the notification of 20 October 1994 from François-Xavier Nsanzuwera.[9] He had been my student at Butare (1984). From May 1990 to 1995, he was the Public Prosecutor in Kigali.[10] In that notification, the Prosecutor expressed his willingness to request the extradition of the person concerned. During the hundred days of the genocide, he had found refuge at the Hôtel des Mille Collines in Kigali.[11] When Ndindiliyimana said in 1999 that the most serious charges against him came from Nsanzuwera, the latter said: 'This man just didn't do his job. For me, such an omission is complicity'.[12]

In the *Gazet van Antwerpen* of 23 May 1996, Professor Filip Reyntjens said that refusing Ndindiliyimana refugee status was a serious mistake: 'Belgium Loses its Last Ruanda Friends'. He complained about the reference in my refusal decision to the so-called human rights organisation CRDDR, 'an organisation covered by the RPF' (Rwandan Patriotic Front). He said moreover that he had been quoted in

[7] African Rights, *Rwanda: Death, Despair and Defiance*, rev edn (London, 1995) 11.

[8] The other two Major Generals, President Juvénal Habyarimana and the Chief of Staff of the Rwandan Armed Forces (FAR), Déogratias Nsabimana, died on 6 April 1994 in the crash of the presidential plane.

[9] F-X Nsanzuwera, *La Battante: renaître après le génocide des Tutsis* (Paris, Ed Fauves, 2018); *Briseurs de destins: Les cerveaux du génocide des Tutsis* (Brussels, PU Saint-Louis, 2024). Nsanzuwera affirmed that Ndindiliyimana was aware of the weapons depots, and when at the dawn of the genocide he received a list of people to kill, he did nothing about it (Koen Vidal, *DM*, 2 February 2000).

[10] On 22 March 1995, François-Xavier Nsanzuwera left Rwanda for Belgium. He gave a press conference on 11 May 1995. See *DM*, 'Prosecutor of Kigali Seeks Asylum in Belgium'; *LS*, 'Le procureur de Kigali's "exile" à Anvers' (12 May 1995). From 1997, he was Secretary General of the International Federation for Human Rights (FIDH) until 2004, when he was hired by the International Criminal Tribunal for Rwanda in Arusha.

[11] F Boudet-Saulnier and F Laffont, *Maudits soient les yeux fermés* (Paris, Arte Ed JC Lattès, 1995).

[12] Marc Hoogsteyns, 'Accused: Rwandans in Belgium' *DM* (23 April 1999).

a misleading manner. On 4 July 1996, the investigating judge in Brussels, Damien Van der Meersch, charged Ndindiliyimana for his attitude during the genocide, based on the Law of 16 June 1993 on serious violations of international humanitarian law.[13]

12.2. Recognition by the Permanent Board (28 May 1998)

On 24 May 1996, he filed an appeal with the Permanent Board against my refusal.[14] More than two years later, on 28 May 1998, this decision was reviewed with a highly reasoned decision.[15] The Permanent Board recognised Ndindiliyimana as a refugee. Several witnesses had been heard. The prosecution witnesses were Gasana Ndoba, the CRDDR coordinator, and Yolande Mukagasana,[16] whose husband had been murdered by gendarmes in Rwanda on 13 April 1994. As defence witnesses, the Permanent Board heard Alain De Brouwer,[17] Joseph Matata, François Nzabahimana, and in particular Professor Filip Reyntjens and Colonel Luc Marchal. Professor Reyntjens stated that the applicant was certainly not part of the organising structure of the genocide. He could be criticised only for lack of courage. Colonel Luc Marchal insisted on the quality of the collaboration of the Gendarmerie with the MINUAR. It seemed incomprehensible and unjust to him to reproach moderate Rwandans who remained in the country, for not having been able to succeed where Belgium and the United Nations had not even tried.[18]

The Permanent Board admitted:

> That the mere fact of having occupied a position of responsibility in a genocidal regime may constitute a sufficient ground to presume responsibility for the crimes committed.
>
> That however this presumption is not irrefutable.
>
> That it is necessary to examine the nature of the power actually held and the possibility of its effective exercise.
>
> That, if the applicant was unquestionably wearing a high-ranking title in the Rwandan State apparatus, the means available to him during the genocide were extremely limited.
>
> That there is no evidence to suggest that any new evidence that could invalidate these conclusions could arise at maturity.

[13] According to Koen Vidal (*DM*, 2 February 2002), the investigating judge said during a closed session of the Rwanda Senate Commission that Ndindiliyimana had not assumed the responsibilities of his office.

[14] His lawyers in Brussels were Me Luc Walleyn, Me Luc Stalars and Me Patrick Dewolf, and in Arusha Me Christopher Black (Toronto) and Me Vincent Lurquin (Brussels).

[15] Koen Vidal (*DM*, 17 July 1998): 'A former Rwandan General may Remain in Belgium'.

[16] Y Mukagasana (with P May), *La mort ne veut pas de moi* (Paris, Robert Laffont, 1997).

[17] Adviser to Christian Democrat International.

[18] L Marchal, *Rwanda: La descente aux enfers. Témoignage d'un peace keeper: décembre 1993–avril 1994* (Paris, Ed Labor, 2001). This Belgian colonel commanded the Belgian contingent of the UN Assistance Mission in Rwanda (UNAMIR; in French: MINUAR).

12.3. Accused by the Prosecutor of the International Criminal Tribunal (20 January 2000)

On 20 January 2000, Carla Del Ponte,[19] Prosecutor at the International Criminal Tribunal for Rwanda,[20] signed an indictment of more than 60 pages concerning Ndindiliyimana. He was charged with conspiracy to commit genocide, genocide, complicity in genocide, crimes against humanity and violations of Article 3 common to the 1949 Geneva Conventions and of Additional Protocol II to those Conventions.[21]

Ndindiliyimana was arrested in Belgium on 28 January 2000 with a view to his transfer to the International Criminal Tribunal.[22] On 12 April, the Cour de cassation withdrew his case from Belgian justice. On 22 April 2000, he was transferred to Arusha (Tanzania),[23] where the Tribunal was located. The indictment was amended on 23 October 2002.[24] On 23 August 2004 the indictment was further amended by the new Prosecutor Hassan Bubacar Jallow.[25] It was not until 17 May 2011 that the Trial Chamber pronounced its judgment.

12.4. Judgment of the Trial Chamber (17 May 2011)

The Trial Chamber[26] of the International Criminal Tribunal for Rwanda delivered its judgment on 17 May 2011.[27] Major General Augustin Bizimungu[28] was

[19] Since 1999, this Swiss lawyer had been Prosecutor of the International Criminal Tribunals for Rwanda (until 2003) and for the Former Yugoslavia (until 2007).

[20] This Tribunal, established by UN Security Council Resolution 955 of 8 November 1994, ceased its activities on 31 December 2015. The Tribunal concluded with 61 convictions and 14 acquittals.

[21] Common Art 3 to the Geneva Conventions: 'Persons taking no active part in the hostilities, including members of armed forces who have laid down their arms and those placed hors de combat by sickness, wounds, detention, or any other cause, shall in all circumstances be treated humanely, without any adverse distinction founded on race, colour, religion or faith, sex, birth or wealth, or any other similar criteria'.

[22] Colette Braeckman (*LS*, 2 February 2000): 'The General has always Enjoyed Serious Protection in Belgium'; (*LS*, 4 February 2000): 'It was after Carla Del Ponte's Visit to Belgium that the Belgian Justice finally got under Way'.

[23] *LS* (26 April 2000): 'Belgium Lets Go a Rwandan General'.

[24] This indictment also concerned Protais Mpiranya, who was the commander of the Presidential Guard Battalion. He was listed as 'on the run'. It was established in May 2022 that he died in October 2006 under a false name as a result of a heart attack in Zimbabwe.

[25] This Gambian lawyer succeeded Carla Del Ponte in 2003. He had been my colleague, as the Representative (1989–92) of his country, on the UN Commission on Human Rights.

[26] Composed of President Asoka de Silva (Sri Lanka) and Judge Taghrid Hikmet (Jordan) and Judge Seon Ki Park (Republic of Korea).

[27] The judgment in case No ICTR-00-56-T (649 pages) contains a blood-chilling account of eyewitnesses to the 7 April 1994 murder of the 10 Belgian paratroopers (§§1746–1889).

[28] Major General and Chief of Staff of the Rwandan Armed Forces since 19 April 1994. He had received training at the commando training centre in Marche-les-Dames (1974/75). He attended courses at the Royal Institute of Defence in Brussels (1982). He was arrested in Angola in August 2002.

sentenced to 30 years in prison, and Major François-Xavier Nzuwonemeye[29] and Captain Innocent Sagahutu,[30] to 20 years each. In the same judgment, the Chamber sentenced Major General Augustin Ndindiliyimana to a sentence corresponding to the period already spent in detention (11 years, 3 months, and 19 days). It ordered his immediate release.[31]

12.4.1. Saint André College of Kigali and the Kansi Parish

On 13 April 1994, gendarmes from the Nyamirambo Brigade killed Tutsi men who had sought refuge at the Saint André College in Kigali (§22); between 20 and 22 April 1994, gendarmes participated in the killing of Tutsi in Kansi parish (§§18–19). The Chamber considers it established that gendarmes participated in the attack on this parish. His wife had made a call to them to ensure the safety of her family at their home in Nyaruhengeri.

In both cases, the Chamber found that he had knowledge of the role of the gendarmes in the killings but did not take measures to punish them (§§19 and 23). In addition, the gendarmes deliberately killed members of the Tutsi group. They had the specific intent to destroy, in whole or in substantial part, the Tutsi group (§§2079 and 2082). The Trial Chamber was satisfied that Ndindiliyimana was aware of the gendarmes' genocidal intent (§§2080 and 2084).

12.4.2. The Responsibility of Ndindiliyimana

In determining his responsibility, the Chamber noted that, as Chief of Staff of the Gendarmerie, he was placed under the supervisory authority of the Ministry of Defence. The primary function of the Gendarmerie was to maintain public law and order and to enforce the laws in force in Rwanda. In time of war, the Gendarmerie participates in the defence of the territory (§1924). On 7 April 1994, on order of the Minister of Defence, the operational command of the relevant units of the Gendarmerie was transferred from the Chief of Staff of the Gendarmerie to the Chief of Staff of the Rwandan army. However, the Gendarmerie retained authority over the units deployed to assist the army regarding administrative and disciplinary matters (§1925).

[29] Nzuwonemeye trained in the Democratic People's Republic of (North) Korea (1979) and at the Belgian School of Military Administrators (1986 and 1988), and from 1990 was commander of the elite reconnaissance battalion RECCE. He was arrested in France on 15 February 2000.

[30] Captain Innocent Sagahutu commanded a squadron of the RECCE battalion. Two of his corporals reportedly broke the resistance of the last four, or two, Belgian peacekeepers by using a LGM (Multiple Grenade Launcher) that he had provided them with or for which he had given his approval for them to take it from his office (§1887). He was arrested in Denmark on 15 February 2000.

[31] Professor Filip Reyntjens reacted with indignation to this judgment: 'This is unprecedented, and this is shocking. This is not serious. This is an acquittal in disguise. Can refraining from sacrificing oneself be considered as guilt?' *Radio Netherlands Worldwide* (23 March 2011).

From that moment on, Ndindiliyimana's powers were 'whittled down'. However, he maintained control and authority over the gendarmes who were not in combat zones (§1927). While he was in fact leading and representing the Gendarmerie, the scope of his de jure authority was dramatically reduced (§§1929–32). The Chamber accepts that he suffered from a lack of resources, that he faced difficulties in communicating with Gendarmerie units operating on the ground and that his force was infiltrated by extremist and rogue elements (§1946).

The Trial Chamber finds, however, that he did exercise de facto authority over the gendarmes who committed the alleged crimes at the Saint André College and Kansi parish (§§1947–48). He failed in his duty to punish the perpetrators of these crimes (§1956). The Chamber finds him guilty of extermination as a crime against humanity for killings in Kansi parish (§2119). He is also guilty of violations of Article 3 common to the Geneva Conventions and of Additional Protocol II for the murder of Tutsi refugees at Saint André College (§2152). Ndindiliyimana has been convicted because of his failure to punish his subordinates. His role carried a duty to serve and protect the people of Rwanda (§2187).

12.4.3. Mitigating Factors

The Chamber finds that several mitigating factors carrying considerable weight have been proven. They are unique and distinguish him from the other accused in this case (§2190). There is considerable evidence that he advocated for the Arusha Accords and cooperated with UNAMIR (§2199). The Chamber referred to the Belgian defence witnesses, Colonel Luc Marchal (§2200) and Colonel André Vincent[32] (§2201) and Ambassador Johan Swinnen[33] (§§2204 and 2213).

On the evening of 7 April 1994, Ndindiliyimana accompanied Lieutenant-General Roméo Dallaire[34] to the morgue. Visibly shocked at the sight of the corpses of the Belgian peacekeepers, he arranged for the bodies to be washed[35] and paid people to make the remains decent (§2214). Then he gave his personal escort to Dallaire.

Prosecution witnesses Dallaire and Alison Des Forges testified that he facilitated UNAMIR search operations (§2217). The Chamber was satisfied that he did not have the support of the Rwandan government. He was marginalised and

[32] He was the head of the Belgian military technical cooperation in Kigali.

[33] J Swinnen, *Rwanda: Mijn Verhaal* (Amsterdam, Polis, 2016). He was Belgian Ambassador in Kigali from 16 August 1990 to 12 April 1994. He successively became diplomatic adviser to Prime Minister Jean-Luc Dehaene and Ambassador to The Hague, Kinshasa and Madrid. In the early 1970s, he was my study companion at the Graduate Institute of International Studies (IUHEI) in Geneva.

[34] R Dallaire, *Shake Hands with the Devil: The Failure of Humanity in Rwanda* (Toronto, Random House, 2003). This Canadian general was the head of UNAMIR.

[35] CB, *LS* (26 April 2000): 'His reputation, if not as a "moderate" at least as a "friend of Belgium" comes from the fact that after the death of the ten Belgian peacekeepers, it was he who ensured that their remains received a funeral toilet'.

threatened (§2234). In the words of Des Forges:[36] 'He saved the lives of a number of people' (§2240). These mitigating factors distinguish him from the other accused in this case. The sentence imposed reflects this difference, notwithstanding the gravity of his crimes (§2243).

12.5. Acquitted by the Appeals Chamber (11 February 2014)

On 11 February 2014, the Appeals Chamber[37] of the International Criminal Tribunal for Rwanda rendered its judgment. The sentences of Augustin Ndindiliyimana and François-Xavier Nzuwonemeye were reviewed[38] and their release ordered. Innocent Sagahutu's 20-year sentence was reduced to 15 years.[39]

As regards Ndindiliyimana, the Appeals Chamber recalled that the essential element of a superior–subordinate relationship is the possession of effective control on the part of the superior in the sense of a material ability to prevent and punish criminal conduct by his subordinates (§55). The Appeals Chamber noted that after 7 April 1994, operational command over most of the Gendarmerie units was transferred to the Rwandan army (§51). The Trial Chamber's failure to provide a reasoned opinion amounts to an error of fact which allows the Appeals Chamber to consider the relevant evidence and actual findings to determine whether a reasonable trier of fact could have found that the gendarmes stationed at his residence were under his command, nor that in fact they participated in the attack in Kansi parish (§§56 and 59). The Appeals Chamber finds that the Trial Chamber erred in concluding that he exercised effective control over the gendarmes of the Nyamirambo Brigade, who participated in the attack against the Saint André College (§75).

12.6. PS: Some Observations

Once released by the International Criminal Tribunal, Ndindiliyimana could not return to Belgium, despite his refugee status. He had to stay in a house at the

[36] A Des Forges, *Leave None to Tell the Story: Genocide in Rwanda* (Human Rights Watch and FIDH, 1999).

[37] Composed of President Theodor Meron (USA) and Judge Liu Daqun (People's Republic of China), Judge Carmel Agius (Malta), Judge Khalida Rachid Khan (Pakistan) and Judge Bakhtiyar Tuzmukhamedov (Russian Federation).

[38] The judgment in case No ICTR-00-56-A is 162 pages long. On 7 February 2014, the Appeals Chamber decided to separate Major General Augustin Bizimungu's appeal from this case. On 30 June 2014, the same Appeals Chamber confirmed his 30-year prison sentence.

[39] In his partially dissenting opinion, Russian judge Bakhtiyar Tuzmukhamedov strongly disagreed with the reduction of Sahutu's sentence since he was 'personally involved in a mortal attack against members of an international UN peacekeeping force. This attack constituted a grave crime which undoubtedly had a most devastating effect on the ensuing events in Rwanda' (§7).

expense of the United Nations with other previously acquitted defendants. They could not find a country willing to accept them. It was not until September 2014, six months after his acquittal by the Appeals Chamber, and more than 14 years after his arrest, that he was able to join his family in Belgium. The abuse of pre-trial detention in this case is blatant.

It happens that preventive detention in international justice gets out of hand. The International Criminal Court did little better. Thus, Jean-Pierre Bemba, former Vice-President of the Democratic Republic of Congo (2003–06), was acquitted by the Appeals Chamber of the International Criminal Court on 8 June 2018 after 10 years and 17 days of pre-trial detention. Laurent Gbagbo, former President of Côte d'Ivoire (2000–11), was acquitted at first instance on 15 January 2019 after spending 7 years and 8 months in pre-trial detention, and Blé Goudé, a former politician from the same country, after 6 years (minus 2 days).[40] On 31 March 2021, the acquittal of these two officials from Côte d'Ivoire was confirmed by the Appeals Chamber.

In Rwanda, a genocide took place that caused between 800,000 and 1,000,000 victims over a period of 100 days. According to the report of three African experts, this was a 'concerted, planned, systematic, and methodical' genocide.[41] This report was prepared within three months of the end of the genocide by experts sent to Rwanda by the UN Security Council. Ndindiliyimana was for 10 years (1982–92) Minister of a regime that, clinging to power, committed genocide. At the beginning of the genocide, he held the highest military rank as Major General. During the first 90 days of this genocide, he remained in office as Chief of Staff of the Gendarmerie. The Gendarmerie's mission was to protect the civilian population. It cannot be denied that he can claim mitigating factors. It is, however, difficult to accept that from a criminal point of view *nothing* can be blamed on him. Yet this was the conclusion of the International Criminal Tribunal for Rwanda.

More than 17 years earlier, I had to rule on his asylum application. Contrary to what is required for a criminal conviction, 'serious grounds' are sufficient for refusing refugee status. I thought there were such reasons based on culpable omissions. The Prosecutor of the Republic of Kigali, the investigating judge in Brussels and successive prosecutors at the International Criminal Tribunal believed that he should be prosecuted. The Trial Chamber found that a sentence corresponding to the long period of pre-trial detention was appropriate.

The Appeals Chamber found that he should be acquitted. The Prosecutor's error may have been in wanting to prove that he 'acted' in a criminal manner. When this proved difficult, the Appeals Chamber acquitted him. Nevertheless, there is a wealth of evidence that he had failed miserably in his duty to protect 'by failing to act'. In the meantime, he was held for more than 11 years. Considering

[40] M Bossuyt, 'The Acquittals of Mr Bemba and Mr Gbagbo by the International Criminal Court' in *Semper Perseverans: Liber amicorum André Alen* (Antwerp, Intersentia, 2020) 847.

[41] See above p 124 (n 8).

mitigating factors and admitting that it was not possible to accuse him of acts, but only of omissions, 11 years in prison – even considering the catastrophic consequences of these omissions – is a long deprivation of liberty. Captain Sagahutu's imprisonment was reduced by the same Appeals Chamber from 20 to 15 years. Yet it was he who provided two of his corporals with the multiple grenade launchers to kill the last four (or two) Belgian peacekeepers. Only the Russian judge disagreed profoundly with this reduction in sentence. He considered him guilty of 'a grave crime which undoubtedly had a most devastating effect on the ensuing events in Rwanda'. In these circumstances, it is permissible to question the validity of the assessments made by the Appeals Chamber.

13

Unhappy with 'Economic Refugees' and My Status (1995–96)

In November 1995, a pastoral letter from the bishops of Belgium provoked a discussion on the (erroneous) notion of 'economic refugees'. I defended the distinction that the Geneva Convention makes between people who can be helped in their own country and those for whom it is impossible because they are persecuted there. On 4 July 1996, I expressed my satisfaction with the results obtained by the asylum procedure. I was less satisfied with my status which was still lingering. That led me to the exit on 5 February 1997, when I left the Commission General.

13.1. The Statement of the Bishops of Belgium (November 1995)

In November 1995, in a statement issued by the Bishops of Belgium on 'Migrants and Refugees among us', it was said: 'The danger of starvation, for so-called economic refugees, is not fundamentally different from the danger of death resulting from persecution on political or religious grounds'.

13.1.1. My Letter to the Cardinal (21 November 1995)

In a letter of 21 November 1995 to His Eminence Godfried Cardinal Danneels, Archbishop of Mechelen-Brussels (1979–2010), I wrote that this thesis was questionable. In my annual reports,[1] I gave the reasons why, not only for legal reasons, the distinction should be maintained between Geneva Convention refugees and people who have left their country for other (often economic) reasons:

1. It is only in the case of refugees within the meaning of the Geneva Convention that our countries have undertaken, under international law, not to return these persons to their country of origin.
2. There is absolutely no criterion for determining who would be welcomed for economic reasons.

[1] In my *Fifth* (1992) §219, and *Sixth Annual Report* (1993) §154.

3. The problems of economic inequality between the north and the south and between the west and the east will not be solved in the least by granting asylum to anyone who applies for it.
4. We can question the fact that people who can afford to take a trip to Western Europe really need our help the most.
5. Our welfare system is not designed to take care of the world's needy.

In a contribution to *Le Soir* of 3 January 1996, I expressed, under the title 'Economic Refugees?', my fear that

> the statement of the Bishops of November 1995, undoubtedly inspired by the most praiseworthy intentions, would contribute to a greater confusion of notions between refugees, on the one hand, and illegal aliens or clandestine migrants, on the other, which does not benefit at all the refugees whose protection is my legal mission.

13.1.2. 'What about "Economic Refugees"?' (Press Conference of 17 January 1996)

At my press conference on 17 January 1996, I spoke about the status of the asylum procedure after eight years of operation. The main message was: 'The number of asylum seekers is declining'. The more well-founded the applications are, the more complex they become. The admissibility procedure proceeded four times faster: its duration was reduced from an average of 450 days to an average of 105 days. For 75 nationalities, no one had ever been recognised as a refugee. The recognition rate was particularly low for Nigerians and Bangladeshi (0.1 per cent), Indians (0.3 per cent) and Ghanaians (0.9 per cent). According to *Le Soir*, the charts and graphs were 'impressive but hard to digest'.

The main complaint concerned the increasingly restrictive policy of the Aliens Office. The admissibility rate for this office, which in 1988 was 48 per cent of the asylum applications, had dropped to 7.7 per cent. The result was that I had, often unnecessarily, to process the same asylum applications twice: once in admissibility and once on the merits. I emphasised that:

> The Geneva Convention is clear. No refugee may be returned to his country of origin, where he fears for his life, liberty, or physical integrity because of his political or religious conviction. This is an obligation we can and must respect. We cannot and should not support all foreigners who prefer to come to our country for economic reasons. There is a critical difference between the two categories.

13.1.3. Opinions Expressed in Newspapers (January–February 1996)

André Lambert, Chairperson of the French-speaking Belgian 'Justice and Peace Commission', wrote an opinion in *La Libre Belgique* of 23 January 1996, under the title 'Nobody Likes to Leave their Country; Sometimes you Have to'.[2] He reacted to the 'weakness and demagogy of the arguments' which, according to him, I highlighted: thus, I missed a good opportunity to strengthen my legal mission.

In an opinion of 24 January 1996 on the Geneva Convention, entitled 'Fortunately, the Bishops are Creating Confusion', Ann Labeeuw[3] wrote that using the concept of 'refugee' in the sense that the Geneva Convention gives it, is a little linguistic game that shows a formalistic approach. According to her, it was a conflict between how to treat people in an ethical way and a cold accounting approach. In her view, a broader access policy than that of the Geneva Convention needed to be considered in a creative way. She thought it was sad that this gave me trouble. On the same page, Johan Leman wrote, under the title 'Refugee Policy is not what is Needed', that the notion of 'true refugee' had to be qualified. He claimed that asylum was also used as an instrument of immigration control and that the principle of equality could not be lost sight of either. Falsified statements and documents were not to be sufficient reasons to ignore residence claims.

In response to these two opinions, I asked the following question in *De Standaard* of 30 January 1996, under the title 'The Refugee Convention is not Outdated':

> How do we determine among the millions of foreigners who would like to come to Belgium rather than stay in their own country, which could, and which could not come to us? Assistance for people who are experiencing economic difficulties must be given in their own countries. Each developing country will have many needy candidates who would like to settle in Belgium. Who will decide and on what criteria? You can't run a policy with good intentions. It is easier to build a good conscience than to pursue a sustainable policy.

As far as the principle of equality is concerned, I felt that it was not because

> it is not possible to return all illegal persons without distinction to their country of origin, that no one can be removed. When it is not a question of rights but of favours, one must be accountable to parliament and – in elections – to the nation, not to judges. Talking about the effective machinery of the deportation process is far in advance of reality. The painful reality is that many foreigners who have good reasons to come to our country do not get visas because the policy fails in removing rejected asylum seekers or other foreigners who have come to our country without valid reasons.

In *La Libre Belgique* of 7 February 1996, I wrote, under the title 'Don't Confuse "Refugee" and "Illegal Migrant"', in reaction to André Lambert's opinion, that

> many of them have had to pay dearly for the traffickers who have helped them to come illegally to our countries and those who most need our help are undoubtedly those who cannot afford a trip to Western Europe. It is not by opening borders to other categories of people than those covered by the Geneva Convention that the economic disparities between north and south and between east and west will disappear.

[2] The same contribution was also published in *Dimanche* (11 February 1996) under the title 'Migrants et réfugiés parmi nous'.

[3] On behalf of 'Kerkwerk Multicultureel Samenleven', a non-profit association linked to the Catholic Church and favouring solidarity within a multicultural society.

13.1.4. The Bishop's Nuance (17 February 1996)

At the General Assembly of the Inter-Diocesan Pastoral Consultation (IPB) on 17 February 1996, Monseigneur Paul Van den Berghe, the Bishop of Antwerp (1980–2008), conceded that the bishops had used the concepts of 'economic refugees' and 'multicultural society' in too vague a way, which led to misunderstandings.[4] Acknowledging that with an overly broad interpretation of the term 'refugee', there are no longer any real refugees, the Bishop declared: 'We were too idealistic. We should have drawn more attention to the need for a migration policy'. The Bishop of Antwerp understood my fear that the reference to the notion of 'economic refugee' implies the risk of disqualifying the true notion of 'refugee'.

13.2. The Commissioner General is Both Happy and Unhappy

On 5 July 1996, after the presentation of my *Eighth Annual Report* (1995), the media reported a 'happy' Commissioner General. Four days earlier in a note to the Minister of the Interior, I had expressed, on the contrary, my unhappiness with the lack of settlement of my status.

13.2.1. 'Satisfied': My Eighth Annual Report (4 July 1996)

On 4 July 1996, I presented my *Eighth Annual Report*. This was not my last annual report, but the last one I would submit myself.[5] According to the media:

> Marc Bossuyt is Happy (*HLN*), [A] happy man. He has less work (*HBvL*); proud (*DM*); confident (*HN*); obviously happy (*Vl'A*); very offensive (*LS*); with verve (*LLB*); sigh of satisfaction (*LNG*).

The press conference was preceded by a visit to the glass house of the Commission General at North Gate I and II (*LS*; *Vl'A*). According to Christian Laporte (*LS*), it was 'a … royal visit':

> Everything was clean and impeccable until the smiles of the employees of the Commission General. Its offices present a very positive image of 'Belgium, a land of welcome' with its various reading and documentation rooms and its largely computerised 'file tracking' services. Optimal working conditions for the team of 125 people

[4] *GvA*; *DS* (19 February 1996).
[5] The following *Annual Report* (the Ninth) (1996) would be published under my responsibility and signed on 5 February 1997. Since I became a judge at the Court of Arbitration on 6 February, it was published by my successor Luc De Smet (9 July 1997).

> where we push the detail to a friendly exotic decoration. Enough to cut short the rumours of relative disorganisation and cold and dehumanised welcome.

I said that I wanted asylum seekers to be received by my services 'politely, if not kindly' (*LLB*) and that I ran the youngest and best computerised public service in the country. There were 190 computers connected in a network, a record (at the time) in administration:

> Of the 230 employees working at the Commission General, 90 per cent are contract employees. The average age is 27 years and two-thirds of the staff are female. 150 people per day are summoned for hearings. Each in-house jurist receives an average of three people. We use 350 interpreters for 145 languages. Per month, we buy for 800,000 BF (€20,000) postage stamps to send notices and decisions, by registered letter[6] (*HBvL*).

The Geneva Convention was not interpreted narrowly or restrictively.[7] In 1995, there were asylum seekers from 118 different countries. There were fewer applications from countries with little chance of recognition, such as Ghana, Nigeria and India. There were more from the Former Yugoslavia (first place with 1.337) and the former Soviet Union (second place with 729). The level of difficulty of the files had increased (*DNG*).

I was concerned about the situation in the appeal bodies: there were 120 appeals pending before the Dutch-speaking Chambers and 1,950 before the French-speaking Chambers (*DS*), although many of these applicants live in Flemish communes (*LS*). The Permanent Board increased the recognition rate from 8.5 per cent to 8.6 per cent (a difference of just 0.1 per cent) (*HBvL*; *LS*). In 1995, 40 per cent of all judgments delivered by the Conseil d'Etat concerned my decisions (*LLB*). Most of the appeals (69 per cent) were granted to French-speaking Chambers (*Vl'A*). Lawyers used language shopping to keep their clients in the country longer (*DS*; *HBvL*). There were only 3 per cent of annulments by the Conseil d'Etat, most often because of a technical error, for example the language used (*LLB*). When a refusal decision was annulled because, according to the Conseil d'Etat, it was not made in the 'right' language, the next decision in the French language did not become positive.

I regretted the negative image of my services, largely due to lawyers speaking unilaterally to the media about their files:

> We do not want to keep people out of the country (*DM*); I am not better paid when I refuse an application (*LLB*); For the lawyers it is a little different (*DM*); The asylum procedure has been criticised because a Zairian was arrested, while he had been living in Belgium for 15 years without ever applying for asylum (*HLN*); Our only link to the closed centres is to make sure that some applicants may leave them! Not without success since 30 per cent of them leave them. (*LS*).

[6] The law requires registered mail. Many refugee applicants do not have valid identification and cannot receive these registered letters. For any eventuality, a copy was sent by non-registered mail. It's unimaginable to see how many documents contain the records of so-called 'undocumented persons'.

[7] 'Otherwise, we could not have granted asylum to 1,500 Turks and 700 Rwandans' (*HBvL*; *FET*; *LS*).

I regretted that I had not had the opportunity for several years to present my annual report to Parliament:[8] 'There may be things there that parliamentarians don't want to hear, or they don't like to face facts as they are' (*HBvL*; *HLN*). I was no longer given the opportunity to present my report to Parliament.

13.2.2. Dissatisfied with My Status and that of My Deputies[9]

Four days before this press conference, on 30 June 1996, I complained once again, in a note to the Minister of the Interior, about my status and that of my deputies. I felt that this status was not appropriate for our function. I've complained about it year after year. I had mentioned it in all my successive annual reports. In the light of a provision of the Flemish decree of 12 June 1991 on universities,[10] this problem became more pressing for me every year. By this provision, after six academic years, I would lose my right to return to full-time teaching at the University of Antwerp. Fortunately, this provision was not retroactive, but a solution had to be found before the end of the 1996/97 academic year. It had become urgent.

13.2.2.1. Unsuitable Status

In a note dated 30 June 1996, I referred to my quasi-jurisdictional, administrative and public responsibilities. Since the creation of the Commission General, these responsibilities had increased significantly:

a. The number of asylum seekers rose from 5,000 in 1988 to 26,000 in 1993.
b. The number of employees increased from 20 to 230.
c. In terms of admissibility, the number of interventions rose from 700 in 1988 to 15,000 in 1994.
d. The number of decisions on the merits had increased from 727 in 1988 to 5,000 in 1994.

In the same note, I compared my responsibilities (CG) with those of the Permanent Board (PB):

a. Since 1 February 1988, the CG had taken 85,000 decisions and the PB 6,950.
b. The CG made 89 per cent of the final refusal decisions and the PB 11 per cent.

[8] Only the first three annual reports were presented to Parliament. On 7 February 1996, I gave the House a presentation on the operation of the asylum procedure *anno* 1996 (*Doc parl*, *Chambre*, No 364/8, 1995/96, 3) as part of the hearings concerning the drafts that led to the Laws of 10 and 15 July 1996 (*M.B.*, 5 October 1996).

[9] Deputy Commissioners Christian Bayi (F) and Marc Bonte (N) were appointed from 1 February 1988. On 9 October 1991, they were appointed to the Permanent Board, respectively, as Assessor (F) and President (N). From 1 August 1992, Xavier De Beys (F) was appointed Deputy Commissioner. From 1 September 1994, Luc De Smet (N) was appointed Deputy Commissioner.

[10] Art 105 of the Decree on Universities of the Flemish Community. An amendment to this decree on 18 May 1999 would extend this period to eight academic years.

c. The CG had made 92.5 per cent (7,325) of the recognition decisions and the PB 7.5 per cent (575).
d. The number of pending cases at the CG had fallen from 22,000 at the end of December 1993 to less than 16,000 at the end of June 1996, whereas during the same period, the number of pending appeals to the PB had risen from 619 to 2,079.

It was stated in the explanatory memorandum of the Refugees Law of 14 July 1987 that the Commissioner General and his two Deputy Commissioners were not 'agents of the State within the meaning of the royal decree of 2 October 1937 on the status of agents of the State'.[11] In a letter dated 28 September 1988, to the Minister of Justice, I asked what the impact was on the social status of the agents concerned. I doubted that sufficient consideration had been given to our legal status as independent agents by granting us an administrative rank of public servants.[12] The royal decree concerning the salary arrangements of the Commissioner General and his deputies was not adopted until 2 April 1990.[13]

13.2.2.2. The Cup was Full

In a letter of 20 October 1992 to the Minister of the Interior, I considered discriminatory the fact that the Law of 18 July 1991 provided, after five years, for the final appointment of the four presidents and eight assessors of the Permanent Board, whereas this was not provided for in the Law of 14 July 1987, for me, or my two deputies.[14] I felt it was necessary to put an end to the precariousness of our situation, which was full of ambiguities and uncertainties. Despite my repeated insistence,[15] my status had still not been settled in 1995.[16] On 2 August 1996, the Council of Ministers approved a bill providing for a permanent appointment to rank 15 of the three Commissioners after an initial period of five years.[17] One of the three would be designated Commissioner General for five years. It was the result of consultations within an inter-Cabinet group chaired by a lady from the Cabinet of Prime Minister Jean-Luc Dehaene.

On 26 August 1996, I informed the Office of the Minister of the Interior that the proposed regulation was unacceptable to me. I was already permanently appointed to the University of Antwerp as a full-time professor, which corresponded to rank 16, even before my appointment as Commissioner General. I therefore found this

[11] *Doc parl, Chambre*, 1986/87, 689/1, 11.
[12] *First Annual Report* (1988) §139.
[13] See the *Third Annual Report* (1990) §139.
[14] The Law of 6 May 1993 made us subject to the social security system for salaried employees. This resulted in a decrease in the net salary of the Deputy Commissioners. It was not known what system was applicable to the calculation of my retirement and survivor's pension (*Seventh Annual Report*, 1994, §168).
[15] Among others to the Minister of the Interior on 13 October 1994 and 13 January 1995.
[16] *Eighth Annual Report* (1995) §§183–85.
[17] *Ninth Annual Report* (1996) §211.

proposal even more incomprehensible since in October 1996 the presidents of the Permanent Board would receive their permanent appointment at rank 16. The cup was full. I had to leave the Commission General as soon as possible.

13.3. En Route to the Court of Arbitration: (September 1996 to February 1997)

On 2 September 1996, at the age of 60, Louis-Paul Baron Suetens, died unexpectedly in his office as a judge at the Court of Arbitration. He was extraordinary professor of administrative law at KU Leuven and a former member of the Conseil d'Etat. He was a kind man and a very competent jurist. On 10 September 1984, he was appointed one of the first 12 judges to the Court of Arbitration. In accordance with the political accounting of the D'Hondt system,[18] this vacant seat belonged to a Dutch-speaking professional jurist to be proposed by the VLD. To meet the legal requirements for this seat, candidates had to be a member of the Cour de cassation or the Conseil d'Etat, a professor at a Belgian law faculty or a 'referendar' (legal assistant) at the Court of Arbitration (always for at least five years). By the Special Law of 6 January 1989, the Court of Arbitration had become competent to review the prohibition of discrimination enshrined in the Belgian Constitution. In 1975, I had defended my doctoral thesis on the prohibition of discrimination in international human rights law at the University of Geneva.[19] I had taught international law at the University of Antwerp (UIA) for more than 10 years, as a professor. I therefore fully satisfied the legal conditions.

Some time before, I had given up – after having asked for 24 hours of reflection – an informal offer of appointment as State Councillor. In my opinion, my academic specialisation was less directed at the Conseil d'Etat. Moreover, the offer was based on a misunderstanding. On 13 October 1994, I had suggested to the Minister of the Interior that the Commissioner General be granted the status of State Councillor in the search for an acceptable settlement of my status. This was misunderstood, as was my wish to become a State Councillor.

13.3.1. The European Commission and Court in Strasbourg

In February 1996, Leo Goovaerts, VLD Senator (1991–99), prompted me to apply for membership of the European Commission of Human Rights in Strasbourg. He was a member of the Belgian delegation of the Parliamentary

[18] This system, proposed in the nineteenth century by Victor D'Hondt, is used to distribute available seats in a proportional electoral system.

[19] M Bossuyt, *L'interdiction de la discrimination dans le droit international des droits de l'homme* (Brussels, Bruylant, 1976).

Assembly of the Council of Europe. On 13 March 1996, this delegation proposed me as the first candidate for this mandate. The outgoing member, State Councillor Jean-Claude Geus, was proposed as the second candidate. There was a constant practice of alternating the linguistic role and the political affiliation of the Belgian holder of this mandate every six years. The government's '*Kern*',[20] however, deviated from this practice, at the insistence of the PS, by instructing Erik Derycke[21] (SP) Minister of Foreign Affairs (1995–99) to nominate the outgoing member. This did not show much appreciation for my role in solving the asylum crisis. The result of my action made some people think that once the crisis was under control, they could do without me. That was at least what the government believed.

The government therefore asked the delegation to change the order of candidates presented in favour of Jean-Claude Geus. On 9 May 1996, the delegation refused to implement this. Ambassador Theo Lansloot, the Belgian Permanent Representative to the Council of Europe in Strasbourg, was nevertheless instructed to lobby his colleagues in favour of the candidate nominated second. On 14 May 1996, the Belgian Official Gazette published a royal decree of 8 March in which Jean-Claude Geus was authorised to serve as a member of the European Commission of Human Rights from 18 May 1996. On 17 June 1996, the Permanent Representatives to the Council of Europe appointed Jean-Claude Geus in this capacity.

Both before (6 June) and after (26 June 1996) this appointment, Hugo Coveliers,[22] leader of the VLD-Group in the Senate (1995–99), questioned the Prime Minister. He implied[23] that the PS supported Jean-Claude Geus because of his role in a case involving the Van Hool Bus Company. A Chamber of the Conseil d'Etat, which he presided over, had on 17 November 1993 overturned the suspension of a decision to order buses.[24] The Chamber ruled that the loss of an order worth €45 million, valued at 204 jobs for three years, could not be considered serious. This Chamber returned the provisional suspension decided on 7 October 1993 by a single State Councillor.[25] The suspension concerned a decision taken on the previous day by the Board of Directors of the Walloon Regional Society for Transport (SRWT) to award the public contract for the supply of public transport buses to a competitor. Finally, the Court of Justice of Luxembourg held in its judgment of 25 April 1996 in that case (C-87/94) that the Belgian State had failed to

[20] The *Kern* ('Core') of the government is composed of the most important ministers.

[21] Erik Derycke would become an excellent colleague at the Constitutional Court (2001–19).

[22] When in 1967/68, I was, as Secretary General at the head of the General Association of Students of the University of Ghent (Gents Studentenkorps), Hugo Coveliers belonged to my left opposition on the GSK General Council as elected member of the Student Trade Union Movement (Studentenvakbeweging, SVB).

[23] The satiric weekly *Père Ubu* of 30 June 1996 was even more explicit in its insinuations.

[24] CdE, Judgment No 44.936 (17 November 1993).

[25] CdE, Judgment No 44.399 (7 October 1993).

fulfil its obligations under the Directive of 17 September 1990.[26] Ultimately, this cost the Walloon taxpayer the equivalent of €6,275 million.

Senator Hugo Coveliers associated moreover the support of Jean-Claude Geus with the condemnation by the Cour de cassation, on 5 April 1996, of prominent PS members in the case of the University Institute of Opinion Polling (UNISOP). He claimed that these members intended to submit requests to Strasbourg. Prime Minister Jean-Luc Dehaene declared that he left these insinuations for Hugo Coveliers. Between 23 July and 8 August 1996, five of those members (Guy Coëme,[27] Jean-Louis Mazy, Jean-Louis Stalport, Merry Hermanus and Camille Javeau) filed petitions against their conviction with the European Commission of Human Rights. In its judgment of 22 June 2000 in *Coëme et al v Belgium* the European Court of Human Rights held that Article 6.1 ECHR had been violated in respect of Guy Coëme. He had been deprived of a fair trial because of the lack of implementing legislation governing the procedure for the trial of ministers. The Strasbourg Court held that the same conventional provision was also violated in respect of the other four applicants. According to Strasbourg, the Cour de cassation was not a tribunal 'established by law' within the meaning of Article 6 ECHR to try them. In addition to the equivalent of €29,000 in costs for the five applicants, the Belgian State still had to pay each the equivalent of €7,500 to these four other applicants for moral damage.

The intention was that Jean-Claude Geus would become the Belgian judge at the Court of Strasbourg, when the Commission and the Court, which were not permanent, merged into a single European Court of Human Rights, on a full-time basis. This merger would take place on 1 November 1998. I was not one of the three candidates put forward on 7 November 1997 by the government for the office of judge of that Court. The Liberals were not part of the government. In the first round of voting at the Parliamentary Assembly of the Council of Europe, Jean-Claude Geus was the only first-order candidate who did not obtain the required majority.

In the second round of voting, on 28 January 1998, Françoise Tulkens, professor at the (francophone) Catholic University of Louvain-la-Neuve (UCL), was elected. She had been an expert at the Dutroux Parliamentary Commission and Chairperson of the (francophone) League for Human Rights. From 1 November 1998 to 12 September 2012, she was a judge at the Strasbourg Court. From 1 February 2011, she became Vice-President of the Court. With her warm personality,[28] she was one of the Court's most activist judges.[29] She left a profound mark, among other things on

[26] Council Directive 90/531/EEC of 17 September 1990 on the procurement procedures of entities operating in the water, energy, transport, and telecommunications sectors.

[27] Guy Coëme had been Minister of Defence (1988–92) and Deputy Prime Minister and Minister of Communications and Public Enterprises (1992–94).

[28] P Lemmens, 'A Grand Lady Leaves the Court' (12 September 2012): *strasbourgobservers.com*.

[29] See E Voeten, 'The Politics of International Judicial Appointments: Evidence from the European Court of Human Rights' (2007) 61 *International Organization* 669. In 2007, Françoise Tulkens was ranked third out of 97 judges in Strasbourg, behind Loukis Loukaidis (Cyprus) and Jan De Meyer

the Court's positions on asylum.[30] Not without concern for balance, King Albert II welcomed us both among the nobility as baron and baroness, by royal decree of 10 July 2009.

13.3.2. My Appointment to the Court of Arbitration

On 12 September 1996, I informed Herman De Croo, Chairperson of the VLD (1995–97), of my interest in the office of judge at the Court of Arbitration. On 27 September, I officially introduced my candidacy to Frank Swaelen (CVP), President of the Senate (1988–99).

On 10 October 1996, I published an interim report. In the first half of 1996, the Netherlands had twice as many asylum applications (10,025) as Belgium (5,591). What was even more striking was that in the Netherlands 4,696 (46.8 per cent) asylum seekers were from Iraq, Afghanistan, Somalia, Iran and Sri Lanka, while only 206 (3.7 per cent) from those countries had applied in Belgium. In Belgium, there were 2,439 asylum seekers from Former Yugoslavia, Romania, Zaire and Armenia, while there were 1,299 (13 per cent) from those countries in the Netherlands. I mentioned a slight increase in demand.[31] Ecolo MP Vincent Decroly said:

> Marc Bossuyt is a competent man at the head of a well-managed administration. He carries out very rigorously a mission that has been entrusted to him: to resolve the backlog of refugee files pending in Belgium. Statistics are one of his favourite strategic weapons, but it is not easy to capture the quintessence of them.[32]

On 20 October 1996, a 'White March' took place in Brussels in protest at the failures in the justice system, observed in the *Dutroux* case. The next day, a journalist warned me that I was in danger of becoming a victim of the White March. Thanks to this march, the political world had understood that the malfunctions could be remedied by putting an end to political appointments in the justice system. By extension, this also applied to the Conseil d'Etat and even to the Court of Arbitration. The vote on the presentation of a judge to the Court of Arbitration was on the agenda of the Senate on 24 October. Guy Verhofstadt, Deputy President of the Senate (1995–99), said immediately that he felt that in any case the VLD should distance itself from such political appointments.[33] For

(Belgium) (ibid 686: Figure 2: 'Estimates of Levels of Activism ECHR judges'). See also M Bossuyt, 'Judicial Activism in Strasbourg' in K Wellens (ed), *International Law in Silver Perspective: Challenges Ahead* (Leiden, Brill/Nijhoff, 2015) 31.

[30] M-B Dembour, 'Françoise Tulkens, Indefatigable Defender of Migrants' Human Rights' (28 August 2012): strasbourgobservers.com.

[31] From an average of 950 applications per month in 1995 to an average of 1,076 in the third quarter of 1996 (*DM*; *HLN*; *GVA*, 10 October 1996).

[32] *LLB* (11 October 1996): 'The Commissioner General Gives himself a Good Report'.

[33] According to a press release of 29 November 1996, the VLD was outraged by the refusal of the majority parties to derogate from the existing appointment procedure. Guy Verhofstadt had introduced

the appointments to the Conseil d'Etat and the Court of Arbitration, the 'pause button' was therefore pressed.

As far as the Conseil d'Etat was concerned, there were six candidates. Coincidentally, the CVP, PSC, VLD, PRL and the PS each supported one. The sixth candidate, Willem Debeuckelaere,[34] was, as chief of staff (1995–98) to Interior Minister Johan Vande Lanotte, supported by the SP. He was sacrificed on the altar of the new political culture. A few months later, on 7 July 1997, eight State Councillors were appointed. As for the Court of Arbitration, the Senate decided for the first time to hold hearings. On 19 December 1996, five candidates were invited *in camera*. The next day, the Senate presented me as the first candidate, by a two-thirds majority secret ballot. The Senate presented Riet Leysen as its second candidate, who for 10 years had been the referendar at the Court of Arbitration of Judge Louis-Paul Suetens. For almost 17 years, she would assist me in an unparalleled way as referendar. When I left the Constitutional Court on 9 January 2014, I was delighted to see that she succeeded me.

Nominated on 17 January 1997 by the Council of Ministers, I was appointed judge at the Court of Arbitration by royal decree of 28 January.[35] I was sworn in on 6 February by King Albert II at Château Belvedère. It was with great sorrow in my heart that I left the Commission General the night before. An interview given a few weeks earlier became my last as Commissioner General.

13.4. Some Thoughts

In December 1996, *De Wereld Morgen* published the exit interview of 'the man who for nine years had led the Commission General with a firm hand'. For many years, I would no longer speak publicly about the problem of asylum in Belgium. That I remained silent as a judge at the Constitutional Court delighted successive governments. This was especially the case when they let the situation slip several times again. What was less joyous is that much of what I said in this interview is still, 25 years later, hot news.

13.4.1. My Exit Interview: 'Much Hypocrisy and Demagogy' (December 1996)

In this interview, Dirk Leyman and Pieter De Gryse noted in their introduction that the theme of asylum seekers and refugees became 'from time to time an

a proposed law providing for an independent 'Wise Men's Commission' which would formulate a qualified opinion on the candidates for the appointment of judge to the Court of Arbitration.

[34] Willem Debeuckelaere became a judge at the Tribunal of first instance and later at the Court of Appeal and Chairperson of the Commission for the Protection of Privacy. He had previously been Chairperson of the (Flemish) League for Human Rights. He is currently Chairperson of the Vermeylen Fund and Executive Secretary of the Federal Institute for Human Rights.

[35] *M.B.* (11 February 1997) 2746.

overheated debate, sometimes stirred by my strong words'. Some excerpts from this interview:

- *Tired of the refugee theme?*
- CG: I don't want to be considered as 'Mister Refugee' until I turn 65. I think I did what I had to do. In terms of its approach and operation, the Commission General is a modern administration, the perfect instrument to recognise those who are refugees and to refuse within a reasonable time those who are not.

- *After a while, do you have 'bruises to the soul'?*
- CG: What bothers me most is that I have been continually exposed to criticism. There is incredible hypocrisy. People who know full well that we are protecting refugees, continue to criticise our operations and approach against any knowledge. In the long run, we've had enough. Belgium gives broad application to the Geneva Convention. We recognise people from 87 different countries. Those who expect us to also recognise people who are not refugees are at the wrong address.

- *Have the new Vande Lanotte Laws once again made asylum policy more restrictive?*
- CG: It was the Wathelet Law (1991) and especially the Tobback Law (1993) that made the most important changes. The main aim of the Vande Lanotte Laws was to adapt Belgian legislation to the Dublin and Schengen Conventions. The indefinite duration of retention has above all a symbolic value. Compulsory reception in open centres during the admissibility phase is not revolutionary. It was already in the previous legislation but was not yet enforced. The opponents seized the opportunity to make media hype. It has everything to do with hypocrisy and demagogy. Looking more closely at what was in the Vande Lanotte project, they discovered that all this was a lot of noise for nothing. In essence, it was directed against the 1993 legislative changes.

- *Are you still arguing for a simplification of the asylum procedure?*
- CG: The current procedure is too cumbersome. There are too many bodies and too many possibilities for appeal. Moreover, the guarantees have become ever wider. The contribution of the Conseil d'Etat consists in a single recognition out of 100,000 decisions. The Permanent Board recognises approximately 80 refugees per year.

- *The most critical predict that the new asylum laws will deter asylum seekers who then go straight into illegality.*
- CG: Nobody benefits from pushing people who are not refugees into the asylum process. I know that I am accused of a fetishism of figures, but 90 per cent of the asylum procedure is used by people who are not refugees. For some nationalities, it's even 99 per cent. That can't be the goal of welcoming all these people here?

- *You suggest two possible solutions for illegality: regularisation for long-standing cases and a stricter deportation policy for others. How do you assess the government's approach to these two instruments?*
- CG: The effective removal of failed asylum seekers is still a rare exception. Critics argue for longer procedures and more safeguards. At the same time, they are pushing for regularisation after two years of procedure. This is a form of hypocrisy.

- *You are calling for a more aggressive attack on the causes of migration. What do you expect from more targeted development assistance?*
- CG: We must not direct development aid to the countries that send us the largest number of asylum seekers. Otherwise, we should have directed our aid in the 1980s, especially to Ghana. Moreover, most asylum seekers do not come from the least developed countries, but from countries that already have a certain level of development. The more westernised countries are, the more their nationals want to come to us. I am a big supporter of more development cooperation, but I do not see it as a direct link to – or impact on – the asylum procedure. It is also an untenable thesis to claim that we should welcome all those from Eastern Europe or Africa because we cannot solve the problems there.

- *Can the image we have in the Third World influence migration movements?*
- CG: The image of the West in the Third World is best served by a rapid asylum procedure, which effectively removes rejected asylum seekers. The noises spread with the speed of lightning over there.

13.4.2. Endless Criticism

Every time the authorities manage to have the asylum procedure and the number of applications under control, every effort is made to criticise the asylum policy. All kinds of actions are being taken to create mistrust of this policy. These actions must convince public opinion that all this is too severe, too repressive, not generous enough. Should we not expect more generosity on our part? Should we not show more humanity and solidarity? We want a warmer society. Meanwhile the attention of the rulers weakens. Since the last crisis, instruments have been developed to deal with higher numbers of asylum seekers. Instead of dismantling these instruments, we could perhaps do better by welcoming a few more people. Otherwise, there will be job losses, especially in the areas of reception and legal aid. Moreover, the necessary budgets are provided to deal with it.

Thus are sown the seeds of new slippages. Other rulers came to power. They did not closely experience the previous crisis. They do not yet know from experience that it is much easier to let the situation worsen than to bring it back under control.

If other official bodies, or bodies subsidised by public authority, join them to put obstacles in the way, we will be in trouble faster than expected.

In 1995, lawyers formed a non-profit association to threaten me with having to justify my decisions to a criminal judge. I had conspired with my staff to take action that they felt was against the law. These measures concerned the excessive number of negative decisions. *There were too few refugee recognitions.* Also in 1995, the Prosecutor's Office requested an investigating judge. I was not given the opportunity to first explain the context of the information provided. This investigating judge forced my collaborators and me to justify the positive decisions we had made or proposed before marshals of the BSR. *There were too many refugee recognitions.* There was no follow-up to prove large-scale fraud by asylum seekers. On the other hand, great means were used in the hope of finding someone at the Commission General who had perhaps had lunch with a lawyer in favour of the recognition of an asylum seeker.

Even in 1995, there were parliamentarians ready to believe any asylum seeker. For them, it was a matter of being able to overwhelm me for having put a human life at risk. I should have opposed her return to her country. They were quite willing to consider a fabricated story by an asylum seeker to be true. After returning from Belgium, her sister was reportedly killed by rape and torture. Joined by journalists from the main French-language newspapers, they gave credit to such stories. Neither these parliamentarians nor these journalists had bothered to contact me beforehand to verify whether this was a credible story. Others, such as Director Johan Leman of the Centre for Equal Opportunities and freelance journalist Pieter De Gryse, also could not resist the temptation to criticise me without first verifying the situation.

14

Peixotin (1996), Maiztegui (1998), Moreno–Garcia (2004) and Jaione (2020)

On 2 October 1996, the Minister of Justice, Stefaan De Clerck, withdrew his ministerial decree of 22 January 1996 ordering the extradition to Spain of the Basque couple Moreno–Garcia. Four and a half months earlier, on 27 May 1996, another Spanish Basque, Enrique Pagoaga Gallastegui, named 'Peixotin', applied for asylum in Belgium. He was exiled to Venezuela. Two years later, on 29 June 1998, another Spanish Basque, Juan Cruz Maiztegui Bengoa, did the same. He was exiled to Mexico. On 30 January 2004, Spain made a new attempt concerning the Moreno–Garcia couple. European arrest warrants (EAWs) were issued to obtain their surrender. Without success. Spain was doing better with its request for Maria Natividad Juaregui Espina, known as 'Jaione'. On 22 November 2020, 40 years after the events of which she was suspected, she was handed over to Spain with the execution of an EAW. But first, the two exiles.

14.1. Another Basque: Exiled in Venezuela (27 May 1996)

'On a Beautiful Day of Pentecost'[1] (26 May 1996), Enrique Pagoaga Gallastegui (b 1954) flew from Venezuela via Frankfurt to Brussels National Airport. He claimed to have Spanish nationality, but the Gendarmerie found that his Spanish passport was false, 'a detail that had escaped strict German control'. The next day he asked for asylum. In Spain, the news quickly became known. The question immediately arose whether a new quarrel with Spain was being prepared.[2] He was known as 'Peixotin', his brother Juan Manuel, named 'Peixoto', being a historical leader of ETA. On 29 May, his fingerprints confirmed his identity. The Spanish authorities reported that they did not contest his nationality. At his hearing by my Office on 4 June, he produced a real Spanish identity card. It had been provided by his mother, but its validity had expired after 1982.

[1] Misjoe Verleyen, *Knack* (19 June 1996).
[2] *LLB*; *LS*; *HLN* (29 May 1996).

14.1.1. Peixotin's 'Complicated Story'

Peixotin had a 'complicated story' behind him, which can be summarised as follows: since the age of 15 he had actively participated in 'the struggle for emancipation of the Basque people'; he was first arrested in 1974, when he was 20 years old; he then claimed to have been tortured; sentenced to four years in prison in 1975, he fled to France and was recognised as a refugee (this status was withdrawn in 1980); from 1976 to 1977 he was in prison in Spain for 14 months; in June 1977, he was transferred to Denmark with 14 others in a Spanish military aircraft; in August 1977 he returned to Spain; in January 1979, he returned to France; in September 1979, he emigrated to Venezuela; in 1982, he returned to France; in July 1987, France deported him to Algeria; on 28 May 1989, he was transferred by a Spanish military plane with 10 others from Algeria to Venezuela, which he left on 25 May 1996.

On 29 May 1996, the Spanish Secretary of State for Security, Ricardo Martí Fluxá, warned Belgium not to grant him asylum, insisting on returning him immediately to Venezuela or Germany. On 30 May, Interior Minister Johan Vande Lanotte refused him access to the territory, sending him back to the country from where he had fled. The Aliens Office had little faith that he would have left Venezuela for fear of persecution. If he was prosecuted in Spain, it would be because he had participated in terrorist actions. On 31 May, he filed an urgent appeal.

On 3 June 1996, with extreme urgency, he also applied to the Conseil d'Etat for a suspension of the decision to refuse him residence, deprive him of liberty and remove him.[3] On the auditor's assent, the Conseil d'Etat rejected the request on 10 June for the refusal of residence and its dismissal, since he had to wait for my decision on its urgent appeal. Deprivation of liberty was not a serious and hardly repairable prejudice. It was justified because he had wanted to access the territory irregularly. The *Knack* wrote: 'Commissioner General Marc Bossuyt must once again pull the chestnuts out of the fire'.

Meanwhile, it turned out that Peixotin had apparently left Venezuela as part of a concerted action with the companions with whom he shared the same fate. *El País* of 2 June 1996 reported that ETA had called from Brussels on its 50 deportees to return to the Basque country.[4] On 5 June, the Spanish Minister of the Interior, Jaime Mayor Oreja, showed little concern: 'I will not waste five minutes with Peixotin'.[5] Later, the *Knack* would write:[6] 'Some 50 Basque Spaniards were scattered in seven African and South American countries. On 7 June 1996, the

[3] According to his lawyer Me Paul Bekaert: 'A Belgian arrested with false documents is still not put on a plane to Venezuela?' (*DS*; *DM*, 3 June 1996).

[4] 'ETA llama desde Bruselas al retorno al País Vasco de sus 50 deportados'.

[5] *El País* (5 June 1996): 'Ni cinco minutos voy perder con Peixotin'.

[6] *Knack* (n 1).

French police arrested ten Basques who were seeking asylum in the Bayonne cathedral and deported them to Spain'.[7]

14.1.2. Peixotin's Application is 'Moot' (27 June 1996)

On 27 June 1996, I decided, based on extensive references to EU law, that the applicant's asylum application 'as a citizen of the European Union was, in the present circumstances, moot'.[8] His fingerprints had confirmed his identity and nationality. Since the entry into force of the Maastricht Treaty on 1 January 1993, every citizen of the European Union enjoys free movement of persons within the Union. So far as an identity card is concerned, even if its validity has expired, if it nevertheless contains all the elements to establish the identity, and the nationality of the person concerned as a citizen of the European Union is established, this person has the right to free movement within the Union.[9]

As regards the banning of the person concerned to Algeria and Venezuela in succession, I observed Article 3, §2, of Protocol No 4 to the ECHR which states: 'No one shall be deprived of the right to enter the territory of the state of which he is a national'. Moreover, Article 11, §2, of the Spanish Constitution states that no Spaniard of origin may be deprived of his nationality. The UN Human Rights Committee[10] found that the failure to obtain a passport for a national violated Article 12, §2, of the International Covenant on Civil and Political Rights.[11] Failure to produce valid documents may be penalised but may not lead to the refusal of the person concerned of his right to freedom of movement and residence.[12]

The first of the reasons given by the Aliens Office (he had left Venezuela without fear) was irrelevant, since he was not Venezuelan. The last reason (he had participated in terrorist actions) clearly exceeded the threshold of the admissibility test. The following observation was of crucial importance:

> In any case, a forced return of the person concerned would be tantamount to the banishment of an EU citizen from the Union, which would be contrary to the international human rights obligations subscribed by the Member States of the European Union.

[7] 'The [French] Government puts an end to the action of Basque refugees in Bayonne' (*Le Monde*); 'The Basque gifts of [Jacques] Chirac [the French President] to Spain. Six nationalists deported to Madrid without judicial intervention. France is zealous' (*Libération*, 10 June 1996).

[8] 'A Basque is at Home in Europe …' (*VI'A*, 28 June 1996). *Le Soir* quoted the Spanish Minister of the Interior: 'I do not envisage any intervention with the Belgian authorities'. *El País* nevertheless referred to 'El explosivo dictamen de Marc Bossuyt'.

[9] See the judgment of 5 March 1991 in *Panagiotis Giagounidis*, CJEU, No C-376/89, *Jur*, 1991, I-1069.

[10] Report of the UN Committee on Human Rights, A/37/40 (1982) §§174–77.

[11] Art 12, §2: 'Everyone shall be free to leave any country, including his own'.

[12] See CJUE, 30 May 1991, *Commission v the Netherlands*, No C-68/89, *Jur*, 1991, I-2637.

There was no Spanish request for extradition and no ministerial order for removal. Neither access to the territory nor residence could be refused to a citizen of a Member State of the European Union.

14.1.3. The Demining Works: Peixotin Granted Access to the Territory (28 June 1996)

It was possible to infer from this decision[13] that, had Peixotin not been a national of a Member State of the European Union, I would have taken a further examination decision. Out of caution for the extreme sensitivity of the Spanish government (and the media) in this matter, I declared the urgent appeal without purpose. This possibility had already been considered, *in tempore non suspecto*, in my refusal decisions of 6 February 1994 in the *Moreno and Garcia* case.

A Spanish request for extradition or a Belgian order for removal would, however, have been a new fact justifying a new application for asylum. In this case, an admissibility decision with the risk of a possible recognition decision – by me or the Permanent Board – might not have been excluded. Both the *Ryan* case and the *Moreno and Garcia* case have shown that the more stubbornly the political authorities (and the media) insist on the extradition of a person, the greater the risk that independent bodies will position themselves in a reserved and unwilling manner. The understanding of the challenges faced by a State facing terrorist actions can be great. However, we cannot expect another EU Member State to cooperate in banning EU citizens. In a democratic society, there is no room for that.

But never despair. Sometimes, wisdom prevails: on 28 June 1996 (the day after my 'moot' decision), the Minister of the Interior, Johan Vande Lanotte, granted Peixotin immediate access to Belgian territory (not as an asylum seeker but as an EU citizen). *De Morgen* of 2 July spoke of a great stir in the Spanish media. *De Standaard* reported on possible prosecution for Peixotin's use of a false passport. For the rest, the case was off the radar.[14] The demining had worked, and the principles were saved.

14.2. And Another Basque (29 June 1998): Exiled in Mexico

On 29 June 1998, a Spanish Basque arrived again at Brussels National Airport, this time from Mexico, via Washington DC. He was on his way to Amsterdam. It was

[13] On 27 June 1996, Pagoaga Gallastegui asked the Conseil d'Etat, with extreme urgency, to suspend this decision and the decision of the Minister of the Interior of 30 May.

[14] On 9 July 1996, the Conseil d'Etat declared in its judgment No 60.818 that on 3 July the applicant had abandoned his request of 27 June.

Juan Cruz Maiztegui Bengoa (b 1945). After finding that his identity documents were false, he applied for asylum. He had been granted refugee status in France from 1975 to 1979. In 1987, his residence permit was withdrawn. In 1992, he travelled from France, where he was staying illegally, to Mexico. He remained there until 28 June 1998.

14.2.1. Persistent Attempts to Drive him Back to Mexico (1 July, 4 and 6 August 1998)

On 1 July 1998, the Aliens Office refused him access to the territory, and he was to be returned to Mexico. This decision was taken because he had tried to gain access to the territory with false documents and because of the lack of fear of persecution in Spain, a democratic State, or in France and Mexico, where he had stayed for more than three months. The next day he filed an urgent appeal with Commissioner General Luc De Smet.[15] On 3 August, the Commissioner General decided that his application was moot. As an EU citizen, he could not be denied access to the territory. Furthermore, there was no Spanish extradition request and a deportation to Mexico would amount to an illegal ban.[16]

On 4 August 1998, however, the Aliens Office[17] decided that he should be returned to Mexico because he did not have the necessary documents to enter the Kingdom. In addition, his use of a false passport could have harmed public order.[18] In a request[19] lodged on 5 August and on the assent of the auditor, the Conseil d'Etat[20] on 6 August suspended with extreme urgency the decision of 4 August 1998 refusing his access of 1 July 1998 and the decision to renew it. Otherwise, he would have been put on the plane to Mexico on 7 August at 12.30 pm. Commissioner General Luc De Smet appeared in person before the Conseil d'Etat to plead against the suspension of his decision of 3 August. The request for suspension was rejected by the Conseil d'Etat because the request did not establish any prejudice caused by the Commissioner General's decision.

On the same day (6 August 1998) a decision was taken, for the third time, to deny him access to the territory and to remove him to Mexico. The reasoning

[15] Luc De Smet had succeeded me from 6 February 1997. From that day on, I had become a judge at the Court of Arbitration (since 7 May 2007 called the 'Constitutional Court').

[16] *DM* (7 August 1998). His lawyer was Me Paul Bekaert.

[17] On 24 April 1998, Louis Tobback succeeded Johan Vande Lanotte as Minister of the Interior. The latter resigned because of Marc Dutroux's escape on 23 April 1998. Five months later (on 26 September 1998), Louis Tobback resigned over the death of Semira Adamu on 22 September 1998.

[18] Previously in my favourable opinion of 14 November 1988 concerning Ryan, I had decided that possession of a false passport was not sufficient to conclude that there was a risk to public order and national security.

[19] His lawyer was Me Paul Bekaert.

[20] CdE, No 75.554 (6 August 1998).

was that a fear of persecution could not be invoked against Spain, a democratic State, nor against France and Mexico, where he had stayed for more than three months. On 7 August, Maiztegui lodged an urgent appeal with the Commissioner General and a request for suspension, in extreme urgency, with the Conseil d'Etat. On 10 August the Conseil d'Etat[21] rejected this request as a matter of extreme urgency because the administrative appeal to the Commissioner General had not yet been exhausted.

14.2.2. Further Examination of an Asylum Application by an EU Citizen (18 August 1998)

On 18 August 1998, Commissioner General Luc De Smet took a further examination decision. He was surprised that the person concerned was denied access to the territory, even though it was a case identical to that of Enrique Pagoaga Gallastegui (Peixotin). He considered that this refusal was contrary to the '*res judicata*' authority of the decision of the Conseil d'Etat of 6 August 1998. That judgment pointed out that the inaccuracy of the facts from which it appeared that he would be in danger in Mexico, was not proven. In a letter dated 3 August, the UNHCR Representative, on a request from the Commissioner General on 13 July, replied that only a substantive examination could clarify the merits of the fear of persecution in Spain. In these circumstances, the Commissioner General considered that it was not possible for him to confirm the refusal of access to the territory, which was poorly justified. With this decision, Maiztegui was free to leave the transit centre.[22] Granting this EU citizen access to the asylum procedure on the merits was apparently the only way to prevent him from being sent back to Mexico.

In *El País* of 20 August 1998, Commissioner General Luc De Smet stressed that this was not an act hostile to Spain. He would not have declared the asylum application admissible if the Ministry of the Interior had not responded to the request of the Spanish Ambassador, Manuel Benavides, to expel Maiztegui. His only objective was to prevent the return to Mexico. The Spanish government declared itself 'surprised' and 'irritated'. The Spanish media were again very harsh towards Belgium. On 27 August 1998, the Spanish newspaper *El Mundo* reported that the most important leaders of ETA had left France for Belgium. However, there was no evidence of this in Belgium. The Minister Louis Tobback had no evidence in this regard. He called this information 'intoxication' and 'manipulation'. The Spanish Minister of the Interior spoke of 'pure speculation'.[23]

[21] CdE, No 75.579 (10 August 1998).

[22] *El País* (19 August 1998); *DM* (20 August): 'The obstinacy and rapidity with which the Interior tried to implement the expulsion raised a certain astonishment. "Pressure from Spain", said Paul Bekaert, his lawyer'.

[23] *IHT* (27 August 1998).

On 3 September 1998, Stéphane Schewebach, the Director General of the Aliens Office, announced that Interior Minister Louis Tobback was preparing an appeal to the Conseil d'Etat against the decision of the Commissioner General concerning Maiztegui's asylum application.[24] The Minister no longer wanted Belgium to be accused by Spain of being a refuge for ETA.[25] He felt that the reasons given for accepting such cases were outdated.

De Morgen of 10 September 1998 mentioned the arrest in France of 14 Basques, including Peixotin. They were promptly transferred to Spain. In the absence of further complaints, the Spanish judge decided to prosecute Peixotin for having in his possession false Spanish documents. In the absence of a formal Belgian complaint, he was released a few days later. In *La Libre Belgique* of 16 September, Me Paul Bekaert said:

> Two cases of Basque exiles arrested in Brussels are not enough to talk about a network. Why is it such a tragedy when Spain does not demand him? If Mr [Stéphane] Schewebach had not yielded to pressure from Spain and had not refused Maiztegui access to the territory, we would not have had to file an asylum application.[26]

In the same newspaper, Commissioner General Luc De Smet declared that he awaited the Minister's announced appeal with great serenity.[27] He referred explicitly to the reservation made by Belgium during the negotiations of the Amsterdam Treaty of 2 October 1997. This Treaty contains a Protocol[28] which aims to limit the possibilities of asylum for nationals of Member States of the European Union. However, Belgium had made a declaration concerning this Protocol in which it stressed that, in accordance with the Geneva Convention, 'it would carry out an individual examination of any request'. In an official communication of 20 June 1997, the Office of the UN High Commissioner for Refugees[29] welcomed the statement of at least one State which intended to receive and consider all asylum applications, regardless of their country of origin.

That same month, on 22 September 1998, Nigerian asylum seeker Semira Adamu died in an aborted attempt to return her to Togo. On 26 September, Louis

[24] 'Tobback no Longer Wants Belgium to be Accused by Madrid of being the "ETA Sanctuary"' (*LLB*, 3 September 1998); 'Tobback Takes the Basque Problem by the Horns' (*LS*, 4 September 1998).

[25] See *El País* (20 August 1998): 'Sanctuario belga'.

[26] Pascale Bourgaux, *LLB* (16 September 1998).

[27] ibid: 'Luc De Smet: "I have no Lesson in Democracy to Learn from Anyone"'.

[28] The Protocol lists the cases in which applications for asylum by nationals of another Member State may be considered or declared admissible for examination by another Member State: (a) if that Member State has invoked the derogation clause of Art 15 ECHR; (b) if the procedure provided for in Art F.l (1) of the Treaty on European Union has been initiated; (c) if the Council has determined the existence of a serious and persistent breach by that Member State of principles mentioned in Art F.1; (d) if that Member State should so decide unilaterally, has immediately informed the Council thereof and is processing the application on the basis of the presumption that it is manifestly unfounded.

[29] The Office of the UN High Commissioner had expressed deep concern about this restriction of EU citizens' access to asylum. That Office was especially concerned that others would follow and that the instrument of international refugee protection could be weakened. The Office stated that it did not share the premise of the Protocol's preamble that it complied with the Geneva Convention.

Tobback resigned as Minister of the Interior. His second term as Minister had lasted only five months. Luc Van den Bossche (SP) succeeded him.[30] There has been no more talk of an appeal to the Conseil d'Etat against the decision of the Commissioner General concerning Maiztegui. Neither have we heard any more about him.

14.3. Once Again Spain: EAWs for Moreno and Garcia[31] (30 January 2004)

The Law on the European Arrest Warrant (EAW)[32] of 19 December 2003 came into force on 1 January 2004.[33] While the previous extradition system remained in force for relations with non-EU Member States, the EAW applied between EU Member States. The differences mainly concern three important points: (a) Belgians too can be 'surrendered' (the new EU-specific term instead of extradited) to other EU Member States; (b) the decision is no longer a political decision by the executive but a purely judicial one; and (c) there is no longer any exception for 'political offences'.

These were for Spain sufficient grounds to try its luck again with EAWs against Moreno and Garcia. Despite their problems with Spanish justice, Moreno and Garcia had become Belgians on 15 October 2001. As a result, they could no longer apply for refugee status in Belgium. On 30 January 2004, a Spanish examining magistrate issued an EAW against each of them. These EAWs were based on the same facts as those for which their provisional arrest in Belgium had been unsuccessfully requested on 20 May 1993. According to *De Morgen*,[34] the Moreno–Garcia couple learned via television that the Spanish authorities had taken a new step to obtain their surrender. They learned this from the Belgian Prime Minister Guy Verhofstadt, who was visiting his Spanish counterpart José Zapatero (2004–11) in Madrid. History sometimes repeats itself.[35] Although in an EAW the government plays no role, heads of government still cannot refrain from exchanging views with each other and communicating to the press on the subject.

[30] Luc Van den Bossche was Minister of the Interior from 28 September 1998 to 11 July 1999.

[31] Their lawyer was Me Paul Bekaert.

[32] This law was adopted in the implementation of Council Framework Decision 2002/584/JHA of 13 June 2002 on the European arrest warrant and the surrender procedures between EU Member States.

[33] The summary of this case is based on C Ryngaert, 'Het Europees aanhoudingsbevel lastens Moreno–Garcia: de aanhouder wint' [2004] *Nieuw Juridisch Weekblad*, ep 89, 1226; see also L Janssens, Note under Cass. 13 April 2004, 'De zaak Moreno–Garcia, een testcase voor het Europees aanhoudingsbevel' [2004–05] *Rechtskundig Weekblad* 1260. On the EAW, see generally H Sanders, *Handboek van het overleveringsrecht* (Antwerp, Intersentia, 2011); C Hanegreef, 'Het Europees aanhoudingsbevel: verholen valkuilen in kaderbesluit' 2002/584/JBZ (Master's Thesis, Ghent University, 2014); S Dewulf, *Europees aanhoudingsbevel* (Mechelen, Wolters Kluwer, 2020).

[34] 28 May 2004.

[35] See above p 78.

14.3.1. Statute-Barred Facts: The Examining Judge Refuses the EAWs (17 March 2004)

After hearing the couple, the Belgian examining judge decided, on 17 March 2004, not to proceed with the execution of the EAWs. He referred to the requirements of Article 4, 4°, of the EAW Law: 'when the public action or the sentence is statute-barred under Belgian law and the facts fall within the jurisdiction of the Belgian courts'.[36] The examining magistrate considered that the Belgian courts had jurisdiction, since the conditions of Article 7, §1, of the Preliminary Title of the Code of Criminal Procedure had been met.[37] Indeed, the judge found that the facts were punishable in both Belgium and Spain, and that the suspects were Belgian and had their main residence in the territory of the Kingdom. He judged that it was sufficient for the latter condition to have been met at the time he made his decision.[38] He did not believe that Belgian courts should have jurisdiction at the time of the events. Since the statute of limitations had expired, the EAWs could not be enforced. The Federal Prosecutor did not dispute that the statute of limitations had expired, but appealed to the Brussels Chamber of Indictment, since he felt that the requirement of being Belgian or having one's main residence in the territory of the Kingdom had to be met at the time of the events. Neither he, nor Moreno and Garcia, could possibly have guessed that the Chamber of Indictment would have to consider this case four more times, and the Cour de cassation three times.

Jurisdiction, as referred to in Article 4, 4°, of the EAW Law, is a prerequisite for invoking the statute of limitations. This is why reference is made to Article 7, §1, of the Preliminary Title of the Code of Criminal Procedure. The condition of being Belgian or, by extension, at least having one's main residence in the territory of the Kingdom, was introduced by the Law of 5 August 2003. The purpose of this law was to temper the Law on Universal Jurisdiction of 16 June 1993.[39] Prior to this amendment, any person could be prosecuted in Belgium for serious violations of humanitarian law, even in the absence of any point of connection. Since then, in the absence of the principle of territoriality commonly used in criminal law, there must be at least one specific connecting factor (either Belgian nationality or principal residence in Belgium).

[36] Janssens (n 33) 1261 points out that the Belgian legislator has made prescription a mandatory ground for refusal.

[37] Art 7, §1, of the Preliminary Title of the Code of Criminal Procedure: '[Any Belgian or any person whose principal residence is in the territory of the Kingdom] who, outside the territory of the Kingdom, is guilty of an act qualified as a crime or misdemeanour under Belgian law may be prosecuted in Belgium if the act is punishable under the legislation of the country where it was committed'.

[38] This corresponds, according to Janssens (n 33) 1261, with the preparatory work for the Law of 8 August 2003, which amended Art 7 of the aforementioned Preliminary Title.

[39] This refers to the Law of 16 June 1993 on the repression of serious violations of international humanitarian law, amended by the Laws of 10 February 1999, 10 April and 23 April 2003 and repealed by the Law of 5 August 2003.

14.3.2. A Refusal by the Chamber of Indictment Despite Three Cassations (23 June 2004)

On three occasions (30 March, 27 April and 26 May 2004), three different Chambers of Indictment in Brussels refused, for various reasons, to execute the EAWs. On three occasions (13 April, 11 May and 8 June 2004), the Cour de cassation[40] overturned these rulings, also for various reasons. Successive judges sometimes looked far and wide for arguments in this case. They did not shy away from one daring argument or another.[41] Finally, execution was refused a fourth time by the Antwerp Chamber of Indictment. In its decision of 23 June 2004, this Chamber ruled that the offence charged had been committed against foreigners, and that the EAWs contained all the elements required for a Belgian authority to institute admissible criminal proceedings against the accused.[42] The EAWs were the 'official notices' required by Article 7, §2, of the Preliminary Title,[43] and the Belgian courts had jurisdiction. As the criminal proceedings were time-barred, the execution of the EAWs was refused.

14.3.3. Observations on the EAWs against Moreno–Garcia: Relief

Five Chambers of Indictment (one in 1993 and four in 2004; four in Brussels and one in Antwerp) opposed the extradition or surrender of Moreno and Garcia to Spain. Fifteen appeal court councillors considered the case. For the Federal Prosecutor, that was enough. Although it is doubtful whether he was satisfied with this latest ruling, he decided to throw in the towel. However, it is not certain that the Cour de cassation agreed with the interpretation of the Antwerp Chamber of Indictment. In any case, it was clear from the outset that the statute of limitations had run out on these facts in 2004. The EAW was a new means of prosecution that gave rise to divergent legal interpretations. Paul Bekaert's contribution to the *Juristenkrant*[44] was mercilessly critical of the EAW: 'The European Arrest Warrant is tinkering at every level'.

Whether the rulings of the Chamber of Indictment and the Cour de cassation in this case really clarified the interpretation of the EAW is not beyond

[40] Cass (13 April 2004) AR P.04.0513.N, *Arr Cass. 2004*, ep 4, 631; Cass (26 May 2004) AR P.04.0660.N, *Arr Cass 2004*, ep 5, 931; Cass (8 June 2004) AR P.04.0842.N.

[41] Ryngaert (n 33) 1228 on the judgment of 26 May 2004 of the Chamber of Indictment of Brussels.

[42] Ryngaert, ibid 1232, speaks of 'artificial reasoning'.

[43] Art 7, §2, of the aforementioned Preliminary Title: 'If the offence has been committed against a foreigner, prosecution can only take place at the request of the Public Prosecutor and must, moreover, be preceded by a complaint from the offended foreigner or his family, or by an *official notice* given to the Belgian authority by the authority of the country where the offence was committed' (emphasis added).

[44] 2005, ep 117, 3.

reasonable doubt. One thing is certain: Moreno and Garcia were not handed over to Spain. They could breathe freely again. In the words of Raquel Garcia, the news came 'as if a doctor who had told us we had cancer, had then come to tell us it was a mistake. From now on, we can finally hope to get on with our lives' (*DM*, 24 June 2004).

14.4. Jaione's Handover: Strasbourg Washes its Hands of the Matter (22 November 2020)

Sixteen years later, Spain had more success, following an intervention by the European Court of Human Rights, with the surrender of Maria Natividad Juaregui Espina (b 1958).[45] This Spanish Basque woman was suspected of participation in a criminal organisation, murder, serious mistreatment and assassination on 19 January 1981, as well as attempted murder and terrorism on 14 June 1981, both in Bilbao. From 1984 to 1988, she lived in France. She then spent 14 years with her life partner in Mexico, where they ran a Basque restaurant. After her partner's extradition to Spain on 11 November 2002, she settled in the Ghent region. Known by her Basque first name 'Jaione', she worked there as a cook, without being registered in the population register.

The EAWs issued by a Spanish judge on 9 July 2004 and 1 December 2005 were declared enforceable, on 16 October 2013, by the Ghent Chambre du conseil. The Chamber of Indictment of the Ghent Court of Appeal, however, overturned this order on 31 October 2013. The Chamber of Indictment described the appellant as follows:

> A young woman in her twenties, who had been active in the Basque armed resistance movement, but who had in the meantime become a 55-year-old woman, professionally active and leading a normal life in Ghent. The execution of the EAW would infringe her fundamental rights, since suspects of punishable acts with alleged terrorist motives must undergo in Spain a special regime of deprivation of liberty, in inhuman conditions that may go hand in hand with torture and very limited contact with the outside world.

The Cour de cassation dismissed the appeal against this refusal of execution on 19 November 2013.[46] The Chambre du conseil, on 29 January 2016, and the Ghent Chamber of Indictment, on 14 July 2016, refused to enforce a third EAW of 8 May 2015. The Cour de cassation rejected the appeal against these decisions on 17 July 2016.[47]

[45] Her lawyer was Me Paul Bekaert.
[46] Cass (19 November 2013) P.13.1765.N.
[47] Cass (17 July 2016) P.16.0847.N.

However, the heirs of the Spanish lieutenant-colonel who was shot dead in 1981 turned to the Strasbourg Court. In its *Romeo Castaño v Belgium* judgment of 9 July 2019, the Court ruled that in this case Belgium had violated Article 2 ECHR (the right to life). As noted in this Strasbourg judgment, on 31 October 2013, the Ghent Chamber of Indictment had referred to the report on the 2011 periodic visit by the European Committee for the Prevention of Torture. In its judgment of 19 November 2013, the Cour de cassation had referred to the risk of imprisonment conditions that could be contrary to Article 3 ECHR. In its judgment of 14 July 2016, the Ghent Chamber of Indictment referred to its earlier judgment. It considered that the observations of the UN Human Rights Committee, dated 14 August 2015, confirmed this.

The Strasbourg Court considered, however, that the Belgian courts should have carried out an updated and detailed examination of the situation prevailing in 2016. They had not sought to identify a real and individualised risk to the person concerned, nor any structural shortcomings in the conditions of detention in Spain. They should have requested additional information. By failing to do so, Belgium had breached its obligation to cooperate under the procedural aspect of Article 2 ECHR. Washing its hands of the matter in advance, the Court pointed out that its finding of a violation did not necessarily imply that Belgium was under an obligation to hand her over to the Spanish authorities.

In this case, the Belgian courts were therefore condemned for violating one of the most fundamental rights: the right to life. The Strasbourg Court at least gave the appearance of having more confidence in the functioning of the Spanish judicial system than in that of Belgium. The Court overlooked that the Belgian government could not defend Belgian judicial decisions in this case without jeopardising its friendly relations with Spain. Despite this Strasbourg ruling, execution of the (fourth) EAW of 16 October 2019 was refused by the Ghent Chambre du conseil on 26 February 2020. However, on 5 November 2020, the Ghent Chamber of Indictment declared this EAW enforceable. The Cour de cassation rejected the appeal against this ruling on 17 November 2020.[48] Jaione was handed over to Spain on 22 November 2020, almost 40 years after the events of which she was suspected.

[48] Cass (17 November 2020) P.20.1127.N. For a favourable commentary, see S Dewulf, 'The Saga Finally Ends. Na een trilogie van procedures kon de overlevering van een vermeend ETA-lid alsnog plaatsvinden' [2021] *Nullum Crimen* 181.

15

A 'Never-Ending Quest' for Human Resources

As soon as they were established, the new refugee authorities were faced with an acute shortage of staff. In an 'ever more insistent and even irritating manner',[1] I warned of the consequences of this shortage. The framework assigned was 22 staff members for the Commission General and 19 staff members for the Permanent Board, each of whom would have two advisers and four jurists. Except for the four advisers, the other staff members were recruited several months before the new Refugee Law came into force on 1 February 1988. It was also very positive that, in the meantime, the eight jurists were provided with training at the Representation of the UN High Commissioner for Refugees and other staff members at the Aliens Office. Measures to strengthen the staff were taken at an exasperating pace. Important lessons can be learned from this experience.

15.1. Step by Step Towards Progress

Steps to strengthen the staff were taken gradually. First, the authorities had to be convinced of their need. Then the decisions had to be made and implemented. Then they had to be adapted to the circumstances that had changed in the meantime. Finally, after more than five years of activity, appropriate measures were taken.

15.1.1. 'Savings' that Cost a Lot of Money

Justice Minister Jean Gol, who had taken the initiative to create the new bodies for refugees, had asked for a realistic staff framework. On the advice of the Finance Inspectorate of 25 November 1986, the staff required had been reduced (-49 per cent), to the point that – already after six months of activity – the Commission General encountered serious difficulties. After the fall of the

[1] *Second Annual Report* (1989) §173.

Martens VI Government, due to the Happart affair,[2] the Martens VII Government took over on 21 October 1987. This government had to organise the 13 December 1987 elections and could only deal with caretaking business. I was appointed Commissioner General, from 4 November on, on the proposal of Minister Jean Gol at the first Council of Ministers of the new government. This was three months before the new refugee proceedings came into force.

Before this entry into force, I had already expressed my concern about the inadequacy of the staff cadre in notes dated 10 November and 21 December 1987 addressed to Eugène Frencken, the Secretary General of the Ministry of Justice, I feared, if this framework was not adapted within a short period of time, an inevitable heap of files. Based on a long experience with the justice system, the Secretary General made me understand in a paternal way that I should not have too many illusions.

The Martens VIII Government was constituted on 9 May 1988, after lengthy negotiations (148 days, the longest ever until then) for the formation of a government. That same day, I requested an urgent meeting with the new Minister of Justice Melchior Wathelet. On 13 June, during a pleasant meeting, I gave him a detailed note on the need to adapt the staff and speed up the recognition procedure.

On 28 June 1988, *Le Monde* announced the resignation of the director of the French Office for the Protection of Refugees and Stateless Persons (OFPRA). He wanted to sound the alarm because the French refugee service did not have enough resources to cope with the influx of applications. OFPRA had 175 staff members, about a third of its German counterpart.[3] In 1988, a well-informed author, Frédéric Tiberghien, wrote: 'The measures adopted have always been too late. They were also insufficient given the scale of the crisis. We can no longer reason as if it were simply a cyclical problem'.[4]

On 8 August 1988, I read the unfavourable opinion of the Inspectorate of Finance concerning my request for expanding my staff. From that moment on, my relationship with the Minister of Justice deteriorated. On 25 October, the Minister even accused me of 'anticipating'. On 12 December, I replied that I had deliberately anticipated the foreseeable development of the refugee question. I felt it was my primary responsibility to get the attention of the political powers before it was too late.

Not only at the Commission General, but also at the Aliens Office, it was becoming increasingly clear that there were not enough staff to process the incoming asylum applications. In his budget speech on 1 March 1989, the Minister of Justice described the situation at the Aliens Office as 'dramatic'. In April 1989, the militiamen placed at the disposal of the reception centre in Petit-Château arrived at the end of their military service. The Aliens Office wanted to replace them with

[2] See above p 3 (n 2).

[3] *First Annual Report* (1988) 83 (Appendix 4).

[4] F Tiberghien, *La protection des réfugiés en France*, 2nd edn (Aix-en-Provence, PU d'Aix-Marseille, 1988) 38.

civil servants. As a result of their departure, refugee applicants were no longer interviewed immediately after their application was submitted. When asked by the *Vlaams Jurist Vandaag* (1st quarter of 1989) whether there was a risk that I would find myself in the same pool of arrears as the UNHCR Representative, because of a shortage of staff, I replied: 'This is not a risk. It already is!'.

On 7 March 1989, Paula D'Hondt was appointed Royal Commissioner for Immigrant Policy (1989–93). Bruno Vinikas (PS) would be her deputy. They were to make general recommendations on immigration policy. To this end, they received a budget of €1 million.[5] The budget of the Commission General and the Permanent Board together amounted to €1.6 million that year. The Royal Commission received eight university trained staff. That was double the staff assisting me in taking a few thousand decisions on asylum applications. Apparently, it wasn't the same Inspector of Finance who had given an opinion on the budget proposal concerning the Royal Commission. On 13 December 1989, I told the *Knack* magazine that with a budget equivalent to €1 million Belgium had 'the cheapest refugee service in the world'.

I presented my *First Annual Report* (1988) to the House of Representatives on 11 May and to the Senate on 8 June 1989. I pointed out the growing backlog. I had already insisted on this during my previous meetings with Miet Smet, Secretary of State for Social Emancipation, on 26 May 1989, and on 30 May with Wilfried Martens, the Prime Minister. To my observation 'To advance something in our country', the Prime Minister replied with a sigh: 'To whom do you say it?'.

On 7 June 1989, and in notes of 11 and 19 July, I also highlighted the growing backlog to the Minister of Justice. Savings in personnel (equivalent to €300,000) ultimately cost the State a lot of money. These savings generated a multitude of additional expenses for CPAS.[6] Moreover, the average availability of civil servants was 27 per cent below the Finance Inspectorate's estimates.[7]

On 14 September 1989, the Finance Inspectorate finally gave a favourable opinion on the extension of the framework I had proposed (14 staff members including five jurists). On 27 October, I informed them that this extension would no longer be sufficient to process asylum applications within a reasonable time. I also indicated that I would welcome any provision of making available jurist-militiamen. In her first report, presented on 23 November, the Royal Commissioner for Immigration Policy referred to the enormous backlog of

[5] The Royal Commission would be succeeded in 1993 by the Centre for Equal Opportunities and the Fight Against Racism. Johan Leman, the chief of staff of the Royal Commissioner, became its director. In 2007, the Centre was succeeded by UNIA (the Interfederal Centre for Equal Opportunities) and Myria (the Federal Migration Centre). In 2018, the UNIA budget amounted to €8.1 million.

[6] In 1989 500 million BF (€12.5 million) (*Second Annual Report* (1989) §116) and in 1990 1 billion BF (€25 million) (*Third Annual Report*, §121: Audit Report of the Civil Service of 26 April 1990, 1).

[7] *Second Annual Report* (1989) §84. This unavailability rose from 32.75% in the first half of 1988 to 39.80% in the first half of 1990 (*Third Annual Report* (1990) §107).

refugee proceedings caused by lack of staff. She rightly described the coming into force of the refugee bodies as a 'missed opportunity'.

On 29 November 1989, I explained that the measures 'which should have been taken a year ago',[8] were not intended to reduce the backlog, but to cope with the pace of applications. In addition, compared with the first half of 1989 (456), the average number of applications each month in the second half of 1989 had almost doubled (to 897). By the end of 1989, it was estimated that the backlog at the Commission General with unchanged staff had increased from a year and a half to four years. The backlog grew by four months a month! Erik Weytjens,[9] an engineer-militiaman in the office of the Minister of Justice, was the first to realise the enormity of these figures. The backlog at the Commission General was 2.5 times greater than at the Aliens Office. At the Aliens Office, it had increased in one year from four to 18 months.

15.1.2. A First Reinforcement: Too Little and Too Late

It was only after two years of activity, in early February 1990, that for the first time a reinforcement (with eight subsidised contract workers and 10 jurist-militiamen) arrived at the Commission General. The Minister of Justice requested an audit of the Commission General from Public Service advisers. In their 26 April 1990 audit report, they wrote that the situation could not be allowed to deteriorate any longer and that strong action was needed. According to the report, 'the only cause of delays at the Commission General has been the lack of staff that this service has suffered since its inception'. The report recommended a statutory framework composed of 45 civil servants, 18 of whom should be university trained, and a temporary framework of 39 civil servants, 25 of whom should be university trained. On 21 May, the Minister of Justice considered that such an extension was not necessary because he counted on a possible increase in efficiency ….

On 24 November 1990, the *Gazet van Antwerpen* wrote:

> Since Marc Bossuyt has been Commissioner General, he has continued in vain to shout from the rooftops that, if his department does not receive more staff immediately, our country is heading for disaster with its refugee policy. The malaise has become a fact.

On 12 December, I reported that almost two-thirds of the staff deemed necessary were missing. The bodies which bore the main responsibility for this dramatic situation recommended a staff of 30 per cent less than I had requested. With the experience of the past three years, I had expected a better understanding.

[8] *Second Annual Report* (1989) §123.

[9] He studied at the Georgia Institute of Technology (1987–89). In 1991/92, he obtained an MBA from INSEAD (the French business school in Fontainebleau).

On 14 January 1991, I continued to insist on a staff cadre of 60. I did so even more emphatically because the number of asylum applications had increased by 62 per cent (from 8,144 in 1989 to 12,845 in 1990). I mentioned a 'snowball effect'. This would attract new asylum seekers since they knew that a long stay with the CPAS was guaranteed. On 23 January, the Finance Inspector, who referred to 'a never-ending quest', recommended to define policies first. The expected savings, he said, depended on the difference between the number of incoming and outgoing applicants in the country. The increase in the number of the latter was by no means commensurate with the growth in the former.[10]

In a letter dated 7 February 1991, I reacted (according to *De Standaard* of 15 February in an unusually sharp manner) by pointing out that the removal of refused asylum seekers was only possible when enforceable refusal decisions had first been taken. And for that, staff were needed. Due to a lack of staff, the number of asylum applications had risen from 459 in June 1989 to 1,474 in March 1990. Thanks to the increase in temporary staff, there had been a significant drop in demand after Easter 1990 (down to 705 in June 1990). Meanwhile, the backlog at the Commission General had increased from 1,842 pending asylum applications at the beginning of September 1989 to 5,144 at the beginning of January 1991. The Finance Inspectorate carried a heavy responsibility in the growth with hundreds of millions of Belgian francs in the budget for the reception of asylum seekers.

In a letter to the Prime Minister dated 18 April 1991, I noted that the backlog at the Commission General had increased from 550 admissible applications at the end of July 1988 to 6,873 at the end of March 1991. On 26 April 1991 (exactly one year after the audit), the Council of Ministers authorised the recruitment of 49 contractual civil servants to fill the vacant statutory places and 126 to make up the backlog. There were 97 civil servants for the Aliens Office, 59 for the Commission General and 19 for the Permanent Board. As far as the jurists at the Commission General were concerned, only two of them were statutory, compared with 35 contractual and 12 militiamen. In the Senate on 5 June 1991, the Minister of Justice paid tribute to the staff at the asylum authorities. He recognised that their task was terribly difficult and trying.

15.1.3. Minister Louis Tobback Competent (Too Late): The Snowball Effect is Triggered

Following the elections of 24 November 1991 ('Black Sunday'), the Dehaene I Government was formed on 7 March 1992. In this government, it was agreed that the Minister of the Interior, Louis Tobback, would become responsible for

[10] *Fourth Annual Report* (1991) §§102–09.

the operation of the Aliens Law. In a note addressed to him on 26 May 1992, I wrote that it was absolutely essential that, in order to prevent asylum proceedings from getting further bogged down in the quicksand, the Aliens Office should: (a) question almost all asylum seekers on the day their application was submitted;[11] (b) notify the majority of the decisions on the admissibility of their application on the same day or within the same week; and (c) notify the inadmissibility decisions after my unfavourable opinion (Annexes 26*ter*) within one week. I feared otherwise the situation would degenerate irremediably before the summer.

The notification of Annexes 26*ter* was problematic. The considerable increase in the number of my opinions (from 200 to 800 per month) was not followed by the notification by the Aliens Office of orders to leave the territory. The enormous effort of my services did not have the desired effect. Within a few weeks, the fruits of efforts over months were lost. From February 1992, I exchanged a vigorous correspondence on this subject with the Aliens Office. I felt that the backlog had to be caught up in the reverse order of the introduction of asylum applications (the LiFo-principle: Last in, First out).[12] In particular, the most recent applications which were the subject of unfavourable opinions had to be treated with absolute priority.

On 12 June 1992, I considered that the 3,620 cases, in which I had given an unfavourable opinion, and which had not yet been followed by the notification of an inadmissibility decision, were the main cause of the growth in asylum applications observed over the past three months. I considered that the Aliens Office had misidentified its priorities. However, it was sufficient to refer, in these decisions, to my unfavourable opinion. Before the summer of 1992 (in June), the announced snowball effect was indeed triggered. It was not until 15 July, thus too late, that Minister Louis Tobback became responsible for aliens' policy.[13] Only then did the number of notifications of Annexes 26*ter* begin to increase.

In preparation for a 'radioscopy' of the Public Service,[14] on 30 July 1992, I drew up a note on the functioning of my services.[15] Among their strengths were: (a) a young administration (an average of less than 30 years of age); (b) a highly motivated staff; (c) a highly flexible staff structure; (d) a spirit of independence; and (e) limited hierarchical control. Among their weaknesses were: (a) the variability of the applicable standards; (b) the changes in flows of asylum applications;

[11] The number of hearings of asylum seekers who had not taken place in the month when their application was submitted to the Petit-Château rose from 109 at the end of January to 4,583 at the end of December 1992 (*Fifth Annual Report* (1992) §23).

[12] ibid §§75–92.

[13] Royal decree of 13 July 1992, *M.B.* (15 July 1992).

[14] Circular of 30 March 1992, *M.B.* (2 April 1992).

[15] *Fifth Annual Report* (1992) 102 (Appendix II). I had set up the following support services: documentation, urgent requests, interpreters, IT, archives, correspondence (reception and dispatch), secretariat, reception, staff, infrastructure, bailiffs and drivers.

(c) the dependence on the operation of other services; and (d) major personnel movements.

In a note[16] dated 7 September 1992 to the Ministers of Justice[17] and the Interior, I summarised the staff situation as follows:

1. Positive effects of the increase in staff: (a) a sharp decrease in the number of Nigerian (-37%), Indian (-40%), Ghanaian (-47%) and Pakistani (-50%) asylum applications;[18] (b) an acceleration in the admissibility procedure from 12 to 5 months; (c) a large increase in the number of opinions issued (3.6 times higher); (d) stabilisation of the overall backlog.
2. Changes in circumstances: (a) asylum applications: 40 per cent more; (b) urgent requests: 2.5 times more; (c) backlog at the Commission General: 4 times higher.
3. Other negative factors: (a) an increase in the number of applications by ex-Yugoslavs (+90%) and Zairians (+52%); (b) the Aliens Office's backlog of admissibility decisions (Annexes 26*bis*) and of notification of inadmissibility decisions based on my unfavourable opinions (Annexes 26*ter*).

While waiting for the backlog at the Aliens Office to be resolved, I proposed to reinforce the staff of my services with 15 additional contractual jurists and to replace the 20 militiamen with 20 contractual civil servants. After the end of the provision of militiamen to ministerial offices, this system was also abolished for the Commission General. On 18 January 1993, military service was itself abolished.

The military staff at Evere always showed great goodwill in the selection of jurist-militiamen. I insisted that the best jurists be selected based on their academic curriculum. Generally, it was a great success. Two of them would even become full professors: Pierre d'Argent in international law at the Catholic University of Louvain-la-Neuve and Dirk Vanheule in constitutional and administrative law at the University of Antwerp. Only once did a few militiamen fail to take their mission to heart. I had them transferred to the Melsbroek Transit Centre where they could stand guard.

Most jurist-militiamen carried out their duties with great dedication and a great sense of responsibility. They also held hearings on urgent requests for reconsideration of inadmissibility decisions at the border. The militiamen were aware of their responsibilities. Their proposals for unfavourable opinions were generally

[16] ibid §142.

[17] The powers relating to the Commission General and the Permanent Board remained with the Minister of Justice until 31 December 1993, *M.B.* (1 January 1994).

[18] For these four nationalities taken together, the rate of admissibility at the Aliens Office had fallen since 1 October 1991 from 29% to 2.8%. Despite an increase in the number of my favourable opinions (from 2.6% to 6%), this resulted in a decrease in the final admissibility rate from 31.6% to 9%. Along with a decline in the number of applications made by asylum seekers of these nationalities, there was a sixfold decline in the number of asylum applications to be considered on the merits (*Fifth Annual Report* (1992) §§32–33 and notes 4 and 7).

followed by an effective return of the asylum seeker to his or her country of origin. Subsequently, the judgments of State Councillors or aliens' judges would less regularly be followed by an effective removal. The militiamen received a daily allowance of 100 Belgian francs (€2.5). Among them were also computer scientists who were much sought after. For one reason or another, all the militiamen were men. Subsequently, the Commission General became heavily feminised.

On 23 October 1992, I wrote to the Minister of the Interior that the growth since April 1992 in the number of asylum seekers who were not questioned immediately,[19] was leading straight to the biggest asylum crisis our country had ever known. All previous notes on the workload and needs of the asylum authorities were outdated. In October 1992, the number of 2,000 asylum applications was crossed for the first time. On 6 November, the Cabinet decided to extend the contract for 39 contractual civil servants of the Commission General. These measures, based on the needs of July 1992, were in the meantime largely outdated. The Inter-Cabinet Working Group had, however, rejected the additional recruitment of 20 contractual civil servants. On 27 November, the Council of Ministers even decided not to renew the contracts of three civil servants at the lowest level to the Commission General …

15.1.4. The Turbo Effect of Minister Louis Tobback: From 3,000 to 1,000 Asylum Applications

On 14 April 1993, I proposed a range of measures to combat the ongoing slippage in the asylum procedure over the past year.[20] The Council of Ministers of 28 May decided on an unprecedented extension of staff: for the Commission General, it was 186 staff members, 138 of whom were university trained. They also had to replace 30 militiamen, including 20 jurists. Recruitment would be spread over three phases: 1 July, 1 October 1993 and 1 January 1994. In a letter dated 28 June 1993, I pointed out that from 1 October an extension of the premises would be essential. As no decision was made to lease additional space in the Shell building, it was not possible to implement the second and third phases as planned. It was not until January 1994 that the Commission General moved to new premisses in the North Gate I (Emile Jacqmain Boulevard, later renamed Albert II Boulevard). At the time of the arrival of the staff of the first phase (1 July 1993), the number of asylum applications had for the first time exceeded the 3,000 mark. With this increase in personnel and the entry into force (on 1 June 1993) of the Law of 6 May 1993, the procedure was considerably accelerated. Taking in account November (with 1,411 applications) and December 1993 (with 1,412), the number of asylum applications had halved.

[19] See above p 186 (n 11).

[20] *Sixth Annual Report* (1993) §91.

As a result of this decline (from an average of 2,400 in 1993 to an average of 1,195 in 1994), it was decided – on my proposal – not to proceed with the planned recruitment of 58 civil servants. Despite this limitation and the delay in recruitment, the backlog in terms of admissibility was proceeding as planned and in terms of the merits even a little faster than expected. It was also possible to strengthen the staff cadre somewhat by designating seven contractual civil servants on probation for permanent appointment and by promoting four statutory civil servants.

On 10 October 1994, Johan Vande Lanotte succeeded Louis Tobback as Minister of the Interior; Tobback became Mayor of Louvain and Chairperson of the Flemish socialists (SP). In a note to the new Minister on 18 October, I recalled that an extension in staff was no longer necessary. On the other hand, recruitment authorisations for 223 staff had to be renewed. At the same time, there was a need to strengthen the staff cadre. The number of statutory civil servants, including those on probation, was only 8.5 per cent.[21]

Some of the civil servants at the Commission General have moved on to have remarkable careers. A very incomplete list contains the following names:

- Serge Bodart, State Councillor and (former) First President of the Aliens Litigation Council.
- Claudia De Maesschalck, Ambassador to Cuba, among others.
- Viviane Scholliers (former) Senior Official (Governor) of the Brussels Capital District.
- Pascal Smet, Commissioner General for Refugees and Stateless Persons (2001–03); Brussels Secretary of State (2003–04, 2019–23); Brussels Minister (2004–09, 2014–19) and Flemish Minister of Education (2009–14).
- Michel Van Bellinghen, President of the Belgian Institute of Postal Services and Telecommunications.
- Birgit Van Hout, regional representative in Brussels of the UN High Commissioner for Human Rights, then Director of the UN Population Fund.

In 1995, the Commission General was faced with great staff mobility, especially of university trained civil servants.[22] That year, 29 of those civil servants left the Commission General partly because of their precarious contracts. These contracts were only extended at the last minute. This was done in 1995 and 1996 by royal decrees of 20 December (*M.B.*, 30 December 1995 and 31 December 1996)! The 1995 royal decree provided for two-year contracts but only for university trained civil servants. The same royal decree granted the Minister of the Interior the authority to recruit 517 contractual civil servants. There were 218 for the Commission General, of which 132 were university trained; the others went to the Aliens Office and the Permanent Board.

[21] *Seventh Annual Report* (1994) §158.
[22] *Eighth Annual Report* (1995) §§155–73.

Thanks to the professionalism and efficiency of the Commission General, in 1995 it was possible to make, on admissibility, four times more decisions, four times faster, than between 1990 and 1991! The overall duration of the admissibility procedure decreased from 14 months and 16 days to 3 months and 15 days. Because since 1 June 1993 I had notified my confirmatory decisions without going through the Aliens Office, the final stage of the admissibility proceedings has been reduced significantly from 4.5 months to 4 days. Thanks to this acceleration in the procedure, the number of asylum applications could be stabilised at an average of less than 1,000 applications per month: 11,901 in 1995; 11,432 in 1996; and 11,538 in 1997.

In my management plan submitted to the Minister of the Interior on 30 September 1996,[23] I considered it necessary to have 162 permanent staff members, of which 99 should be university trained. Until the backlog was eliminated (scheduled for the end of July 1999), I needed 57 additional contract staff, 30 of whom were university trained. If the flow were to rise to an average of over 1,000 asylum seekers per month, I would have to receive per 100 additional asylum applications 6.5 university trained civil servants. Numerical targets were set for the average processing time of the files: in admissibility (after transmission of the file by the Aliens Office) 12 or 90 days, depending on whether asylum seekers stayed in a closed centre or not; for files on the merits: 120 days once the backlog was cleared.

15.2. 'What have We Learned?'

From the start, the shortage of staff at the Commission General was obvious. On the advice of the Finance Inspectorate of 25 November 1986, less than half of the staff requested by the competent Minister (Jean Gol) was granted. After half a year of activity, the Commission General could not even process half of the asylum applications submitted. This increased their number. With the staff cadre originally requested, the Commission General could have operated for an additional year – perhaps even two more years (until mid-1990) – without a significant backlog.

15.2.1. The 'Snowball Effect'

Complaints about the length of the asylum procedure are frequent. However, it is rare for a refugee application to require lengthy screening. In most cases, it is possible to quickly determine whether an asylum application is justified or not. It

[23] *Ninth Annual Report* (1996) 194 (Annex I).

is giving the reasons for negative decisions (positive decisions are not motivated) that demands time. These motivations must also resist the ingenuity of applicants' legal counsels. They must also be able to resist the critical eye of administrative jurisdictions, such as the Aliens Litigation Council and the Conseil d'Etat. Jurisdictions tend to attach more importance to formalities than to the reality of a well-founded fear of persecution. That's why it is preferable that decisions be prepared by jurists.

At the beginning of the Commission General (1988/89), it was demonstrated that decisions can be made quickly. The law required the Commissioner General to give an opinion within 24 hours on inadmissibility decisions taken by the Minister of Justice (or his delegate) regarding applications made at the border. In fact, this concerned applications at the National Airport. For two years, I kept strictly to this very short deadline. Since, for someone arriving at the airport, there were few disputes as to his country of origin, it was possible, in the event of an unfavourable opinion, to take the person concerned, often immediately, back to that country. In this case, this can be done at the expense of the airline that transported the applicant to Belgium. It is therefore not surprising that the percentage of applications lodged at the National Airport fell from 85 per cent from 1986 to 1987 to 3.4 per cent in 1991.[24]

When an asylum procedure takes a very long time, it is generally not because of the complexity of the application. What lasts long is the time before the file is processed: 'There are still many more waiting before you'. Often, asylum authorities face a backlog. This was not only the case in Belgium but also in neighbouring countries. On 1 February 1988, the Belgian Commissioner General for Refugees and Stateless Persons was the only asylum authority without a backlog. With great wisdom, it was decided to leave the processing of applications submitted before this date with his predecessor (the Representative in Belgium of the UN High Commissioner for Refugees). There was thus a unique opportunity to process incoming refugee applications without delay. The advice of the Inspectorate of Finance had the effect that after only a few months this chance was lost. As the Royal Commissioner for Immigration Policy wrote on 23 November 1989, this was a 'missed opportunity'. A chance like that never comes back.

Rapid processing of asylum applications decreases their number. Asylum seekers who know that they have little chance of being recognised as refugees do not feel called upon to apply, knowing that it will quickly lead to a negative decision. It is not worth undertaking such a journey – often difficult, dangerous and costly – when the chances of being very quickly back in the country of departure are great. On the other hand, for many applicants from less prosperous countries, it is still worth taking a chance, even when the risk of a negative decision is high, if there is the possibility of a lengthy procedure. The guaranteed right of reception

[24] *Second Annual Report* (1989) §21.

is for many sufficiently attractive if they can take advantage of it for a long time. It is also generally known that an ultimate refusal is not always followed by an effective removal.

The asylum procedure is likely to have a 'snowball effect'. When the process is slow, there are more applications; which further slows down the process; which leads to more applications and so on. Once the snowball effect is triggered, it is very difficult to stop it. Its growth is not purely linear but often exponential. When applications cannot be processed immediately, this almost always leads to an increase in the number of applications: first 10 per cent more applications, then 20 per cent, then 40 per cent, then 80 per cent, etc. The snowball can only be stopped at the cost of enormous efforts. It is not a 10 per cent increase in personnel that will be necessary, but a doubling and even a tripling of its number.

15.2.2. Costly 'Savings'

The Finance Inspectorate had lost sight of the fact that the 'savings' in staff at the refugee authorities would cause huge additional costs to the budget for the reception of asylum seekers. Because of these 'savings', we received many more asylum seekers – and for much longer. The saving of a few million Belgian francs in the Justice budget led to several tens of millions of Belgian francs in additional costs to the Social Emancipation budget. The costs of the asylum procedure are only a fraction of what is necessary for the reception of asylum seekers. These can moreover be doubled by the medical care of asylum seekers. It was penny-wise and pound-foolish.

Of course, the Inspector of Finance was right when he observed on 23 January 1991 that the number of outgoing applicants did not correspond to the number of entrants. Many efforts to make refusal decisions are lost because the implementation of these decisions leaves a lot to be desired. Thus, it is like 'mopping the floor under an open tap'. The Finance Inspectorate put its finger on a wound that is not healing. It is easier to obtain from successive governments a continuous increase in the capacity of asylum authorities, both for the procedure and the reception, than to obtain an effective and efficient policy of expulsion. Fortunately, an acceleration in the procedure can – even without such a policy – ease the pressure on asylum authorities. One day, this pressure will become so strong that it will be necessary to turn to the solution of effective removals.

In the case of a backlog, the acceleration of the procedure has the most effect when applied to the most recently introduced asylum applications: the LiFo-principle. The intended effect can be achieved when the principle is applied to nationalities for which the percentage of favourable decisions is low. A quick negative decision has a clear deterrent effect. This is obviously not the case with rapid positive decisions. The principle is 'Last in, First out', not 'First in'. It is essential that this principle be applied by all bodies in the chain of decisions.

At the time, it proved difficult to win the assent of the Aliens Office to this idea. For some jurisdictions, this always seems very difficult.

15.2.3. The 'Cascade Effect'

The 'cascade effect' is another permanent feature of the asylum procedure. Once a backlog has been resolved in a proceeding, it results in a new backlog in the proceeding that follows it directly into the decision chain. The elimination of the backlog at the Aliens Office led to the appearance of new backlogs at the Commission General. I had to make more decisions on admissibility and on the merits. Once the delay was made up at the Commission General, further delays were formed at the Permanent Board and the Conseil d'Etat.

When the new Refugee Law came into force on 1 February 1988, the Martens VII Government was in caretaking mode. The Martens VIII Government was not sworn in until 9 May 1988. The new Minister of Justice, Melchior Wathelet, apparently trusted the Inspector of Finance more than the Commissioner General. That I continued to insist, and especially that I got support in the media, irritated the Minister a lot. My annual report was an important leverage. The presentation of the *First Annual Report* (1988) to the House of Representatives on 11 May 1989 had a great impact. Since I was not heard by the Minister of Justice, I complained on 26 May 1989 to Miet Smet, the Secretary of State for Social Emancipation. Responsible for the reception of asylum seekers, for whom she had set up the Petit-Château on 14 November 1986,[25] she had to suffer the consequences of the slippage in the asylum procedure. On 30 May 1989, I was received by Prime Minister Wilfried Martens. It was not until the day before the presentation of my *First Annual Report* to the Senate on 8 June, that I was received by the Minister of Justice.

It proved impossible in Belgium to react quickly to slippages. Hence my disillusioned remark to the Prime Minister: 'To advance something in our country'.[26] Even when the Public Service audit (26 April 1990) had undoubtedly shown that a considerable acceleration in the procedure was necessary, it took exactly another year for the Council of Ministers to decide on reinforcements. Then we still had to recruit new staff and train them. It was also necessary to make available to them additional premises, and all that this entails. Meanwhile, the situation was deteriorating at an ever-increasing rate. On several occasions, however, I have been able to show that an increase in personnel not only leads to a multiplication in the number of decisions taken, but also to a considerable decrease in the number of applications.

[25] According to M Smet, *Ik kijk alleen vooruit: Mijn leven als politica* (Tielt, Lannoo, 2018) refugees were first included in the agenda of the Council of Ministers on 29 October 1986 (82). It wouldn't be the last time.

[26] See above p 183.

15.2.4. The Transfer from the Justice Ministry to the Interior Ministry

For a Minister of Justice who has been managing a budget poorly funded for decades, asylum seekers were not the top priority. His attention was obviously first to the functioning of justice. Second came the prisons. Prisons do not have significant influence in the political world, and much less so among public opinion. Asylum seekers were only a tertiary concern. I relied on my independent status to denounce, both in Parliament and in public opinion, the slippage in the asylum procedure. That made me an embarrassing troublemaker. Because of the slippage, we had to open reception centres for asylum seekers all over the country. It was only when that caused turmoil that my voice was heard. A highlight was the broadcast *Panorama* on 5 September 1991 on BRTN TV with a report on a new Red Cross Centre for the reception of asylum seekers in Lint, near Antwerp.

The following Sunday, 8 September 1991, Interior Minister Louis Tobback said, much to the displeasure of Prime Minister Wilfried Martens, that he found the operation in Lint to be absurd. With that, I said: 'If you distribute asylum seekers across the country, you also distribute resentment. If thousands of asylum seekers must wait so long for the recognition process to end, they must be taken care of in the meantime'.[27] On 18 December I introduced, in a tense atmosphere, an information evening on the operation of the Red Cross Refugee Candidate Centre in Lint. Only about three hundred inhabitants of this community were admitted, based on their identity cards. A few hours later, asylum seekers arrived in Lint, a town of 7,000 inhabitants.[28]

Encouraged by the words of Minister Louis Tobback, I went to him in desperation and in complete confidentiality. Among other things, I argued in favour of a transfer of the Aliens Office to the Ministry of the Interior. The Aliens Office, which together with State Security was part of the Directorate-General for Public Security, had been under the responsibility of the Ministry of Justice since soon after the creation of Belgium. I thought that, as is the case in France, the Aliens Office would be better under the responsibility of the Ministry of the Interior. This Ministry had also, in the context of reform of the State, lost many of its powers to the benefit of the three Regions.

The Aliens Office and the Commission General are very different services. First, they have a different mission: for the Commissioner General, it is the protection of refugees; for the Aliens Office, it is the control of the access of foreigners to the territory and their stay. The Commission General was a much younger department, both in terms of its creation (1988 compared with 1835) and the average age of its staff (under 30). The Commission General was made up mainly of jurists, whereas

[27] *DS* (10 September 1991).
[28] *GvA* (19 December 1991).

the Aliens Office employed mainly non-university trained staff. The Aliens Office worked under the authority of the Minister of Justice; the Commission General is an independent authority.

This is also the explanation I gave on Friday 2 July 1993 as an answer to King Baudouin's question: 'And how are your relations with Mr [Stéphane] Schewebach?' He asked this question at the end of the audience granted in the Chateau of Laeken. After my reply, he ended the audience with the words, 'I will receive him immediately'. Two hours later, at the reception of the Ambassador of the United States, the Administrator of Public Security addressed me with these words: 'The King said that we should get along better'.

I thought that my independence would be better assured if the staff at my disposal depended administratively on a minister other than the one responsible for the Aliens Office.[29] This could be the Prime Minister (as was the case for the Secretary of State for Social Emancipation and the Royal Commissioner for Immigration Policy) or the Minister of Foreign Affairs (who had delegated this competence to the United Nations and as was the case in France with the Director of OFPRA), or the Minister of Justice, if he was no longer in charge of the Aliens Office. The result of the elections of 24 November 1991 ('Black Sunday') increased the urgency of making serious changes to asylum policy.

During the negotiations for the formation of a new government, the outgoing Minister of the Interior, Louis Tobback, skilfully used that mission of the outgoing Minister of Justice, Melchior Wathelet, to successfully obtain the transfer of asylum authorities to the Interior Ministry. After being long asked by me, Minister Melchior Wathelet agreed to visit the Commission General for the first time. This visit was scheduled for 19 December 1991. That morning, I received the message that the visit could not take place. It was indeed the day when the King appointed the Minister to form a new government.

After the end of his formative mission (31 January 1992), I continued to insist on receiving his visit. At the beginning, the Minister said that it no longer made sense since the competences of the aliens' policy would be transferred to the Minister of the Interior. I said to the Minister of Justice that my staff members would appreciate his visit. Many of them were appointed, after I personally selected them, on his recommendation, The Minister finally visited the Commission General before the formation of the new government. It was a grand style visit. He knew how to charm the staff. When he left the Shell building, he said, 'You were right to insist. This was also the case for other issues'. We had made peace.

Immediately after the formation of the Dehaene I Government (7 March 1992), Minister Louis Tobback explained to me the need to place all the authorities involved in the asylum procedure under the responsibility of the same minister. The Minister of the Interior was already responsible for the Conseil d'Etat. He feared that the functioning of the asylum authorities would be flawed if one of

[29] *Second Annual Report* (1989) §§131–32.

the authorities concerned did not receive the same attention as the others. The future showed that he was right. The asylum authorities have never complained about this transfer. Minister Louis Tobback also asked me to accept a renewal of my mandate. This was still to be done on the proposal of the Minister of Justice. By royal decree given in Motril (Spain) on 31 July 1992, I was again appointed Commissioner General for a period of five years. Exactly one year later, King Baudouin died. The royal decree, which was sent to me on 7 September 1992, came into force on 3 November 1992.

The transfer of responsibility from the Justice Ministry to the Interior Ministry for aliens' policy (effective from 15 July 1992 on) came just too late. By June 1992, the snowball effect had begun. A gigantic effort would be necessary to stop it. The Minister did not back down from any effort. But it took time. With reinforcements of personnel – never seen before – decided on 28 May 1993 and the entry into force on 1 June 1993 of the amended Aliens Law, he set the pace. Very quickly, the number of asylum applications was under control. For more than three years (1995–97), this number was maintained at an average of less than 1,000 per month. It was important that my management plan of 30 September 1996 provided that an increase in the number of asylum seekers would automatically lead to an increase in the number of university trained civil servants (6.5 per 100 asylum applications).

15.2.5. The Junction of Responsibility for the Procedure and for the Reception

Minister Louis Tobback would have liked to go even further in asylum policy. He fully understood that the division of responsibility for the asylum procedure, on the one hand, and for the reception of asylum seekers, on the other, constituted an important handicap for the conduct of a responsible asylum policy. The reception was mainly through CPAS. Hospitality costs were reimbursed by the Ministry of Public Health. From December 1992 onwards, pilot projects were implemented in the cities of Antwerp,[30] Ghent, Liège[31] and Namur. They were intended to promote coordination between the various bodies in the processing of the files of asylum seekers dependent on the CPAS.[32] I have lent active cooperation to it. I considered the presence on these lists to be a determining factor in the priority processing of files. I didn't care about the criticism. I felt that no one had a fundamental right to a lengthy procedure.

[30] In May 1993, there were 2,234 asylum seekers dependent on the CPAS of Antwerp.

[31] In February 1994, there were 4,283 asylum seekers dependent on the CPAS of Liège, of whom 1.559 (36%) were rejected.

[32] *Fifth Annual Report* (1992) §164.

I forwarded to the Ministry of Public Health lists of asylum seekers who had been subject to an enforceable refusal decision. This Ministry gave little follow-up on the pretext of not having received confirmation from the Aliens Office.[33] Thus, in violation of the law, CPAS gave aid to hundreds of rejected asylum seekers. At the same time, CPAS refused – again in violation of the law – assistance to hundreds of asylum seekers whose applications were still being processed. In my contacts with the local authorities, I proposed that they respect the law. In 1993 and 1994, the Ministry of Public Health provided me sporadically with lists of asylum seekers. These were asylum seekers for whom CPAS had received an acceptance in principle of reimbursement by the State. On 3 September and 15 December 1993, I pointed out that, when I had communicated that their application was rejected, aid could only be continued if the Aliens Office explicitly agreed.

On 30 September 1994, I expressed my concern to Jacques Santkin (PS), Minister of Public Health (1994–95), about the high number of rejected applicants (7,931 or 40 per cent!) at the expense of the CPAS. I felt that it was necessary to explain the increasing burden of providing aid to asylum seekers, not by the slow progress of the asylum procedure, but by the ill will of the Ministry of Public Health. That Ministry refused to consider the information I was giving it. On 7 October, I reported that almost 8,500 asylum seekers had wrongly received aid for almost a year. The cost could be estimated at the equivalent of €50 million.

In 1995, I sent lists of rejected asylum seekers to several institutions throughout the Kingdom, including CPAS, as well as to the Minister of Public Health. On 23 June 1995, Marcel Colla (PS) became Minister of Public Health (until 1 June 1999). It was not until October 1996 that I received from that Ministry a list of the asylum seekers who were being supported. On 22 February 1996, I expressed my concern about the absence of such lists to Jan Peeters (SP), Secretary of State for Social Emancipation (1995–99). I was saying that only the regular and reciprocal exchange of data would make it possible to follow closely their progress and their updating.

Because of the close links between the CPAS and the Ministry of Public Health regarding the reception of asylum seekers, a transfer of responsibilities in this area to the Interior Ministry was not obvious. During the formation of the Dehaene II Government, which took office on 23 June 1995, Louis Tobback took care as Chairperson of the SP that a member of his party, Jan Peeters, would be responsible for the reception of asylum seekers as Secretary of State for Social Emancipation. Another member of his party, Johan Vande Lanotte, remained as Minister of the Interior responsible for aliens' policy. As has been shown above, the Ministry of Public Health was not, however, institutionally ready to meet the needs of the asylum policy.

[33] *Sixth Annual Report* (1993) §132.

Linking the responsibility for the asylum procedure and the responsibility for reception has still taken years. The antagonism between the federal administrations concerned culminated in 2008 to 2009 with the governments of Leterme I and Van Rompuy (CD&V/cdH; Open VLD/MR, PS). On 20 March 2008, Marie Arena, a French-speaking socialist, became Minister of Social Integration and Annemie Turtelboom, a Dutch-speaking liberal, became Minister of Migration and Asylum Policy. For the first time, a member of the government would not share her attention for migration and asylum policy with other competences, generally considered more important. Because one federal administration worked to prevent another federal administration from successfully pursuing an aliens' policy, the development of an effective policy proved impossible. Yves Leterme (CD&V) resigned as Prime Minister on 22 December 2008 because of the Fortis case.[34] On 30 December, Herman Van Rompuy[35] (CD&V) succeeded him (until 25 November 2009). The paralysis of the asylum policy became so untenable that the Van Rompuy Government had to be changed on 17 July 2009: Annemie Turtelboom became Minister of the Interior, Melchior Wathelet Jr (cdH) Secretary of State for Migration and Asylum Policy, and Philippe Courard (PS) Secretary of State for Social Integration.

The asylum policy remained flawed as long as there was no link between the two responsibilities. This was not achieved until Maggie De Block (Open VLD) became Secretary of State for Asylum, Migration and Social Integration on 6 December 2011. She thus became responsible in the Di Rupo Government (2011–14) for both the asylum procedure and the reception of asylum seekers. Since the creation of Fedasil by the Reception Law of 12 January 2007, this federal agency is the main guarantor of the reception of asylum seekers. The integration of the two competences was the key to the success of the asylum policy. Maggie De Block and her successor Theo Francken[36] (N-VA) became very popular.

[34] W Van den Eynde, *Fortisgate: een stresstest voor justitie* (Louvain, Van Halewyck, 2016).

[35] Herman Van Rompuy (since 2016 count) would become President of the European Council from 1 January 2010 to 30 November 2014.

[36] T Francken and J Vermeersch, *Continent zonder grens* (Doorbraak, 2018).

16

Asylum Legislation: 'Ping-Pong' between Legislator and High Courts

Before the creation of the new bodies for refugees, the recognition of refugee status was delegated by order of 22 February 1954 to the Representative in Belgium of the UN High Commissioner for Refugees (UNHCR). The asylum procedure was simplicity itself. The asylum applications were submitted to the Aliens Office. This Office could refuse access of an asylum seeker to the territory and residence. This was only possible on a limited number of grounds. These included the late submission of the application and the stay of more than three months in a third country. Since these conditions had to be met before the merits of the application could be considered, this phase was called – for convenience (at least for jurists) – the 'admissibility procedure'. When the Aliens Office made a positive decision on access or residence, the application became 'admissible' and was forwarded to the UNHCR.

The UNHCR, a UN subsidiary agency, judged the merits of the asylum application. The intervention of a lawyer was not provided for. UNHCR's decisions were not reasoned. The Belgian language laws were not applicable.[1] It was therefore not possible to challenge the language in which a decision was taken. There was no possibility of appeal against the refusal decisions on the merits. Indeed, the Conseil d'Etat had no jurisdiction over decisions taken by an international authority. The Conseil d'Etat could be seized only of requests for annulment of decisions of inadmissibility taken by the Aliens Office. These requests had no suspensive effect. There was also no suspension procedure before the Conseil d'Etat. For this reason, asylum appeals before the highest administrative court were rare.

16.1. The Gol Law (14 July 1987): Belgium Takes the Asylum Procedure into its Own Hands

For years, the UNHCR had been asking to be discharged from its jurisdiction to determine refugee status in Belgium. The Belgian situation had become

[1] It is only with the Law of 10 July 1996 (Arts 2 and 8, §2, of the Aliens Law) that the use of languages in matters of asylum would be regulated in a more appropriate manner (see the *Ninth Annual Report* (1996) §§237–59).

exceptional. Rather than exercising this jurisdiction itself, the UNHCR preferred to monitor the way in which States Parties to the Geneva Convention were fulfilling their obligations. The way in which the UNHCR exercised its jurisdiction in Belgium did not correspond to its own recommendations. Only when the number of asylum applications in Belgium began to increase,[2] did the government decide to take this competence into its own hands. The competent Minister, Jean Gol, Minister of Justice, was inspired by the French system. There, refugee status was granted by the French Office for the Protection of Refugees and Stateless Persons (OFPRA).

16.1.1. The New Refugee Bodies: The French Model

The Gol Law[3] of 14 July 1987 created a new independent administrative authority: the Commissioner General for Refugees and Stateless Persons (in French: CGRA). The Commissioner General was given autonomous decision-making powers to recognise, refuse, confirm or withdraw refugee status. The Commissioner General's negative decisions had to be reasoned. The only possibility of appeal against the decisions of the Commissioner General on the merits was a new administrative tribunal: the Permanent Refugees Appeals Board.[4] That Permanent Board consisted of at least two Chambers, one Dutch-speaking and one French-speaking. Each Chamber was composed of four members: a judge in active service who held the office of president; a lawyer; an official of the Ministry of Justice; and an official of the Ministry of Foreign Affairs.

The bill retained the former duality: the Aliens Office remained competent for access and residence; the Commissioner General and the Permanent Board became competent to determine refugee status. There was a widening of the grounds on which access and residence could be refused. Henceforth, an asylum application could also be refused when it was fraudulent or manifestly based on grounds foreign to the Geneva Convention. To meet parliamentary reservations about this enlargement, it was decided that these new grounds for refusal could be invoked only by the Minister.

In addition, it was decided to involve the Commissioner General in these refusal decisions. The Minister agreed that in the event of an inadmissibility decision, an urgent request for reconsideration could be made. This request had to be addressed to the body that had made the refusal decision: the Aliens Office or the Minister. The Commissioner General's opinion was sought on their request. But it had to be done quickly: the request had to be submitted, within the country, within three working days and, at the border, within 24 hours; the Commissioner

[2] *Doc parl, Chambre*, 1986–87, No 689/1, 2.
[3] *M.B.* (18 July 1987).
[4] *Doc parl, Chambre*, 1986–87, No 689/1, 5.

General had to give his opinion, within the country, within seven days and, at the border, within 24 hours. These opinions were binding on the Minister's delegate, when it was the delegate who made the decision. If the Minister had made the decision himself, he was not bound by the Commissioner General's opinion. If the Minister disregarded this advice, he had to give reasons for his decision. It was still possible to bring a request to the President of the Tribunal of first instance within two days, which was to be decided in the form of an interlocutory order within 15 days.

16.1.2. The New Refugee Law: A Cumbersome Procedure

The Minister of Justice himself signed more and more refusal decisions (60 per cent in 1988, 80 per cent in 1989, 85 per cent in 1990). Since 9 May 1988, it was Melchior Wathelet. It was a very cumbersome procedure: the Aliens Office, the Office of the Minister of Justice, the Minister of Justice, the Office of the Minister of Justice, the Aliens Office and again the same route in case of an urgent request for reconsideration, completed in the middle by my opinion. Even though I gave my opinions within the very short time limits prescribed by law, the decision on admissibility often took several weeks.

I made sure that I delivered my opinions very quickly. It was for me a matter of honour. In 1988 and 1989, I gave 521 and 544 opinions within the country within seven days and 188 and 294 opinions at the border within 24 hours respectively. This was to the detriment of processing on the merits asylum applications declared admissible. The absolute priority was given to the asylum procedure at the border, not only because it was prescribed by law, but also (a) because it was the only procedure that made it possible to take enforceable decisions at short notice; (b) to ensure that the removal from the territory (which was at the border effectively implemented) was done with the necessary guarantees; and (c) because in the meantime asylum seekers were frequently retained, at least those staying at the National Airport, in degrading living conditions.

Giving opinions at the border requires a trip to the National Airport for the hearing of the asylum seeker. For the first two years, the hearing was generally conducted, in turn, by one of the two Deputy Commissioners. Immediately after the hearing, a reasoned opinion was drafted, typed, signed and faxed to the Minister of Justice and/or the Aliens Office. All this was done within 24 hours of the notification by the Aliens Office of the request to the Commission General. The Aliens Office was kind enough to notify requests only during working days. In trying to speed up the procedure, some pragmatic measures were taken. On 2 August 1989, the Minister of Justice decided to move the relevant section of his Cabinet to the building in Rue de la Régence where the Commission General was established. On 20 November 1989, a liaison section of the Aliens Office was also established in this building. A change in the law was urgently needed.

16.2. The Wathelet Law (18 July 1991): Levelling the Angles

In my *First Annual Report*,[5] I had already proposed legislative changes to make the procedure more efficient. On 9 November 1989, four SP senators introduced a bill.[6] The bill basically contained my proposals. This was also the case with the bill drafted by the Minister of Justice, Melchior Wathelet and the Secretary of State for Social Emancipation, Miet Smet. Their preliminary draft was approved by the Council of Ministers on 9 May 1990. Introduced as a bill, on 2 October 1990, by six senators,[7] it became the Wathelet Law of 18 July 1991. This law entered into force on 1 October 1991.

16.2.1. Limiting the Ministerial Intervention: A Step in the Right Direction

By these legislative amendments, the decisions of inadmissibility could be taken not only by the Minister but also by his delegate. Urgent requests for reconsideration were now made directly to the Commissioner General. There was a slight increase in the prescribed delays: at the border, from 24 hours to two working days and, within the country, from seven days to seven working days. The Commissioner General's opinions became binding unless overruled by the Minister of Justice within a very short period (five working days). In the previous three years, the Minister ignored my opinion in 26 cases (16 per cent) in 1988, 24 (14 per cent) in 1989 and 63 (11 per cent) in 1990. On 9 July 1990, the Minister of Justice wrote to me that in most cases in which the Aliens Office had proposed not to follow my opinion, he did follow me anyway. As from 1 October 1991, the Minister only ignored my opinion in 1 per cent of cases. Once he became responsible (15 July 1992), the Minister of the Interior always followed me.

The entry into force on 1 October 1991 of the Wathelet Law reduced asylum applications from 10 October onwards by 25 per cent. At the end of December 1991, this decrease reached 45 per cent. Through the efforts of the Aliens Office to catch up, the Commission General could not keep up with the processing of urgent requests. It was no longer possible for me to meet the statutory deadlines for giving my opinions. The Wathelet Law of 18 July 1991 could have ensured efficient and rapid processing of asylum applications. The law did not, however,

[5] Year of activity 1988, §§36–44.

[6] They were SP Senators Paul Pataer, Fred Erdman, Orphale Crucke and Maxime Stroobant (*Doc parl*, Senate, 1989/90, No 801/1).

[7] They were Senators Fred Erdman, Robert Gijs, France Truffaut, Pierre Wintgens, Jef Valkeniers and Willy Seeuws (*Doc parl*, Senate, 1990/91, No 1076/1).

take into account the introduction of the power of the Conseil d'Etat to suspend administrative decisions by a law dated the following day (19 July 1991). This law was adopted on the initiative of Interior Minister Louis Tobback. He did so at the instigation of his chief of staff Johan Vande Lanotte, a former auditor at the Conseil d'Etat and lecturer in constitutional and administrative law. The Minister of the Interior did not become responsible for aliens' policy until a year later. The Conseil d'Etat rightly pointed out in its 1994/95 Annual Report that 'it was not established that the legislator had clearly realised that his previously stated desire to prohibit any type of referral to foreigners was rendered futile' (p 244).

The damage was done. Very quickly, it appeared that the Conseil d'Etat was not at all capable of processing – within the 45-day period imposed by law – requests for suspension submitted by asylum seekers. The Conseil d'Etat itself spoke of 'rapid congestion' (ibid). Retention at the border had just been limited to two months. Thus, it was often enough to submit a request for suspension to the Conseil d'Etat to be admitted to the territory. This led to a considerable increase in asylum applications, especially at the National Airport where the reception conditions were unacceptable.

The Wathelet Law required me, in the event of an unfavourable opinion, to explicitly mention 'whether the foreigner can be returned to the border of the country from which he fled and where, according to his declaration, his life or liberty would be threatened' (Article 63/3, §2, 2°, of the Aliens Law). It was only in exceptional circumstances that my unfavourable opinion did not go hand in hand with the statement that I had no objection to the removal. In rare cases, I used this provision to draw the Minister's attention to serious humanitarian considerations specific to the refugee application in question. This new legislative provision, together with a ground of inadmissibility known as the 'double five per cent' rule (Article 52, §1, 7°, of the Aliens Law), brought me to consider the merits of an asylum application already in the admissibility phase.

16.2.2. The Double Five Per Cent Rule: An Original Attempt

In my contacts with the Secretary of State for Social Emancipation, I had pointed out that the asylum procedure was heavily burdened by asylum applications from many persons from countries with very low recognition rates. I was referring, for example, to asylum seekers of nationalities who accounted for more than 5 per cent of applications and for whom the recognition rate was less than 5 per cent. For that category of applicants, I believed there had to be an expedited process. Since the grounds of inadmissibility are listed in an exhaustive manner, other grounds cannot be invoked. Sometimes, none of these grounds can be invoked, even though the examination of the urgent request revealed that the application was manifestly unfounded. My collaborators were confronted with sharp lawyers, arguing the following paradoxical thesis:

> You may be satisfied that my client's application is unfounded, but it is not late; my client has not spent more than three months in a third country; you cannot prove that his application is fraudulent and, since he claims to be persecuted because of his political convictions, his application is not manifestly based on grounds foreign to the Geneva Convention. You must therefore declare his application admissible.

Even when the alleged fear of persecution did not hold, my collaborators could not therefore propose to declare the application inadmissible because this phase of the proceedings did not concern the merits of the application. For this reason, I felt that I should be given the opportunity to conclude, at this stage of the proceedings, that these applications were manifestly unfounded.

My astonishment was great when I read a government amendment, probably on the initiative of the Secretary of State for Social Emancipation, introducing as a new ground of inadmissibility a 'double five per cent' rule:

> If the foreign national comes from a country from which, in the previous calendar year, at least 5 per cent of asylum seekers came, and to the extent that it is apparent from the last annual report of the Commissioner General for Refugees and Stateless Persons that less than 5 per cent of the final decisions that have been taken have granted refugee status to asylum seekers from that country, and provided that it does not provide any evidence of a serious risk to its life or freedom under the Geneva Convention relating to the Status of Refugees.

While this was a meritorious attempt, the wording of this legislative provision was not very satisfactory. It gave the impression, as stated in the opinion of the Conseil d'Etat of 2 June 1991, that the application of these asylum seekers could be declared inadmissible 'solely because they come from a given country'. It is true that the applicant's country of origin is one of the most relevant factors in assessing the reality of his or her persecution. In fact, the identification of these countries was based on the recent experience of the Belgian authorities in refugee matters. It would have been better to mention specific percentages as examples in the Explanatory Statement. I found the notion of 'safe country' more questionable. This concept was introduced in Switzerland by an urgent decree of 22 June 1990. The new Belgian legislation indicated 'as precisely as possible and on objective and relevant grounds' for which asylum seekers an accelerated procedure could be followed. For this reason,[8] I held in my opinion on 2 October 1991 that the maintenance of a more formal admissibility procedure for most nationalities for which the same abuses had not been established was not contrary to the Geneva Convention.

[8] *Fourth Annual Report* (1991) §87 (Annex II).

The Representative in Belgium of the UN High Commissioner for Refugees also stated in his opinion[9] on 3 July 1991 that

> the formula [of the double 5 per cent] was not contrary to the Geneva Convention … insofar as it is simply a reversal of the burden of proof while keeping the two stages of the procedure, even accelerated, with verification of the merits.

In accordance with the rules of administrative law, the burden of proof rests in the merits stage on the applicant. This is not a very heavy burden: it is sufficient that the fear of persecution is 'plausible'. In the admissibility stage, however, it is for the authority to prove that one of the grounds of inadmissibility is applicable. With the 'double five per cent' rule, there was a ground in the admissibility phase for which it was up to the applicant to demonstrate that there were serious indications that his life or liberty was threatened. This was tantamount to placing the burden of proof on the applicant at an earlier stage in the proceedings.

Since the entry into force of the Law of 18 July 1991 on 1 October 1991, the percentage of admissibility decisions taken by the Aliens Office for Ghanaians, Indians, Pakistanis and Nigerians had fallen from 29 per cent to 2.8 per cent. The number of applications from those countries fell by 45 per cent (2,067 instead of 3,713).[10] On 5 December 1991, a royal decree of 25 November 1991 came into force, making the double five per cent rule applicable for a very short time (until 31 December 1991) to asylum seekers from countries with a very low recognition rate: Poland (0.77 per cent), Ghana (0.41 per cent), India (0.23 per cent) and Pakistan (0 per cent).

In my opinion of 3 February 1992, I noted that during 1992 the following countries were subject to the double five per cent rule:

Country	Applications %	Positive decisions %
Romania	15.56	4.49
Ghana	8.53	0.75
India	8.26	0.00
Yugoslavia	7.58	4.62
Nigeria	5.02	0.00

The percentages were calculated in respect of 15,272 asylum applications submitted in 1991 and 9,834 final decisions taken in 1991. That year, there were no positive final decisions on 444 Nigerian refugee applications and 951 Indian applications. I was proposing that Yugoslavia should not be included in the list because the final decisions in 1991 were mainly about asylum applications made before the outbreak of the armed conflict in that country. On the other hand,

[9] *Doc parl, Chambre*, 1990/91, No 1647/4, 8.
[10] *Fifth Annual Report* (1992) §§33–34.

because the positive decisions concerning the Romanians were mainly about asylum applications submitted before 1991, I proposed to include this country in the list, although the percentage of these decisions was only slightly lower than that concerning the Yugoslavs. A royal decree was issued on 7 May 1992 which brought the countries, except Yugoslavia, under the application of the 'double five per cent' rule (*M.B.*, 20 May 1992).

In January 1992, some non-profit associations (Amnesty International – French-speaking Belgium, the Movement against Racism, Anti-Semitism and Xenophobia, the League for Human Rights, and the Union of Lawyers for Democracy) brought requests for annulment before the Court of Arbitration. The Belgian National Order of Lawyers joined these requests. The 29 *Bâtonniers* (lawyers' presidents) approved this move on 10 January.[11] Because of these requests, the Aliens Office did not take decisions of inadmissibility based solely on this ground. I didn't either.

It is remarkable that on 23 September 2020, the Commission of the European Union proposed an accelerated procedure for asylum seekers from countries with a recognition rate of less than 20 per cent. An expedited procedure was proposed based on a set percentage of recognitions. A certain percentage of the total was not required. It is important to note that apparently the European Commission understood that its Asylum Procedure Directive was far too cumbersome to process applications from asylum seekers of nationalities with a low recognition rate. A simplified procedure was essential to process such applications more quickly. When the European Procedure Directives of 1 December 2005[12] and 26 June 2013[13] were adopted, or a fortiori in Belgium in 1993, this awareness had not yet happened.

In its judgment No 20/93 of 4 March 1993, the Court of Arbitration annulled the provisions concerning the double five per cent rule: 'By imposing a reversal of the burden of proof on a single category of foreigners who declare themselves refugees, the four provisions under attack go beyond what is necessary to achieve the objective pursued' (B.2.8). The Court of Arbitration argued that this goal could be achieved by applying another ground of inadmissibility, namely an application 'manifestly based on grounds foreign to the Geneva Convention' (see Article 51, §1, 2°, of the Aliens Law) (ibid*)*. However, if the applicant invokes one of the grounds of the Geneva Convention, stating, for example, that he is being persecuted for political reasons, his application is not based on 'foreign grounds'. His application could not be declared inadmissible on that ground, even when it was already clear that his alleged fear was unfounded.

[11] *DM* (20 February 1992).

[12] Council Directive 2005/85/EC of 1 December 2005 on minimum standards on procedures in Member States for granting and withdrawing refugee status.

[13] Directive 2013/32/EU of the European Parliament and of the Council of 26 June 2013 on common procedures for granting and withdrawing international protection (recast).

However, if the problem was that the burden of proof was reversed for only one category of foreigners, it could be solved by making it possible to invoke this ground for *all* categories. So said, so done. On the initiative of the responsible minister – now Interior Minister Louis Tobback – a quick reaction from the legislator prevented the decision of the Court of Arbitration from putting spokes in the wheels of the asylum procedure. Later, that would not always be the case.

16.3. The Tobback Law (6 May 1993): A Dynamic Approach

The Tobback Law[14] of 6 May 1993 extends the scope of the above ground to all nationalities. From now on, asylum seekers of any nationality could be refused in the admissibility stage when their application was considered manifestly unfounded

> because the foreigner does not provide evidence that there are, as far as he is concerned, serious indications of a well-founded fear of persecution within the meaning of the aforementioned International Convention (Article 52, §1, 7, of the Aliens Law).

A source beyond all suspicion inspired this provision: Article 35.3 ECHR provides that the Court of Strasbourg may declare applications inadmissible when they are 'manifestly ill-founded'. Thus, the too rigid distinction between the admissibility phase and the substantive phase disappeared.

Under the same law, 'urgent requests for reconsideration' to the body that made the decision were replaced by 'urgent appeals' to the Commissioner General. I received decision-making authority in respect of urgent appeals brought before me. Since there was now a suspensive appeal before an independent and specialised administrative authority with decision-making competence, the possibility of suspension before a third body (the Conseil d'Etat) was no longer considered necessary. Neither the Geneva Convention nor the subsequent EU Procedure Directive require the intervention of a third instance. The interventions of the President of the Tribunal of first instance in the form of interlocutory orders had been only occasional. Since 1 October 1991, this jurisdiction was reserved for (rare) cases in which the Minister overruled my opinion. Now that this was no longer possible, this intervention was considered superfluous.

[14] *M.B.* (21 May 1993).

16.3.1. The President of the Tribunal has no Jurisdiction: A Rearguard Fight

Since the independent body, which has jurisdiction as to the merits of the case, had received in a suspensive appeal a decision-making power on the removal at the border, the President of the Tribunal of first instance was explicitly deprived of jurisdiction in the matter of interlocutory orders concerning foreigners (Article 63, §2, of the Aliens Law). At first, some presiding judges of a Tribunal of first instance still encountered difficulties with the loss of this responsibility. On 8 October 1993, the President of the Tribunal of first instance in Brussels declared himself competent to judge the refusal of access and the deportation of a Zairean asylum seeker. I published a legal contribution on this issue in a legal journal in French and in Dutch.[15]

I drew particular attention to the specific characteristics of the asylum procedure: 'In addition to the obvious interest of most asylum seekers in using all possible means to extend their stay in our country', I noted:

1. The partly subjective nature of the fear invoked;
2. The material impossibility of verifying in the countries of origin the veracity of the stories advanced by sending interrogatory commissions;
3. The inherent insecurity of future developments in countries of origin; and above all
4. The great diversity of asylum applications (from more than 110 different countries).

I also wondered based on what information the civilian judge could take decisions on asylum:

1. Did he maintain regular contact with the Belgian embassies, with the authorities of neighbouring countries confronted with the same questions or with the UN High Commissioner for Refugees?
2. Did he have collaborators with experience in this field who specialised in the development of the respective situation in more than a hundred different countries?
3. Did he have specific and constantly updated documentation on the subject?
4. Did he have an overview of the asylum applications made in Belgium, as well as of the necessarily varied and evolving practice adopted by the competent authorities?
5. How did he rule out the risk of inconsistency in his decisions influenced by media-induced impressions, or by the partisan information provided by the advice of those concerned, often reduced to mere statements with no authentic evidence?

[15] In *Le Journal des Procès* of 8 March (18–24) and 1 April 1994 (12–14) and in the *Rechtskundig Weekblad* of 30 April 1994.

Thereafter, the use of this procedure became rare. The resistance of the Conseil d'Etat was more tenacious.

16.3.2. Enforcement Notwithstanding Any Remedy: An Ambivalent Solution

Although the Minister of the Interior himself introduced the suspension procedure to the Conseil d'Etat, he was looking for a way to counter the heavy obstacles it had caused to the asylum procedure. The Conseil d'Etat was attached to the suspension procedure it had recently acquired. In conversations with the office of the Minister of the Interior, the First President (1991–96) of the Conseil d'Etat, Paul Tapie, proposed granting the Commissioner General additional responsibility. It would be up to him to mention whether he considered his confirmatory decision under appeal and the removal order 'enforceable notwithstanding any remedy' (see Article 63/5, paragraph 5, of the Aliens Law). According to the administrative principle of the '*privilège du préalable*' (enforcement without prior intervention of a judge), this was already the case. What was new was that, if necessary, the Council became incompetent 'to order the suspension of measures that are enforceable notwithstanding any remedy, pursuant to section 63/5' (Article 70, paragraph 2, of the Aliens Law). A leave to appeal was introduced, which is well known in Anglo-Saxon law. That leave was only required for the request for suspension not for the request for annulment.

I was not happy with this ambivalent solution which did not eliminate the suspension procedure in all cases. As an appeal body, I first had to take reasoned decisions on the refusal, made by the Minister or his delegate, of access to the territory or residence for asylum seekers. Either I decided that a further examination was necessary, or I confirmed the denial of access or residence. In addition, in the event of a confirmatory decision, I had to give another opinion on the applicant's return to the country from which he had fled. But in addition, I had to declare that I considered that my decision could be enforced notwithstanding any remedy. In my view, these were three elements of a single decision that form a coherent whole. I was not inclined to provide three separate motivations. I wanted to avoid separate legal challenges for each of these three elements.

Without contradicting myself, I could only consider in very exceptional cases that a confirmatory decision was necessary but that it could not, however, go hand in hand with a removal to the country of origin, and/or that it could not be enforced in case of appeal. Only in very exceptional cases could these elements of the decision require a separate individual motivation. Moreover, when the civil judge declares his decisions enforceable notwithstanding any appeal, in accordance with Article 1398 of the Judicial Code, he also does not give any specific reasons. Despite my lack of enthusiasm for the solution adopted, I discharged this additional responsibility from the entry into force of these legislative provisions on 1 June 1993 until their annulment on 14 July 1994. In most cases, I accompanied my confirmatory decisions with the following declaration:

> In addition, the Commissioner General considers that there are no reasons to declare the decision contested in urgent appeal and the removal order non-enforceable notwithstanding any remedy. In accordance with the last paragraph of Article 63/5 of the Law of 15 December 1980, the decision contested in urgent appeal and the removal order are therefore enforceable.

From mid-1993, when I received decision-making power on urgent appeals, I entrusted the defence of my confirmatory decisions before the Conseil d'Etat to my own jurists. The Aliens Office usually used lawyers attached to the Bar. Initially, the Conseil d'Etat declared that it had no jurisdiction to hear appeals for the suspension of confirmatory decisions, which I had declared enforceable notwithstanding any remedy. As a rule, the Conseil d'Etat concluded that such requests for suspension were inadmissible.

After a few months, the Conseil d'Etat suddenly felt that the wording I was using 'did not satisfy or was not explicitly motivated'. On 8 February 1994, a State Councillor sitting alone granted a suspension, after having judged that my declaration of enforcement did not satisfy:

> The Commissioner General having to formally declare whether the decision is enforceable notwithstanding any remedy, and not the reverse; that, moreover, the words 'non-enforceable notwithstanding any remedy' are meaningless; the Commissioner General's decision must be positive and not doubly negative'.[16]

Then I modified my declaration as follows: 'The Commissioner General sees no reason why the decision contested in urgent appeal, or the removal order could not be enforced'.

In a letter to the Minister of the Interior dated 21 February 1994, I pointed out that of the 1,485 requests for suspension in French made before September 1993, only 3.4 per cent had been the subject of a judgment. Since 1 June 1993, I had made more than 4,000 confirmatory decisions. I still had to consider more than 8,000 urgent appeals, as well as more than 2,000 urgent requests for reconsideration. I observed that, not being associated with the choice of the time, means and conditions for the effective execution of the removal order, I could not produce a statement of reasons which would be relevant at the very moment of the actual removal of the person concerned.

Following the suspension granted on 8 February 1994, I appeared in person at the beginning of March 1994 before the Conseil d'Etat. I recalled the lack of competence of the Conseil d'Etat for such requests for suspension. The

[16] CdE, No 46.086 (8 February 1994).

auditors of the Conseil d'Etat endeavoured to declare these requests admissible. The auditors considered that a standard wording did not sufficiently justify the 'enforceable formula'. In a charged atmosphere, I stressed that the Conseil d'Etat had to declare itself incompetent. To be able to declare an action admissible, a court must first declare that it has jurisdiction. The law explicitly stated that in these cases the Conseil d'Etat was not competent. The Conseil d'Etat was drowning in the high number of asylum applications. The legislator had thrown it a lifeline. The castaway seemed unwilling to seize it. Some behaved as supporters of the maxim: '*Fiat justitia et pereat mundus*' ('May justice be done and the world perish').

One of the cases in which I appeared in person led to the (French) judgment of 7 March 1994.[17] Contrary to the auditor's opinion, the Conseil d'Etat ruled that the request for suspension was inadmissible. Admittedly, the Council felt that the 'formal mention' should be justified. However, in the Council's view, the failure or lack of motivation did not have the effect of rendering the 'formal mention' non-existent. In accordance with Articles 63/5, 69 and 70 of the Aliens Law, a request for suspension could not be dealt with. In a series of (French-speaking) judgments of 11 May 1994,[18] the Conseil d'Etat held that, in such cases, it had no jurisdiction to deal with requests for suspension. As regards questions to be referred to the Court of Arbitration for a preliminary ruling, on 30 March 1994 the Conseil d'Etat ruled in a (French-speaking) judgment[19] that 'the speed with which the Conseil d'Etat had to decide when it received a request for suspension could not, as a general rule, be reconciled with the obligation to ask a question for a preliminary ruling'.

On 10 June 1994, however, the Conseil d'Etat suspended such confirmatory decisions in several (French-speaking) judgments and referred questions to the Court of Arbitration.[20] At that time, I was already at my third enforceable formula:

> *For all the above reasons*, the Commissioner General also formally declares that the contested decision in urgent appeal and the removal order are enforceable notwithstanding any remedy, in accordance with the last paragraph of Article 63/5 of the Law of 15 December 1980.

Curiously, requesting a preliminary ruling had suddenly become reconcilable with the 'speed' with which the Conseil d'Etat had to decide. The Conseil d'Etat considered that it should ask the Court of Arbitration whether it was competent to rule on suspension requests. Without waiting for the answer, the Conseil d'Etat declared itself competent. The previously formed backlog of such requests had already shown that the Conseil d'Etat did not take the speed prescribed by law

[17] CdE, No 46.443 (7 March 1994).
[18] CdE, No 44.445–44.449 (11 May 1994).
[19] CdE, No 46.784 (30 March 1994).
[20] CdE, Nos 47.153, 47.873, 47.877, 47.879 (10 June 1994).

(45 days) very seriously. Requests for annulment of the legislative provisions in question, brought on 3 November 1993 by (French-speaking) non-profit associations, namely the Movement against Racism, Anti-Semitism and Xenophobia, the Union of Lawyers for Democracy and People's Rights was already before the Court of Arbitration. The Conseil d'Etat, however, referred several questions to the Court for a preliminary ruling on these legislative provisions. In doing so, the Conseil d'Etat showed its support for the requests of these associations.

In a note dated 30 June 1994 to the chief of staff of the Minister of the Interior, I pointed out that the Conseil d'Etat did not decide on any request for suspension within the 45-day period imposed by law. In the last 12 months, 820 judgments (78 per cent) had rejected the requests for reasons unrelated to the merits of the case. In recent weeks, this figure was even close to 90 per cent. I pointed out that the flip-flop in the case law caused great legal uncertainty. The different jurisprudence of the different linguistic Chambers of the Conseil d'Etat resulted in the applicants abandoning one linguistic role in favour of another.

16.3.3. Suspension before the Conseil d'Etat Reinstated: A Thunderbolt (14 July 1994)

Although the Court of Arbitration acknowledged in its judgment No 61/94 of 14 July 1994,[21] that no provision requires that the legislator introduces a procedure of administrative interim measures, it considered that:

> However, where Parliament considers that it is desirable to provide for the possibility of a request for the suspension of administrative acts, it may not refuse that request to certain categories of subjects of law – in this case, certain categories of foreign nationals who declare themselves refugees – if there is no reasonable justification (B.5.7).

The Court of Arbitration found that asylum seekers could not be deprived of a 'useful remedy' (B.5.9.6). The exclusion of the possibility of suspension by the Conseil d'Etat was described as 'disproportionate', 'especially since it allows the administrative authority itself to designate decisions whose suspension it prohibits from requesting from the Conseil d'Etat' (B.5.9.8). The 'leave to appeal' process (see above p 209) went too far for the Court of Arbitration, certainly when it was for the Commissioner General to decide. The Court of Arbitration annulled the contested legislation (Article 69*bis*, paragraph 2, and Article 70, paragraph 2, of the Aliens Law). Thus, the Court re-establishes the jurisdiction of the Conseil d'Etat to hear requests for suspension of my confirmatory decisions for refusal. In the long run, this would lead to a slippage in the asylum procedure.

The Court of Arbitration ignored the fact that these claimants had already exercised a 'useful remedy' before the Commissioner General. Indeed, the 'effective

[21] See above p 99 (n 16).

remedy' of Article 13 ECHR does not require a judicial body. Later, the European Court of Human Rights explicitly stated in its judgment in *Chahal v the United Kingdom* (§152) of 15 November 1996 that the 'effective remedy' required by Article 13 ECHR should not necessarily be offered by a judicial body. The level of protection depends more on the professional qualifications of the competent authorities than on the jurisdictional nature of the proceedings. Court proceedings are characterised by formalities which are not suitable for asylum. For my part, I felt that it had been a mistake to have settled the exclusion of the suspension procedure in the Aliens Law for 'certain categories of aliens'. This regulation should have been included in the coordinated laws on the Conseil d'Etat for all administrative decisions that had already been the subject of a suspensive appeal organised before an independent body. This is the process that will be used later, when the Aliens Litigation Council is created, to establish a procedure for filtering appeals in cassation before the Conseil d'Etat.[22]

I did not understand why the exclusion from the suspension procedure was 'disproportionate', while other strong measures were considered 'proportionate'. There was no problem that: (1) failed asylum seekers no longer received any social assistance (other than urgent medical aid) (B.4.3); (2) they can be retained in a specified place (B.7.5); and (3) they can be returned to their country of origin, before the Conseil d'Etat has been able to pronounce itself, even in suspension (B.5.9.7). All this was not serious, provided they had a judicial remedy.

The Minister of the Interior, Louis Tobback, sought a reply to this judgment based on the Court of Arbitration's dictum concerning the latter measure: 'Nothing prohibits the competent authority from executing the negative decision of the Commissioner General or his deputy confirming the decision of the Minister or his delegate'. The Minister put an end to the 'arrangement'[23] by which he had unilaterally promised the Conseil d'Etat not to execute the legally enforceable decisions if a remedy in suspension was brought before it. Despite a contrary decision of the Council of Ministers of 25 March 1995, the Aliens Office clung to this 'arrangement'. Henceforth, we had to see who would be the quickest: the Aliens Office to implement the decision of removal or the Conseil d'Etat to suspend it.

16.3.4. The Asylum Procedure before the Conseil d'Etat: Problems of All Kinds

On 18 October 1994, I repeated, in a note addressed to Minister Johan Vande Lanotte, my proposal to limit the jurisdiction of suspension via the coordinated

[22] Art 20 of the coordinated Laws on the Conseil d'Etat, introduced by the Law of 15 December 2006.

[23] In its judgment in *Čonka v Belgium* of 5 February 2002, the Strasbourg Court stated that Art 13 ECHR requires a suspensive appeal: 'the requirements of Article 13 … take the form of a guarantee, and not of a mere statement of intent or a practical arrangement' (§83).

laws on the Conseil d'Etat. A week before, Louis Tobback had been replaced as Minister of the Interior by his former chief of staff. This proposal could have avoided many misfortunes. I drew attention to problems which had their origin (almost exclusively) in the (French-speaking) procedure before the Conseil d'Etat. The French-speaking Chambers did not hesitate to substitute their assessment of 'serious harm' for that of the administrative authority. Sometimes they went so far as to appreciate the human rights situation in the countries of origin. Without hearing the applicant, it is difficult to get a sense of the truth of his story. Most of the requests (70 per cent) were rejected for purely procedural reasons specific to the Conseil d'Etat. I noticed that many requests were not serious. They were often unworthy of the highest administrative jurisdiction. Since the judgment of the Court of Arbitration, the number of requests for suspension had increased considerably. In its 1994/95 Annual Report (p 260), the Conseil d'Etat noted that it was 'overwhelmed' by these requests. On 27 October 1994, the backlog had increased to more than 1,000 requests pending in suspension (325 N and 738 F). Between June 1993 and December 1994, the Conseil d'Etat had granted only 13 annulments and 27 suspensions; 1,408 requests were denied.

There were great differences in the assessment of the Dutch-speaking and French-speaking Chambers of the Conseil d'Etat. According to the Dutch-speaking Chambers, the 'grievous and irreconcilable harm' which is legally required to be able to suspend could not have resulted from my confirmatory decision. This prejudice could only result from the removal order issued by the Aliens Office. This measure had become enforceable again following my confirmatory decision. According to the French-speaking Chambers, this prejudice was inherent in the 'quality' of asylum seeker. Yet by simply asking for asylum, any foreigner unilaterally confers to himself this 'quality'. Whatever his country of origin and whatever the specific circumstances of the person concerned, a removal of an asylum seeker was, according to the French-speaking Chambers, always a serious prejudice to the person concerned. I insisted that the General Assembly of the Conseil d'Etat ensure the unity of jurisprudence. Since I could not be divided into linguistic roles myself, I felt that the differences in case law between the two linguistic roles of the Conseil d'Etat were undermining the federal character of the asylum policy.

In my opinions accompanying my confirmatory decisions, I had to rule on the removal of the applicant to the country where he claimed to fear for his life, his physical integrity, or his freedom. To be able to suspend, the Conseil d'Etat regularly claimed that I had committed a 'manifest error of appreciation'. In doing so, the Conseil substituted its assessment for that of the administrative authority legally competent to assess that fear. Unlike this independent authority, the Conseil d'Etat was not specially equipped to make this assessment in full knowledge of the facts.

In 1995, 1,240 requests and in 1996, 1,431 requests were brought before the Conseil d'Etat against confirmatory decisions (new procedure) or decisions refusing urgent requests for reconsideration (old procedure). From July 1996, however, there was a significant decrease in these requests since the Cour de cassation had affirmed that their introduction did not entail a right to social assistance (see below p 223). Sixty-nine per cent and 74 per cent respectively of these requests were attributed to the French-speaking Chambers of the Conseil d'Etat. One lawyer alone accounted for 9 per cent of all requests in 1995 and 6.8 per cent in 1996. None of his requests resulted in a suspension or an annulment. On 31 December 1996, there was a backlog of 1,961 asylum cases (compared with 1,421 the previous year). The number of requests pending in 1994, 1995 and 1996 had averaged 414 days. The law required a pronouncement within 45 days.

In 1995, the Conseil d'Etat had delivered 2,534 judgments suspending or annulling decisions upon such requests, compared with 2,215 in 1996. In 1995, these judgments accounted for 40 per cent and in 1996 36 per cent of all judgments delivered by the Conseil d'Etat. During these two years, there were respectively 3.5 per cent and 5.3 per cent suspensions of confirmatory decisions. For urgent requests for reconsideration, there were respectively 7.6 per cent and 10.8 per cent suspensions. There were respectively 0.97 per cent and 1.91 per cent annulments. Without exception, they were exclusively, both in suspension and in annulment, judgments delivered by French-speaking Chambers. By comparison, my favourable opinions or further examination decisions fluctuated between 17 per cent and 35 per cent.[24]

[24] Precisely 34% in 1988; 31% in 1989; 35% in 1990; 25% in 1991; 18.5% in 1992; 17% in 1993; 21.8% in 1994; 33.6% in 1995; and 22.1% in 1996.

17

The Conseil d'Etat: The Bottleneck in the Asylum Procedure

The failure of the Conseil d'Etat to process requests for suspension of rejected asylum seekers within the 45-day period prescribed by law made the asylum procedure very vulnerable. This weakened the effects sought by the efforts undertaken. The Vande Lanotte Laws of 10 and 15 July 1996 did not change anything. The Onkelinx Law of 30 December 1992, which set out when social assistance would end, caused a great deal of confusion. The labour jurisdictions granted social assistance as long as the endless proceedings in the Conseil d'Etat remained pending. The endless disputes over this question increased the burden on the Conseil d'Etat. Even the judgment of the Cour de cassation of 4 September 1995 did not bring the labour jurisdictions into line. The interpretation given to the Onkelinx Law by the Vande Lanotte Law of 15 July 1996 was challenged before the Court of Arbitration. Following the judgment of 22 April 1998 of this Court, the workload of the Conseil d'Etat exploded. It was drowning in requests from asylum seekers. The whole asylum process followed the same path.

17.1. The Vande Lanotte Laws (10–15 July 1996): Grunts in the Margin

Childbirth was difficult for the legislative amendments introduced by Minister Johan Vande Lanotte. These were not fundamental measures. The suspension procedure before the Conseil d'Etat was maintained. No one questioned whether this remedy was 'useful'. The problem would be solved by appointing additional State Councillors.

17.1.1. Adaptation to Dublin and Schengen: No Procedural Relief

Minister Johan Vande Lanotte had to adapt the Aliens Law to the Dublin Convention of 15 June 1990 and the Schengen Agreement of 19 June 1990. This was not a simplification of the asylum procedure. It added to that procedure an additional phase to determine which State was responsible for processing an asylum application. Such a phase only makes sense when the removal to another European country is more effective and faster than to the country of origin.

Even though these were not fundamental measures, parliamentary proceedings were proceeding painfully. Many hearings were held. Various bodies and organisations dealing with refugees and foreigners, including myself (7 February 1996),[1] were heard. The organisations were worried. Minister Louis Tobback had taken measures, including the Law of 6 May 1993, which had considerably reduced the number of asylum applications. Despite the noise made by these organisations and the media, the legislative amendments were passed by the House, virtually unamended, on 4 April 1996. After being evoked by it on 30 April, the Senate adopted them in turn, on 27 June 1996, without any change.

I was worried too. I was concerned that the proposed legislative amendments would maintain an overly onerous asylum procedure. Despite all this hype, it was only a few grunts in the margin. The dramatic drop in asylum applications was not enough to resolve the backlog only with additional staff. The backlog was expected not to be resolved before mid-1999. This was without considering the arrears of the Permanent Board and the Conseil d'Etat.

Even before the adoption of the new laws, I had expressed my doubts to the Minister of the Interior in a letter of 18 March 1996. I knew that he planned to expand the number of State Councillors and Chambers of the Permanent Board. I felt that consideration should be given to granting the Office of the Commissioner General the status of an administrative jurisdiction. The Legislative Section of the Conseil d'Etat had proposed this in an opinion of 14 October 1992.[2] Since the asylum procedure was greatly hampered by the reinstatement of the suspension procedure in the Conseil d'Etat, this option had to be considered. In addition, some of the advantages of an administrative authority over an administrative jurisdiction disappeared with the laws of 29 July 1991 concerning the formal reasons for administrative acts, and of 11 April 1994 on the publicity of the administration.

I indicated my preference for an asylum procedure with a maximum of three bodies, namely:

1. At first instance: the Aliens Office.
2. One (only) suspensive appeal to the Commission General converted into an administrative jurisdiction where, depending on the complexity of the appeal, the Commissioners in charge would take, immediately or after further examination, an enforceable decision. Only the asylum seekers retained in a specified place could, in the event that confirmation of the decision is not possible, benefit from a subsequent (intermediate) decision for further examination.
3. A non-suspensive appeal in cassation before the Conseil d'Etat.

[1] *Doc parl, Chambre*, 1995/96, No 364/8.
[2] *Doc parl, Chambre*, 1992/93, No 555/1, 47, point 4, §4.

In view of the working cultures of the authorities concerned, a Commission General converted into an administrative jurisdiction would have considerably (and favourably) differentiated from a Permanent Board converted into an Aliens Litigation Council. This would be all the easier since the Commissioner General, as a quasi-judicial body, already met several of the requirements of a jurisdiction: summons by registered letter, hearings, assistance by a lawyer and an interpreter, the possibility of submitting documents, and reasons given for decisions. Only two features of a jurisdiction were missing: the person who heard the applicant was not the one who decides, and the applicant did not have prior access to the file.

Minister Johan Vande Lanotte, who had already spent a lot of political energy in getting the laws of 10 and 15 July 1996 approved, was not willing to pass the proposed simplification. The number of asylum applications was under control. Most incoming refugee applications were processed quickly. In my opinion, this was a unique opportunity to try to develop a system for effectively returning to their country of origin newly arrived and failed asylum seekers. But there was no interest in my proposals. A much-needed simplification of the procedure could have avoided considerable overload and enormous costs. This overload and cost would result from the future slippage of the asylum procedure and the establishment of expansive jurisdictional structures. Legal challenges to social assistance for asylum seekers would be fatal for the existing asylum procedure. Ping-pong balls became tennis balls.

17.1.2. Asylum Recourse to the Conseil d'Etat: A 'Useful Remedy'?

By the Law of 4 August 1996, adopted at the initiative of Minister Johan Vande Lanotte, a significant increase in the number of State Councillors and members of the Auditorium, the Coordination Office and the Registry was authorised. In addition, the Councillors of State would be assisted by several jurists. The Conseil d'Etat could be grateful to its former auditor. The justification given for this significant growth in staff was the need to catch up with the backlog at the Conseil d'Etat. It was largely made up of claims from foreign nationals, particularly failed refugee applicants.

In the light of the justification given, the question arose as to whether the efforts made by the French-speaking Chambers in 1994 to retain jurisdiction over the suspension of my confirmatory decisions had anything to do with it.[3] Without this surplus of French-speaking asylum cases, there would have been a significant imbalance between the workload of the Dutch-speaking Chambers and that of the French-speaking Chambers. On 15 September 2006, the Aliens

[3] *Ninth Annual Report* (1996) 36, note 49.

Litigation Council was created.[4] The loot was cashed. The aliens' litigation could largely be entrusted to an administrative jurisdiction of first instance. It is currently composed of 62 aliens' judges. On 1 September 2009, a (Flemish) Permits Litigation Council was to be established with seven administrative judges. The number of Councillors of State remained unchanged.

The only practical effect of the intervention of the Conseil d'Etat was the postponement in time of the removal of rejected asylum seekers. This resulted in a longer reception period (and additional costs). The longer the reception period, the more difficult it is for the authorities to remove someone to his country of origin – and the more painful it is for the person concerned. It was also an important factor in attracting asylum applications. In addition, jurists in my services had to devote additional efforts to defend hundreds of my decisions before the Conseil d'Etat.

From the moment when the Commissioner General obtained decision-making power in the matter of removal, the intervention of the Conseil d'Etat had no real added value. It seemed above all that it was a matter of giving good conscience to some, under the pretext of respect for great principles. Or was it mainly the employment of lawyers that had to be ensured? I lost the motivation to cooperate in keeping up good appearances. Denouncing this hypocrisy could jeopardise the exercise of my mandate. This prompted me to consider looking at other horizons. On 5 February 1997, I left the Commission General. Before doing so, I had verified how many decisions annulled by the Conseil d'Etat had led to the recognition of refugee status. There was only one case. What we call a 'useful remedy'!

17.2. Social Assistance: The Nerve of Asylum

More than a right of residence, the introduction of an asylum application aims to obtain a right to social assistance. If money is the nerve of war, welfare is the nerve of asylum. Hence the importance of determining when this right ends. The Onkelinx Law of 30 December 1992 caused widespread confusion. On 4 September 1995, the Cour de cassation provided clarity. When it turned out that labour jurisdictions did not respect the Cassation judgment, the Vande Lanotte Law of 15 July 1996 intended to put an end to it. In its judgment of 22 April 1998, however, the Court of Arbitration favoured an interpretation of its own. The consequences were unprecedented. Only at the end of 2000 will the peak be reached.

[4] M Bossuyt and L De Geyter, 'De rol van de asieljurisdicties in de Belgische asielprocedure' in J Rozie, F Deruyck, L Huybrechts and F Van Volsem (eds), *Na Rijp beraad: liber amicorum Michel Rozie* (Antwerp, Intersentia, 2014) 39.

17.2.1. Obligations Towards Foreigners Staying Illegally in the Territory

The state does not have the same obligations towards those who stay illegally in its territory as it does towards those who stay there legally.[5] A foreigner who has entered or is staying in the territory without authorisation is not entitled to make the same claims as foreigners who have obtained this authorisation. It is rare for asylum applications to be made by foreigners who have, as required, obtained prior authorisation to stay in the country. For this reason, the asylum procedure began with a decision on access to or stay in the territory. It is generally accepted that foreigners who apply for asylum have a right to social assistance from the state pending a decision on entry or residence. They benefit a fortiori from this right once they have obtained access or residence for the purpose of deciding on their asylum application.

Determining when the entitlement to social assistance ends is critically important. An order to leave the territory is legally binding: the person concerned is obliged to leave the territory. It is clearly preferable that the person concerned complies voluntarily with this obligation rather than being forced to do so. Removal by force is only possible when the order is enforceable. The enforceability can be postponed by deadlines and appeal procedures. As a rule, the order to leave the territory indicates the time within which it must be executed. In the case of an organised appeal, as was the case with the urgent appeal before the Commissioner General, the execution of the order is suspended for the period necessary to bring such an appeal. If it is further provided that the appeal is suspensive, the order cannot be enforced if the appeal is not closed. When it has finally been found that the applicant is not a refugee, it will follow, as a rule, that the order to leave the territory will have to be executed. This will be done voluntarily, if possible; by constraint, if necessary (*cf* chapter eighteen, p 234–241).

It is difficult to expect failed asylum seekers to voluntarily leave the country, when – in case they do not – they continue to receive social assistance. Once the application for asylum is refused, the residence situation of the persons concerned is the same as that of other foreigners staying in the territory without authorisation. They are therefore not (or no longer) entitled to social assistance.

[5] See the judgments of the Court of Arbitration No 203/2004 of 21 December 2004 ('The State must not recognize itself, in the face of the needs of those who stay illegally in the territory, the same duties as those who stay legally in the territory' (B.11.5)) and No 66/2006 of 3 May 2006 ('for foreigners staying illegally in Belgium, the State has not the same obligations as for those staying legally in the country' (B.6.3)).

17.2.2. The Onkelinx Law (30 December 1992): Confusion on All Levels

Laurette Onkelinx, Minister of Health, and Social Integration (7 March 1992–4 May 1993), took the initiative to clarify the CPAS Law of 8 July 1976. Amended by the Law of 30 December 1992, Article 57, §2 of that Law provided that

> the Centre shall only provide the strictly necessary assistance to enable to leave the country to:
>
> 1) a foreigner who has declared himself a refugee, has asked to be recognised in that capacity, is however not authorised to remain in the Kingdom in that capacity and to whom a *definitive* order to leave the country has been notified;
> 2) a foreigner who is staying illegally in the Kingdom and to whom a *definitive* order to leave the country has been notified.

17.2.2.1. A 'Definitive' Order: A Nonsense in Administrative Law

When I saw this text in the office of Interior Minister Louis Tobback, I was appalled by its wording. I expressed my displeasure in no uncertain terms. I could not understand that such an important initiative for asylum policy had been taken without my having had the opportunity to make my point. I saw it as a lack of trust based on partisan politics. All members of the government concerned by the asylum policy had not yet understood that without cooperation it would not be possible to overcome the asylum crisis. That would not happen any more in the future. But the damage was done. Unfortunately, my fear that the notion of 'definitive order' would lead to great confusion and many legal challenges became reality. I did not foresee that the entire asylum policy would collapse because of this confusion.

Every jurist knows when a judgment in criminal or civil matters is 'definitive': (a) when the judge in first instance has pronounced and the time limit for appeal has elapsed, or (b) in case of appeal, when the time limit for the recourse in cassation against the judgment in appeal has elapsed, or (c) in the case of a recourse in cassation, when the Cour de cassation has denied it. Once a court proceeding is definitively dealt with, no judge, no minister or anyone can reverse the decision. It is definitive.

In administrative law, it's quite different. Any order to leave the territory may at any time be withdrawn by the competent authority. This can be done even after the administrative judge has ruled that the order is legal. Often there are opportunities for recourse: sometimes before administrative authorities, more and more before administrative jurisdictions and always (on first or last instance) before the Conseil d'Etat. The mere introduction of an appeal before the Conseil d'Etat – for annulment or (since the Law of 19 July 1991) for suspension – has no suspensive effect. Decisions of an administrative authority are supposed to be legal. If an administrative judge has not ruled otherwise, an administrative decision is binding. That is exactly what is meant by the already mentioned (see above p 209) principle of administrative law '*le privilège du préalable*': administrative decisions are enforceable without prior intervention by a judge. Therefore, the legislative provision regarding CPAS should have referred to an 'enforceable' order, not a 'definitive' order.

17.2.2.2. The Cour de cassation (4 September 1995)

Initially, this new provision of the CPAS Law (Article 57, §2) was not frequently applied. The Ministry of Public Health did not often respond to the lists I provided. These lists included the names of asylum seekers who had been subject to an enforceable refusal decision. The Ministry claimed that it did not receive confirmation from the Aliens Office. It was not clear whether a suspension had been requested from the Conseil d'Etat. The Ministry initially considered that decisions were definitive only after the Conseil d'Etat refused to suspend them. There were even labour courts and tribunals that ruled that decisions were definitive only after the Conseil d'Etat – whenever – ruled on a request for annulment. Some argued that the order, while enforceable, would not be definitive. Laurette Onkelinx, the Minister of Public Health and Social Integration, also contributed to the confusion. In a circular dated 2 March 1993,[6] it was stated that in the event of an appeal to the Conseil d'Etat, the order would not be definitive. According to a circular (corrigendum) of 27 April 1993,[7] the order was definitive when no *suspensive* appeal was possible.

In a note of 13 October 1994 addressed to the (new) Interior Minister Johan Vande Lanotte, I insisted that misunderstandings must be avoided. It should be clear when social assistance should be stopped. It had not to be as soon as a 'definitive' decision was made but an 'enforceable' decision refusing refugee status. I proposed that all cases in which a decision was enforceable should be mentioned in the law:

a. A decision of inadmissibility made by the Minister or his delegate for which the time limit for filing an urgent request or an urgent appeal has expired.
b. An unfavourable opinion of the Commissioner General confirmed by the Minister or his delegate or a confirmatory decision of refusal to stay taken by the Commissioner General.
c. A refusal decision taken by the Commissioner General for which the time limit for filing an appeal with the Permanent Board has expired.
d. A refusal decision by the Permanent Board.

Unlike many CPAS, more labour courts and tribunals considered that the order was not 'definitive' when it was still subject to appeal before the Conseil d'Etat.

[6] 'Tijdschrift voor Vreemdelingenrecht' (1994) 314.
[7] ibid 326.

This jurisprudence was largely responsible for a high number of dilatory appeals[8] brought before the Conseil d'Etat. Fortunately, the Cour de cassation kept a cool head. In judgments of 4 September[9] and 4 December 1995,[10] the Court recalled[11] that a definitive order to leave the territory was an order which could no longer be the subject of an appeal with suspensive effect before an administrative authority or the Conseil d'Etat. It was not an order against which no appeal was more possible before any authority or jurisdiction likely to take a decision on foreigners. Since neither the request for annulment nor the request for suspension had a suspensive effect, the order was definitive, despite the introduction of such requests before the Conseil d'Etat. Even in the case of appeals to the Conseil d'Etat, there was no longer a right to social assistance.

The Conseil d'Etat acted swiftly on requests for suspension 'in extreme emergency' (but only in that case). This made it possible to suspend removal decisions deemed to be contrary to the law before their implementation. Moreover, this was in line with the Court of Arbitration's ruling in No 61/94 of 14 July 1994: 'only a suspension decision taken by the Conseil d'Etat, possibly in extreme urgency by a President … will prevent expulsion from the territory' (B.5.9.7). Recourse to this procedure in extreme urgency occurred only rarely. In its 1994/95 Annual Report, the Conseil d'Etat observed that many asylum seekers preferred the ordinary procedure because it could last forever.

17.2.2.3. An Interpretative Law (15 July 1996)

Despite the judgments of the Cour de cassation, several labour jurisdictions continued to grant social assistance. They continued to make contrary judgments. Marcel Colla was Minister of Health (1995–99) when the initiative was taken to pass interpretive legislation. The provision in question (Article 65) was part of the Vande Lanotte Law of 15 July 1996 (see above p 216–217). In section 57, §2 of the CPAS Law, the term 'definitive order' has been replaced by the term 'enforceable order'. In addition, that provision explicitly provided that the task of a CPAS was limited to providing urgent medical assistance to a foreigner who was illegally staying in the Kingdom. The concept of 'urgent medical assistance' was defined by the royal decree of 12 December 1996. This assistance could be both curative and preventive.

In judgments of 21 October[12] and 7 November 1996,[13] the Cour de cassation confirmed that the introduction of appeals to the Conseil d'Etat did not entail

[8] Actions brought in order to benefit from the long duration of a procedure, including the extension of social assistance.

[9] Cass (4 September 1995) S.94.0133. F, *Arr Cass* 1995, 734.

[10] Cass (4 December 1995) S.95.0038. N, *Arr Cass* 1995, 1070.

[11] For a comment on these two judgments, see M-C Foblets and F Bernard, 'L'aide sociale aux étrangers en séjour illégal: la saga de l'ordre de quitter le territoire définitif de l'article 57, §2, de la loi sur les CPAS' [1996] *Recente arresten van het Hof van Cassatie* No 97.

[12] Cass (21 October 1996) S.96.0021.N, *Arr Cass* 1996, 941.

[13] Cass. (7 November 1996) S.96.0088.F, *Arr Cass* 1996, 1019.

social assistance. This view of the Cour de cassation corresponded not only to that of the government, but also to the will of the legislator. The legislative branch, the executive branch and the judiciary agreed on this interpretation.

17.3. The Judgment of 22 April 1998: The Court of Arbitration Understood it Otherwise

The Court of Arbitration understood it otherwise. On 24 March 1997, three French-speaking non-profit associations (the Movement against Racism, Anti-Semitism and Xenophobia; the League for Human Rights; and the Lawyers' Union for Democracy) asked for the annulment of the amendments made by the Law of 15 July 1996 to the Aliens Law of 15 December 1980 and the CPAS Law of 8 July 1976. I had been a judge at the Court of Arbitration since 6 February 1997. The date for the hearing of this case was 11 February 1998. On that day, one of the francophone judges was not available. Therefore, as the last appointed Dutch-speaking judge, I could not sit. The absence of these two judges affected the balanced composition of the seat. On 22 April 1998, the Court of Arbitration delivered its judgment No 43/98.[14]

17.3.1. Social Assistance as Long as the Appeals Brought before the Conseil d'Etat are not Decided

It was to be inferred from this judgment of 22 April 1998 that at the time of its judgment No 51/94 of 29 June 1994,[15] the Court of Arbitration would have understood that an order to leave the territory would only be 'definitive' when no further appeal was pending before the Conseil d'Etat. The Law of 15 July 1996 having clarified – by replacing the word 'definitive' with the word 'enforceable' – that there was no longer any entitlement to social assistance despite appeals pending before the Conseil d'Etat, the Court considered that this measure was 'excessive' (B.35). The Court held that the contested measure brought about a 'disproportionate limitation' on the right to social assistance and the right to the effective exercise of a judicial remedy (B.36). The Court relied on the finding that there was a filtering procedure for dilatory appeals (B.35): 'The rules of procedure applicable before the Conseil d'Etat allow requests for suspension and for annulment which are manifestly inadmissible or manifestly unfounded to be rejected without delay' (B.34).

[14] See also M Bossuyt and R Leysen, 'Het Arbitragehof en het vreemdelingenrecht' in M Bossuyt et al, *Burgerschap, inburgering en migratie* (Brussels, Larcier, 2006) 47.

[15] In Judgment No 51/94 of 29 June 1994, the Court found no discrimination in limiting social assistance to urgent medical assistance to foreigners who had received a definitive order to leave the territory.

The Court struck down the word 'enforceable' in section 57, §2, of the CPAS Law. But what was to be understood by 'an order to leave the territory' which was not qualified, neither by the word 'definitive', nor by the word 'enforceable'? The Court gave its own interpretation. The effect of the annulment was clarified by prefacing the annulment with the following sentence:

> The effect of this annulment is that Article 57, §2, must be interpreted as not applying to a foreign national who has applied to be recognised as a refugee, whose application has been refused and who has been ordered to leave the country, *as long as the appeals brought before the Conseil d'Etat have not been decided* against the decision of the Commissioner General for Refugees and Stateless Persons taken pursuant to Article 63/3 of the Law or against the decision of the Permanent Refugees Appeals Board (emphasis added).

Consequently, once an appeal was lodged with the Conseil d'Etat, social assistance was maintained, not only until the end of the suspension proceedings against the Commissioner General's confirmatory decision, but also until the end of the annulment proceedings against this decision. Moreover, not only was the admissibility procedure to be completed by the Conseil d'Etat, but this also applied to the procedure on the merits, since even if the contested decision was taken by a jurisdiction (the Permanent Board), social assistance was maintained until the end of a possible (cassation) procedure before the Conseil d'Etat. Thus, national solidarity was extended in favour of foreigners for whom the competent authorities had decided that they had to leave the territory and that they could be removed from it. Although I was not part of the seat, as a judge emeritus of the Court, I better refrain from commenting on this judgment. Allow me, however, to point out that the use of the word 'definitive' in the Onkelinx Law of 30 December 1992 was the cause of the collapse of the asylum procedure. The consequences of this blunder were even greater than I had feared at the time it was made.

17.3.2. The Consequences of the Judgment of 22 April 1998: All Records Broken

As might be expected, the judgment of 22 April 1998 created an ever-greater burden of appeals before the Conseil d'Etat.[16] The dykes had burst. The Conseil d'Etat's backlog of confirmatory decisions taken by the Commissioner General rose from 1,059 at the end of 1998 to 2,177 (+105 per cent) at the end of 1999 and to 8,791 (+248 per cent) at the end of 2000.[17] This is an exponential growth.

[16] See P Gilliaux, 'Le Conseil d'Etat et le contentieux des étrangers: L'irrésistible attrait de l'inefficace' (1 October 1999) *Journal des Procès* 15.

[17] In its Annual Report 2000/01, the Conseil d'Etat pointed out that, following the judgment of 22 April 1998 of the Court of Arbitration, the Registry had to issue certificates to asylum seekers who had lodged an appeal with the Conseil d'Etat. On average, it was 150 to 200 certificates a day. In addition, the Registry had to keep a full monthly correspondence with the CPAS or with the applicants' counsel.

The number of appeals made by asylum seekers had even increased to represent more than 80 per cent of all appeals before the Conseil d'Etat! But this does not mean that the Conseil d'Etat allocated 80 per cent of its staff to the handling of appeals against decisions of the Commissioner General, far from it. Yet, either the asylum dispute was equivalent to other administrative challenges, and then equivalent efforts had to be made to deal with them; or less effort was required and then there was no justification for the formation of significant backlogs. These backlogs were all the less justifiable as asylum seekers are at the charge of the state for the duration of the procedure. Those who have recourse to the Conseil d'Etat in other matters are not. Moreover, the mere introduction of an appeal before the Conseil d'Etat has the consequence, for asylum seekers only, of obtaining in fact immediately what they are looking for: a prolonged stay in the territory. After the judgment of 22 April 1998, a right to social assistance was added automatically. It was therefore not surprising that after two months the snowball effect was triggered again. It would continue without interruption for two and a half years.

Taking advantage of the bridge of Ascension, I undertook, to change my ideas a little, a university mission from 16 to 23 May 1998 in Rwanda and Burundi. Accompanied by my colleague from the University of Antwerp (UIA), Professor Henri Swennen, I visited the National University of Rwanda in Butare and the University of Burundi in Bujumbura.[18] We were looking at the possibilities of resuming cooperation with the law faculties of these two universities. As coordinator of the Flemish Interuniversity Council (Vl.I.R.), I would resume cooperation with the law faculty in Bujumbura. In Rwanda, we visited two Tutsi genocide memorials: the long rows of skulls in the small church of Nyamata and the sight of the bodies under the lime in the Murambi Technical School near Gikongoro (where 60,000 bodies had been unearthed) made a strong impression on us.[19]

17.3.2.1. The Saint-Pierre Hospital: Heart Concerns (14 July 1998)

Less than three months after the judgment of the Court of Arbitration of 22 April 1998, on 14 July 1998, I suffered a heart attack at the Court. It was only a short time before the Court, after having pronounced the last judgments of the year of activity, would suspend its activities for the summer break. I was quickly transported to Saint-Pierre Hospital in Brussels, close to the Ministry of Justice. Early evening, a stent was inserted into my arteries to dilate them. During the night, suddenly my heart stopped beating. Since I was under cardiac surveillance, a few

[18] V Sagaert, 'De betekenis van Marc Bossuyt voor de Burundese rechtstaat. "*Mushingantahe*" als eretitel' in A Alen, V Joosten, R Leysen and W Verrijdt, *Liberae cogitationes: Liber amicorum Marc Bossuyt* (Antwerp, Intersentia, 2013) 543.

[19] In a letter of 7 June 1998 to Professor Josse Van Steenberge, Rector of the University of Antwerp (UIA), Professor Filip Reyntjens of the University of Antwerp (RUCA) described our visit to these two 'places of pilgrimage' as 'obligatory genocide tourism'.

electric shocks immediately fixed it. The Chief Medical Officer, who came by in the morning, said to me: 'Now we don't worry about you any more. It was different last night'.

Saint-Pierre Hospital is widely frequented by foreigners whose status of stay varies greatly. The care is excellent. Doctor Michel de Marneffe, a very dynamic doctor, had done the dilation urgently. A very nice woman doctor of Turkish origin oversaw the cardiac surveillance. Another woman doctor of Tunisian origin, wearing a scarf, gave me a stress test. A doctor of Rwandan origin gave me post-operative care. When I asked him where he went to university, he said, 'In Bujumbura. Do you understand?' I understood: he was a Rwandan refugee in Burundi. During night conversations, a Flemish aid, a rather rare species over there, told me: 'We have here patients who have as their only proof of identity an order to leave the territory issued five years earlier'. I felt at home.

Among the few visitors allowed by my wife to cardiac surveillance was my successor, Commissioner General Luc De Smet. He knew how to please me. He brought the latest statistics from the Commission General. However, looking at these statistics was not good for my heart. June 1998 showed a sharp rise of 33 per cent. With 1,510 asylum applications, this represented a one-third increase from the monthly average of 1,132 in the previous five months. I was very worried. I advised Luc to sound the alarm. I was concerned that without quick action, the snowball effect would be triggered. It became a reality: that same month (July 1998), there were more than 2,000 asylum applications (2,035).

17.3.2.2. The Ultimate Skid (End 2000)

On 17 August 1998, Commissioner General Luc De Smet drew the attention of Interior Minister Louis Tobback to the enormous growth in asylum applications. Among the most important pull factors, he cited the fact that incoming asylum seekers were not immediately questioned by the Aliens Office, and the 22 April 1998 judgment of the Court of Arbitration. He emphasised the need for urgent action to prevent the well-known 'snowball effect'. Later it appeared that this effect manifested itself as never before. By the end of 1998, the number of applications for the first half of the year (7,171) had doubled in the second half of the year (14,796). This continued in the same way: from 11,909 in 1997, the number of asylum applications rose to 21,967 in 1998; then to 35,808 in 1999; and finally to the never reached number of 41,982(!) in 2000. This annual record was 3.5 times higher than the average (12,006 asylum applications) of the three years (1995–97) before the slide. That cost the taxpayer a fortune.

Meanwhile, the ministers of the Interior had succeeded each other: after the death of Semira Adamu on 22 September 1998, Louis Tobback resigned on 26 September 1998. He was a second time Minister of the Interior for only five months. Luc Van den Bossche (SP) succeeded him for less than 10 months until

12 July 1999. In early 1999, the 'dioxin crisis' broke out.[20] After the elections on 13 June 1999, Guy Verhofstadt became Prime Minister on 12 July 1999. Antoine Duquesne (PRL, later MR) became Minister of the Interior (until 11 July 2003).

Just before he became Prime Minister, I had the opportunity to urge Guy Verhofstadt to give an urgent response to any requests for reinforcement from the asylum bodies. Since June 1998, asylum applications had risen sharply, for the fourth time since 1 February 1988. In addition, the removal policy had collapsed because of the death of Semira Adamu. Previous increases had also begun in early summer (July 1989, July 1991 and June 1992). It was to be feared that in July 1999 the number of asylum applications would once again peak.

The first skid (with a peak in March 1990) was cleared, thanks to reinforcements of staff by subsidised contract civil servants and militiamen; the second (September 1991), with reinforcements of personnel and the Wathelet Law of 18 July 1991; the third (June 1993) thanks to draconian reinforcements of personnel and the Tobback Law of 6 May 1993. It seemed unlikely to me that it would be possible to control the fourth skid with only additional personnel. I wrote to him:

> The slippage of the asylum policy is not a fatality that one must undergo and before which our country would be powerless. In the case of flooding, the causes are not eliminated by the expansion of flood zones and the distribution of buckets to bring water back to ditches and rivers. Raising the dykes and stopping the water flows is much more effective. Streamlining the process and effective removals are more effective than the multiplication of reception centres and the growth in the number of staff to move files from one jurisdiction to another.

After a few months at the head of the government, Guy Verhofstadt took the asylum policy into his own hands with the determination that characterises him. At the head of a Task Force, he did not shy away from any effort to move things forward. When the Russians were slow to issue pass documents, he did not hesitate to address (his then friend) Vladimir Putin, President (2000–08; 2012–) of the Russian Federation.

He relied mainly on Pascal Smet. After having been my student at the University of Antwerp, he worked at the Commission General from 1991. Very quickly, Pascal was 'promoted' from protection officer handling files to a supervisor and then to a section head. All these promotions were only functional. They had no effect on the rank or remuneration of the 'promoted' members. As head of the 'Asia' section, Pascal was so effective that his section, which dealt mainly with applications from India and Pakistan, was cut short. When the crisis broke out in Yugoslavia, almost his entire section was able to be transferred to a new section: 'Former Yugoslavia'. After some time in the Cabinet of Interior

[20] Political crisis provoked by the detection of dioxin in animal food products, mainly eggs and chickens.

Minister Johan Vande Lanotte, in 1998 he succeeded Luc De Smet as Deputy Commissioner. At the end of October 1999, Guy Verhofstadt appointed this former Chairperson of the Flemish Young Socialists (1990–92) as deputy chief of staff to Minister Antoine Duquesne. From 1 January 2001, Pascal Smet was appointed Commissioner General. Prime Minister Guy Verhofstadt had put a knife at the throat of Luc De Smet. Used as a scapegoat, he was forced to resign. He was appointed as an asylum expert in the Ministry of Foreign Affairs for six years.

On 4 January 2006, Luc De Smet died in the car that was transporting him from his office in Brussels to the hospital. The previous two days, he had still come to his office. On 14 January 2006, I gave a speech at his funeral in Louise-Marie in the Flemish Ardennes:

> When Luc became my deputy [on 1 September 1994], I could blindly entrust him with the recognition policy. It gave me more time to lead the Commission General in security through the sometimes big storms of asylum. When he succeeded me [on 6 February 1997], he knew how thankless and risky the mission was. Nevertheless, he engaged with enthusiasm and tenacity. Luc was especially the man of individual files and good advice. He was more interested in the trees than in the forest. This forest is full of traps and shotguns. When he warned against the imminent slippage [from August 1998], he was not listened to. One tried to make him bear the responsibility for that slippage. For the refugees and his staff, he was a good commissioner general. He did not always know how to avoid administrative obstacles and political pitfalls. His relations with the competent ministers were laborious. He failed in making the media into an ally against unfair criticism. His precarious status left him with no choice but to throw away the glove.[21]

On 15 September 2003, Steve Stevaert, Chairperson of the SP (2003–05), had removed Pascal Smet, originally from Beveren, from the Commission General to become Secretary of State for Mobility in the Brussels Government. This was the beginning of a successful political career (see above p 189).

Following Pascal's departure from the Commission General, Dirk Van den Bulck, Deputy Commissioner since July 2002, acted as Commissioner General. On 1 January 2005, he was appointed as such. He had previously worked at the *Foyer* of Johan Leman in Molenbeek. From 1992 to 1999, he oversaw asylum issues in the Cabinet of Interior Ministers Johan Vande Lanotte, Louis Tobback and Luc Van den Bossche. In 1999, he was appointed assessor of the Permanent Board. His term as Commissioner General was renewed for five years in 2010, 2015 and 2020. On 31 March 2023, he retired. The next day, Sophie Van Balberghe, whom I had recruited at the Commission General in 1993, ensured his succession. This is the fourth time that one of the two Deputy Commissioners succeeded as Commissioner General, but for the first time, it was a woman and a francophone.

[21] 'In Memoriam' (2006/1) *Wereldbeeld* 5.

18

Semira Adamu, Removals and Regularisations (1998–2020)

Semira Adamu, a Nigerian woman, died on 22 September 1998, during a sixth repatriation attempt, resulting in the resignation of Interior Minister Louis Tobback on 26 September. Following this event, the Vermeersch I Commission (1998–99), the Vermeersch II Commission (2004–05) and the Bossuyt Commission (2018–20) were established. They had to make recommendations for a more humane and effective policy of removals. On 12 December 2003, four gendarmes involved in her attempted repatriation were criminally convicted. At the end of this chapter, I will develop the pitfalls that arise with regularisations presented as alternatives to removals.

18.1. The Death of Semira Adamu (22 September 1998): A Drama in Zaventem

On the evening of Tuesday 22 September 1998, Nigerian asylum seeker Semira Adamu died at the Saint-Luc University Hospital in Woluwe-Saint-Lambert. This sad event took place a year and a half after I left the Commission General. It marks a very exceptional and important place in Belgian asylum policy. We can assume that there is some interest in knowing the exact circumstances of this tragedy.

18.1.1. Semira Adamu: Figurehead of Resistance against Removals

Coming from Togo, she applied for asylum at Brussels National Airport on 25 March 1998. She was on her way to Berlin with a fake Portuguese passport. She claimed to have fled her country because her stepmother forced her to marry a 65-year-old man. This man would have already been married to two or three other women. Few in the media doubted this. Only *De Morgen* made mention of an anonymous witness who had known her very closely for six months. He said: 'This little story of forced marriage was an invention. She told me explicitly herself'. After her death, Reverend Herman Boon, the Catholic chaplain at the airport, said: 'She laughed at the fact that Belgium could believe in her history of forced marriage. This story did not hold. At the centre, no one believed it'. A social worker at the closed Reception Centre 127*bis* said: 'Indeed, the story of a forced marriage was not true'.

According to Commissioner General Luc De Smet, in his press release of 24 July 1998, it was not correct to say that Belgium did not accept asylum applications alleging gender-related persecution:

> The condition of access to the asylum procedure is that the applicant provides a coherent and credible narrative, which was not the case here. She could not claim refugee status because she had travelled to Belgium for reasons other than the grounds of persecution.

This press release was issued on the fourth failed attempt at her repatriation, on 21 July, because the press had not properly reported on the facts concerning her application and the asylum policy.

18.1.2. Her Stay at the Closed Reception Centre 127*bis* (March–September 1998)

On 21 July 1998, there was a fire – probably intentionally started – at Reception Centre 127*bis* in Steenokkerzeel.[1] Thirty-one illegal aliens had taken the opportunity to escape; seven of them were taken back immediately. The Collective against removals went there to demonstrate with torches. Accused of having cut the double fence surrounding the closed centre, 17 of them were placed at the disposal of the prosecutor. For about two months they tried to prevent removals. At the airport, they talked to the passengers or the pilot. This was also the case on 21 July. They were accompanied by Ecolo MP Olivier Deleuze.[2] The protest action in Steenokkerzeel followed the failed attempt to expel Semira Adamu on the same day. She had been placed in a segregation cell for four hours. This prevented her from escaping with the others. The Collective demanded that Semira should stay in Belgium. Her man of trust at the Collective later said: 'We were outside, in front of the Centre 127*bis* shouting our telephone numbers at the windows. She was one of the first to call us'.

18.1.3. Reactions to the Death of Semira Adamu (22–24 September 1998)

Her tragic death on 22 September 1998 was widely reported in newspapers. The most striking headlines of 23 September appeared in French language newspapers:

> Semira's Death Challenges Brutal Deportation Techniques (*LLB*).

[1] *LS* (22 July 1998).
[2] Olivier Deleuze was MP (1981–86; 1995–99; 2010–12); Secretary of State for Energy (1999–2003); and (since 2012) Mayor of Watermaal-Boitsfort.

> The Expulsion of a Refugee Turns into a Tragedy in Zaventem (*LS*).
>
> Deceased, Semira may Remain in Belgium Forever (*LS*).

On the day of her death, Minister Louis Tobback declared that he 'deeply regretted this incident'. Vincent Decroly, Ecolo MP (1995–2003), immediately called for a moratorium on all removals for at least six months. Heard the following day in the Senate Committee on the Interior, under the presidency of Joëlle Milquet[3] (PSC), Minister Louis Tobback said:

> What happened is probably the darkest day of my political career. I didn't sleep well last night. If it appears that the Gendarmerie committed a fault in the attempt to expel fatally, I will resign. I hope that the organisations that encouraged this young girl to resist her deportation violently will also assume their responsibilities.

In the evening, Minister Louis Tobback gave the following overview of the facts during a two-hour press conference:

- On 7 August 1998, her asylum procedure was completed, including her appeal to the Conseil d'Etat. She was not counted as a 'member of a particular social group' based on women's rights since her statements had proven to be false.
- Previous attempts to repatriate her had been made on 21 and 26 April, 28 June, 21 July and 11 August. There was an escort of 11 gendarmes because four failed asylum seekers were involved. She was tied by her hands and feet. She created disorder as soon as the first passengers boarded. A padded cushion was used. There's video footage of the incident. The padded cushion, abolished in 1993, was reintroduced in 1996, after positive advice from a doctor and a psychologist. The staff had requested it because there were several bites and there was fear of AIDS contamination.
- In 1997 there were 6,937 repatriations, 295 of which were escorted, and the cushion was used twice. Until then, there had been more than 5,000 repatriations in 1998, of which 193 were escorted, and the cushion was used twelve times (*DS*, 25 September 1998).

Minister Louis Tobback accused the Collective against removals of having a big responsibility: 'The Collective maintained the illusion that it was enough to shout and struggle to stay in our country'. The Collective, which had already acted on 21 July, was demonstrating with 100 to 150 people in front of the hospital when her death was announced. Among the demonstrators was Arthur Haulot (85). This great resistance fighter, who survived the Nazi concentration camps of Mauthausen and Dachau, started off the singing of the partisans with a squeaky voice. MPs Vincent Decroly and Olivier Deleuze, as well as Me Georges-Henri Beauthier, Chairperson of the (French-speaking) League for Human Rights, were also present. Then they went to the closed Reception Centre 127*bis* at Steenokkerzeel where they drilled two gates. Finally, they went to the Grand-Place in Leuven.

[3] From 2008 to 2014, Joëlle Milquet would be Deputy Prime Minister, combined with Employment until 2011 and then with the Interior.

From there they wanted to go to the private home of Minister Louis Tobback. They were prevented by a platoon of gendarmes who responded with a charge.

A steward, who wanted to remain anonymous, also pointed to the Collective as being co-responsible for Semira's problems:

> The expulsion policy has been a problem for a long time. Some passengers are confronted with members of the Collective at the check-in counter. They encourage them to make trouble. The illegals to be expelled are in a position of weakness. The Collective makes them believe something. It gets them off the plane. The next week we have them back on board.

Under the title 'Not too "Simple"', Yves Desmet wrote:

> In any case, there must be a selection policy. Therefore, there are people who will be refused and sent back. But there is a world of difference between a theoretical political line and the screams of a terrified woman dragged on a plane. We cannot fall into the hypocrisy of many politicians. Publicly they say that we must put an end to the influx of refugees. Then they write letters of support for 'this Nigerian' who is so popular on their local football team (*DM*, 24 September 1998).

18.1.4. Minister Louis Tobback Resigns (26 September 1998)

Prime Minister Jean-Luc Dehaene reported that he had consulted with the Minister of the Interior. He supported him in the correct execution of the government's aliens' policy. The government parties CVP and SP said that the asylum policy should not be changed. On Thursday evening, 24 September, Louis Tobback asked the Prime Minister to offer his resignation as Minister of the Interior to the King. His colleagues insisted that he stay.

It turned out that one of the accompanying gendarmes, a 40-year-old man, had already been disciplined beforehand. A handcuffed man, who was to be expelled, had been beaten in his cell by him. In January 1998, he was suspended for one month on three-quarters of his salary. However, he was left in the Gendarmerie detachment at the airport. Forced deportations were suspended. The drama has been used widely to criticise the Vande Lanotte Law. No one specified which provision of this law had caused the death of Semira Adamu. The Association of francophone magistrates took the opportunity to plead in favour of administrative tribunals of first instance.

On Friday 25 September, early in the evening, the doors of closed Reception Centre 127*bis* at Steenokkerzeel were opened. All 69 asylum seekers were released. A first group of rejected asylum seekers learned that they had five days to leave the territory. A second group, which was still in appeal proceedings, had 30 days to do the same. A third group of 21 who were in 'border procedure' was transferred to the closed reception centre 'De Refuge' in Bruges-Saint-André. There, 30 women were released. The principal would have said that they were all prostitutes: 'So we know where to find them'. Ludwig Verduyn spoke of 'a rare example of football panic. Beyond madness'. In *De Morgen*, 220 academics also expressed their concern and disgust.

The farewell ceremony for Semira Adamu took place in Brussels in the Cathedral of St Michael and Gudule on Saturday 26 September 1998. Thousands of people attended. King Albert II and Queen Paola had a wreath laid on her white coffin. Minister Louis Tobback decided not to follow up on the pressing request of his colleagues. The same day, the King accepted his resignation. Luc Van den Bossche succeeded him as Deputy Prime Minister and Minister of the Interior (until 12 July 1999).

On the same day, Commissioner General Luc De Smet issued a (second) press release. He stressed that

> the rebellion against forced marriage may, in certain circumstances, constitute grounds for recognition of the status of refugee in Belgium. The first decision was in April 1993. However, the fundamental condition is that the applicant spontaneously makes a credible and coherent asylum story. This condition was not met in the case of Semira Adamu.

Moreover, he gave the benefit of the doubt, 'without naively applying it'. He also pointed out that the asylum procedure was often used by prostitution networks to provide temporary residence documents to women, forced or not, to prostitute themselves.

In an interview with the Belga agency after his resignation, Louis Tobback said that he was

> concerned by the growing gap between the overwhelming silent majority (at least in Flanders) and French-speaking opinion leaders. However, the three major French-speaking political parties voted for the Asylum Law. But they have problems with its application. He said he was disgusted by this hypocrisy. They refuse to accept the consequences of the law they have passed (*LS*; *LLB*, 29 September 1998).

In a point of view in *De Morgen* of 28 September 1998, Bart Brinckman wrote:

> Louis Tobback left anyway. Every day, the Minister is forced to turn his heart into stone and break dreams by sending people back to their country of origin. A policy of expulsion remains inevitable for the person concerned, whether he likes it or not. Comparing it with deportation or Nazi terror reveals a terrible lack of historical knowledge and leads to de facto trivialisation of fascism and support for the *Vlaams Blok*.

The VLD declared that it was necessary to put an end to the expulsion of the rejected by airliners. The government had to resort not to C-130 aircraft but to charters, which normally take tourists to sunny places.

18.2. The Sequels to Semira Adamu (1998–2020): More Humane and Efficient

Following the death of Semira Adamu, commissions were set up to ensure a more humane and efficient conduct of removals. On 4 October 1998, Minister Luc Van den Bossche launched the Vermeersch I Commission; on 13 January 2004, Minister Patrick Dewael did the same with the Vermeersch II Commission; and on 7 March 2018, Secretary of State Theo Francken with the Bossuyt Commission.

On 12 December 2003, the Correctional Tribunal of Brussels disciplined four gendarmes who accompanied Semira Adamu in the failed attempt to repatriate her.

18.2.1. The Vermeersch I Commission (21 January 1999): The Inevitable Recourse to Legitimate Violence

After the death of Semira Adamu, the (new) Minister of the Interior, Luc Van den Bossche, set up a Commission responsible for 'the evaluation of instructions on removal'. This Commission, chaired by Professor Emeritus Etienne Vermeersch,[4] presented its final report (31 pp) to the Minister of the Interior on 21 January 1999. The Commission[5] has concluded that it will sometimes be inevitable to resort to coercion against persons who do not leave voluntarily. This 'legitimate violence' must meet the criteria of legality, opportunity and proportionality. In the context of removals, two aspects are decisive: effective compliance with legal requirements, and respect for the human rights of those to be removed. Forced deportation is considered the last link in any immigration policy (the *ultimum remedium*) when all other means have failed.

The Vermeersch I Commission made recommendations for a policy of human removals:

1. Clarify coercion guidelines.
2. Prohibit measures that pose risks to those concerned or express the frustrations of law enforcement.
3. Control and evaluate the use of violence.
4. Curb any infringement of these directives.
5. Use means of transport other than conventional scheduled flights.
6. Develop existing voluntary return arrangements.
7. Drastically reduce the duration of recognition procedures.
8. Improve the conditions for retaining foreigners.
9. Improve staff communication.
10. Organise a structured consultation between departments.

18.2.2. The Correctional Tribunal (12 December 2003): Heavy Penalties

On 12 December 2003, the Correctional Tribunal of Brussels delivered its judgment in the case concerning the death of Semira Adamu. Three marshals from

[4] Etienne Vermeersch, Full Professor at the University of Ghent (since 1967), was Vice-Rector of that university from 1993 to 1997. He died on 18 January 2019.

[5] The Vermeersch I Commission was also composed of Professor Stephan Parmentier (rapporteur) and Professor Léon Cassiers, a lieutenant-colonel, a lieutenant and a marshal of the Gendarmerie and representatives of the Air Inspection, Sabena and the Belgian Pilots Association.

the Gendarmerie who had forcibly detained her, were sentenced to one-year suspended sentences and an effective fine of €500 for assault and battery leading to death. The Gendarmerie captain, who was present on the plane, was sentenced to a 14-month suspended sentence and an effective fine of €500. The Belgian State was held civilly responsible for the fines and responsible *in solidum* for the costs of the gendarmes. The guardian uncle of Semira received €5,000 as moral damage and her five brothers and sisters €2,000 each.

The next day, the newspapers (especially Dutch speaking) were particularly accurate in their accounts of this judgment (in the Dutch language):

1. On the cause of her death:

   The autopsy concluded that the cause of her death was due to an initial cerebral oedema that resulted in transient cardiac arrest and breathing dysfunctions. The development of this oedema was due to a combination of circumstances: her position on the aircraft, pressure on her chest and face, previous chronic stress, and severe stress while she was being restrained. This led to a brain injury, due to a lack of oxygen in the blood.

2. On the person of Semira Adamu:

   The interrogations showed that her family knew nothing about the forced marriage that she said led her to flee her country. Her fake passport and plane ticket had been paid for by her cousin Tina who lived in a prostitution district in Milan [Italy]. She had already been convicted of heroin trafficking. It was only after her death that her family learned that Semira had gone to Europe (*HV*; *HN*).

3. On the context of her deportation:

   Her expulsion had become the issue of the success or failure of the government's expulsion policy [*De Tijd*]. Her expulsion took place in a context of serious tensions around repatriations, which had given rise to a real psychodrama. During 1998, the resistance of failed asylum seekers against their repatriation increased. This resistance was reinforced by the actions of the Collective against removals (*DS*).

4. On the Collective against removals:

   The Collective used illegal means against decisions taken by our democratically elected bodies that had rejected her asylum application. We cannot tolerate that. The Collective gave her the vain hope that she could stay in Belgium without regard to the danger she was in resisting her repatriation. And without warning her that in Belgium she should live illegally [*HN*]. Semira Adamu had become the figurehead of the policy of expulsion of illegals. She was quite excited by the Collective (*GvA*).

5. On the instructions of the Gendarmerie:

   The working group of the Gendarmerie, which had introduced the cushion, showed a reprehensible indifference to the medical literature in which the dangers of these techniques were addressed. It is appalling that the working group has only barely explained the cushion technique in its guidelines. The training of the gendarmes at the airport was insufficient. Due to a chronic lack of personnel, the

> instruction concerning the use of the cushion had been cancelled. The man who was to train his colleagues had never received any instructions himself [*HN*]. The guidelines were deficient and deadly. They ignored the great danger of sudden death during prolonged use of the cushion (*DS*).

6. On the pressure of hierarchical authority:

> The Gendarmerie airport detachment did not have enough men and too few staff in general to implement the repatriations. The Minister nevertheless insisted on the repatriation of many failed asylum seekers. There were political and perhaps also financial reasons for not arranging separate flights for the repatriation of illegals (*HN*).

7. On the responsibility of the Gendarmerie officer:

> The Gendarmerie captain was, on board the plane, the highest-ranking police officer. He could act personally and correct things in situations that could threaten the lives of others. He didn't do it. He was passive and inattentive (*HV*; *HN*).

8. On the responsibility of the accompanying marshals:

> The failures of the others concerned do not excuse the mistakes of the gendarmes. We do not see at any time in the video that they control if Semira has calmed down and if she can still breathe gently. The force used was excessive and held too long [*HV*; *HN*]. When she relieved herself, they thought it was 'a trick', but it was the beginning of her coma [*HLN*]. The Home Office guidelines, though rare and insufficient, say that escorts must constantly assess a returnee's health. Among other things, they must check if the nose is blocked by the cushion. They did not act aggressively or passionately during the repatriation. They gave no sign of contempt for the victim. They had no intention of hurting her. There were no intentional beatings (*DS*).

None of the parties appealed that judgment.

In general, the newspapers considered the sentences to be heavy, especially since they were 'involuntary' injuries that resulted in death: 'the sentence seems heavy' (*LS*) 'quite severe', 'more severe than it appears' (*LLB*) and 'relatively heavy sentences' (*DS*). According to Louis Tobback, the judgment showed that he had made the correct decision by resigning. According to Professor Emeritus Etienne Vermeersch, the cushion should be definitely banned: 'The Solution: "Put these People on a Plane without Passengers". They will Cause less Trouble' (*HLN*). All the newspapers reported that the 65 federal police officers at the airport had indicated that they would no longer ensure, until 1 January 2004, the escorted removal of foreigners.

18.2.3. The Vermeersch II Commission (31 January 2005): Ethical Justification for Coercive Measures

Following the judgment of 12 December 2003, the Minister of the Interior, Patrick Dewael, again (on 13 January 2004) appointed a Commission, chaired by Professor

Emeritus Etienne Vermeersch,[6] to evaluate the instructions on expulsion (II). The final report (104 pp) of this Commission,[7] under the title 'Fundamentals of a humane and effective policy of removal', was submitted to the Minister of the Interior on 31 January 2005. The Commission rejects a policy of 'open borders' since 'social security, which is already struggling, could collapse in the short term'. The Commission hopes that the public and its representatives will understand that for the staff members of institutions that carry out aliens' policy, 'this can sometimes be a heavy and harsh mission for them as human beings'. The Commission is of the opinion that the use of coercive measures stemming from a logic of refusal of an 'open borders' policy is 'fully justified from an ethical point of view' and stresses that this does not imply any 'negative judgment' on the people to be removed. The report contains 34 recommendations for a humane and effective deportation policy.

In addition, the Commission defends several points of view:

1. Address the backlog of first-in refugee applicants.
2. Granting humanitarian residence permits to families whose children are well integrated and to people who have made themselves useful to society.
3. To establish assessments concerning the number of people who have left the territory after the refusal of their asylum application.
4. Provide special protection to individuals who can prove they are at individual risk.
5. Accelerate the processing of appeals pending before the Conseil d'Etat.
6. Make the aliens' policy and the policy of removals a coherent whole.
7. Extend the retention of persons who cannot be removed because they object, until the time of their removal.
8. Prohibit the administration of medicines to facilitate removals.
9. Prohibit all acts of violence against immobilised persons.
10. Provide protection to police officers who are victims of violence.

18.2.4. 'Sudanese Transmigrants Badly Treated' (8 February 2018): 'Not Truthful'

A few years later a new phenomenon occurred with 'transmigrants'. These are foreigners who are illegally staying in the country but have the objective of

[6] Professor Emeritus Etienne Vermeersch would become a particularly active member of the Commission 'Norms and Values', constituted by the Flemish Minister of the Interior Marino Keulen (2004–09), and chaired by me. The Commission was also composed of Ludo Abicht, Abied Alsulaiman, Naima Charkaoui, Marie-Claire Foblets and Rik Torfs. On 4 May 2006, the Commission presented its report on the content of social orientation courses to the Flemish Parliament (*Doc parl, Parl fl*, 2005–06, No 860-1).

[7] The Vermeersch II Commission was also composed of Professor Stephan Parmentier (rapporteur) and Professor Léon Cassiers, as well as representatives of the Minister of the Interior, the SPF Interior, the OE, the Federal Police, the AIG (the General Inspectorate of the Federal and Local Police), the Directorate-General for Aviation, the Belgian Pilots Association and SN Brussels Airlines.

travelling to the United Kingdom. In addition to the English language, an important factor attracting them is the absence on the island of the obligation to carry identity documents. These transmigrants frequently refuse to apply for asylum. They fear being sent back, based on the Dublin Regulation, to the country through which they entered the Schengen Area. In 2017, a hundred transmigrants made Maximilien Park in Brussels their place to stay. The impotence towards this phenomenon, causing a lot of trouble, was the despair of political leaders. The transmigrants did not hesitate to attack truck drivers on the motorway parking lots.

Secretary of State, Theo Francken, decided to call for a Sudanese identification mission. After identification by an official Sudanese delegation in September 2017, nine Sudanese who did not want to apply for asylum, were removed to their country in October 2017. On 20 December 2017, Koert Debeuf[8] said that they had been treated badly when they returned to Khartoum.[9] On 22 December, the government asked Commissioner General Dirk Van den Bulck to investigate. In his report of 8 February 2018,[10] the Commissioner General reported on contacts with the International Organization for Migration (IOM) in Khartoum. One of the persons, who – according to his statements – was ill-treated, had showed up that day at the IOM office in Khartoum to collect his return bonus. His testimony regarding abuse was therefore not truthful. It planted a shadow of incredibility on these allegations. However, the Commissioner General believed that the risk of violation of Article 3 ECHR should have been examined before identification by the authorities of their country of origin.

In its judgment *MA v Belgium* of 27 October 2020, the Strasbourg Court held that Belgium had violated Article 3 ECHR (the prohibition of torture) because of the treatment of a Sudanese national in Belgium.[11] The Court found that there had been procedural shortcomings in the way the Sudanese identification mission had been organised in September 2017. Pending a judicial decision on its retention, the President of the Tribunal of first instance had prohibited the applicant's removal to Sudan. Because this ban had been ignored, the Court also found that Article 13 ECHR (effective remedy) had been violated. The Court admitted that an 'implicit demand for international protection' might a priori satisfy. This (new) practice would consist of an examination by the Commissioner General, at the request of the Aliens Office, of the situation of persons who have not applied for asylum (§112).

[8] Koert Debeuf, a former cabinet staffer (2003–08) of Prime Minister Guy Verhofstadt, is director of the Tahrir Institute for Middle East Policy and editor of EU-Observers. From 2011 to 2014, he lived in Cairo.

[9] *HLN* (20 December 2017).

[10] See: www.cgvs.be/nl/actueel/soedan-report.

[11] Bart Brinckman, *DS* (28 October 2020); Koert Debeuf, *DS* (2 November).

18.2.5. The Bossuyt Commission (2018–20): Promoting Transparency and Dialogue

For a long time, the idea was to set up another commission to evaluate the policy of expulsion. The release of the report on alleged inhumane treatment in Sudan on 8 February 2018 accelerated the creation of a new commission. On 7 March 2018, Theo Francken, Secretary of State for Asylum and Migration, constituted a Temporary Commission on 'the evaluation of the policy of voluntary return and forced removal of foreigners'. This Commission, which I chaired, was asked to evaluate the practical implementation of the legal and regulatory provisions in the context of the policy of return and cooperation between the various actors. The Commission was composed of the heads of the departments concerned (AIG, CGRA, OE, Fedasil and the Federal Police),[12] as well as a representative of the Belgian Pilots Association and a representative of the air carriers.

18.2.5.1. The Interim Report (22 February 2019): Grey Areas Cleared

The interim report[13] (107 pp) of the Bossuyt Commission was presented to Maggie De Block, Minister of Asylum and Migration, on 22 February 2019. On 9 December 2018, Theo Francken and the other N-VA members of the government resigned from the Michel I Government (MR/Open VLD, N-VA, CD&V) because of a disagreement on the adoption of the Marrakech Compact.[14] Maggie De Block, Minister of Social Affairs and Public Health, then again became also responsible for Asylum and Migration (until 30 September 2020). In the introduction to this interim report, I paid tribute to Professor Emeritus Etienne Vermeersch, who had died on 18 January 2019, the month before the interim report was presented:

> As President of the two commissions that preceded the present commission, Professor Emeritus Etienne Vermeersch did a tremendous job. He considered it himself his most thankless task. His merit is only greater. His reports were innovative with respect to the use of force, in case of physical resistance to forced return, the conditions of that recourse and the means to be used and not to be used.

[12] They are Inspector-General Thierry Gillis (AIG), Commissioner-General Dirk Van den Bulck (CGRA), Director-General Freddy Roosemont (OE), Director of Strategic Support Fanny François (Fedasil) and Director-General André Desenfants (Federal Police).

[13] See: dofi.ibz.be/sites/dvzoe/FR/Documents/Def-Rapportinterimaire_Fr.pdf.

[14] The Compact was adopted without a vote in Marrakech on 13 December 2018. The resolution approving the Compact was adopted on 19 December 2018 by the UN General Assembly by 152 votes to 5 (USA, Hungary, Israel, Poland and the Czech Republic) and 12 abstentions (Algeria, Australia, Austria, Bulgaria, Chile, Italy, Latvia, Libya, Liechtenstein, Romania, Singapore and Switzerland). Slovakia and 23 other countries did not vote.

> He was a philosopher who had his feet on the ground, even though he was sometimes on slippery ground. He was not a man to jump to conclusions without considering the needs and realities of the world in which he lived. He believed that the convictions he defended should be the same even if he himself should assume political responsibility for them. He was aware that his positions could have consequences for society, which was a major concern for him. That's what made him so special.

The main objective of the interim report was to promote transparency and dialogue on the policy of removals. Regarding transparency, the interim report responds to the criticism – expressed at its constitution – that the policy of removals is 'surrounded by many persistent grey areas'.[15] As far as dialogue is concerned, the interim report was largely built around multiple contributions from all kinds of bodies and NGOs. They had raised their concerns and grievances with the Commission.

18.2.5.2. The Final Report (15 September 2020): Efficiency is Lacking

The final report[16] (155 pp) of the Bossuyt Commission was presented on 15 September 2020 to Maggie De Block, Minister of Asylum and Migration. The Commission considered that, thanks to the implementation of most of the recommendations of the two Vermeersch Commissions, the humane way of removals was guaranteed. Efficiency, on the other hand, left much to be desired. The social and budgetary costs of a hesitant approach or the absence of a harmonised approach can hardly be overestimated. Migration, one of the major challenges of our time, requires a coherent and rational approach. A migration policy without a return policy is failing.

In the final report, the different components of the removal process are analysed in detail. The obstacles to overcome are identified. To improve the process, 62 recommendations of a varied nature were formulated. A balance sheet is drawn up of the cost of the return and removal policy. The lack of cooperation, not to mention the resistance to which the various services are too often confronted, increases costs. It is a luxury that our society can hardly afford.

The irregular stay in the territory is harmful for both society and the people concerned. Social assistance for persons residing irregularly in the territory is limited to urgent medical assistance. It is difficult for those persons to meet their basic needs in a legal way. They are exposed to many forms of exploitation.[17] Tolerating irregular residence, as well as misperceptions in countries of origin, lead foreigners to take deadly risks for themselves and their children in trying to reach our countries. It is a mistake to believe that such a tolerance is humane.

[15] Stephan Parmentier, *DS* (21 January 2017 and 12 March 2018).

[16] See: dofi.ibz.be/sites/dvzoe/FR/Documents/CommissionBossuyt_Rapport-Final_FR.pdf.

[17] J Knockaert 'Undocumented people in Belgium have only five options to survive: begging, charity of friends, sex work, criminal acts, and undeclared work' *DS Weekblad* (14 December 2019) 14.

An attitude that allows abuses to persist and encourages them to multiply is anything but humane.

18.3. Regularisation Commissions: Multiple Pitfalls

Regularisations are often presented as an alternative to removals. The Regularization Law of 22 December 1999 launched a large-scale campaign to regularise illegal aliens. Almost 36,000 files were submitted concerning about 55,000 people. Three years later, this whole process, which lasted much longer than expected, was still ongoing. The percentage of applications approved was more than 81 per cent. From 15 September to 15 December 2009, a new regularisation campaign was conducted. About 50,000 people have been regularised. In addition, a few thousand people were regularised each year, without specific campaigns, based on Articles 9*bis* (for humanitarian reasons)[18] and 9*ter* (for medical reasons)[19] of the Aliens Law.

It is appropriate to indicate the many pitfalls which accompany regularisations entrusted to independent commissions. A regularisation is always the recognition of a failure. It may be the result of an asylum procedure which has lasted too long, neglect in carrying out orders to leave the territory or a lack of vigilance in the detection of persons staying in the territory without being authorised. Derogation from the legal procedures for granting residence permits undermines the credibility of these procedures. Persons who have not followed legal procedures or have not followed orders to leave the territory are privileged to the detriment of those who have. The latter can therefore rightly feel discriminated against.

Large-scale regularisation procedures are an attraction factor that encourage people to try their luck outside the existing residence procedures. Even if not accepted for regularisation, they think they know what they need to do to have a chance at the next opportunity. A simple announcement of the possibility that there may be a regularisation procedure may be enough to induce people to come irregularly. Regularisation procedures do not encourage people residing irregularly in the territory to leave it spontaneously. At the very least, they create the illusion that those who do not follow through on an order to leave the territory will after a certain time still have the chance to obtain a residence permit. There are no reasons to assume that a negative decision on a regularisation application will be followed by a voluntary return.

[18] Art 9*bis*: 'In exceptional circumstances and on the condition that the foreigner has an identity document, the residence permit may be requested from the mayor of the locality in which he is staying'.

[19] Art *9ter*: 'A foreigner who suffers from an illness that poses a real risk to his life or physical integrity or a real risk of inhuman or degrading treatment when there is no adequate treatment in his country of origin or in the country in which he is staying'.

18.3.1. Regularisation as a Favour

It is better to entrust cases for which individual regularisation may be justified to the competent administration under the political responsibility of the Minister or Secretary of State concerned. Thus, several disadvantages in a formal regularisation procedure may be avoided, thanks to the discretion with which these administrative regularisations take place. Exercising discretionary jurisdiction is less transparent, but it avoids a lot of pitfalls. Some feel that regularisations are too strict, while others consider them to be too flexible. It is up to the competent member of the government to strike the right balance. It is a political responsibility to which that member must be held accountable to the nation in elections. By entrusting the procedure for the recognition of refugees to independent bodies (the Commissioner General and the Aliens Litigation Council) the government has abandoned all control over these recognitions. By establishing regularisation commissions, this abandonment extends to the granting of residence permits to categories of foreigners who have not followed the legally prescribed procedures.

18.3.2. Regularisation as a Right

Once the legal criteria and the independent commissions are established, a favour is transformed into a right with all the legal consequences that this entails. In the case of a right, the applicant may claim regularisation by law. This requires a procedure in which the person concerned must have the opportunity to present his arguments. He is entitled to be assisted by a legal counsel of his choice (paid for by the State). He has the right to be heard assisted by an interpreter (paid for by the State). He is entitled to a reasoned decision. He can challenge this decision before the Aliens Litigation Council and then in cassation before the Conseil d'Etat. He also has the right to be heard before these appeal bodies, again assisted by a lawyer and an interpreter (paid for by the State).

Once the law has transformed regularisation into a right, a series of side effects must be considered. First, the question arises whether the application for regularisation is sufficient to suspend the deportation procedure, including the order to leave the territory. If this is the case, it can be expected that many foreigners, who do not meet the criteria to be regularised, will apply for it anyway. This goes hand in hand with the question whether, by this application, their stay becomes temporarily regular. Crucial then is the question of whether this mere application creates a right to social assistance for those who otherwise would not (or no more) be entitled to it. The chance is great that as soon as someone is dealt with in an organised regularisation procedure, labour courts will grant social assistance. Many will then apply to get social assistance for as long the regularisation procedure, including the appeal, is open.

18.3.3. Status of a Candidate Regularised

By transforming regularisation into a right, a status of candidate-regularised, analogous to that of candidate-refugee, is established, despite the differences between both statuses. Indeed, unlike the candidate-regularised, the candidate-refugee claims to fear for his life, his physical integrity, or his freedom. Refugee status is a right guaranteed by an international convention. However, when regularisation also is recognised by law as a right, there is a risk that the differences between the two statuses will be deemed discriminatory.

The disadvantages of establishing a candidate-regularised status can be avoided by providing for an admissibility phase during which the applicant would not benefit from any of these advantages. It would then be a purely administrative procedure in which the competent administration (the Aliens Office) could check in a non-contradictory manner whether the conditions are satisfied prima facie. Only if so satisfied, the file would then be forwarded to the regularisation commission. The question remains whether the Conseil d'Etat will consider that decisions in this phase should also be reasoned and would require a possibility of appeal with suspensive effect. The impossibility for the applicant to refer directly to the regularisation commission could be considered discriminatory. Supporters of regularisation do not wish such a phase of admissibility, which would be less transparent since they usually do not trust the Aliens Office.

18.3.4. A Good Idea Only in Appearance

Regularisation commissions are not characterised by a balanced composition. Lawyers and representatives of NGOs who apply for the position generally believe that they have a vocation to take care of the interests of foreigners. Thus, there is at least a majority (if not a consensus) in the commission to take favourable decisions. Inevitably, the burden of the Aliens Office and the Aliens Litigation Council would become heavier, thereby jeopardising the asylum procedure and other residence procedures. This would entail a slowdown in these procedures, while it is precisely their acceleration that is desired.

The establishment of independent regularisation commissions would undermine the credibility of existing procedures. It would not encourage voluntary return, on which we should focus. Social assistance costs would increase. The country becomes a more attractive country of destination. An important aspect of aliens' policy would be removed from the political responsibility of the government.

Independent regularisation commissions would take positive decisions. The Aliens Litigation Council would finally take the negative decisions. Labour courts would judge entitlements to social assistance. The Conseil d'Etat would judge the possibilities and methods of appeal. Attempts to legally restrict these disadvantages, as well as the classes of beneficiaries, would likely not withstand review by the courts. It would be up to the Constitutional Court to judge whether these restrictions pass the test of non-discrimination.

The government would be held accountable for the operation of the regularisation process without being able to determine the results of it. Many of those who were associated with the ordeal of the 1999–2002 regularisation commissions believed that we would not quickly embark on such an adventure again. More than 20 years later, there is a risk that this memory has faded.

19

Some Reflections

Before concluding with a supplement consisting of two chapters on the jurisprudence of the Strasbourg Court on matters of asylum, I would like to offer some reflections concerning the 'famous asylum seekers'. These reflections will be followed by a few anecdotes relating to Nigerian asylum applications which were met with particularly little success, contrary to Rwandan applications which were often successful. Finally, I will review the push and pull factors that explain why asylum seekers leave their country to go to a specific country.

19.1. The Cases of Famous Asylum Seekers

Much of what we now know, was not known at the time when difficult decisions had to be made about some cases of famous asylum seekers. Years later, we know how it all ended. The passage of time makes it possible to evaluate with more serenity the decisions taken at the time. These cases concern an Irishman, four Spanish Basques, two Islamists (one Tunisian and one Algerian) and two Rwandans. I recognised only one of them as a refugee (Walid Bennani); another (Augustin Ndindiliyimana) was recognised by the Permanent Board.

19.1.1. The IRA Terrorist: Father Ryan

Patrick Ryan's recent confession (24 September 2019), more than 30 years after his asylum application in Belgium, was staggering. There is nothing to prevent calling him a terrorist. It was shocking to hear that he has dozens of lives on his conscience. That his only regret is that there have not been more attacks is even more so. Coming from a Catholic priest, his confession is beyond belief. Was Belgium naive and irresponsible in this affair? This still remains questionable.

From the very beginning, there were serious doubts about Ryan's innocence. The fact that he had timers in his possession was intriguing. This made us think of time bombs, one of the IRA's favourite modus operandi for carrying out its attacks. And – hoping the Bar wouldn't mind – he had seven lawyers from four different countries, a bit much for an innocent asylum seeker. By arresting him, Belgium has assumed its share of responsibility in the fight against terrorism.

As the extradition request revealed, the United Kingdom had been watching him for a long time. For years he travelled through many European countries. He was rarely arrested and never extradited. Belgium, at least, arrested him. Belgium even passed him on to his government.

Ireland was in a better position than Belgium to assess whether an Irish citizen could be extradited to the United Kingdom. His Irish lawyer had also explicitly warned that, if the United Kingdom so requested, the Republic of Ireland could not refuse this request. In addition, Ryan, who was on a hunger strike, made it clear that he preferred death to extradition to the United Kingdom. Seven years earlier (in 1981), Margaret Thatcher (British Prime Minister since 1979) had left 10 young hunger strikers to die in the Maze prison. Belgium had not to interfere in the conflict between Ireland and the United Kingdom.

That Margaret Thatcher was furious was easy to understand. At the time of the bombing in Brighton in 1984, she barely escaped death. Five of her companions had lost their lives there. She suspected that Ryan was associated with the bombing. In 2019, he admitted that he was. Margaret Thatcher's anger in Parliament, in the media and with the Belgian and Irish Prime Ministers had the effect of jeopardising Ryan's chances of a fair trial in the United Kingdom. Whether her outbursts of rage were caused by the search for political gains or by a lack of self-control, has little importance. They prevented the Irish government from acceding to the British extradition request. It had not only become politically impossible; her attitude provided a legal justification for this impossibility to extradite. The vagueness of the extradition request did not help either.

And there was yet another reading: Jean-Claude Matgen wrote in *La Libre Belgique* on 1 December 1988 that the British had only asked the Belgian police to keep an eye on him pending a possible meeting of IRA activists. If this is true, over-zealous police action is at the root of a big quarrel between the United Kingdom, on the one hand, and Belgium and Ireland, on the other. All this could have been avoided. It has not served the fight against terrorism.

19.1.2. The Four Basques: Moreno–Garcia, Peixotin and Maiztegui

The Spanish request for extradition of Moreno and Garcia mentioned 800 people who died in ETA attacks. Just to be clear, Moreno and Garcia did not murder 800 people. They were accused of providing accommodation and transportation to Juan Ramón Rojo, who committed an attack that claimed the life of a Guardia civil officer. For that, Juan Ramón Rojo has been held for 21 years in a Spanish prison. On the correct criminal classification of the acts of Moreno and Garcia (concealment or participation), there is a legal dispute. There is also a legal dispute as to whether these acts fall within the scope of an applicable provision of an extradition treaty. There is even a dispute over whether that would be the 1977 European

Convention or the 1870 bilateral treaty. In any case, the Chamber of Indictment of the Brussels Court of Appeal ruled that 'it was politically motivated'. This is hardly debatable. Until that time, there was a consistent practice in Belgium of not going against a negative opinion of the Court of Appeal. By referring to that practice, the case could have been completed resolutely and quickly. Spain would not have been happy, but a succession of political discussions and diplomatic incidents for years could have been avoided.

The charges against Moreno and Garcia were based on the statements of Juan Ramón Rojo. They were obtained under pressure of serious ill-treatment. This was immediately apparent from a written statement from a Spanish medical doctor. This has been confirmed by the *Audiencia Nacional*. All of this compromised the charges against Moreno and Garcia. It was an important part of my admissibility decision. It permanently weakened the Spanish demands.

In this case, Spain has taken many blows: the negative opinion of the Court of Appeal, my declaration of admissibility, the release by the President of the Tribunal of first instance, the suspension judgments of the Conseil d'Etat, and finally the decision of non-extradition of the investigating judge and its confirmation by four Chambers of the Court of Appeal. There was only my refusal of recognition, the confirmation of this refusal by the Permanent Board and the extradition decision of the Minister of Justice to put a little comfort in the heart of the Spaniards. The ministerial decision could not be implemented. The Conseil d'Etat blocked it. The Minister withdrew his decision.

Frankly, I have never seriously considered granting refugee status to nationals of a Member State of the European Union. However, I did not want my refusal decision to be used as an argument in favour of extradition. The Spanish reactions were not likely to facilitate a refusal decision. These reactions, especially after my declaration of admissibility and after the release by the President of the Tribunal of first instance, were excessive. Spain continually demanded respect for the Spanish rule of law. But Spain had the greatest difficulties in respecting Belgian rule of law. No decision of a Belgian authority expressed a lack of confidence in Spanish justice. All decisions taken by independent Belgian bodies were based on the applicable legal rules. The outrageous nature of Spanish criticism did not strengthen that confidence.

In the *Peixotin* case, Spain was trapped by its past. Peixotin's asylum application revealed that Spain had sent 50 Basques into exile in various countries outside any legal proceedings and without legal grounds. The pressure exerted on the Belgian government by the Spanish Secretary of State for Security and by the Spanish Ambassador in Brussels was shocking. A Spanish national, who was not prosecuted, nevertheless had to be kept outside the European Union. Belgium had to send him back to Venezuela. I was not prepared to do that. Thanks to good communication with the Minister of the Interior, this case was cleared. Based on his European citizenship, Peixotin was granted access to the European Union.

Two years later, another Basque (Maiztegui) arrived in Belgium. He came from Mexico. It was claimed that there would be a Basque route that – based on my previous decisions – led to Belgium. This was contradicted by the facts. Neither had left Latin America with the intention of seeking asylum in Belgium. The one from Venezuela was on his way to France. The other, from Mexico, was en route to Amsterdam. Excellent police checks at the airport had found that they did not have valid identity documents. Although they were citizens of the European Union, the Aliens Office refused them access to the territory. This forced them to seek asylum in Belgium. When Maiztegui applied for asylum, the Commissioner General was no longer the same, but the policy of that Office was unchanged. Again, the Commissioner General decided that the asylum application was moot. The understanding with the Minister of the Interior was apparently not optimal. The Minister was no longer the same. The Aliens Office decided three times to send him back to Mexico. The Conseil d'Etat and the Commissioner General joined forces to prevent it. To achieve this, the Commissioner General decided that further examination was necessary. No one in Belgium ever heard any more about Maiztegui.

19.1.3. The Two Islamist Fundamentalists: Bennani and Zaoui

A year and a half apart, two Islamist fundamentalists applied for asylum in Belgium. One (Bennani) belonged to Ennahdha and came from Tunisia; the other (Zaoui) belonged to the Islamic Salvation Front (FIS) and came from Algeria. One was recognised, not without much difficulty and patience; the other was refused, pursuant to the exclusion clause.

Bennani's recognition process took five years and eight months. The Aliens Office refused him access to the territory as well as – three months later – the stay in Belgium. Each time, I went against these decisions by giving a favourable opinion. Each time, the Minister of Justice persisted, confirming the refusal. Each time, the Conseil d'Etat suspended this ministerial decision. The Conseil d'Etat needed three weeks to suspend the refusal of access to the territory, 13 months to suspend the refusal to stay, and four years and three months more to annul the refusal to stay. Less than two months later he was recognised as a refugee. His wife and children had already been recognised three years earlier.

After President Ben Ali was ousted from power in 2011, Bennani returned to Tunisia. That same year he became a parliamentarian for Ennahdha. He remained so until 2019. I have no doubt about my decisions at the time regarding Bennani. For those who do, I would like to point out that to be recognised as a refugee, the person must have a well-founded fear of persecution based on his conviction. This conviction must not necessarily benefit from the sympathy of the Belgian population.

The flight of Zaoui to Belgium was even more difficult. Under the exclusion clause, he was denied refugee status (first by the Deputy Commissioner, secondly by me). The Permanent Board confirmed this refusal. In Belgium, he was deprived of his liberty for a long time: first, in pre-trial detention and then, in administrative retention. He was sentenced several times: in Algeria to death (in July 1993); in Belgium on appeal (after having been acquitted at first instance) to a suspended sentence of four years (in November 1995); and in France to a sentence (also suspended) of three years (in November 2001). It must be recognised that this is not very convincing. By way of comparison: Bennani was sentenced, in Tunisia only, to 20 years (in 1987) and to five years for passive complicity (in February 1992). He would not have informed the authorities of a project of which he had knowledge. A strange charge. Ennahdha was also known to be less violent than the GIA, with which Zaoui was – rightly or wrongly – associated.

After four years in Belgium, Zaoui went illegally to Switzerland (in November 1997). A year later, Switzerland sent him to Burkina Faso. Two years later, he went to Malaysia. After almost three years (in December 2002), he arrived in New Zealand. Here again, he was initially not welcome. The exclusion clause was applied to him. In August 2003, the New Zealand appeal body granted him refugee status. It apparently felt that his suspended sentences in Belgium and France, and his death sentence in Algeria, were not sufficiently convincing to apply the exclusion clause. In 2014, he became a New Zealand citizen. The fact that Auckland is 17,700 km further away from Algiers than Brussels may have contributed to this difference in treatment.

19.1.4. The Two Rwandans: Rwabukumba and Ndindiliyimana

All sources and Rwanda experts agree that *Akazu* was the core of evil in Rwanda. President Juvénal Habyarimana's in-laws occupied a central place there. Séraphin Rwabukumba was frequently mentioned by name as the financier. Neither Belgian justice nor international justice succeeded in assembling enough evidence to bring him to justice. This did not remove the suspicions that weighed on him. To apply the exclusion clause, you need 'serious reasons', not evidence. It is difficult to admit that all the Rwandan experts were grossly mistaken. Although he was refused refugee status, he managed with many of his dependent family members to obtain a residence permit in Belgium. Refugee status would have been too honourable for someone who had been so close to one of the most horrific genocides in history.

I had a similar opinion about Major General Augustin Ndindiliyimana. As Chief of Staff of the Rwandan Gendarmerie, he held an exceptional strategic position at the time of the genocide. He made no attempt to thwart the genocide. In my view, such an omission was incompatible with refugee status. The Permanent

Board ruled otherwise. After many developments, the International Criminal Tribunal for Rwanda acquitted him on appeal. At the request of that Tribunal, he was arrested in Belgium. The Prosecutor of this Tribunal had accused him of the worst crimes. I could not be accused of having granted refugee status to a person who, at the request of the International Criminal Tribunal, was arrested in Belgium on serious charges.

19.2. Some Anecdotes

These anecdotes concern Nigerian asylum applicants, as well as Rwanda, a country that is particularly dear to me.

19.2.1. Fraud of Nigerian Asylum Seekers

Nigerian asylum applications were not successful. This has nothing to do with the assessment of the human rights situation in that country. This only shows that Nigerians who applied for asylum in Belgium had left their country for reasons other than persecution based on one of the grounds of the Geneva Convention. In nine years, out of 3,900 Nigerian asylum applications, there were only four recognitions, three of them by the Permanent Board (thus only one by me). The overall recognition rate for Nigerians was 0.1 per cent.

I regularly reviewed the statistics of my Office, most often in the evening or at the weekend to find out the status of individual asylum applications.[1] I checked, nationality by nationality, what was the percentage of positive decisions in admissibility of the Aliens Office; what were the percentages of admissibility and recognition of my Office; and the number of applications without a decision at each stage of the procedure. And what was the evolution of those percentages over time. It helped me answer critical questions, wherever they came from. It helped me to ask critical questions of my own staff.

I was struck by the fact that out of thousands of Nigerian applications there was for years only one recognition. I was intrigued when I noticed one day that the number of Nigerian recognitions had increased by 100 per cent (from 1 to 2). When Luc De Smet was finally appointed Dutch-speaking Deputy Commissioner on 1 September 1994, I asked him to take a final look at the proposals for recognition. He signed them too. At the UNHCR Representation, he had long

[1] In an RTBF broadcast of 13 March 1996, under the title 'Un si beau pays', I was criticised for spending my time on statistics. I told Marianne Klaric, a RTBF journalist, that 'I thought it necessary to provide figures to demonstrate the inaccuracy, the fanciful and even often false nature of statements made about the Belgian asylum procedure, sometimes even by people who know better. These figures are disturbing, especially because they prove irrefutably that too often realities do not correspond to the prevailing preconceptions in the field'.

experience in handling individual cases. He liked to delve into them. He often returned home to Louise-Marie (Maarkedal) with several crates of files. Until late at night, he scribbled his observations, in his characteristic handwriting.

After seeing that the number of Nigerian recognitions had doubled, I went to see Luc one evening in his office:

> I saw that you recognised a Nigerian.
>
> *Yes, but it is a strong case.*
>
> Ah, yes.
>
> *Yes, it's not like the other Nigerian cases. He is the editor of an opposition newspaper.*
>
> Ah, well. Did you check everything? Have you contacted our embassy in Lagos.
>
> *No, we can't do that for every application.*
>
> Of course not, but perhaps for the recognition of a Nigerian. It is exceptional.
>
> *No problem at all. It's still possible.*
>
> Do it.

Three weeks later, Luc came to my office with a smile:

> *I got a phone call.*
>
> Oh, yes? And from whom?
>
> *From someone at the Belgian Embassy in Lagos.*
>
> And?
>
> *The editor of that newspaper was in his office. And he's not our refugee.*
>
> Okay, so we're going to have to take away his refugee status.
>
> *It will be done.*

In the first weeks of the introduction of Printrak for the verification of fingerprints of asylum seekers (end 1993), there were 11 per cent of applications by a same person under different identities. This was also the percentage for Nigerian applications (for Indians it was almost 25 per cent). I remember one of them doing it under four different identities. Fortunately, he was refused four times. Twice his application was declared inadmissible by the Aliens Office, followed by a confirmatory decision of refusal on urgent appeal. Twice his application was declared admissible by the Aliens Office, but I then refused to accept it on the merits. All this time he could stay in Belgium. He was interrogated eight times. Eight decisions had been taken. Six motivations had to be written. Thanks to Printrak, we would no longer waste that much time.

The protection officer dealing with Nigerian applications once told me a famous story. A well-documented Nigerian asylum seeker appeared before him for a hearing. In support of his request, he presented an extract from a Nigerian newspaper. His photo was there with the mention that he was wanted for his political activities. The protection officer, apparently suspicious, had taken the trouble to go to the Nigerian Embassy. He found the right page of the newspaper on the day in question. Everything matched, except for the picture of the applicant and the accompanying text that was not there. His application was rejected.

At one point, I learned that there were experts in African languages at the Royal Museum of Central Africa in Tervuren. It was possible to consult them. A few Liberians, not many, were recognised as refugees, but we weren't really convinced. It was possible to give them a language test and have them checked in Tervuren. Liberian refugees have been summoned. We asked them to translate a few English words into their mother tongue. This was recorded on tape and sent to Tervuren. More than half of them spoke – not a Liberian – but a Nigerian language. Two months later, statistics showed a lower number of Liberian recognitions than before. Finally, out of 1,870 Liberian applications, 31 refugees were recognised, including seven by the Permanent Board.

19.2.2. Rwanda, the 'Land of a Thousand Hills'

Rwanda is known as the 'Land of a Thousand Hills'. According to Rwandan legend, it is in this country that *Imana* (God) who travels the world by day, comes to rest at night. Rwandans (and Burundians) are very homely. After the genocide of the Tutsi in 1994, hundreds of thousands of Tutsi refugees left the diaspora as soon as possible to return to their country. 'Ruanda-Urundi'[2] being particularly dear to me, the genocide touched me greatly.

Rwandan asylum applications were very successful for obvious reasons. It is not surprising, first, that people from our former overseas territories apply for asylum in Belgium. Second, the stories they told were by no means imaginary. Their fear of persecution was real and based on ethnic grounds. At the beginning of the Commission General, there were only a few Rwandan asylum applications (4 in 1988; 7 in 1989). The year of the genocide (1994) there were 659. When I left the Commission General, there had been – out of a total of 1,067 final decisions concerning Rwandans – 899 recognitions (84 per cent).

One of the first elements to be checked for each asylum application is the nationality of the applicant. Fraud is common. Albanians pretended to be Kosovars, Ghanaians to be Sudanese, Guineans to be Sierra Leoneans, Lebanese to be Armenians, Nigerians to be Liberians, Pakistanis to be Afghans and Zairians to be Rwandans. We were sometimes contacted by foreign embassies to assist their country's refugee services in identifying Burundians or Rwandans.

In Belgium, Rwandan nationality fraud was rare. They were at the wrong address. Sometimes, however, it happened that so-called Rwandans showed up, not even knowing the name of their President. Some will reply that there are also

[2] Under the League of Nations, the territory under mandate, which was to become a trusteeship territory under the United Nations, was called Ruanda-Urundi (in Swahili). Since their independence, these countries have been called Rwanda (in Kinyarwanda) and Burundi (in Kirundi).

Belgians who do not know the name of our Prime Minister. In Belgium, it is possible, but not in Rwanda. There was no one in Rwanda who did not know who the President was. His photo hung on the walls of all official buildings and many unofficial buildings. His image was on the banknotes. Every day, he could be heard on the radio. Poor or not, every family in Rwanda had a portable battery radio.

In 1981 and 1984, I went to Rwanda for a few months to teach international law at the National University of Rwanda in Butare. In this city, which was called Astrida at the time of the Belgian tutelage (until mid-1962), there was the '*Groupe scolaire*' of which the Brothers of Charity of my primary school in Ghent had told me so much. In Butare, we were awakened every morning by the weather report of the Flemish shortwave radio. Rwandans were awakened by Rwandan Radio. It often began with a message to the '*Militants et militantes*' (in Zaire, they were '*Citoyens et citoyennes*'; in Burundi, simply '*Mesdames et Messieurs*'). From the time of their birth, all Rwandans were by right members of the single party. The message went as follows:

> This morning, His Excellency Major General Habyarimana Juvénal, President of the Republic of Rwanda and President of the National Revolutionary Movement for Development, sent a telegram to his counterpart, His Excellency Mr X, the President of the Republic of a country – often African or Latin American – and the people of that country with his best wishes on the National Day of that Republic. He assured him of the unwavering friendship and sentiments of sincere brotherhood that exist between the people of this country and the people of Rwanda. He is confident that cooperation between our countries and our peoples will be deepened with a view to lasting peaceful coexistence between our two nations.

Twice I had the opportunity to greet President Juvénal Habyarimana. The first time, in the second quarter of 1981, when early in the morning I was waiting with two colleagues from the University of Antwerp (Filip Reyntjens and his future brother-in-law Jean-François Beyer) for the arrival of a Belgian professor at the (modest) Butare airport. The main road from Kigali to Butare was not yet asphalted. Neither was the landing site at the airport. Suddenly, two limousines arrived. They stopped a hundred yards from us. The imposing figure of the Rwandan President came out of the first car. As Ambassador Johan Swinnen described him so well: 'A slender, strong figure with a dark, firm head and round, worried eyes'.[3] He had visited the university hospital where his brother was a surgeon. On 21 June 1981, my daughter Anneleen, would be born there. After some hesitation, which he had noticed, we went to meet him. He shook our hand and smiled: 'You come to greet me, while I'm not even white?'

The second time was in Kigali at a 'Conference on the Application of Human Rights in Africa' from 15 to 17 March 1989. I was invited by the US State Department. The Rwandan Minister of Justice, Théoneste Mujyamana, opened and closed the conference. In 1987 and 1988, he was my colleague at the UN Commission on Human Rights. At the end of the conference, some participants were invited to a

[3] J Swinnen, *Rwanda: Mijn Verhaal* (Amsterdam, Polis, 2016) 32.

meeting with the President at his residence. The seats were installed by his swimming pool. The President assured us that he attached great importance to respect for human rights.

Seven months later, from 9 to 12 October 1989, a Colloquium was organised in Bujumbura on 'Human Rights for a Dynamic of Peace'. I was invited there as Chairperson of the UN Commission on Human Rights. On 10 October 1989, I received a petition from Rwandan refugee communities around the world. They worked for an unconditional return to their country. They accused the Rwandan government of wanting to keep them in exile forever, under the pretext that there was not enough space in Rwanda. Less than a year later, they tried to return to their country by armed force.

President Juvénal Habyarimana was an affable man. This same person had imprisoned many dignitaries, all Hutu, of the previous Rwandan regime.[4] While claiming to protect the Tutsi from the worst,[5] his close entourage was preparing a genocide after the RPF incursion.[6] Two days after the raid, he landed at Melsbroek military airport early in the morning of 3 October 1990. He came from New York where he attended the UN General Assembly. He went to the Château of Laeken. He knew how to charm people. At dawn, he accompanied King Baudouin to the chapel to pray, kneeling side by side. This deeply religious and devout man deserved all the support of Belgium in resisting the brutal attack from abroad.

President Juvénal Habyarimana was a great master of the 'double game'.[7] He did not tell the Belgian Ambassador the same thing as the French Ambassador. In French, he did not say the same thing as in Kinyarwanda. To François Mitterrand,[8] the French President (1981–95), he presented himself not as a perfect Christian but as a freethinker in favour of secularism. He made a great impression on him by quoting verses by Jacques Prévert. A francophile president of great literary scholarship deserved all the support of France against anglophone aggressors. They didn't even speak the language of the country they wanted to conquer. The French President lost sight of the fact that it was not French but Kinyarwanda which is the language of the Rwandans. And that language they spoke.

On 6 April 1994, five years after the meeting around the presidential pool in Kigali, a rocket knocked down the Falcon plane (a gift from France) with the Presidents of Rwanda and Burundi on board. The plane ended its flight next to this

[4] S Barahinyura, *Quinze ans de tyrannie et de tartuferie au Rwanda: 1973–1988. Le Général major Habyarimana* (Frankfurt, Ed Inuba, 1988).

[5] Swinnen (n 3) 166.

[6] See among others, Jean-Berchmans Birara (181), Justin Mugenzi (190), inhabitants of Kibuye (239), Boniface Ngulinzira (272), Janvier Afrika (310) and Jean-Pierre (477), cited by Swinnen, ibid.

[7] As noted by our ambassador in Nairobi at the time, C Funes-Noppen, *Des hommes, des femmes et des bêtes*, Vol II (Aix-en-Provence, Persia, 2012) 209. Ambassador Johan Swinnen (n 3) 234 and 493 spoke of a 'double language'.

[8] On the responsibility of France, and in particular of President Mitterrand, in the genocide on the Tutsi, see V Duclert, *La France face au génocide des Tutsi. Le grand scandale de la Ve République* (Paris, Tallandier, 2024).

same pool. Very early in the morning of the next day, the most horrible genocide in Africa began. For a hundred days, day after day, on average 8,000 to 10,000 Rwandans, most Tutsi, were exterminated. This was not done in gas chambers, but with machetes. The Tutsi were massacred, not for what they had done, not for what they had said, not even for what they had thought. They were murdered for what they were: Tutsi. This problem had to be solved once and for all. To this end, even babies had to be killed and foetuses had to be removed from their mothers' wombs. The Tutsi were to be eradicated at the root. For years I had been active in the human rights bodies of the United Nations. Belgium had been responsible for the administration of this country for decades. I had taught international law there three times. In that country, the cruellest violations of human rights took place on an unimaginable scale.

19.3. The Push and Pull Factors

It is not possible to address the issue of refugees and asylum seekers without talking about push and pull factors, at the risk otherwise of being accused of being blind to the causes of migration currents. What causes people to leave their country and what is being done to prevent these causes? Traditionally, a distinction is made between push factors and pull factors. For years, I explained this in many places. This earned me a few art books and several bottles of wine, of varied quality. Gradually, my belief in the importance of push factors began to falter. Over time, I became convinced that pull factors weigh the most, by far.

19.3.1. The Push Factors

Push factors cause asylum seekers to leave their country. The most important of these factors are human rights violations, armed conflicts and economic inequality. Of course, all efforts to eliminate or reduce the flow of illegal migration are welcome. The more successful these efforts are, the greater the chance of alleviating pressure on the asylum procedure. However, we must not delude ourselves: it is very difficult to influence the causes of migratory currents.

19.3.1.1. Violations of Human Rights

There are not many ways to prevent human rights violations abroad.[9] A fundamental requirement is to always speak unambiguously in favour of respect for human rights, regardless of the nature of the bilateral relations between the

[9] M Bossuyt, 'Human Rights as an Element of Foreign Policy' *Bulletin of Human Rights* (Geneva, United Nations, 1989) 27.

countries concerned. On the other hand, trade relations are, contrary to what is often supposed, not very suitable for carrying out a human rights policy. Trading is not done out of charity but on a balance of mutual interests. Restricting trade relations because of human rights violations, harms no less your own interests. Moreover, if there was only trade with countries that respect human rights, world trade would be greatly reduced.

In the event of human rights violations, it is often too quickly envisaged as ending development cooperation. This is rarely justified. Two possibilities: either this cooperation mainly benefits the privileged of the regime, and it is therefore not a justifiable cooperation; or it benefits those who are most in need and, as victims of these violations, they should not be punished again.

We must be very careful with economic sanctions.[10] It is a mistake to expect 'unscrupulous dictators' to change their policies because their people would suffer from these sanctions. A dictator who does that would not be 'unscrupulous'. Nor can the people in the following elections choose another leader: in a dictatorship, there are no elections or at least no elections allowing the people to choose a better leader. The sole criterion must be the effectiveness of sanctions, not the persistence of violations. Sanctions rarely affect those responsible for human rights violations. Too often they are only an additional sanction for the victims of these violations. These disadvantages can be avoided by 'smart sanctions' of a financial nature or concerning the non-delivery of visas targeting specific persons.

19.3.1.2. Armed Conflicts

Few countries have the means to put an end to armed conflicts. In many cases, it is also very difficult to know whether military interventions can achieve the intended objectives. A strong intervention in Afghanistan after 11 September 2001, did not prevent 20 years later that there are still many Afghans coming to Europe. The invasion of Iraq in 2003, which was contrary to international law, did not produce a better result. The 2011 intervention in Libya, which consisted mainly of NATO bombing, did not prevent the country's coasts from being transformed into bases of departure for desperate African migrants. Criminal human traffickers shamelessly enrich themselves by exploiting the misery and illusions of these poor wretches. In Syria, where there was no Western intervention, there was a very large displacement of people. A policy capable of preventing migratory flows caused by armed conflicts is not easy to find.

19.3.1.3. Economic Inequalities

There are vast economic inequalities in the world between countries, often compounded by rapidly increasing demographics. These inequalities also push

[10] M Bossuyt, 'Adverse Consequences of Economic Sanctions on the Enjoyment of Human Rights' E/CN.4/Sub.2/2000/33 (Geneva, United Nations, 2000).

people to leave their country in the hope of finding a better future. And although they are not refugees within the meaning of the Geneva Convention, their determination to leave their country is nonetheless firm. Once they arrive, they try their luck by applying for asylum. It is not the neediest who leave their country. Only those who are privileged in their own country can afford such a trip. It is profoundly tragic that unfortunate people are selling their meagre possessions (and sometimes those of their entire family or even their entire village) to pay human traffickers and risk their lives on their way to Europe.

Of course, there are still human rights violations, armed conflicts and economic inequalities. That will not change any time soon. However, that is no reason to welcome all the victims of these misfortunes. The solution is not to be found here, but in their own countries, by working for change on the ground or, in the meantime, by providing humanitarian aid. If this assistance cannot be provided on the ground, we must look to neighbouring countries. The lower cost of hosting in these countries enables helping a lot more people than here. Thus, problems resulting from cultural uprooting can also be avoided. Mass migration[11] to the European Union is not the solution to poverty in Africa or to conflicts in the Middle East. The European Union must profess this message clearly. If this does not happen, more and more irregular migrants will be attracted and drownings at sea will continue. The biggest victims of this lack of clarity are migrants, and the biggest beneficiaries are human traffickers.

19.3.2. The Pull Factors

Pull factors are factors that attract asylum seekers to a particular country rather than to other countries. These factors are numerous: the level of general well-being, a good reception system with allowances and a good level of education for children as well as good medical care, the presence of family members and compatriots, linguistic familiarity, a high percentage of recognition and – above all(!) – the chance to stay in the country, even after a negative decision, and to obtain a residence permit and, ultimately, even nationality.

Substandard reception conditions will not deter asylum seekers. In their own country and on their way to the host country, they have often had to face greater deprivation. They see them as a temporary lack of comfort. A reception in kind is less attractive than a reception in cash, especially since they generally overestimate

[11] R Beck '*The Gum Ball Analogy*' (10 September 2010): www.youtube.com/watch?v=LPjzfGChGlE notes that there are 3 billion people in the world with incomes below US$2 per day. In addition, 2.6 billion people have lower incomes than Mexico. Migrants to the United States come mainly from this latter group. More than 99% of the first group is not able to emigrate. They can only be helped where they live. Every year the group of needy grows by 80 million people. Even if the number of migrants in the United States doubled from 1 to 2 million a year, the effect on poverty reduction in the world would be negligible.

the purchasing power of their allowances. An important factor in deterring applications for asylum is a procedure that can quickly lead to a negative decision. Nothing is more discouraging than to receive on the day of the application an order to leave the territory. If confirmed by a rapid appeal procedure followed by effective deportation, the number of unfounded asylum applications will fall rapidly. Moreover, it is on pull factors that host countries can exert the greatest influence.

An increase in the number of asylum applications is often wrongly attributed to push factors. It is not uncommon for governments to stress the importance of push factors in discharging their own responsibilities. The media usually swallow it without critical thinking. Thus, the rise in asylum applications in 1992 was attributed to the deteriorating situation in Kosovo. On closer examination, this rise was caused for more than half by asylum seekers of other nationalities. And there is more: half of those who said they came from Kosovo did not come from there. They were Albanians. In fact, the Kosovars had breached the dyke. We didn't close it. Many non-Kosovars have slipped in ….

The great asylum crisis of 2015 in the Mediterranean was attributed to the armed conflict in Syria.[12] This conflict had been going on for four years. All this time, war refugees were in Jordan, Lebanon and Turkey. It was said that after four years, the stay in neighbouring countries became unbearable. The occupation of Afghanistan by the Soviet Union for nine years (1979–89) had led to the flight of one million Afghans to Iran and three million to Pakistan. Despite a stay of more than four years in Iran or Pakistan, there were not many Afghans who went to the European Union.

The 2015 asylum crisis brought more than a million asylum seekers to the European Union. Most of them were not Syrian. Applicants from different countries had understood that it was easier to reach Lesbos (Greece), which is 5 km from Turkey, rather than making the crossing (at least 300 km) to Lampedusa (Italy). Turkey, yet a candidate-member of the European Union, adopted an attitude that was far from innocent. The Italian Coast Guard tried to dissuade irregular migrants on their way to Lampedusa by bringing them back to Libya. The Strasbourg Court condemned this practice in 2012. Since then, anyone from anywhere can be admitted to the European Union if he arrives by boat. This is not likely to discourage migrants from risking their lives in the Mediterranean. Once they arrive on land in the Schengen area, they can, thanks to the eponymous Agreement, continue their journey to the country of their preference. They are barely at risk of being sent back to the country where they landed. This is the consequence of the dismantling of the Dublin Regulation by the same Court in 2011.

The Dublin Regulation (2003) is based on the oldest pillar of European asylum policy. To avoid asylum shopping between different host countries, the Dublin

[12] M Bossuyt, 'The European Union Confronted with an Asylum Crisis in the Mediterranean' (2015) 32 *Journal européen des droits de l'homme* 581.

Convention was adopted in 1990. It stipulates that the country through which an asylum seeker arrived in the European Union is responsible for processing his application. Thus, each Member State is made responsible for the surveillance of its external border part of the Union. Italy and Greece, the main countries of arrival, felt abandoned by the European Union. They have waived their obligation to register and fingerprint asylum seekers. The risk for asylum seekers to be returned to their country of entry was virtually eliminated. It therefore seems useful to study the development of the asylum jurisprudence of this Court. Those who think it is of interest only to legal experts are grossly mistaken. It also explains why, in Mark Elchardus' words, the Strasbourg Court's responsibility for facilitating illegal immigration is 'overwhelming'.[13]

[13] M Elchardus, *Reset: Over identiteit, gemeenschap en democratie* (Aalter, Ertsberg, 2021) 378, and esp chs 15 and 16.

20

An Extra: Criticism by a 'Renegade'

Over the years, the European Court of Human Rights has become more involved in the field of asylum. The European Convention on Human Rights (ECHR) was signed on 4 November 1950. It entered into force on 3 September 1953. The first judgment (*Lawless v Ireland*) of the European Court dates from 14 November 1960. The applicant, who had a predestined name, was a former member of the Irish Republican Army (IRA). He complained that his detention in 1957, without trial under Irish exceptional legislation, was too long. The ECHR, like the universal human rights conventions, contains no provisions on asylum. The Universal Declaration of Human Rights, adopted on 10 December 1948, contains a provision concerning asylum, namely Article 14.1: 'Everyone has the right to seek and to enjoy in other countries asylum from persecution'. However, this Declaration is not a formally legally binding text. It is therefore not surprising that it took a long time before the Strasbourg Court considered applications by asylum seekers.

The first Strasbourg decision concerning an asylum seeker (*Cruz Varas*, 20 March 1991) only came more than 30 years after the *Lawless* judgment. It took an additional five years for the adoption of the *Chahal* judgment (15 November 1996), the first in which a breach of an asylum seeker's right was found. This was a 'potential' or '*virtual*' violation. This means that it had not yet taken place. The Court found that there would have been a serious risk of violation if the applicant had been returned to his country. This is not the finding of a fact. It is an estimate by the Court that something might happen. Nor is it a direct violation by the State (ie, the United Kingdom) which is a State Party to the ECHR. The responsibility of this State Party is only *indirect*. The State Party would be responsible if another State (ie, India), which is not a State Party to the ECHR, did something that, if committed by a State Party in its own country, would be contrary to the ECHR. In this respect, it is generally an indirect liability for potential violations. The Court does not examine facts that happened; it speculates on what might happen in the future.

From 6 February 1997, I was a judge at the Court of Arbitration (since 7 May 2007, the 'Constitutional Court'). I no longer spoke on asylum issues in Belgium. The Constitutional Court was sometimes faced with such issues, but as a sitting judge, I could not comment. On 7 October 2007, I became President of the Constitutional Court. For this reason, I retired as extraordinary professor emeritus at the University of Antwerp on 30 September 2007, two years earlier than required. This gave me more time for legal publications. The judgments on asylum by the

Strasbourg Court seemed to me an appropriate subject for study. They deserved more attention. My experiences as an academician specialised in the international protection of human rights, as an expert in UN human rights bodies, as a former Commissioner General for Refugees and as a judge at the Constitutional Court complemented and enriched each other.

20.1. Judges on Thin Ice

I wrote a book (189 pp) on these judgments, which was published in 2010 by Bruylant, as was the case in 1976 with my doctoral thesis defended in Geneva on 7 July 1975. This book is in French. With Dutch, it is one of the two main languages spoken in Belgium. With English, it is one of the two working languages of the Strasbourg Court. Later, I wrote more often in English. The young Dutch speakers seem to be more familiar with this language. At the international level, French is falling further and further behind English. The title of the book became *Strasbourg et les demandeurs d'asile: des juges sur un terrain glissant.*

I found this expression in a separate opinion of Wilhelmina Thomassen, who had been the Dutch judge (1998–2004) in Strasbourg. She used this expression in a judgment of 5 July 2005: *Said v the Netherlands.* This judgment concerned the expulsion by the Netherlands of a rejected asylum seeker to Eritrea. 'Having to assess the reliability of the account given by the person concerned and bearing in mind the subjective elements which are inherent in making such an assessment', she wrote (in original English) '*judges will to a certain extent find themselves on thin ice*'. This was nicely translated into French by '*les juges sont parfois amenés à s'aventurer sur un terrain glissant*'. The two expressions seemed well chosen: judges on slippery ground or on a layer of thin ice. In French, they risk slipping; in English, they may get through the ice.

In my commentary (p 103) on the Strasbourg cases on asylum, I wrote:

> The Court's decisions on asylum are generally welcomed with enthusiasm by lawyers, with fervour by scientific researchers, with complacency by journalists, with submission by national judges and with resignation by politicians. In the name of dynamic and teleological interpretation, the Court is gradually moving forward on the road of an ever greater 'juridisation' of the European society, without worrying too much about what the States wanted by becoming parties to the Convention.

At the ceremony on my departure from the Presidency of the Constitutional Court at the Palais des Académies in Brussels on 12 December 2013, Egbert Myjer,[1] who was the Dutch judge (2004–12) at the European Court of Human Rights, said:

[1] Egbert Myjer was Advocate General (1991–96) at the Hague Court and substitute Prosecutor General (1996–2004) at the Amsterdam Court. He is the author of numerous publications and, with Peter Kempees, of a magnificent fairy tale (applicable to the Court): E Myjer and P Kempees, *Jack and the Solemn Promise: A Cautionary Tale* (Nijmegen, Wolf Legal Publishers, 2010).

> A good majority of the 47 judges of the Court have heard of Marc Bossuyt and have read one or more works of his hand. Marc has a creative imagination (and humour) but he also knows what he's talking about. He has a quality that is part of the tools of a judge but that often remains unused: he is courageous, and he is not afraid to express his opinion when he considers it necessary. At a time when, with all his theoretical and practical experience, he felt that the European Court was going too far in its jurisprudence in the matter of foreigners, he wrote about it and published on it in several international journals. He was starting the conversation. He did so in a rather nuanced way. And even while he was writing his publications in his personal capacity, this kind of publication written by someone with such a high status in national law were also read in Strasbourg.

In his preface[2] to a book which I published in 2016, Paul Mahoney,[3] the British judge (2012–16) at the Strasbourg Court, wrote:

> There is an all-too-common intolerance in European human rights circles of anyone who dares to break ranks by questioning or, even worse, criticising the rulings or approach of the Strasbourg Court. Such persons are regarded almost as renegades or traitors; they are not true human rights 'patriots'. Sad to say, but self-questioning and openness to criticism are generally lacking as qualities in many leading lights of the European human rights movement. In his book, as in his writings throughout his distinguished career, Marc Bossuyt provides a refreshing breath of fresh air. In looking not only at the remarkable, ground-breaking achievements of the Strasbourg Court but also at its possible errors, he has not been afraid to break the taboo of human rights 'patriotism'.

20.2. The Precursors of Indirect Violations

The precursors[4] to the concept of 'indirect violations' date back to 1973 and 1989. These were not virtual violations at all. In the first case, the applicant's husband had indeed been executed in Morocco. In the second case, the risk of the applicant being sentenced to capital punishment in the United States was very real.

20.2.1. Moroccan: Lt-Col *Amekrane v the United Kingdom* (Com 11 October 1973)

On 16 August 1972, the Boeing 727, which brought home King Hassan II, king (since 1961) of Morocco, was attacked by Moroccan air force fighters. The plane

[2] P Mahoney, 'A Penetrating and Salutary Analysis of the European System of Human Rights Protection' in M Bossuyt, *International Human Rights Protection: Balanced, Critical and Realistic* (Cambridge, Intersentia, 2016) (ix–x).

[3] Paul Mahoney was previously (since 1974) an official and then Deputy Registrar and Registrar (2001–05) of the Strasbourg Court and (the first) President (2005–11) of the EU Civil Service Tribunal in Luxembourg.

[4] The summary of these cases and judgments up to June 2010 is based on Bossuyt, above p 64 (n 3).

landed undamaged, and the King escaped unharmed. The commander-in-chief of the air force, Lieutenant-Colonel Mohamed Amekrane, landed in Gibraltar in a helicopter at 6.34 pm where he applied for asylum. The next day, at 10.40 pm, he and his colleagues were handed over to Moroccan officials and taken to Rabat. Morocco's Ministry of Foreign Affairs had given assurances that they would be treated properly. On 3 January 1973, the Military Court of Kenitra handed down the death penalty against him for participating in the plot. He was executed 10 days later.

A petition lodged on 16 December 1972 by his German wife, also on behalf of her two children, with the European Commission of Human Rights, was declared admissible on 11 October 1973. The Commission believed that the request posed sufficiently complex problems in the field of Article 3 of the ECHR to require an examination on the merits. On 19 July 1974, the Commission adopted an amicable settlement. The applicants had accepted the ex gratia payment of £37,000 from the British government. That government stated that this regulation did not imply any admission of violation of anyone's rights. Only 16 years later, would the Court itself take indirect responsibility into account.

20.2.2. A German from Virginia: *Soering v the United Kingdom* (7 July 1989)

A German national, Jens Soering, was accused of killing his Canadian friend's parents in March 1985 in Virginia (USA). On 11 August 1986, the American authorities requested his extradition from the United Kingdom. The Federal Republic of Germany did the same on 11 March 1987. His girlfriend, who was extradited to the United States on 8 May, was sentenced on 6 October 1987 – for complicity in murder – to 90 years in prison. With the consent of the Divisional Court of the House of Lords, the British Home Office decided on 8 August 1988 to extradite Soering to the American authorities. Seized one month before this decision, the European Commission took a provisional measure on 11 August asking the British government not to extradite him.

On 7 July 1989, the European Court ruled in plenary session that

> it would hardly be compatible with the underlying values of the Convention were a Contracting State knowingly to surrender a fugitive to another State where there were substantial grounds for believing that he would be in danger of being subjected to torture, however heinous the crime allegedly committed (§88).

There was a problem because the ECHR itself does not prohibit capital punishment. Article 2(1) of the ECHR provides the following exception to the prohibition of intentionally inflicting life deprivation on anyone: 'the execution of a sentence of a court following his conviction of a crime for which this penalty is provided for'. Only Protocol No 6 to the ECHR, adopted on 28 April 1983, abolishes the death penalty, but only in peacetime. Only Protocol No 13 to the ECHR, adopted on 3 May 2002, abolishes the death penalty 'in all circumstances'. However, a human rights court could not be expected to tolerate the death penalty. The extradition ban was based on the extreme conditions on death row in American prisons:

> Having regard to the very long period of time spent on death row in such extreme conditions, with the ever present and mounting anguish of awaiting execution of the death penalty, and to the personal circumstances of the applicant, especially his age and mental state at the time of the offence, the applicant's extradition to the United States would expose him to a real risk of treatment going beyond the threshold set by Article 3 (§111).

Since the Federal Republic of Germany also requested extradition, there was no risk of impunity.

In the *Soering* case, the violation of Article 3 was certainly 'virtual', but not at all imaginary. The Court used this precedent to develop its jurisprudence on asylum seekers. I will explain how the Court went down the road of indirect liability for virtual violations. From the outset, the scope granted to Article 3 ECHR went further than what had been accepted by the States by becoming parties to the Geneva Convention. Between 1991 and 2005, there were only 15 judgments in 15 years concerning asylum seekers. After the judgment of the Grand Chamber in *Mamatkulov and Askarov v Turkey* of 4 February 2005, there were in four and a half years 45 more judgments. The number of violations increased tenfold (from 1 to 10 a year). Before *Mamatkulov and Askarov*, in 15 years there were four violations out of 12 judgments (33 per cent); then, in four and a half years, there were 28 violations out of 35 judgments (80 per cent) concerning Article 3 ECHR.

20.3. The Restraint Phase (before *Mamatkulov and Askarov*)

At first, the Court still took a rather restrained attitude. But soon it began to attribute to Article 3 ECHR a scope beyond the protection offered by the Geneva Convention. From 2001 to 2002, there was the *Čonka* case, the first asylum case against Belgium.

20.3.1. The First Two Asylum Judgments (1991)

In 1991, the first two judgments of the Court in matters of asylum occurred: *Cruz Varas*, in which no violation was found, and *Vilvarajah et al*, in which the Court showed great restraint.

20.3.1.1. A Chilean under Pinochet:[5] Cruz Varas v Sweden *(20 March 1991)*

It was in its judgment in *Cruz Varas v* Sweden of 20 March 1991 that the Court (in plenary session) first pronounced on a request from an asylum seeker. Although it was a deportation and not an extradition, the Court applied the same principle (§70). There are important differences. In the case of extradition, the initiative comes from the State of destination which is not a State Party. The person may expect (at least) legal action. An expulsion, inversely, is made on the initiative of a State Party, where the State of destination is not one. Most often, the latter is even indifferent about the person who will be deported.

Sweden had found that Hector Cruz Varas's claims were not plausible, that his story had different internal contradictions and that his credibility was lacking in many respects. On 6 October 1989, he was returned to Chile. His wife and son remained clandestinely in Sweden. In view of the democratic developments taking place in Chile (the state of emergency lifted in August 1988 and presidential elections on 14 December 1989), the Court decided, by 18 votes to 1, that his expulsion did not expose him to a real risk of inhuman or degrading treatment. Only Jan De Meyer, the Belgian judge (1986–98), considered that the situation in Chile was not yet sufficiently reassuring in October 1989.

20.3.1.2. Five Tamils: Vilvarajah et al v the United Kingdom *(30 October 1991)*

In its judgment in *Vilvarajah et al v the United Kingdom* of 30 October 1991, the Court ruled, by 8 votes to 1, that the removal in February 1988 of five Tamil asylum seekers to Sri Lanka had not violated Article 3 ECHR. Yet they had faced varying degrees of hassle on their return. For this reason, they were allowed to return to the United Kingdom in 1989. The Court noted that 'a mere possibility of ill-treatment is not in itself sufficient to give rise to a breach of Article 3' (§111). It follows from that judgment that the Court was still (excessively) restrained.

20.3.2. Protection Beyond the Geneva Convention (1996–2002)

Chahal (1996) was the first judgment concerning an asylum seeker in which the Court found a (virtual and indirect) violation of Article 3 ECHR. In *Ahmed* (1996), *HLR* (1997) and *Jabari* (2000), the Court, based on Article 3 ECHR, also granted broader protection than that prescribed by the Geneva Convention. Finally, there is the *Čonka* case (2001–02), the first asylum case against Belgium.

[5] General Augusto Pinochet, President of Chile (1974–90).

20.3.2.1. A Sikh Separatist: Chahal v the United Kingdom *(GC, 15 November 1996)*

The judgment in *Chahal v the United Kingdom* of 15 November 1996 was the first in which the Grand Chamber of the Court, by 12 votes to 7, found a (virtual) violation of Article 3 ECHR in the event of the applicant's expulsion to his country. During a visit to India in 1984, he was detained for 21 days and reportedly received electric shocks on various parts of his body. Under the Prevention of Terrorism Act, he had been detained in the United Kingdom for more than six years, awaiting deportation. By 13 votes to 6, the Court, still being restrained, considered that this period was not excessive. As for his expulsion, the Court considered that he would likely be a prime target of the security forces because of his notoriety for supporting the cause of Sikh separatism. According to the majority of the Court, this awareness would increase the risk. For the minority, it was the opposite. The Court referred to the involvement of the Punjabi police in killings and kidnappings, also outside the State of Punjab, and to allegations of serious human rights violations by members of the security forces in other Indian states. The Court considered that the scrutiny of his fear of a real risk of treatment contrary to Article 3 ECHR must be carried out without regard of any perceived threat to the national security of the expelling State.

20.3.2.2. A Somali: Ahmed v Austria *(17 December 1996)*

In its judgment *Ahmed v Austria* of 17 December 1996, the Court held that the applicant's expulsion to Somalia would constitute a (virtual) violation of Article 3 ECHR. He was disqualified from refugee status after being sentenced to two and a half years in prison for attempted theft, having been previously sentenced to three months in prison on a suspended sentence for other offences. According to the Court, his deportation would have been possible only after his refugee status was withdrawn when the circumstances that justified granting it were no longer relevant.

20.3.2.3. A Colombian and Drug Traffickers: HLR v France *(GC, 29 April 1997)*

In its judgment *HLR v France* of 29 April 1997, the Grand Chamber admitted that persecution does not necessarily have to come from persons in the public service. The applicant claimed that he feared reprisals from drug traffickers. Nevertheless, the Court decided, by 15 votes to 6, that there would be no violation of Article 3 ECHR in the event of the applicant's expulsion to Colombia.

20.3.2.4. An Iranian Adulteress: Jabari v Turkey *(11 July 2000)*

In its judgment in *Jabari v Turkey* of 11 July 2000, the Court held that there would be a 'potential' breach of Article 3 ECHR if an Iranian woman who claimed to be prosecuted for adultery was deported to Iran. She had been recognised as a refugee by the UNHCR Representative in Turkey because of her membership of a particular social group, namely that of 'women who have transgressed social mores'. The Court merely held that stoning was provided for in the criminal legislation and that the authorities could have recourse to it. Fortunately, there are not many reports of such stoning in Iran.

In previous cases, the protection guaranteed by Article 3 ECHR is, as the Court itself observed (*Chahal*, §80), broader than that provided for in the Geneva Convention. Where there are serious reasons to believe that there is a real risk of torture, the exceptions in the Geneva Convention to the prohibition of refoulement do not apply. These are the exceptions provided for in Article 32 (national security or public order, as was the case in *Chahal*) and Article 33 (convicted of a particularly serious crime, as was the case in *Ahmed*) of this Convention. According to the Court, danger does not necessarily have to emanate from persons who are members of the public service, as was the case in *HLR*. The ground of persecution of 'membership of a particular social group' is also broadly interpreted by the Court, as in the case of *Jabari*.

20.3.3. Slovak Roma: *Čonka v Belgium* (Decision 13 March 2001; 5 February 2002)

Among the judgments preceding the judgment of the Grand Chamber (GC) in *Mamatkulov and Askarov* (4 February 2005), mention should be made of *Čonka v Belgium*. The case concerned the deportation to Slovakia of a group of failed asylum seekers including the Čonka couple and their children. Čonka claimed to have left Slovakia because he was attacked by skinheads on 4 November 1998. He had already bought his plane tickets before this incident. The man did not respond to the summons of the Commissioner General. The woman was heard while in prison for theft.

In its inadmissibility decision of 13 March 2001, the Court considered that the allegation of treatment contrary to Article 3 ECHR was manifestly unfounded. The Court attached great importance to the absence of any evidence of violence or ill-treatment suffered by the persons concerned since their return to Slovakia. The process of marking the seat numbers allocated to them in their hands with a ballpoint pen before boarding at the airport had not met the minimum threshold of gravity required by Article 3 ECHR. The same procedure was used for humanitarian transport of Kosovar refugees to Belgium.

In its judgment of 5 February 2002, the Court ruled, by 4 votes to 3, that the prohibition of collective expulsion of aliens in Article 4 of Protocol No 4 had been violated. The deportation orders in issue were made to enforce an order to leave the territory in which the only reference to the personal circumstances of the applicants was the fact that their stay in Belgium had exceeded three months. This caused some uncertainty about collective removals. Fortunately, this uncertainty was lifted in *Sultani v France* (20 September 2007). The Court did not find a violation of Article 4 of Protocol No 4, although the flight to Afghanistan was described as 'grouped' and 'collective', because the applicant's situation was examined individually.

The Čonka couple had received a written notice to attend Ghent police station 'to enable the file concerning their application to be completed'. The number of asylum applications from Slovaks rose from an average of 22 per month in the first seven months of 1999 to 359 in the first 24 days of August 1999. After arriving at the police station, the couple was transferred to a closed centre for repatriation. That was the only element missing from the file. The Belgian government spoke of the 'unfortunate' wording of the notice and a 'little ruse'. The Court noted that this was not the result of 'inadvertence' but that it was chosen deliberately by the authorities to mislead aliens about the purpose of the notice to make it easier to deprive them of their liberty. The Court held that this was contrary to Article 5 ECHR on the illegitimate deprivation of liberty. The Court did not specify how it should have been done. Article 5.4 ECHR was violated because their deprivation of liberty was too long without them being able to address a judge. Article 5.1 ECHR was violated because their deprivation of liberty was too brief to be able to address a judge before being repatriated.

20.4. *Mamatkulov and Askarov v Turkey* (GC, 4 February 2005): 'An Excess of Power'

Mamatkulov and Askarov were two Uzbeks extradited in 1999 by Turkey to their country's authorities. This was not a problem for the majority of the Court (14 to 3). The problem was that the extradition had taken place despite the interim measure it had indicated. On 18 March 1999, the Court requested that they should not be extradited. Until then, it was accepted that such provisional measures were not legally binding.[6] This was decided by the Court in its judgment in *Cruz Varas* (20 March 1991) by 10 votes to 9. The majority reached this conclusion because the ECHR does not contain a provision on provisional measures. In addition, the Committee of Ministers of the Council of Europe had refused to act on a recommendation of the Consultative Assembly of the Council of Europe to draft an additional protocol to this effect. This view was further confirmed by the Court in *Čonka* (13 March 2001). Four years later, the Court (14 to 3) suddenly changed its mind. The provisional measures became mandatory.

[6] Art 36 of the Commission's Rules of Procedure provided that: 'The Commission, or where it is not in session, the President may indicate to the parties any interim measure the adoption of which *seems desirable* in the interest of the parties or the proper conduct of the proceedings before it'. Currently, Rule 39 of the Court's Rules of Procedure says, 'to indicate to the parties any interim measure which they [the Chamber, or, where appropriate, the President of the Section] consider *should* be adopted'.

To justify this change, the Court refers to the practice of the UN Committee on Human Rights and the UN Committee against Torture, as well as that of the International Court of Justice and the Inter-American Court of Human Rights. These references are not convincing. The two UN Committees do not have the competence to adopt legally binding decisions or judgments. Therefore, their provisional measures cannot be legally binding either. The Statute (26 June 1945) of the International Court of Justice and the Statute of the American Convention on Human Rights (22 November 1969) both contain a provision on provisional measures. The ECHR contains none.

The three minority judges, Lucius Caflisch[7] (Liechtenstein), Riza Türmen (Turkey) and Anatoly Kovler (Russian Federation), argued strongly in their dissenting opinion:

a. Since 2001, there has been no change which would justify a diametrically opposite conclusion.
b. The International Court of Justice relies on a provision of its own constitutive treaty (Article 41 of its Statute), while no such provision is found in the ECHR; there is a wide difference between the mere interpretation of a treaty and its amendment.
c. Proposals to this effect have been rejected by the government experts.
d. There is a customary rule allowing international courts to formulate interim provisional measures, but that does not include the power to prescribe such measures.
e. What the Court has done is a matter of legislation rather than of judicial action; its conclusion that it is empowered to issue binding provisional measures is *ultra vires* (excess of power).

If a government went against an indicated interim measure, it assumed a great risk. In the event of acts contrary to the ECHR, refusal would be considered as aggravating any breach of Article 3 ECHR. If nothing harmful happened to the applicant, it was proof that the competent services of the government concerned had properly assessed the situation. From now on, there would be a violation, even if the government concerned had assessed the situation more correctly than the Court.

What was expected, by all those familiar with asylum, happened: the number of applications for provisional measures by asylum seekers exploded: 112 in 2006; 883 in 2007; 3,185 in 2008; 2,402 in 2009; 3,775 in 2010. On average, in 2010, there were 15 requests each working day that the Court had to respond to immediately.

[7] He was a professor of international law and director of the Graduate Institute of International Studies (IUHEI; now IHEID) in Geneva, legal adviser to the Swiss Ministry of Foreign Affairs, judge in Strasbourg (1998–2006) and Chairperson of the UN Commission on International Law. L Caflisch, 'Provisional Measures in the International Protection of Human Rights: the Mamatkulov case' in P-M Dupuy, B Fassbender, MN Shaw and KP Sommermann (eds), *Common Values in International Law: Essays in Honour of Christian Tomuschat* (Kehl, NP Engel, 2006) 493.

In a statement issued on 11 February 2011, the President of the Court expressed concern about 'the alarming rise in the number of requests for interim measures that must be dealt with urgently, when human resources are not infinite'.[8]

The Court 'knew or must have known'[9] that this would be the inevitable effect of its *Mamatkulov and Askarov* judgment. Provisional measures 'most often in cases involving the law of aliens and the right of asylum' were a matter of concern to the governments of the States Parties. At its High-Level Conference in Izmir (Turkey) on 27 April 2011, the Committee of Ministers of the Council of Europe expressed concern that 'the number of interim measures requested [had] greatly increased, thus further increasing the workload of the Court'. The Conference recalled that 'the Court is not an immigration Appeals Tribunal or a Court of fourth instance'.[10]

There was a growing awareness that the increase in requests for interim measures was becoming unmanageable. The Court had initially kindly granted these requests: 23 per cent in 2008, 27 per cent in 2009 and 38 per cent in 2010. In 2011, this rate dropped suddenly to 11 per cent. In absolute terms, this was a decrease from 1,434 requests for interim measures granted in 2010 to 250 in 2011 (a decrease of 83 per cent). Unsurprisingly, the number of applications subsequently began to fall: from 3,775 in 2010 to 2,778 in 2011. This shows that a change in the attitude of the Court can curb the influx of applications.[11] By assigning legally binding force to its provisional measures, the number of asylum seekers applying to the Court has increased sharply. By indicating provisional measures, the Court intervenes in the day-to-day management of asylum and immigration policy, without having to assume responsibility for their consequences. In these asylum cases, the Court is increasingly substituting itself for the competent and specialised national authorities. The Court began to assess the credibility of asylum seekers and the risk they run in the event of repatriation. The Court has thus become an 'Asylum Court'.[12]

[8] In the Annex to the statement of 11 February 2011 of the President of the Court, there is question of 4,786 requests. 'The Court's Interim Measures: Rule 39 Decisions by year (2008–2011)' cited 3,755 applications. No explanation is given for this difference in figures.

[9] Quoted from *MSS v Belgium and Greece* (21 January 2011) §334.

[10] M Bossuyt, 'Des limites à la jurisdiction de la Cour de Strasbourg' in E Lambert Abdelgawad, D Szymczak and S Touzé (eds), *L'homme et le droit: en homage au Professeur Jean-François Flauss* (Paris, Pedone, 2014) 117.

[11] M Bossuyt, 'Is the European Court of Human Rights on a Slippery Slope ?' in S Flogaitis, T Zwart and J Fraser (eds), *The European Court of Human Rights and is Discontents: Turning Criticism into Strength* (Cheltenham, Elgar, 2013) 27.

[12] To demonstrate this, I published in the *European Constitutional Law Review* (2012) 203 an analysis of the Court's decisions on asylum under the title 'The Court of Strasbourg Acting as an Asylum Court'. Egbert Myjer responded, in A Alen, V Joosten, R Leysen and W Verrijdt, *Liberae cogitationes: Liber amicorum Marc Bossuyt* (Antwerp, Intersentia, 2013) 419, by publishing a contribution entitled 'The European Court of Human Rights is no European Asylum Court'. In the same *Liber amicorum* (107), Geert De Baere rightly asked for more attention for another court: the Court of Justice of the European Union. He published a chapter under the title 'The Court of Luxembourg acting as an asylum court'.

21

The Court of Strasbourg as an Asylum Court (Since 4 February 2005)

Since the *Mamatkulov and Askarov* judgment (4 February 2005), there have been so many asylum rulings that it is necessary to be very selective in the choice of those who deserve special attention. This choice is obviously partly subjective, with a weakness for cases against Belgium. The objective is to only make those who are not familiar with them understand how important jurisprudence is for asylum. It will be shown that, to a large extent, asylum policy is not determined by politicians, but by judges.

21.1. A Congolese DSP Officer and a Credulous Court: *N v Finland* (26 July 2006)

Just five months after *Mamatkoulov and Askarov*, the judgment in *N v Finland* (26 July 2005) illustrates the credulity of the Strasbourg judges. The Court found that the account of a Congolese asylum seeker, who claimed to have been part of President Mobutu Sese Seko's Special Presidential Division (DSP), was 'sufficiently consistent and credible' (§155). This was the conclusion of a mission by two judges at the Court who went to Finland to question him. Perhaps a mission to Kinshasa would have been more useful.

His asylum application was deemed not credible and was rejected, first in the Netherlands, then in Finland by the Immigration Directorate, the Administrative Court and the Supreme Administrative Court in Helsinki. The following elements pointed in this direction: he had not been able to provide any identity card, travel document or certificate of education; he had appeared under four different names; he claimed to originate from the Ngbandi tribe (Mobutu's tribe) but he did not speak the language; he had been found guilty on two accounts of shoplifting; the Court itself acknowledged that his testimony had been evasive on many points and that the account of his journey to Finland was not credible. The protection officer in Finland, who had refused his application at first instance, had five years' experience in processing Congolese asylum applications. In 2000, he had investigated in Kinshasa. Between 70 per cent and 80 per cent of the documents submitted by Congolese asylum seekers had been falsified. The Court nevertheless considered that the situation in the Democratic Republic of Congo would still expose this asylum seeker – eight years after Mobutu's regime was toppled – to a real risk of treatment contrary to Article 3 ECHR. By appointing Mobutu's son as State Minister in his government after the July 2006 elections, the new Congolese President Joseph Kabila (2001–19) demonstrated that he was not relentlessly against the faithful of the former president. In any case, the Court was no longer going to send judges on missions to verify the credibility of asylum seekers.

21.2. Reception in Closed Centres in Belgium (2006–11)

The convictions of Belgium for violation of Article 3 ECHR because of the living conditions in closed centres do not concern indirect responsibility or virtual violations. Belgium was convicted five times because the Court considered that it had treated asylum seekers in an inhumane manner. In three cases (*Mubilanzila Mayeka and Kaniki Mitunga*, *Muskhadzhiyeva et al* and *Kanagaratnam et al*), children are involved.

21.2.1. Tabitha: *Mubilanzila Mayeka and Kaniki Mitunga* (12 October 2006)

On 25 September 2000, Mubilanzila Mayeka left the Democratic Republic of Congo for Canada. She left her three-year-old daughter, Tabitha Kaniki Mitunga, with her grandmother. On 17 August 2002, Tabitha arrived at Brussels National Airport accompanied by her uncle, a Dutch national. Not in possession of the documents required to continue her journey to Canada, she was sent back to Kinshasa on 17 October. Her dismissal had been preceded by dozens of contacts with a wide range of individuals and authorities. Another uncle, a student in Kinshasa, had promised the Belgian Embassy that he would wait for her at N'Djili airport (DRC). He wasn't there. The embassy shouldn't have counted on it. It should have taken care of Tabitha itself when she arrived. On 12 October 2006, Belgium was sentenced by the Court for inhumane treatment of mother and daughter.

Tabitha, was she treated inhumanely at the Transit centre? Although at the time there were no special provisions for minors in those centres, she had been looked after by two women who were themselves mothers:

> According to the director of the Transit centre No 127, she had played with other children; her uncle [in the Netherlands] and her mother [in Canada] had telephoned her nearly every day. She had been allowed to telephone them free of charge under the supervision of a team of social workers; her lawyer had paid her a number of visits and had brought her telephone cards, confectionary and money; she had often played outside, had watched large numbers of videos, done drawings and arithmetic, and had been comforted if she showed any signs of distress after telephone calls from her family (§37).

It is doubtful that Tabitha in Kinshasa (or her twin sister in Brazzaville) was able to call their mother regularly in Canada. A five-year-old child in a daycare centre does not have the same freedom of movement as an adult. Tabitha's lawyer had offered to entrust her to an 18-year-old Belgian woman. The father of this young woman was however under arrest for violating the morals of minors. Upon her return, Tabitha had been taken in by an air hostess, as is usually the case with unaccompanied minors.

The mother, was she treated inhumanely when her daughter was staying at the transit centre at the National Airport? It was the mother who had abandoned her daughter with her grandmother for two years. The Court acknowledged that 'the mother's conduct was questionable and did not appear to have been entirely fault-free'. The situation would have been different in Canada if the mother had not failed to mention the existence of the twins. Belgian Prime Minister Guy Verhofstadt intervened with Prime Minister Jean Chrétien of Canada (1993–2003). Later, six days after her return to Kinshasa and at the expense of the Belgian authorities, Tabitha was able to leave for Canada to join her mother. For violation of Article 3 ECHR and, as far as Tabitha was concerned, of Article 5 (unlawful deprivation of liberty), Belgium was ordered to pay €25,000 for moral damage to Tabitha and €10,000 to her mother. No one seemed to care about her twin sister in Brazzaville.

21.2.2. Two Palestinians: *Riad and Idiab* (24 January 2008)

Two Palestinians arrived separately from Freetown (Sierra Leone) at Brussels National Airport at the end of December 2002. For two months and 11 days they stayed in various closed centres (Transit Centre 127, Bruges and Merksplas). In early March 2003, they were taken to Beirut. Despite their release ordered by the Chambre du conseil and the Chamber of Indictment, they spent 12 and 17 days respectively in the transit area of the airport. The Court found there a violation of Article 5 ECHR. The Court also held that Article 3 ECHR had been violated because they had to stay for more than 10 days in conditions in which there was 'a complete failure to take care of their essential needs'. It is indisputable that the transit zone is not an appropriate place to receive people who are not admitted to the territory. For violation of Articles 3 and 5 ECHR, Belgium had to pay each of the applicants €15,000 for moral damage.

21.2.3. A Chechen Mother: *Muskhadzhiyeva et al* (19 January 2010)

Fingerprints showed that a Chechen mother, accompanied by four young children, had, contrary to her claims, been in Poland for at least a year and a half. While waiting for their asylum application to be examined, they were taken to an open centre. As they had left this centre, they were then placed in a closed centre.

The Chambre du conseil decided within two weeks that their stay was necessary for their transfer to Poland. A week later they refused to leave. After 12 more days, the Chamber of Indictment confirmed the decision of the Chambre du conseil. They were transferred to Poland the next day. Although the children were not separated from their mother, the Court found in their case a violation of Article 3 ECHR because of unsatisfactory living conditions. For violation of Articles 3 and 5.1 ECHR, Belgium had to pay a total of €17,000 to the mother and her children for moral damage.

21.2.4. A Sri Lankan Mother: *Kanagaratnam et al* (13 December 2011)

Accompanied by her three young children, a Sri Lankan woman arrived in Belgium via Kinshasa (DRC) with the help of a smuggler and in possession of a fake Indian passport. When two months later the date of their departure for Kinshasa was determined, the Court took an interim measure. Subsequently, they refused to leave. Six weeks later, the Aliens Office granted them access to the territory. Because of the living conditions at the centre, the Court considered that Article 3 ECHR had been violated. Referring to its judgment in *Nunez v Norway* (28 June 2011), the Court stressed the importance of the requirement of Article 3 of the Convention on the Rights of the Child that 'the best interests of the child shall be a primary consideration'. In a dissenting opinion,[1] two judges in that judgment considered that this consideration was not necessarily decisive. In their view, a fair balance had to be struck 'between the right to respect for family life and the State's legitimate public interest in ensuring effective – and not merely cosmetic or illusory – immigration control'. For violation of Articles 3 and 5.1 ECHR, Belgium had to pay a total of €46,650 to the mother and the children for moral damage.

21.2.5. A Cameroonian Woman: *Yoh-Ekale Mwanje* (20 December 2011)

After being rejected for asylum in the Netherlands, a Cameroonian woman, who had engaged in a relationship with a Dutch national in Belgium, found herself there illegally in that country. In view of her repatriation, she stayed twice, for a total of three months, in a closed centre. When it was decided to repatriate her, the Court took an interim measure. Six weeks later, she was released.

On her first visit, her lawyer informed the centre's doctor that she was infected with HIV. During her second stay, it appeared that she had interrupted her antiretroviral therapy for about a year. For this reason, her initial therapy had to

[1] Ljiljana Mijović (Bosnia and Herzegovina) and Vincent A de Gaetano (Malta).

be modified. Two days before her second placement at the centre (22 December 2009), she went to the Institute of Tropical Medicine in Antwerp for consultation. The Court found a violation of Article 3 ECHR, combined with Article 13 ECHR ('an effective remedy') because she was not examined for the first time until 9 February 2010 and because she had not received the medicines prescribed on 26 February until 1 March. For this reason, Belgium had to pay her €14,000 for moral damage.

The Court makes it particularly difficult to apply the exception to the deprivation of liberty provided for in paragraph (f) of Article 5.1 ECHR.[2] A 'cosmetic or illusory' migration control seems to the Court to be more than sufficient. At the same time, the threshold of Article 3 ECHR is continually falling. The absolute nature of the prohibition of torture is justified by a high threshold. The month following this judgment, a third judgment (*MS*) came in less than two months in which Belgium was sentenced for the inhumane treatment of an asylum seeker. This Belgian case was linked to terrorism.

21.3. Terrorism-Related Belgian Cases (2012 and 2014)

It concerns the expulsion of an Iraqi (*MS*) to Kurdistan and the extradition of a Tunisian (*Trabelsi*) to the United States. Both had previously been sentenced in Belgium to five years and ten years' imprisonment respectively for terrorist acts.

21.3.1. An Iraqi Terrorist Deported to Kurdistan: *MS v Belgium* (31 January 2012)

The Iraqi MS[3] had been in Belgium since 15 November 2000. He was arrested on 21 May 2003 by virtue of criminal association, forgery and usage of forgery and suspected of links with the terrorist organisation al Qaeda. His five-year sentence was reduced on appeal on 21 May 2003 to 45 months. After his release on 27 October 2007, he was kept for a period of three years, including two in closed centres (Merksplas, Vottem and Bruges). The Strasbourg Court considered that for 10 months and 2 days, in the absence of a realistic prospect of expulsion within a reasonable time, this was irregular. During this period, he was the subject of 11 judgments of first instance, 10 judgments on appeal, six in cassation, five of the Aliens Litigation Council and three of the Conseil d'Etat,

[2] Art 5.1(f) ECHR: 'the lawful arrest or detention of a person to prevent his effecting an unauthorized entry into the country or of a person against whom action is being taken with a view to deportation or extradition'.

[3] M Bossuyt, '*You cannot try them, you cannot detain them and you cannot deport them* (Observations sous C.E.D.H., M.S. c. Belgique, 31 janvier 2012)' [2012] *Journal des Tribunaux* 351.

as well as two decisions and three opinions of the Commissioner General. For 13 months he was under house arrest at Saint-Nicolas. On 26 April 2005 and 2 February 2009, the Commissioner General refused his refugee status under the exclusion clause. The latter refusal was confirmed by the Aliens Litigation Council on 4 March 2009. While he was still in Bruges, they were looking for a country willing to take him in. Only Burundi agreed to do so, but MS refused to go.

During negotiations with the Belgian authorities, he claimed €50,000 to return to Iraq. He said he needed the money to pay his lawyers and bribe judges. He finally accepted a Belgian counterproposal for €10,000 and was repatriated to Iraq. After a three-week stay in a prison in Erbil (Kurdistan), he was released on bail on 23 November, provided he did not leave his home. In addition to violations of Article 5 ECHR because of its continued retention, the Court found that his return to Iraq had violated Article 3 ECHR. There had been no 'free consent' upon his departure and the Belgian authorities had not sought diplomatic assurances.[4] However, it could be admitted that he had accepted the €10,000 and he did not want any contact made with the Iraqi Embassy. By 4 votes to 3, the Court decided not to grant him the €25,000 claimed for moral damage.

Six days before this judgment, on 25 January 2012, the British Prime Minister David Cameron (2010–16), told the Parliamentary Assembly of the Council of Europe, referring to such judgments:[5]

> Of course, no decent country should deport people if they are going to be tortured. But the problem today is that you can end up with someone who has no right to live in your country, who you are convinced – and have good reason to be convinced – means to do your country harm. And yet there are circumstances in which *you cannot try them, you cannot detain them, and you cannot deport them*. Together, we have to find a solution to this (emphasis added).

When it is certain that someone will be tortured, he cannot be deported, regardless of the crimes he has committed. It is not permissible to admit a degree of torture proportionate to its degree of criminality or dangerousness. The problem is who is responsible for assessing that information and those risks? The Court does not confine itself to marginal control but substitutes itself without restraint to the national authorities.

[4] The Court was very suspicious of such diplomatic assurances in the event of extradition or expulsion to Tunisia or to the States of the former Soviet Union.

[5] See especially *Othman (Abu Qatada) v the United Kingdom* of 17 January 2012 (eight days before). On the basis of a Memorandum of Understanding with the Jordanian government, the expulsion of Othman would not violate Art 3 ECHR. Yet his extradition could not take place. The Court had decided to grant extraterritorial effect to Art 6 ECHR. There would be a risk that during his trial evidence would be admissible even though obtained from third parties under torture.

21.3.2. A Tunisian Terrorist Deported to the United States: *Trabelsi v Belgium* (4 September 2014)

Nizar Trabelsi[6] is a Tunisian who was sentenced on 30 September 2003 to 10 years in prison for attempting to blow up the Kleine-Brogel Belgian army base. This judgment was upheld on appeal on 9 June 2004. After serving his sentence, he was detained for the implementation of an extradition request from the United States. The United States charged him with the provision of resources with the intention of murdering American nationals and destroying real estate occupied by the United States. They gave assurances that he would not be prosecuted before a military commission and that he would be detained in a civilian facility in the United States. When, on 6 December 2011, Trabelsi became aware of the ministerial order for extradition, he immediately requested provisional measures from the Strasbourg Court. On the same day the Court acceded to the applicant's request. The Minister of Justice feared that Belgian courts would order his release because of delays in extradition. Four times she asked the Court to lift the provisional measures. Four times the Court refused to act on it. When the Conseil d'Etat rejected his request to annul the ministerial decree of 23 September 2013, Trabelsi was extradited – despite the provisional measure – 10 days later (on 3 October) to the United States. Belgium considered that its obligations under the Extradition Convention of 27 April 1987 with the United States deserved priority over those under Article 39 of the Court's Rules of Procedure.

In its judgment of 4 September 2014, the Court considered that Belgium had violated Article 34 ECHR. By extraditing Trabelsi – despite the provisional measure – Belgium had hindered the effective exercise of its right of individual petition. The Court also held that Article 3 ECHR had been violated because of the possibility of imposing an incompressible life sentence. This was the first time that the Court reached such a conclusion in the case of extradition. Even in a national context, it was only in its judgment in *Vinter et al v the United Kingdom* of 9 July 2013 that the Court ruled for the first time that such a sentence would violate Article 3 ECHR. Belgium had to pay him €60,000 for moral damage.

This decision was highly speculative and three times hypothetical: there would have been a violation: (a) if Trabelsi were convicted;[7] (b) if he were be sentenced to an incompressible life sentence; and (c) if in 25 years there were no mechanism in the United States to decide on his eventual release. In the absence of such a mechanism, Belgium should have immediately released him. There was no other legal basis for detaining him. Despite the Court's denials (§119), it tried to impose the evolution of its own European standards on other States. If a third State does

[6] M Bossuyt, 'The European Court of Human Rights and Irreducible Life Sentences, The *Trabelsi v Belgium* Judgment of 4 September 2014' (2014) 14 *Human Rights Law Journal* 269.

[7] On 14 July 2023, he was found not guilty by a US federal court.

not respect European standards, it is the State Party that will be condemned. This approach is not conducive to international cooperation in criminal law, based on reciprocity. The mechanical combination of the continuous lowering of the threshold of Article 3 ECHR, on the one hand, and the expansion of its scope by granting it extraterritorial effects on the other, approaches the frontier of what can still be considered reasonable.[8]

21.4. Three Disastrous Judgments (2011, 2012, 2016)

Three judgments had disastrous consequences. These are the *MSS* judgment which dismantled the Dublin procedure and the *Hirsi Jamaa et al* judgment which declared the maritime borders of the Member States of the Council of Europe open to anyone who applies for asylum, even on the high seas. Finally, the *Paposhvili* judgment is mentioned because in that judgment the Court wishes, in addition to the existing asylum procedure, to introduce a new medical asylum procedure.

21.4.1. An Afghan Interpreter: *MSS v Belgium and Greece* (GC, 21 January 2011)

MSS[9] was an Afghan interpreter. With the help of a trafficker to whom he had paid US$12,000, he arrived in Greece on 7 December 2008. Considering that the Belgian soldiers in Afghanistan were 'very friendly', he continued his journey to Belgium on 10 February 2009. Under the Dublin Regulation, he was returned to Greece on 15 June 2009, where he was held for four days in unacceptable conditions. The Court had already considered conditions of detention of asylum seekers contrary to Article 3 ECHR. These were detentions in Greece for 17 months (*Dougoz*, 2001) and for three months (*SD* and *Tabesh*, 2009; *AA*, 2010). In cases against Belgium, periods of two months (*Tabitha*, 2006), 17 days (*Riad and Idiab*, 2008) and four days (*SS*, 2011) were considered sufficient to establish such a violation. We are close to the danger of 'trivialisation' and 'banalisation' of Article 3 ECHR.

In addition, the prohibition on torture was transformed by the Court into an obligation to provide benefits to asylum seekers.[10] The Court did not find it

[8] In *Harkins and Edwards v the United Kingdom* (17 January 2012) (§38), reference is made to the reference of British Justice Lord Hoffmann to *Napier v Scottish Ministers* (2005) SC 229, in which the use of a toilet seal in a Scottish prison cell was found to be contrary to Art 3 ECHR. This would make extradition impossible towards a State where conditions in prison would be equivalent (or worse).

[9] M Bossuyt, 'Belgium Condemned for Inhuman and Degrading Treatment due to Violations by Greece of EU Asylum Law, *M.S.S. v. Belgium and Greece*, Grand Chamber, European Court of Human Rights, January 21, 2011' [2011] *European Human Rights Law Review* 581.

[10] For a (prior) critique of this development, see M Bossuyt, 'Should the Strasbourg Court Exercise more Self-Restraint? On the Extension of the Jurisdiction of the European Court of Human Rights to

contradictory that MSS asserted that he was 'with no means of subsistence' and 'in permanent fear of being attacked and robbed' (§238). The Court noted the considerable difficulties faced by Member States at the external borders of the European Union. In 2009 (when MSS arrived), there were 15,930 asylum applications in Greece. In 2010 (during the deliberations of the Court), there were 19,941 asylum applications in Belgium. Due to direct violations of the ECHR, Greece had to pay MSS €1,000 and Belgium, due to indirect violations of the ECHR, €24,900. Henceforth, the Member States of the European Union had to undergo a rigorous examination of the situation of asylum seekers in the country concerned before being able to transfer an asylum seeker to another Member State of the European Union. Gradually, it appeared that this situation was 'unacceptable' in several Member States. These asylum seekers could stay in the country of their preference.

As can be seen from the judgment of the Grand Chamber in *Tarakhel v Switzerland* of 4 November 2014,[11] Switzerland could not transfer to Italy an Afghan family with six minor children who had lived in Iran for 16 years. Switzerland had first to obtain from the Italian authorities individual guarantees, on the one hand, that the applicants should be taken charge of in a manner adapted to the age of the children and, on the other, that the family would be kept together. These two judgments (*MSS* and *Tarakhel*) have shaken the fundamental principle of 'mutual trust' in the European Union. They helped to encourage the Court of Justice of the European Union to give in its Opinion 2/13 of 18 December 2014 a negative opinion on the accession of the European Union to the ECHR.[12]

21.4.2. Africans Arriving by Boat: *Hirsi Jamaa et al v Italy* (GC, 23 February 2012)

Eleven Somalis and 13 Eritreans were part of a group of 200 people who had left Libya on three boats. They were intercepted on 6 May 2009 by three Italian Coast Guard ships in the Maltese maritime zone 35 miles from Lampedusa. They were brought back to Tripoli (Libya). The Court ruled that Article 3 ECHR was violated because they were at risk of ill-treatment in Libya and repatriation to Somalia and Eritrea. Article 4 of Protocol No 4 prohibiting collective expulsions was also violated, as their personal situation had not been examined. Italy had to pay each claimant €15,000 for moral damage.

Social Security Regulations' [2007] *Human Rights Law Journal* 321. See also M Bossuyt, 'Les droits sociaux: une catégorie spécifique de droits de l'hommes?' in L Berg, M Enrich Mas, P Kempees and D Spielman (eds), *Cohérence et impact de la jurisprudence de la Cour européenne des droits de l'homme: Liber amicorum Vincent Berger* (Oisterwijk, Wolf, 2013) 43.

[11] M Bossuyt, 'Tarakhel c. Suisse: La Cour de Strasbourg rend encore plus difficile une politique commune européenne en matière d'asile' [2015] *Revue suisse de droit international et européen* 3.

[12] M Bossuyt, 'The Principle of "Mutual Trust" in Opinion 2/13' in S Imamović et al (eds), *The EU Fundamental Rights Landscape after Opinion 2/13* (Maastricht, Maastricht Faculty of Law, 2016) 15.

The combination of these two judgments had disastrous consequences, although it took time to become aware of it. The *MSS* judgment in fact rendered the Dublin procedure inapplicable in respect of several States, as the transfer of asylum seekers to the main countries of arrival in the Schengen area became particularly difficult. The European Union did not dare to suspend the Schengen Convention in relation to the countries to which the Dublin procedure could no longer be applied. Logic demanded it, but it ran up against a political taboo. Once in the territory of one of the Schengen countries, the eponymous Convention made it possible for asylum seekers to continue their journey without difficulty to other countries, considered more attractive, in that area.

The decision in *Hirsi Jamaa et al* made the chance of receiving assistance to reach one of the Schengen countries much greater. The number of people who wanted to try it has increased tremendously. Human traffickers pushed asylum seekers into ever more dangerous small boats. Contacts were established with ships of NGOs, and even with navy ships belonging to the Schengen countries, to come and rescue them. They later landed on the shores of one of those countries.

The collapse of the Dublin procedure, as well as the onshore welcome of those venturing into the Mediterranean Sea, made it much more interesting to travel from Turkey to one of the Greek islands than from North Africa to Lampedusa. Tens of thousands of people in the Middle East and Africa decided to try their luck. This led to great chaos in 2015. Although many will refuse violently – and even with indignation – to acknowledge it, more than the push factor – Bashar al-Assad, President of Syria (since 2000) – and the pull factor – Angela Merkel, Federal Chancellor of Germany (2005–21), those two decisions were the cause of the great asylum chaos in 2015.

These judgments have prompted hundreds of thousands of people to try their luck. Some even sell all their assets to pay travel expenses as well as smugglers. Some faced the greatest dangers, especially during their travels through Africa and Libya. Along the way, their human rights were not respected. Many risked their lives, and frequently that of their wives and children, to reach the coasts of Greece, Italy, Malta and Spain. Often, they paid exorbitant prices. Thousands perished, often by drowning.

The Court doubtless hoped that, with its *MSS* judgment, fewer people would receive a bad reception in Greece. On the contrary, many more people have suffered in many States. Fortunately, the Court did not award €24.900 to every asylum seeker who was not well received in Member States of the Council of Europe. Initially, the impression was created that there was a great willingness to welcome many asylum seekers. It was wrongly estimated that these were mostly war refugees from Syria.

It soon became clear that the situation was not tenable. The tide has changed. Even obscure means were used. For those who do not close their eyes, it is difficult to dismiss the disastrous consequences of these two judgments. Of a different kind is the Court's attempt to impose on the States Parties to the ECHR – in addition to an asylum procedure for refugees within the meaning of the Geneva Convention – a medical asylum procedure.

21.4.3. An Illegal Georgian: *Paposhvili v Belgium*[13] (17 April 2014; GC, 13 December 2016)

Despite criminal convictions for multiple thefts and several refusals to stay, the Georgian national Georgie Paposhvili was able to stay in Belgium for seventeen and a half years. His two asylum applications, the second under a false identity, as well as his three humanitarian regularisation applications and his two medical regularisation applications, were refused. He did not follow up on the order to go – under the Dublin Convention – to Italy, which had agreed to accept him. Several times forced deportation was not executed on humanitarian grounds (pregnancy of his wife, illness of children). For the Court, this amounted to a 'tolerance' of foreigners in irregular residence. The condemnation of Belgium can only encourage States to proceed to removals with more efficiency and determination.

During his stay in Belgium, except for the periods during which he was in prison, in a closed centre for illegals aliens or in hospital, he was guilty of an impressive number of ordinary crimes. As a result, he was sentenced in two sentences to 21 months' imprisonment (suspended except for the duration of his preventive detention) and to three years of effective imprisonment. He has been treated for several diseases, notably a chronic lymphocytic leukaemia, as well as other conditions, namely active pulmonary tuberculosis, hepatitis C, chronic obstructive pulmonary disease and a stroke. His stay in Belgium was a huge expense. In addition to the cost of the judicial proceedings (correctional tribunals, Court of Appeal, Conseil d'Etat, six judgments of the Aliens Litigation Council), including the legal assistance for all these proceedings, as well as the cost of various prison stays totalling more than three years, foremost reference must be made to the cost of multiple medical consultations and his frequent hospitalisation, accompanied by extremely expensive therapies and medicines.

In its Chamber judgment of 17 April 2014, the Court found that there were no compelling humanitarian and compassionate considerations to oppose the expulsion of Paposhvili. For these diseases, drugs could be found in Georgia. The Chamber referred to the judgment of the Grand Chamber in *N v the United Kingdom* of 27 May 2008. In that judgment, the deportation to her country of a Ugandan woman infected with HIV was not considered contrary to Article 3 ECHR:

> Aliens who are subject to expulsion cannot in principle claim any entitlement to remain in the territory of a Contracting State to continue to benefit from medical, social, or other forms of assistance and services provided by the expelling State. Only in a very exceptional case, where humanitarian grounds against the removal are compelling, the decision to remove an alien who is suffering from a serious mental or physical

[13] M Bossuyt, 'La Cour de Strasbourg souhaite que les Etats parties instaurent une procedure d'"asile medical" (obs. sous Cour eur. dr. h., Gde Ch., *Paposhvili c. Belgique*, 13 décembre 2016)' [2017] *Revue trimestrielle des droits de l'homme* 651.

> illness to a country where the facilities of that illness are inferior to those available in the Contracting State, may raise an issue under Article 3 [§42]. An obligation on Contracting States to provide free and unlimited health care to all aliens without a right to stay in their territory would place too heavy a burden on them (§44).

The three minority judges in *N*,[14] on the other hand, rejected the claim that 'finding a breach of Article 3 in the present case would open the floodgates to medical immigration and make Europe vulnerable to becoming the "sick bay" of the world'. In its judgment in *Yoh-Ekale Mwanje v Belgium* of 20 December 2011, six[15] of the seven judges expressed the hope that the Court might one day review its jurisprudence on this point: 'The difference between a person who is on his deathbed or someone who is known to be sentenced on short notice seems small in terms of humanity'.

The request to refer the *Paposhvili* case to the Grand Chamber was accepted on 20 April 2015. Paposhvili died on 7 June 2016. The Grand Chamber's desire to review the jurisprudence of the Court was so great that it nevertheless pursued the case. His widow insisted on it. Despite being sentenced to four months in prison, she was regularised on 29 July 2010. However, the risk that Belgium would expel Paposhvili had become non-existent following his death. Six months later, in its judgment of 13 December 2016, the Grand Chamber retroactively noted 'hypothetical violations'.[16] By the applicant's death, these were in fact 'fictitious violations'. For the same reason, it seems rather cynical to regard the finding of a breach as satisfactory for the moral damage that the applicant might have suffered.

As a general principle, the Grand Chamber says that the very exceptional cases which may raise an issue under Article 3 ECHR should be understood to refer

> to situations involving the removal of a seriously ill person in which substantial grounds have been shown for believing that he or she, *although not at imminent risk of dying*, would face a real risk, on account of the absence of appropriate treatment in the receiving country or the lack of access to such treatment, of being exposed to a serious, rapid and irreversible decline in his or her state of health resulting in intense suffering or to a significant reduction in life expectancy (§183).

The problem with this judgment is not so much that the disease threshold is lowered. At the general meeting of 12 December 2014, the Aliens Litigation Council had already adopted a broad interpretation of Article 9*ter* of the Aliens Law. According to this interpretation, an illness may justify the granting of a residence permit if it is a serious illness, even if it does not present an imminent risk of death. Problematic is that a favour is transformed by the Court into a right. By declaring

[14] Judge Françoise Tulkens, Judge Giovanni Bonello (Malta) and Judge Dean Spielmann (Luxembourg).

[15] Judge Danutė Jočienė (Lithuania), Judge Françoise Tulkens (Malta), Judge Dragoljub Popović (Serbia), Judge Işıl Karakaş (Turkey), Judge Guido Raimondi (Italy) and Judge Paulo Pinto de Albuquerque (Portugal). This hope was maintained by ordering (despite the *N v the United Kingdom* judgment) interim measures prohibiting the deportation of sick persons.

[16] 'There would have been (*il y aurait eu*) a problem if the applicant had been removed *(avait été éloigné)* to Georgia without the Belgian authorities having assessed (*eussent évalué*) the risk faced by him'.

these provisional measures mandatory, the Court has already experienced that the consequences of transforming a practice into a legal obligation can be profound. It is commendable to encourage States to show compassion, humanity and generosity. Anyone who believes that the role of the Strasbourg Court is not to transform benevolence and humanitarian grounds into a legal obligation should not be considered as lacking in humanity. It is the nature of a 'government of judges' that those who make the decisions do not bear the consequences.

The consequence of the conversion of a favour into a right, is that the Court wishes to impose on the States Parties the establishment of a medical asylum procedure. In its *Paposhvili* judgment, the Court has the benevolence to provide detailed instructions to legislators of States Parties, inspired by the procedure for the recognition of refugee status. All States Parties to the ECHR are also parties to the Geneva Convention. However, none of these States is party to a convention on medical asylum. One author, Nicolas Klauser,[17] observed that of the 47 States Parties there are only two that have a medical asylum procedure: Belgium (Article 9*ter* of the Aliens Law)[18] and France. There are three (Germany, Italy and Switzerland) that grant medical asylum without having a specific procedure for this purpose. That precisely one of these two countries, which is the most advanced in this direction, is condemned for violation of Article 3 ECHR, is nevertheless paradoxical, but not unique.[19] In the end, the States that have the most advanced medical care system will bear the burden of lowering the threshold. In most countries, good health is a condition for legal migration. Poor health is considered by the Strasbourg Court as a reason why someone who is illegally in the territory of a Member State of the Council of Europe, must be able to continue to be taken in charge.

Following the *Paposhvili* judgment, the case of *Savran v Denmark*[20] should also be mentioned. In finding a violation of Article 3 ECHR in its judgment of 1 October 2019, a majority of four judges[21] of a Chamber of the Court tried to broaden the scope of this provision in this sensitive area. The case concerns the return to Turkey of a Turkish national suffering from paranoid schizophrenia and convicted of aggravated aggression resulting in the death of a man. In their dissenting opinion, three judges[22] considered that the majority has departed from

[17] N Klauser, 'Malades étrangers: la CEDH se réconcilie (presque) avec elle-même et l'humanité' (February 2017) *La Revue des droits de l'homme* 1.

[18] See above p 242 (n 19).

[19] M Bossuyt, 'Unduly Harsh Treatment of Sweden in Asylum Cases in Strasbourg?' [2016] *Human Rights Law Journal* 323.

[20] M Bossuyt, 'La Cour persiste dans sa volonté de faire instaurer une procedure d'asile médical (obs. sous Cour eur. dr. h., Gde Ch., *Savran c. Danemark* (7 décembre 2021)' [2022] *Revue trimestrielle des droits de l'homme* 701.

[21] The majority of the Chamber was composed of Chamber President Paul Lemmens (Belgium), Judge Faris Vehabović (Bosnia and Herzegovina), Judge Carlo Ranzoni (Liechtenstein) and Judge Jolien Schukking (Netherlands).

[22] Judge Jon Fridrik Kjølbro (Denmark), Judge Iulia Motoc (Romania) and Judge Stéphanie Mourou-Vikström (Monaco).

the strict jurisprudence of the *Paposhvili* judgment, which applied Article 3 only if the foreigner to be deported was on the 'threshold of death'.

Before the Grand Chamber, the German, British, French, Dutch, Norwegian, Russian and Swiss governments intervened in support of the Danish government. In its judgment of 7 December 2021, the Grand Chamber ruled, by 16 votes to 1,[23] that the applicant's deportation to Turkey had not resulted in a violation of Article 3. On the other hand, the Grand Chamber found, by 11 votes to 6, that there had been a violation of Article 8 (respect for privacy). The six minority judges[24] considered this judgment to be 'a regrettable development in its case-law, providing increased protection to individuals who have perpetrated very serious criminal offences'.

It goes without saying that the European Court of Human Rights has great merit in having strengthened the protection of human rights of the inhabitants of the Member States of the Council of Europe. It is less certain that the Court's interference in asylum policy has benefited refugees within the meaning of the Geneva Convention. It is not enough to have good intentions. The Court, as well as the Member States of the Council of Europe, has little control over developments in States that are not parties to the ECHR. Without being able to control the causes of these developments, it suggests how to manage the consequences. As the Court moved into the realm of indirect liability and virtual violations, it found itself in the realm of speculation about future facts rather than the more familiar realm of finding facts. It stepped on slippery ground or thin ice. Sometimes it slipped up. Sometimes it even went through the ice.

[23] Judge Georgios Serghides (Cyprus).

[24] Judge Jon Fridrik Kjølbro, Judge Dmitry Dedov (Russian Federation), Judge Branko Lubarda (Serbia), Judge Armen Harutyunyan (Armenia), Judge Gabriele Kucsko-Stadlmayer (Austria) and Judge Alena Poláčková (Slovakia).

22

Epilogue

This Epilogue first points out some important differences between the asylum situation at the time I left the Commission General and that of 25 years later. Secondly, I would like to stress the importance of European interference in asylum policy and comment on the European Union's response to the asylum crisis. Finally, I ask whether the current asylum model is sustainable.

22.1. Twenty-Five Years after

Since I left the Commission General 25 years ago, our asylum policy, like that of other European countries, has changed a great deal. However, let us first mention an important constant: the growth in the cost of procedure and reception. During the nine years of my mandate, the overall cost of the procedure (Commission General and Permanent Board) increased from €1.5 million to €9.5 million. In 2008, it amounted to €35 million, and €53 million in 2018. The reception cost, which can be up to 10 times the cost of the procedure, rose during the period of my mandate from €12.5 million to €150 million. The record was reached in 2023 with more than €1 billion, without counting the medical costs for asylum seekers and foreigners staying irregularly on the territory.

The most important changes in the processing of asylum applications concern the nationality of asylum seekers, the extension of beneficiaries of international protection, and the further 'juridictionalisation' of the procedure.

22.1.1. The Evolution in Nationalities

During my mandate, there were already considerable differences between the nationalities of asylum seekers in Belgium. Comparing 1988 to 1996, I note that there are only three nationalities (Zairean, Turkish and Pakistani) which are among the 10 most important in those two years. Constant (twice at number three) was only one country (Zaire), for obvious historical reasons. In 2019 (the last year before the pandemic), Afghanistan, Syria, Palestine, Iraq and El Salvador were among the top five countries. None of these five countries was among the top 10 in 1988 or 1996. With countries like Afghanistan, Syria and Iraq at the top, decision-making has not become easier. The time has passed when most asylum seekers could not claim international protection.

22.1.2. The Expansion of Beneficiaries of International Protection

At the time, it was widely assumed that only 'political refugees' were considered for protection. Even Ghanaian asylum seekers, who found themselves massively in prostitution, argued political stories. Their standard story was a variation on the same theme: their partner was suspected (often unbeknownst to them) of hiding weapons at home to commit a coup (aborted). These stories were ill-founded but not 'clearly foreign to the Geneva Convention criteria'. At that time, there were also refugees recognised on grounds other than their 'political convictions', but this was rather rare and there was no publicity for it.

Today, it is mainly war refugees who demand international protection. In addition to refugee status under the Geneva Convention, a slightly weaker status has been introduced in subsidiary order, which is called 'subsidiary protection'. This has considerably increased the number of potential beneficiaries of international protection. This statute wanted to meet the consequences of the extraterritorial effect that the Strasbourg Court had granted to Article 3 ECHR. According to the EU Qualifications Directive (2004), this subsidiary protection is first introduced for those in their own country who risk 'the death penalty or execution, or torture or inhuman or degrading treatment or sanctions'. However, the number of beneficiaries of international protection has increased mainly by also granting subsidiary protection because of 'a serious and individual threat to a civilian's life or person by reason of *indiscriminate violence* in situations of international or internal *armed conflict*'. The number of people in the world who may feel threatened by indiscriminate violence or armed conflict is easily in the millions. This was not the case with the Geneva Convention.

Today, in addition to subsidiary protection, international protection is also often sought on the grounds of 'membership of a particular social group'. This is the ground for which the description in the Geneva Convention is the least precise. The Strasbourg Court also interpreted it flexibly when it included the group of women who, by committing adultery, transgressed social mores. In Belgium, it is often about sexual orientation, forced marriages, female excision, sexual violence and domestic violence. Some of these grounds can be invoked by large groups of people. Verifying the risk of persecution, based on some of these grounds, can be particularly difficult.

22.1.3. The 'Juridictionalisation' of the Asylum Procedure

In the past, it was sometimes said that the refusal of failed asylum seekers to return to their country of origin was due to the poor quality of the asylum procedure. In any case, it has not been shown that an applicant refused by me was persecuted after his return to his country, for reasons given in his asylum application.

The improvement of the quality of the asylum procedure has been a constant concern: the training of employees has intensified, the hearings last longer and the motivations have become more elaborate. But while there is no reason to doubt the independence of the Commissioner General, he is not a judge. For those who believe that salvation can only come from judges (judicial fetishism), this is an unforgivable defect.

In the final years of my mandate, the asylum jurisdiction (the Permanent Board) took only 10 per cent of the final decisions, both positive and negative. The Aliens Office took 17 per cent of the final negative decisions, and I took 72 per cent. I also took 90 per cent of the recognitions. Nowadays, any refusal, even for manifestly unfounded reasons, is subject to appeal to the Aliens Litigation Council.

At the urging of the European Union, in 2006 Interior Minister Patrick Dewael fulfilled the dream of the asylum lobby and all those who believe that judges are infallible. The refusal of an asylum application became enforceable only after the intervention of aliens' judges exercising full jurisdiction. The Conseil d'Etat was only competent to annul administrative decisions without being able to substitute to the competent administrative authority. Since 2006, the Commissioner General must no longer deal with appeals against the many clearly unfounded asylum applications. These appeals are now also dealt with by aliens' judges who are competent to recognise refugees themselves. The Permanent Board had this power only for asylum applications previously declared admissible.

The promoters of this 'juridictionalisation' ensured that it would be a 'light' procedure. Nevertheless, no fewer than 26 aliens' judges were appointed, each assisted by several collaborators. This procedure was by no means 'light'. Gradually, the number of judges rose to 62. Those who thought that once refused by an aliens' judge exercising full jurisdiction, rejected asylum seekers would happily board the plane taking them back to their country of origin, must be disappointed. The resistance against removals has not diminished either. Campaigns attacking home visits[1] and the retention of persons accompanied by minor children[2] are only the most visible manifestations. That this attracts a disproportionate number of minors is a consequence that seems to be accepted.

In the meantime, asylum seekers can apply to the courts for no less than six procedures: to the Aliens Litigation Council to contest: (1) the refusal of their asylum application; (2) the refusal of their humanitarian or medical regularisation; (3) their removal from the territory; (4) the decision to transfer to another EU Member State under the Dublin Regulation; to labour jurisdictions (5) their assignment to a reception centre managed by Fedasil; and to the courts of inquiry (Chambre du conseil and Chamber of Indictment), (6) their retention for the purpose of their expulsion. A new Migration Code should put some order in it.

[1] Bossuyt Commission Final Report, above p 241 (n 16) 22.
[2] Bossuyt Commission Interim Report, above p 240 (n 13) 79.

How far aliens' judges are willing to go is shown by some suspension judgments in 2016.[3] With these judgments, they wanted to force the Secretary of State for Asylum and Migration, Theo Francken, to have the Belgian Embassy in Beirut issue humanitarian visas to a Syrian couple. Anyone, wherever he was in the world, should be entitled to choose which State Party to the ECHR had to allow him to enter its territory when he risked being treated contrary to the ECHR. This view was reinforced by penalties of €1,000 per day imposed by the Tribunal of first instance and the Court of Appeal of Brussels.[4] The Secretary of State refused to follow up. He considered that these jurisdictions, by interfering with his discretionary powers, violated the constitutional separation of powers. Fortunately, neither the Court of Luxembourg (in 2017), nor the Court of Strasbourg (in 2020) have taken the path indicated by these Belgian judges.[5]

22.2. European Interference

To a large extent, changes in asylum policy are the result of European interference. In the past, the asylum crises in Belgium were due to deficiencies in Belgian asylum policy. EU Member States could, each for themselves, take the necessary measures to control the situation. It was different with the asylum crisis of 2015. This was due to deficiencies in European asylum policy. Increasingly, the regulation of asylum has been taken over by the European Union. The Union is therefore responsible for its consequences. Admittedly, the case law of the Strasbourg Court may be invoked as a mitigating factor. But it is up to the Union to deal with it. Strasbourg, Luxembourg, or Brussels, whatever, it is always Europe that the EU citizen holds responsible.

22.2.1. The Strasbourg Court

In recent years, the Court of Strasbourg has been heavily involved in the asylum policy of the Member States of the Council of Europe. During my mandate, it was still very limited. It was not until 1991 that the Strasbourg Court issued its first judgment on asylum. It was only in 1996 that this Court found for the first time a virtual violation of Article 3 ECHR, if an asylum seeker was removed to his country of origin. It was also then that the Court lifted certain restrictions provided for in the Geneva Convention: the danger to national security or the conviction for a

[3] In (French) suspension decisions of 7, 14 and 20 October 2016.

[4] In a (French) judgment of 25 October and a (French) judgment of 7 December 2016.

[5] See the judgment of 7 March 2017 of the Grand Chamber of the Court of Luxembourg in *X and X v Belgium* (C-638/16 PPU), on a question referred for a preliminary ruling by a general meeting of the Aliens Litigation Council of 8 December 2016, and the decision of 5 May 2020 of the Grand Chamber of the Court of Strasbourg on application of 10 January 2018 of the Syrian couple (*N et al v Belgium*).

particularly serious crime are no longer valid as an exception to the expulsion ban; moreover, persecution must no longer emanate from State agents.

In 2005, the Court declared that its provisional measures had become mandatory. Since then, it has been involved in the daily conduct of asylum policy. The popularity of these provisional measures among asylum seekers has considerably increased the number of asylum judgments. Since then, the Court has frequently found violations of the prohibition of torture of Article 3 ECHR in respect of asylum seekers. Article 3 has thus become, especially in its procedural aspect, an instrument that promotes illegal immigration. Several EU Member States have been prevented from applying the Dublin Regulation. The maritime borders of the Member States of the Council of Europe have been declared open for anyone arriving in a boat. For those who wish to apply for medical asylum, the Court has even prescribed a whole procedure.

Although the ECHR does not guarantee a right to asylum, the Strasbourg Court has nevertheless continually raised the requirements it imposes on the asylum procedure. The 'effective remedy' of Article 13 ECHR does not require a judicial appeal body. However, according to the Court this appeal must have an automatic suspensive effect. In a 2016 judgment against Sweden,[6] the Court behaved as if it were competent to act, regarding the asylum procedure, as legislator for 47 (now 46) Member States of the Council of Europe.

22.2.2. The European Union

The right to asylum is not enshrined in any of the universal human rights treaties. The European Union has nevertheless enshrined this right in Article 18 of the Charter of Fundamental Rights (Nice, 2000). At the end of 2009, at the same time as the Lisbon Treaty (2007), this Charter became legally binding on the European Union. This has enshrined in Union Law not only a right to asylum, but also a judicial remedy in the asylum procedure. In its Qualification Directive (2004), the European Union had already imposed this legal obligation on the Member States. What was not required by Strasbourg, the European Union imposed on itself.

22.2.2.1. The Asylum Directives

The EU's asylum directives are not limited to formulating some general principles to which national asylum procedures must comply. They have developed a comprehensive asylum procedure, a kind of common denominator – at a high level – of the 27 national asylum procedures. Member States have tried to have elements of their own procedures taken up as much as possible. The result is

[6] See the judgment of the Grand Chamber of 23 August 2016 in *JK et al v Sweden*; see Bossuyt, above p 284 (n 19).

a compromise of unimaginable complexity. Since – following the 2015 asylum crisis – the European Commission has been more involved in this issue, it has begun to understand that this complexity prevents flexible processing of asylum applications. Given the weight of the asylum lobby, it is to be feared that it will still be a long time before the Member States and especially the European Parliament will act.

EU directives have certainly not simplified asylum procedures. The harmonisation of criteria between Member States has not yielded much either. This does not diminish the attractiveness of countries which enjoy the preference of asylum seekers. Conversely, countries that do not enjoy their preference have not become more attractive. It is envisaged that the European Asylum Agency will have the competence to recognise refugee status to achieve greater uniformity.

The experience of the Belgian Commission General leads to a certain scepticism. In Belgium, there is only one body – or rather one person – who recognises refugee status in the first instance. However, the percentage of recognition varies according to the national language in which these decisions are taken. This is, a fortiori, the case with the Aliens Litigation Council where different individual judges take the decisions. The percentage of recognition is 10 times higher in French than in Dutch.[7] Will there also be European asylum judges? How can we avoid divergent decisions being taken according to the language or the nationality of the judges? Time will tell if this is a step in the right direction. The awarding of EU salaries will not reduce the cost of the procedure.

22.2.2.2. The Return Directive

The European Union Return Directive (2008) does not seem to be based on much experience in overcoming the obstacles faced by an effective return policy. In most EU Member States, this policy is still in its infancy. This is an area in which the added value of the European Union is however more obvious than with the Reception Directive (2003), the Qualification Directive (2004) and the Procedure Directive (2005). For the return, the cooperation of the countries of origin is essential. The European Union and the 27 Member States together have much more leverage than the Member States, individually. However, it is only recently that the European Union proposed to take the returns policy seriously.

22.2.2.3. The Luxembourg Court

In applying EU directives, the Court of Luxembourg plays an important role. This Court is very awake when the Strasbourg Court infringes the principle of mutual trust between the Member States. In other respects, it suffers from the same

[7] The recognition rate of the Aliens Litigation Council in the period from 2017 to 2019 was 12.18% in the French-speaking Chambers and 1.20% in the Dutch-speaking Chambers.

ailments. Sometimes, it even engages in competition with the Strasbourg Court to obtain the favour of asylum seekers and defenders of their interests. This escalation is not likely to facilitate an effective asylum and returns policy.

22.3. The EU Response to the Asylum Crisis

The Strasbourg judgments of 2011 (*MSS*) and 2012 (*Hirsi Jamaa et al*) had created the conditions for 'asylum chaos'. The door was wide open for those who came by sea. The risk of being sent back to the country of entry was virtually eliminated. It is surprising that it lasted until 2015 before becoming unmanageable. The Court considered that the application of the Dublin Regulation was the cause of an unacceptable situation in Greece. Its non-application subsequently caused unacceptable situations for asylum seekers in several Member States of the Council of Europe: Albania, Austria, Bulgaria, Croatia, Germany, Hungary, Northern Macedonia, Romania, Serbia and Slovenia. There are now refugees recognised in Greece, Italy or Poland who come to Belgium because they consider that social services there are better than in the country where they are recognised ….

On 31 August 2015, Angela Merkel pronounced her famous words: '*Wir schaffen das*' ('We make it'). In many countries from Africa and the Middle East to the Far East, this was understood as an invitation to come to countries like Germany, Sweden and Belgium. In 2015, the passage through Europe of these asylum seekers led to unprecedented chaos. The wind had changed fast. The leaders of the European Union, including Angela Merkel, understood that the persistence of such an influx was untenable. That change of course was obscured. The asylum crisis had meanwhile caused a resurgence in xenophobia. Political forces that did not have much respect for human rights were revived. Faith in the European project suffered a serious setback.

The European Union wanted to tackle the crisis with a repartition plan. This plan was a failure due to the rapid increase in the number of asylum seekers and the resistance of several Eastern European States. These States are aware of the not always positive experiences of Western European countries in terms of migration from Turkey and the Maghreb.[8] They rightly said they were not responsible for the asylum crisis. They were not the ones who failed to respect their EU obligations by not registering asylum seekers upon arrival. It was not them, either, who attracted this influx of asylum seekers.

The repartition plan had many weak points: it offered no solution for the influx of irregular migrants; it did not increase pressure to better monitor external borders; it did not sufficiently take into account the large number of asylum seekers that some Member States had already accepted; the proposed figures were only a fraction of the asylum seekers already present in the European Union, and

[8] See T Naegels, *La nouvelle Belgique: une histoire de l'immigration 1944–1978* (Tielt, Lannoo, 2021).

even less of those who wished to come. In addition, once asylum seekers have arrived in the Member State to which they will be assigned, they can – thanks to Schengen – go unimpeded to the country of their preference. No wonder this plan could not be realised.

The failure of the European Union to prevent this chaos has not gone unnoticed. On 23 June 2016, 51.89 per cent of British voters supported leaving the European Union. During the campaign on this issue, migration occupied an important place. The 'Brexiteers' accused the European justice system of preventing the expulsion of terrorists. However, it was not the Court of Luxembourg but the Court of Strasbourg which was responsible.[9] If there had been 0.95 per cent more votes for remaining in the European Union (instead of against), Brexit would have been avoided. The asylum crisis had probably caused more than 1 per cent of the British to lose their confidence in the European Union. Less than five months later, Donald Trump was elected as forty-fifth President of the United States. He had made the fight against mass immigration his battle horse. His successor, President Joe Biden, also knows that he cannot afford to passively endure migratory pressure. By June 2021, he had sent Vice President Kamala Harris to Guatemala with the message 'Do not come!'

On 23 September 2020, five years after the great asylum crisis of 2015, the European Commission announced a '*new Pact on Migration and Asylum*'. The Commission considers that 'the EU must overcome the current stalemate'. It recognises that 'the current system no longer works'. It rightly points out the concerns of Member States (other than those at the EU's external borders) that, 'if procedures are not respected at the external borders, their own national systems for asylum, integration or return will not be able to cope in the event of large flows'. The possibility of abandoning the basic principle of the Dublin Regulation is examined. It's a risky business.

There is a risk that, if asylum seekers can continue their journey to the country of their choice, the deplorable conditions of Lampedusa and Lesbos will move to these countries. Much faster than expected, such conditions had already become a reality in Brussels in 2022. Neither the penalties – up to €278.5 million in March 2023 – imposed by labour tribunals seized by more than 10,000 requests, nor the finding of a violation of Article 6.1 ECHR by the Strasbourg Court in its judgment in *Camara v Belgium* of 18 July 2023, had any impact on that situation.

The Pact talks about 'pre-entry screening of all people crossing the EU's external borders without permission or who having been disembarked after a search and rescue operation'. More specifically, this involves identification, health checks and security checks, fingerprinting and registering in the Eurodac database. It should also be determined quickly whether the person is considered for asylum. To do this, we will have to seriously adapt the heavy Procedure Directive (2013). A fast – and therefore simplified – procedure will be needed not only in the main

[9] See especially *Othman (Abu Qatada) v the United Kingdom*, above p 277 (n 5).

countries of arrival, but in all Member States, for those who have crossed the EU borders irregularly.

There is also talk of a 'common EU system for returns' and an 'EU Return Coordinator'. This is necessary. Indeed, 'the EU and its Member States must act in unity using a wide range of tools to support cooperation with third countries on readmission'. The 2008 Return Directive will also need to be adapted to make a more vigorous returns policy possible. In view of the many obstacles facing returns, the Union needs a directive that facilitates rather than complicates them. And, of course, the management of the external borders will have to be improved. There is still work to be done, a lot of work, and indeed hard work. It would be reckless to abandon the Dublin principle before we have achieved all this.

22.4. Is the Present Asylum Model Sustainable?

Nowadays, it has become much easier to travel, even from distant countries. The Schengen Agreement (1985) lifted internal border controls.[10] This free movement should not apply to foreigners who reside irregularly in the territory. Control should not be mandatory but should not be prohibited. In earlier times it was accepted that each country controlled its own borders. Because of increased mobility and lack of internal border controls, for a long time this has not been the case. This is even more true when organised gangs of traffickers push, with the complicity of transit countries, illegal shipments across external borders. From there, they can continue their journey to the countries of their preference without being disturbed. These countries, including Belgium, are under heavy pressure.

In the coming decades, we cannot expect the desire for immigration to weaken. Neither poverty in Africa nor conflicts in the Middle East will disappear quickly. The European model of asylum is bureaucratic, inefficient, cumbersome and costly. In addition, it depends on the goodwill of third States to keep millions of people outside Europe who push at its doors. Meanwhile, the European Union is exposed to blackmail from some neighbouring countries. Think of Belarus (vis-a-vis Lithuania and Poland), Libya (vis-a-vis Italy), Morocco (vis-a-vis Ceuta and Melilla) and Turkey (vis-a-vis Greece and Cyprus). The current asylum model is not sustainable when migrants are deliberately sent to destabilise the European Union. The European Union cannot condemn itself to blackmail. European public opinion, politicians and even European judges will have to become aware of it. Otherwise, the very survival of the European Union will be in danger. A repetition of the 2015 crisis could cause a political earthquake in key countries such as Italy, France and even Germany. It would shake the European Union to its foundations.

[10] Currently, the Schengen area covers the territory of 24 EU Member States (excluding Cyprus, Croatia and Ireland), as well as Iceland, Liechtenstein, Norway and Switzerland.

Do we have a moral duty to welcome with open arms some of the irregular immigration? Should we take charge of anyone who succeeds in reaching our country? Can we still determine who we want to welcome or not? Or do we have to give up that choice to human traffickers? There is no natural mechanism that distributes the needy foreigners among different countries. There is nothing natural about a mechanism that is the result of the criminal activities of smugglers. It is therefore not our moral duty to submit to their lucrative business model. Illegal immigration must be firmly discouraged. More resources for Frontex will not be enough. Current asylum and return procedures prevent effective action against illegal immigration. A simplification is necessary. Why not provide that those who enter the European Union illegally cannot obtain a permanent residence permit and even less the nationality of an EU Member State? It is surprising that in the current circumstances, deterrence actions in some countries of origin are sometimes (temporarily) successful. These actions announce that coming illegally to the European Union, does not pay. It is a lie: it pays well. And that must change.

BIBLIOGRAPHY

Strasbourg Cases

Lawless v Ireland, 14 November 1960
De Becker v Belgium, 27 March 1962
Amekrane v the United Kingdom, Com 11 October 1973
Becker v Denmark, Com 3 October 1975
Soering v the United Kingdom (plen), 7 July 1989
Cruz Varas v Sweden (plen), 20 March 1991
Vilvarajah et al v the United Kingdom, 30 October 1991
McCann et al v the United Kingdom, GC, 27 September 1995
Chahal v the United Kingdom, GC, 15 November 1996
Ahmed v Austria, 17 December 1996
HLR v France, GC, 29 April 1997
Coëme et al v Belgium, 22 June 2000
Jabari v Turkey, 11 July 2000
Dougoz v Greece, 6 March 2001
Čonka v Belgium, dec, 13 March 2001; 5 February 2005
Mamatkulov and Askarov v Turkey, 6 February 2003; GC, 4 February 2005
Said v the Netherlands, 5 July 2005
N v Finland, 26 July 2006
Mubilanzila Mayeka and Kaniki Mitunga v Belgium, 12 October 2006
Sultani v France, 20 September 2007
Riad and Idiab v Belgium, 24 January 2008
N v the United Kingdom, GC, 27 May 2008
SD v Greece, 11 June 2009
Tabesh v Greece, 26 November 2009
Muskhadzhiyeva et al v Belgium, 19 January 2010
AA v Greece, 22 July 2010
MSS v Belgium and Greece, GC, 21 January 2011
Nunez v Norway, 28 June 2011
Kanagaratnam et al v Belgium, 13 December 2011
Yoh-Ekale Mwanje v Belgium, 20 December 2011
Othman (Abu Qatada) v the United Kingdom, 17 January 2012
Harkins and Edwards v the United Kingdom, 17 January 2012
MS v Belgium, 31 January 2012
Hirsi Jamaa et al v Italy, GC, 23 February 2012
Vinter et al v the United Kingdom, 17 January 2012; GC, 9 July 2013
Trabelsi v Belgium, 4 September 2014
Tarakhel v Switzerland, GC, 4 November 1914
JK et al v Sweden, GC, 23 August 2016
Paposhvili v Belgium, 17 April 2014; GC, 13 December 2016
Romeo Castaño *v Belgium*, 9 July 2019
N et al v Belgium, GC, dec 5 May 2020
MA v Belgium, 27 October 2020
Savran v Denmark, 1 October 2019; GC, 7 December 2021
Camara v Belgium, 18 July 2023

Books

African Rights, *Rwanda: Death, Despair and Defiance*, rev edn (London, African Rights, 1995).

Barahinyura, S, *Quinze ans de tyrannie et de tartuferie au Rwanda: 1973–1988, Le général major Habyarimana* (Frankfurt, Ed Inuba, 1988).

Bossuyt, M, *L'interdiction de la discrimination dans le droit international des droits de l'homme* (Brussels, Bruylant, 1976).

——*Strasbourg et les demandeurs d'asile: des juges sur un terrain glissant* (Brussels, Bruylant, 2010).

——*International Human Rights Protection: Balanced, Critical, Realistic* (Cambridge, Intersentia, 2016).

Braeckman, C, *Rwanda: Histoire d'un génocide* (Paris, Fayard, 1994).

Boudet-Saulnier, F and Laffont, F, *Maudits soient les yeux fermés* (Paris, Arte Ed JC Lattès, 1995).

Chrétien, J-P, *Rwanda: les médias du génocide* (Paris, Karthala, 1995).

Dallaire, R, *Shake Hands with the Devil: The Failure of Humanity in Rwanda* (Toronto, Random House, 2003).

Des Forges, A, *Leave None to Tell the Story: Genocide in Rwanda* (Human Rights Watch & FIDH, 1999).

De Temmerman, E, *De doden zijn niet dood – Rwanda, een ooggetuigenverslag* (Grand-Bigard, Globe, 1995).

Destexhe, A, *Qui a tué nos Paras* (Brussels, Ed Luc Pire, 1995).

Dewulf, S, *Europees aanhoudingsbevel* (Mechelen, Wolters Kluwer, 2020).

Duclert, V, *La France face au génocide des Tutsi. Le grand scandale de la Ve République* (Paris, Tallandier, 2024).

Elchardus, M, *Reset: Over identiteit, gemeenschap en democratie* (Aalter, Ertsberg, 2021).

Francken, T and Vermeersch, J, *Continent zonder grens* (Doorbraak, 2018).

Goffin, A, Rwanda, *le 7 avril 1994: Dix commandos vont mourir* (Brussels, Ed Luc Pire, 1995).

Guichaoua, A, *Les crises politiques au Burundi et au Rwanda (1993–1994)* (University of Lille, Karthala, 1995).

Kinzer, S, *A Thousand Hills: Rwanda's Rebirth and The Man Who Dreamed It* (Hoboken NJ, Wiley, 2008).

Marchal, L, *Rwanda: la descente aux enfers. Témoignage d'un peace keeper: décembre 1993–avril 1994* (Paris, Éd Labor, 2001).

Martens, W, *De Mémoires: Luctor et emergo* (Tielt, Lannoo, 2006).

Misser, F, *Vers un nouveau Rwanda?* (Brussels, Luc Pire and Karthala, 1995).

Myjer, E and Kempees, P, *Jack and the Solemn Promise: A Cautionary Tale* (Nijmegen, Wolf Legal Publishers, 2010).

Mukagasana, Y (with May, P), *La mort ne veut pas de moi* (Paris, Robert Laffont, 1997).

Funes-Noppen, C *Des hommes, des femmes et des bêtes*, Vol II (Aix-en-Provence, Persia, 2012).

—— *Chroniques impertinentes* (Brussels, 180 éditions, 2021).

Naegels, T, *La nouvelle Belgique: une histoire de l'immigration 1944–1978* (Tielt, Lannoo, 2021).

Nsanzuwera, F-X, *La Battante: renaître après le génocide des Tutsis* (Fauves Ed, 2018).

——*Briseurs de destins: Les cerveaux du génocide des Tutsis* (Brussels, PU Saint-Louis, 2024).

Prunier, G, *The Rwanda Crisis. History of a Genocide* (London, Hurst & Co, 1995).

Reyntjens, F, *L'Afrique des Grands Lacs en crise* (Paris, Karthala, 1994).

—— *Rwanda: Trois jours qui ont fait basculer l'histoire* (Paris, Ed L'Harmattan, 1995).

Sanders, H, *Handboek van het overleveringsrecht* (Antwerp, Intersentia, 2011).

Schamp, W, *10 jaar Politieke Campagnes: een huurling vertelt* (Antwerp, Hadewijch, 1996).

Schnyder, F, *The Status of Refugee in International Law* (Leiden, Sijthoff, 1966).

Smet, M, *Ik kijk alleen vooruit: Mijn leven als politica* (Tielt, Lannoo, 2018).

Swinnen, J, *Rwanda: Mijn Verhaal* (Amsterdam, Polis, 2016).

Thompson, A (ed), *The Media and the Rwanda Genocide* (London, Pluto Press, 2007).

Tiberghien, F, *La protection des réfugiés en France*, 2nd edn (Aix-en-Provence, PU d'Aix-Marseille, 1988).

Tindemans, L, *Een Politiek Testament: Mijn plaats in de tijd. Dagboek van een minister* (Tielt, Lannoo, 2009).

Thatcher, M, *The Downing Street Years* (London, Harper Press, 1993).

Van den Eynde, W, *Fortisgate: Een stresstest voor justitie* (Louvain, Van Halewyck, 2016).

Verschaeve, F-X, *Complicité de génocide* (Paris, Ed La Découverte, 1994).

Chapters in Edited Volumes

Bossuyt, M, 'La Belgique et la Commission des Droits de l'Homme de l'ONU (1986–1991)' in *La Belgique et 50 ans de Nations Unies* (Brussels, Ed Vif, 1995) 467.

—— Is the European Court of Human Rights on a Slippery Slope?' in S Flogaitis, T Zwart and J Fraser, J (eds), *The European Court of Human Rights and is Discontents: Turning Criticism into Strength* (Cheltenham, Elgar, 2013) 27.

—— 'Les droits sociaux: une catégorie spécifique de droits de l'homme?' in L Berg, M Enrich Mas, P Kempees and D Spielmann (eds), *Cohérence et impact de la jurisprudence de la Cour européenne des droits de l'homme: Liber amicorum Vincent Berger* (Oisterwijk, Wolf, 2013) 43.

—— 'Des limites à la juridiction de la Cour de Strasbourg ?' in E Lambert Abdelgawad, D Szymczak and S Touzé (eds), *L'homme et le droit: en hommage au Professeur Jean-François Flauss* (Paris, Pedone, 2014) 117.

—— 'Judicial Activism in Strasbourg' in K Wellens (ed), *International Law in Silver Perspective: Challenges Ahead* (Leiden, Brill/Nijhoff, 2015) 31.

—— 'The Principle of "Mutual Trust" in Opinion 2/13' in S Imamović et al (eds), *The EU Fundamental Rights Landscape after Opinion 2/13* (Maastricht, Maastricht Faculty of Law, 2016) 15.

—— 'The UN Optional Protocol on the Abolition of the Death Penalty' in M deGuzman and DM Amann (eds), *Arcs of Global Justice: Essays in honour of William A Schabas* (Oxford University Press, 2018) 109.

—— 'Father Ryan, an Irish Asylum Seeker in Belgium (1988)' in K Lemmens, S Parmentier and L Reyntjens (eds), *Human Rights with a Human Touch: Liber amicorum Paul Lemmens* (Antwerp, Intersentia, 2019) 223.

—— 'The Acquittals of Mr Bemba and Mr Gbagbo by the International Criminal Court' in M Bossuyt, *Semper Perseverans: Liber amicorum André Alen* (Antwerp, Intersentia, 2020) 847.

Bossuyt, M and De Geyter, L 'De rol van de asieljurisdicties in de Belgische asielprocedure' in J Rozie, F Deruyck, L Huybrechts and F Van Volsem (eds), *Na Rijp beraad: liber amicorum Michel Rozie* (Antwerp, Intersentia, 2014) 39.

Bossuyt, M and Leysen, R, 'Het Arbitragehof en het vreemdelingenrecht' in M Bossuyt et al, *Burgerschap, inburgering en migratie* (Brussels, Larcier, 2007) 47.

Brody, R and Weissbrodt, D, 'Major Developments at the 1989 Session of the UN v on Human Rights' in F Newman and D Weissbrodt (eds), *International Human Rights: Law, Policy and Process* (Cincinnati, Anderson, 1990) 133.

Caflisch, L, 'Provisional Measures in the International Protection of Human Rights: the Mamatkulov case' in P-M Dupuy, B Fassbender, MN Shaw and KP Sommermann (eds), *Common Values in International Law: Essays in Honour of Christian Tomuschat* (Kehl, NP Engel, 2006) 493.

De Baere, G, 'The Court of Luxembourg Acting as an Asylum Court' in A Alen, V Joosten, R Leysen and W Verrijdt, *Liberae cogitationes: Liber amicorum Marc Bossuyt* (Antwerp, Intersentia, 2013) 107.

Mahoney, P, 'A Penetrating and Salutary Analysis of the European System of Human Rights Protection' in M Bossuyt, *International Human Rights Protection: Balanced, Critical and Realistic* (Cambridge, Intersentia, 2016) (ix–x).

Myjer, E, 'The European Court of Human Rights is no European Asylum Court' in A Alen, V Joosten, R Leysen and W Verrijdt, *Liberae cogitationes: Liber amicorum Marc Bossuyt* (Antwerp, Intersentia, 2013) 419.

Sagaert, V, 'De betekenis van Marc Bossuyt voor de Burundese rechtstaat. "*Mushingantahe*" als eretitel' in A Alen, V Joosten, R Leysen and W Verrijdt, *Liberae cogitationes: Liber amicorum Marc Bossuyt* (Antwerp, Intersentia, 2013) 543.

Articles

Bossuyt, M, 'Human Rights as an Element of Foreign Policy' *Bulletin of Human Rights* (Geneva, United Nations, 1989) 27.

—— 'La Convention des Nations Unies sur les droits de l'enfant' [1990] *Revue universelle des droits de l'homme* 141.

—— 'L'incompétence du juge civil des référés en matière d'asile' (1994) (18 March) *Le Journal des Procès* 18.

—— 'L'incompétence du juge civil des référés en matière d'asile' (1994) (1 April) *Le Journal des Procès* 12.

—— 'Le C.G.R.A. et les personnes déplacées de l'ex-Yougoslavie' [1995] *Revue du droit des étrangers* 467.

—— 'La Cour d'arbitrage: Contrôle d'égalité ou contrôle d'opportunité? A propos de la faculté de suspension par le Conseil d'Etat des décisions confirmatives du Commissaire général aux réfugiés et aux apatrides' [1996] *Revue trimestrielle des droits de l'homme* 467.

—— 'Should the Strasbourg Court Exercise more Self-Restraint? On the Extension of the Jurisdiction of the European Court of Human Rights to Social Security Regulations' [2007] *Human Rights Law Journal* 321.

—— 'Témoignage d'une présence belge au sein des organes des Nations Unies en matière de droits de l'homme' [2008] *Revue trimestrielle des droits de l'homme* 329.

—— 'Judges on Thin Ice: The European Court of Human Rights and the Treatment of Asylum Seekers' [2010] *Inter-American and European Rights Journal* 3.

—— 'Belgium Condemned for Inhuman or Degrading Treatment due to Violations by Greece of EU Asylum Law, M.S.S. v Belgium and Greece, Grand Chamber, European Court of Human Rights, January 21, 2011' [2011] *European Human Rights Law Review* 581.

—— 'The Court of Strasbourg as an Asylum Court' [2012] *European Constitutional Law Review* 203.

—— 'You cannot try them, you cannot detain them and you cannot deport them (Observations sous C.E.D.H., M.S. c. Belgique, 31 janvier 2012)' [2012] *Journal des Tribunaux* 351.

—— 'The European Court of Human Rights and Irreducible Life Sentences, The *Trabelsi v Belgium* Judgment of 4 September 2014' (2014) 14 *Human Rights Law Journal* 269.

—— 'Tarakhel c. Suisse: La Cour de Strasbourg rend encore plus difficile une politique commune européenne en matière d'asile' [2015] *Revue suisse de droit international et européen* 3.

—— 'The European Union Confronted with an Asylum Crisis in the Mediterranean' (2015) 32 *Journal européen des droits de l'homme* 581.

—— 'Unduly Harsh Treatment of Sweden in Asylum Cases in Strasbourg?' [2016] *Human Rights Law Journal* 323.

—— 'La Cour de Strasbourg souhaite que les États parties instaurent une procédure d'"asile médical" (obs. sous Cour eur. dr. h., Gde Ch., arrêt Paposhvili c. Belgique, 13 décembre 2016)' [2017] *Revue trimestrielle des droits de l'homme* 651.

—— 'La Cour persiste dans sa volonté de faire instaurer une procédure d'"asile medical" (obs. sous Cour eur. dr. h., Gde Ch., arrêt *Savran c. Danemark*, 7 décembre 2021)' [2022] *Revue trimestrielle des droits de l'homme* 701.

Bossuyt, M and Vandeginste, S (2001) 'The Issue of Reparation for Slavery and Colonialism and the Durban Conference against Racism' (2001) 22 *Human Rights Law Journal* 341.

Das, H and Pertegás Sender, M, 'Het dossier Moreno en Garcia: recht en diplomatie' (May 1996) *Vlaams Jurist Vandaag* 4.

Denys, L, 'De uitlevering naar het land van oorsprong van een kandidaat-vluchteling, onderdaan van een EG-lidstaat' [1994] *Tijdschrift voor Vreemdelingenrecht* 39.

Dewulf, S, 'The Saga Finally Ends. Na een trilogie van procedures kon de overlevering van een vermeend ETA-lid alsnog plaatsvinden' [2021] *Nullum Crimen* 181.

Foblets, M-C and Bernard, F, 'L'aide sociale aux étrangers en séjour illégal: la saga de l'ordre de quitter le territoire définitif de l'article 57, §2, de la loi sur les CPAS' [1996] *Recente arresten van het Hof van Cassatie* No 97.

Gerritssen, M, 'Een hoogst opmerkelijke beslissing' [1994] *Tijdschrift voor Vreemdelingenrecht* 31.

Gillet, E, 'Les candidats réfugiés dans le maquis du référé' [1992] *Jurisprudence de Liège, Mons et Bruxelles* 834.

Gilliaux, P, 'Le Conseil d'Etat et le contentieux des étrangers: L'irrésistible attrait de l'inefficace' (1 October 1999) *Journal des Procès* 15.

Janssens, L, 'De zaak Moreno-Garcia, een testcase voor het Europees aanhoudingsbevel' (Note on Cass 13 April 2004) [2004–05] *Rechtskundig Weekblad* 1260.

Klauser, N, 'Malades étrangers: la CEDH se réconcilie (presque) avec elle-même et l'humanité' (February 2017) *La Revue des droits de l'homme* 1.

Ryngaert, C, 'Het Europees aanhoudingsbevel lastens Moreno-Garcia: de aanhouder wint' (2004) Nieuw Juridisch Weekblad ep 89, 1226.

Van Den Wijngaert, C, 'La Belgique et l'exception pour délits politiques en matière d'extradition: analyse critique de la pratique judiciaire et administrative' [1979] *Revue du Droit Public* 833.

Voeten, E, 'The Politics of International Judicial Appointments: Evidence from the European Court of Human Rights' (2007) 61 *International Organization* 669.

Verbruggen, F, 'Ook zonder Madrid en Dublin blijft de uitlevering van Moreno en Garcia mogelijk, als Spanje een degelijk dossier heeft' [1997] *Panopticon* 162.

Vermeulen, G and Vander Beken, T, 'Uitlevering Basken aan Spanje: Juridische Bedenkingen bij een Politieke Zaak' [1995–96] *Recente arresten van de Raad van State* 221.

Other

Bossuyt, M, 'Adverse Consequences of Economic Sanctions on Human Rights' E/CN.4/Sub.2/2000/33 (Geneva, United Nations, 2000).

—— (2001) 'Procedural Confusion at the Main Committee of the Durban World Conference against Racism *Human Rights Monitor* No 56 12.

Dembour, M-B, 'Françoise Tulkens, indefatigable defender of migrants' human rights' (28 August 2012): *strasbourgobservers.com*.

Gerritsen, M, *Wordt Vervolgd* (Amnesty International – Nederland).

Hanegreef, C, 'Het Europees aanhoudingsbevel: verholen valkuilen in kaderbesluit' 2002/584/JBZ (Master's Thesis, Ghent University, 2014).

Heirman, M, 'Ruanda: Het land van duizend leugens' *IPIS-brochure* No 79 (Antwerp, 1995).

Lemmens, P, 'A Grand Lady Leaves the Court' (12 September 2012): *strasbourgobservers.com*.

Misser, F, 'Radio la mort' *Témoignage chrétien* (3 June 1994).

REGISTER OF PERSONS

Marc baron Bossuyt

Doctor juris (University of Ghent),
Docteur ès sciences politiques (University of Geneva),
Doctor honoris causa (University of Hasselt),
Diplôme d'honneur (University of Burundi).

Certificate of International Relations of the Bologna Centre
of the School of Advanced International Studies of the Johns Hopkins University.
Diploma of International and Comparative Law of Human Rights
of the International Institute of Human Rights (Strasbourg).
Certificat d'Etudes supérieures
of the Graduate Institute of International Studies (Geneva).

Former Visiting Professor at the
School of Law of the University of Santa Clara (California),
Faculties of Law of the University of Burundi (Bujumbura) and
of the National University of Rwanda (Butare) and
College of Law of the National Taiwan University (Taipei).
Former Fellow of the Stellenbosch Institute of Advanced Study (STIAS).

Former
Chairperson of the UN Commission on Human Rights,
Chairperson of the UN Sub-Commission on the Promotion
and the Protection of Human Rights,
Vice-Chairperson of the UN Committee on the Elimination of Racial Discrimination (CERD)
Chairperson/Rapporteur of the Working Group of the Declaration of the World Conference against
Racism, Racial Discrimination, Xenophobia and Related Intolerance (Durban).

Grand Cordon of the Order of Leopold,
Grand Cross of the Order of the Crown,
Grand Officer of the Order of Leopold II.
Honorary Citizen of Edegem.

President emeritus of the Constitutional Court,
Extraordinary Professor emeritus of the University of Antwerp,
Honorary Commissioner General for Refugees
and Stateless Persons.
Member of the International Commission
against the Death Penalty.

www.ingramcontent.com/pod-product-compliance
Ingram Content Group UK Ltd.
Pitfield, Milton Keynes, MK11 3LW, UK
UKHW020239290926
15470UKWH00002B/623

9 781509 982677